THE
COMBING OF
HISTORY

THE
COMBING OF
HISTORY

David William Cohen

THE
UNIVERSITY OF CHICAGO PRESS
Chicago
and
London

David William Cohen is professor of history and anthropology and director of the International Institute at the University of Michigan.

1222734

The University of Chicago Press, Chicago 60637
The University of Chicago Press, Ltd., London
© 1994 by The University of Chicago
All rights reserved. Published 1994
Printed in the United States of America

03 02 01 00 99 98 97 96 95 94   1 2 3 4 5

ISBN 0-226-11277-2 (cloth)
ISBN 0-226-11278-0 (paper)

Library of Congress Cataloging-in-Publication Data

Cohen, David William.
    The combing of history / David William Cohen.
        p.   cm.
    Includes bibliographical references and index.
    1. History—Methodology.   2. United States—History.
    3. Uganda—History.   4. Kenya—History.   I. Title.
    D16.C55   1994
    901—dc20   93-34883

∞ The paper used in this publication meets the minimum requirements of the American National Standard for Information Sciences—Permanence of Paper for Printed Library Materials, ANSI Z39.48-1984.

CONTENTS

List of Illustrations *vii*

Acknowledgments *ix*

Preface *xiii*

ONE
The Production of History *1*

TWO
Namuluta v. Kazibwe *24*

THREE
The Economy of Debate *50*

FOUR
Silences of the Living,
Orations of the Dead *78*

FIVE
Pim's Doorway *112*

SIX
Ditmar's Revenge *147*

SEVEN
Tisdale Divide *182*

EIGHT
The Constitution of
Expertise *216*

Conclusion *241*

Bibliography *251*

Index *261*

Louis S. B. Leakey, 1903–72,
a postcard *120*

The Way We Were–24 from
The Wisconsin Alumnus,
November/December, 1985,
p. 19 *123*

The Map of Africa, from the
National Museum of African Art,
Washington, D.C. *136*

The display area, *The Map of
Africa,* from the National
Museum of African Art,
Washington, D.C. *137*

The exterior doors to the *Burial
Room,* Dickson Mounds, Illinois,
April 1992 *145*

Tom Tisdale, June, 1992, at
Haywood's Gulch, speaking on
the murder of his grandfather
Tom A. Tisdale, November 30,
1891 *205*

In February 1985, Rhys Isaac, Alf ACKNOWLEDGMENTS
Lüdtke, Hans Medick, and Gerald
Sider posed the challenge that resulted in this book. They asked the difficult questions, then and in the years that followed. In 1980, however, the American historian Herbert G. Gutman raised the issue of memory and history in a way that has shaped and inspired this program of research and writing over some eight years, through an original position paper, through many conference and seminar discussions, through a number of discrete writing projects, and into this volume. If there has been a disappointment through the years, it is in not having been able to revisit these issues with Herb, who died in 1985, or with the late Paul Cowan, whose stories in the *Village Voice* provided the opening for Herb's consequential intervention in a 1980 meeting of anthropologists and historians in Paris, or with the Nairobi lawyer Silvanus Melea Otieno, whose corpse became a site for *the production of history* at his death in December 1986.

If there has been pleasure, it is in the rich exchanges that have developed with colleagues at Johns Hopkins and Northwestern, and with friends and others, who have been so generous with commentary and criticism, including David Anderson, Anthony Appiah, Adam Ashforth, Mark Auslander, Ralph A. Austen, Ruth Behar, Robert Berdahl, Caroline Bledsoe, Keith Breckenridge, Stephen Bunker, Catherine Burns, Matthew Cenzer, Christopher Chase-Dunn, Catherine Cole, Jean Comaroff, John Comaroff, Fred Cooper, Clifton C. Crais, James Currey, Philip D. Curtin, Greg Dening, Garrey Dennie, Toby Ditz, Milad Doueihi, Johannes Fabian, Gillian Feeley-Harnik, Michael M. J. Fischer, Ashraf Ghani, John B. Godfrey, Patrick Hagopian, Jerome Handler, Suzette Heald, Neil Hertz, Abdullahi Ali Ibrahim, Bogumil Jewsiewicki, Richard Kagan, Ivan Karp, Corinne A. Kratz, Windsor Leroke, Jonathan Lewis, Lisa Lindsay, John Lonsdale, Kristin Mann, George Martin, Dismas A. Masolo, Truman Metzel, Jr., Sidney W. Mintz, Thomas H. Murphy, Bethwell Allan Ogot, Grace Ogot, Elijah Oduor Ogutu, Duncan Okoth-Okombo, Ikem Stanley Okoye, Tejumola Olaniyan, Roland Oliver, Kathy Peiss, John G. A. Pocock, Sally Price, Orest Ranum, Richard Rathbone, Jeff Rice, Richard Roberts, Renato Rosaldo, Franz Rottland, Peter Sacks, Jonathan Sadowsky, Jane Schneider, Erica Schoenberger, Richard M. Shain, Keith Shear, Gavin Smith, Christopher Steiner, Nancy Struever, Carol Summers, Lynn Thomas, Michel-Rolph Trouillot, Michael Twaddle, Luise White, Ed Wilmsen, Eric Wolf, and Olivier Zunz. I am grateful to so many good colleagues, members of seminars, and others who offered criticism and suggestions at "a hundred meetings" over eight years.

Alberta Arthurs, Timothy Burke, Ben Cohen, Jennifer H. Cohen, Dwight Conquergood, Carolyn Hamilton, Karin Hausen, Rhys Isaac, Richard H. Levy, Alf Lüdtke, Shula Marks, Emily Martin, Hans Medick, Santu Mofokeng, Richard Price, Rea Tajiri, and Katherine Verdery provided maps into terrains of perspective I would never have known to visit. Several special individuals who would not agree that their names be mentioned here were unstinting in their loyalty, support, and affection throughout the entire project.

A brilliant and beautiful collaborator in two, and maybe yet three, projects of research and writing, E. S. Atieno Odhiambo showed the possibility of making, as one, the pen and the keyboard. He has generously acquiesced in my publishing here portions of work that developed within a common project extending back almost ten years.

Gabrielle Spiegel has engaged this work with a most constructive criticism, and so much encouragement, from the first jottings to the last revisions, bringing insight to a field of work at one time most distant from her own, and demonstrating through mutual readings the possibilities of accounting the past in diverse settings.

My late father, Wallace M. Cohen, a master of words, tumbled to the task of counsel, support, and editor. My sister Anne and my brother Edward at certain times seemed unable to comprehend their brother's descent into the mines of history production, but always provided love and support. My former spouse, Susan Hadary Cohen, provided support and inspiration through the prehistory and early gestation of this project and has continued, by her life, her commitments, and her art, to inspire. In life, in illness, in death, my mother, Sylvia Stone Cohen, has stood over this project—courageous in a terrible illness for too many years, her silences full of history, her story so well kempt, her struggles so carefully combed to protect those she brought to life.

Staff at Johns Hopkins and Northwestern—Betty Whildin, Sharon Widomski, John B. Godfrey, Akbar Virmani, Sandra Collins, Roseann Mark, Sheri Carsello, and Linda Kerr—have created space and time (where there was none) for this work to proceed and did their best to comb over the traces of chaotic and disruptive periods of travel, research, and writing.

Johns Hopkins University, Northwestern University, the Rockefeller Foundation, the John Simon Guggenheim Foundation, the National Science Foundation, the Max-Planck-Institut für Geschichte, and the Maison des Sciences de l'Homme provided support for periods of study and research, and for meetings critical to the development and completion of this project.

Staff of Colonial Williamsburg, the Johnson County (Wyoming) Historical Society, the Johnson County Library, the National Museum of African Art, the National Park Service, the University of Wisconsin Alumni Association, Great Expectations Bookstore, the Library of Reed College, the Office of the Secretary, Haverford College, the Melville Herskovits Library of African Studies, the Milton S. Eisenhower Library, and the Louis Leakey Foundation assisted with various, multiple, and sometimes difficult inquiries.

Credits

A portion of the Preface appeared in David William Cohen, *Toward a Reconstructed Past: Historical Texts from Busoga, Uganda* (London: British Academy and Oxford University Press, 1986); and in David William Cohen, "The Undefining of Oral Tradition," *Ethnohistory* 36, 1 (Winter, 1989): 9–17.

Portions of chapters 1 and 6 first appeared in David William Cohen, "The Production of History," a position paper for the Fifth Roundtable in Anthropology and History, Paris, 1986.

Portions of chapter 2 first appeared in David William Cohen, "'A Case for the Basoga': Lloyd Fallers and the Construction of an African Legal System," in *Law in Colonial Africa*, edited by Kristin Mann and Richard Roberts (Portsmouth, N.H.: Heinemann, 1991; London: James Currey, 1991), 238–54.

Portions of chapter 4 draw on material published in David William Cohen and E. S. Atieno Odhiambo, *Siaya: The Historical Anthropology of an African Landscape* (London: James Currey, 1989; Nairobi: Heinemann Kenya, 1989; Athens: Ohio University Press, 1989); and in David William Cohen and E. S. Atieno Odhiambo, *Burying SM: The Politics of Knowledge and the Sociology of Power in Africa* (Portsmouth, N.H.: Heinemann, 1992; London: James Currey, 1992).

Portions of chapter 5 draw on material published in David William Cohen, "Doing Social History from Pim's Doorway," in Olivier Zunz, ed., *Reliving the Past: The Worlds of Social History* (Chapel Hill: University of North Carolina Press, 1985), 191–232; on material published in David William Cohen and E. S. Atieno Odhiambo, *Siaya: The Historical Anthropology of an African Landscape* (London: James Currey, 1989; Nairobi: Heinemann Kenya, 1989; Athens: Ohio University Press, 1989); and on material published in David William Cohen and E. S. Atieno Odhiambo, *Burying SM: The Politics of Knowledge and the Sociology of Power in Africa* (Portsmouth, N.H.: Heinemann, 1992; London: James Currey, 1992).

Portions of chapter 8 draw on David William Cohen, "La Fontaine and Wamimbi: The Anthropology of 'Time-Present' as the Substructure of Historical Oration," in *Chronotypes: The Construction of Time,* edited by John Bender and David Wellbery (Stanford: Stanford University Press, 1991), 5–24; and on material published in David William Cohen and E. S. Atieno Odhiambo, *Burying SM: The Politics of Knowledge and the Sociology of Power in Africa* (Portsmouth, N.H.: Heinemann, 1992; London: James Currey, 1992).

The photographic reproduction of "The Map of Africa" from the National Museum of African Art, Washington, D.C., along with the photograph of the area in which the map is displayed, are provided by permission of the museum. "The Map of Africa" was designed in 1987, with credit to the artist David Ravitch et al., and photographers Jeffrey Ploskonka and James Young. The photograph of the display area is credited to Jeffrey Ploskonka.

The photograph "The Way We Were–24" is reproduced from *The Wisconsin Alumnus,* November–December 1985, 19.

The postcard image of Louis Leakey and others is reproduced by permission of the Leakey Foundation.

In the opening pages of his *Book of Laughter and Forgetting,* Milan Kundera offers a story of the beginnings of the Communist regime in Czechoslovakia in 1948. On a frigid February day in Prague, the new Czech leader Klement Gottwald moved out onto a balcony to address an immense crowd. Kundera calls it a "crucial moment in Czech history—a fateful moment of the kind that occurs once or twice in a millennium." Standing next to Gottwald was Vladimir Clementis, a foreign policy expert in the Czech Communist party and a hero in the struggle against Nazi suppression of the Leftist press in 1938–39. As the crowd roared, Clementis took off his fur cap and put it on the bare head of Gottwald.

While Kundera's narrative is full of power, he omits certain contextualizing detail. Clementis was part of the Communist party contingent that took refuge in the West during the period of Nazi control of Czechoslovakia while Gottwald had been the leader of the so-called Muscovite contingent. For many in the crowd, when Clementis put his cap upon Gottwald's head it signaled the reunification of the party.

Later, according to Kundera's narrative, the Communist party printed hundreds of thousands of these posters with Clementis's fur cap atop Gottwald's head. The poster captured the founding moment of a Communist Czechoslovakia. But several years later Clementis was tried for treason and hanged. The photograph was remade with Clementis airbrushed out. Kundera has written, "Where Clementis once stood, there is only bare palace wall. All that remains is the cap on Gottwald's head."

In this brief passage, Kundera, a writer of fiction, has asked his readers to recognize that there are essential truths in the past—the weather in Prague, a crowd in a square, Clementis and Gottwald together on a balcony, Clementis's cap, the act of placing the cap on Gottwald's head, a roaring crowd—but that such truths may also be obliterated.

In setting before his readers this tale of Clementis's cap, Milan Kundera has sought to impress upon us a view of the essential problem of *past:* that our knowledge of past is always at risk, essential pieces of knowledge of essential moments have been effaced, the most critical elements may have been made to disappear, but most important, that what comes down to us as knowledge from the past has been subjected to all kinds of suppression. Kundera has reminded us that—in his words—the "struggle of man against power is the struggle of memory against forgetting."

Yet, as we read Kundera's text, we may note the ways in which the past,[1] the forces of history, the quest for memory, have a way of rein-serting themselves, of placing a story of a fur cap before us, in our pres-ent, or in the present of those we study. And one may note that the historian's challenge is enlarged and multiplied beyond the reconstruc-tion or recovery of Kundera's essential truths to the reconstruction and also comprehension of the laminate processes and programs of oblitera-tion and recovery, which include Kundera's act of narration and my own act of reading Kundera, as well as the act of air-brushing.

As a historian of precolonial Africa who has, necessarily, sought to reconstruct the past in the absence of officially constituted archives and written documents,[2] my goals of writing history have certainly, if not also constantly, confronted the "struggle of memory against forgetting." One may well recognize the fragility of memory and wonder about the virtue and authority of works of history constructed out of what people claim, or are called, to remember. But one may also recognize the diffi-culty of "memory" as a concept, or as a construction, or as a field. Con-sider the variations of meanings among a state that has virtually obliter-ated a person, a president of the United States who asserts, "I have no recollection of those events," and an eighty-year-old man in Busoga, Uganda, in 1966, who is unable to "remember" where his father is buried.

Kundera's story reopens this ground in an important way, calling one to recognize not only the fragility of memory but also how complex and challenging the notion of "forgetting" is.[3]

*

In 1983, the British Academy invited me to bring out an edition of oral materials on the precolonial past of Busoga, Uganda, collected during fieldwork in 1966–67 and 1971–72. As I re-read hundreds of texts—and more specifically focused on the less than twenty that came to constitute

1. Recent events in eastern Europe, particularly in Czechoslovakia and Hungary, under-line, at least metaphorically, the extraordinary power that lay in the *absence*, the missing Clementis.

2. Karen Tranberg Hansen has told me about a taxi-bus she saw in Nigeria with the inscription painted on the side: "No documents, no history."

3. Observers of recent American presidents and their nominees to high office may note the way in which declarations that "I don't recall" or "I don't remember" have supplanted the Fifth Amendment of the late 1940s and 1950s as a shelter—and a very different sort of shelter—from responsibility, confrontation, and prosecution.

the corpus of the British Academy volume[4]—my attention moved ever so slightly from questions about what these texts really said about the past to how these texts, and the knowledge within them, came to be. I was interested in how one might approach the manner of construction of these reservoirs of evidence on the past and was intrigued by the challenge laid before the academy of historians with the recognition of "individuals making and holding historical knowledge in all their complexity and individuality—considerably concerned with interests, objectives, recreation, and esteem, and rather less concerned with performing history according to some given cultural design."[5] Reacting to prevalent and influential opinion that "reliable" or "verifiable" knowledge of the African past was—to the extent available—conserved in formal traditions carefully handed down through lineages or guilds of specialists—historians and storytellers, such as griots, I wrote,

> In Busoga, when one seeks the rich, formal narrative, there is bound to be a sense of profound disappointment concerning the articulation of the knowledge of the past. If one listens with a more open definition of historical knowledge, however, one finds that it is not located more formidably in poetic verse or extended narratives of a formulaic kind; it is constantly voiced, addressed, and invoked all through everyday life in Busoga by everyone, and this voiced knowledge constitutes a remarkable reservoir of evidence on the past.[6]

I was moved by the observation that while the academic guild of African historians debated methods and experiences of handling specific texts, and also oral tradition generally, people across Africa were themselves producing, using, and actively debating their pasts in ways virtually inaccessible to guild interests in evolving something like a science of oral historiography.[7] Immensely important historical practice lay out-

4. David William Cohen, *Toward a Reconstructed Past: Historical Texts from Busoga, Uganda* (London: British Academy and Oxford University Press, 1986). See also "The Undefining of Oral Tradition," *Ethnohistory* 36, 1 (1989): 9–17.

5. "Undefining of Oral Tradition," 16.

6. Ibid., 13. If one notes here a strident response to the approaches to "oral tradition" forwarded by Jan Vansina (*Oral Tradition: A Study in Methodology* [London: Oxford University Press, 1965] and *Oral Tradition as History* [Madison: University of Wisconsin Press, 1985]) that is just the point.

7. Over a number of years in history and anthropology seminars (the Atlantic Program) at Johns Hopkins University, I similarly regarded as largely vacuous and unproductive the efforts of faculty colleagues, visitors, and students to discern the essential qualities of, and distinctions between, the two "disciplines" of anthropology and history. What

side the discourse of the guild historians yet within the social worlds that historians studied. I lived with, and sought to understand, the tensions that linked this observation with a concern for enhanced and replicable historical method which I shared with many colleagues in a relatively new field of academic historical practice. With the British Academy project, I came to recognize[8] more fully that my own practice—and that of guild colleagues—operated not only upon, but also within, these social worlds. The techniques, interests, and production of the guild historian were a piece of broader historical practice.

In February 1985, a small group of anthropologists and historians met at Johns Hopkins in Baltimore, Maryland, to discuss interests that crossed the notional boundary between the two disciplines. Over lunch, I was asked to work with the anthropologist Gerald Sider on a position paper on the topic of historical practice, which could become the subject of the next and Fifth Roundtable in Anthropology and History. I accepted this as a commission and began working on the planning of the Fifth Roundtable and on the drafting of a position paper.

Since early 1985, this exploration and drafting have led through a series of projects lying within a field that I have come to refer to as "the production of history." Several of these projects have culminated in papers or book chapters or books; some are out in print, some forthcoming, and other work is in progress. In 1991, I began to assemble some of this writing into one volume, drawing sections of writing back from disparate volumes, journals, conferences, and lectures. What first was reckoned a simple task of editorial assembly has become a more substantial challenge of rethinking each piece, and each piece in connection with the others, as they are joined into the whole. Across the eight years from the first stages of work on the position paper to the completion of this volume, I have sought to sustain an "open text"—one that permits the entry of diverse material; one that allows itself digression; one that

---

seemed far more vital, and also productive, was to examine how guild practices inscribed as "anthropological" and "historical" operated in broader fields of practices of producing knowledge, in the broadest sense, of culture, society, and past.

8. In a recent critique, Jan Vansina has narrated my shift in the following way: "Among historians the foremost champion of postmodernism has been D. Cohen. . . . He had gradually come to the idea that there was something wrong with historical 'evidence' after starting from a very positivist stance in the mid '60s, moving to an almost allegorical way of interpreting oral traditions in the early 1970s and showing how historical consciousness is made and preserved in his *Womunafu's Bunafu* (1977). By the mid 1980s and teaming up with the political scientist [sic] A. [sic] Adhiambo [sic] he reached the position in Siaya [sic] that both culture and historical evidence are the creation and the present moment and only have meaning in this moment. Hence culture and history are perpetually 'invented,' a

experiments with forms of argumentation and exposition; one that explores, if in a stumbling and experimental way, attentions that seem to belong properly to other and specific specializations; one that seeks to join in a less than laborious manner insightful work and important experience located in several regions of the world; one that remains alert to the manner of its own practice without abandoning the potential of such practice to comprehend the world.

One of the first of these position paper projects was the investigation in 1985 and 1986 of an intervention by the American historian Herbert G. Gutman at a Paris conference in 1980; this led to the construction of an account of the work of the late *Village Voice* reporter Paul Cowan and of his "discovery" in Lawrence, Massachusetts, of the story of Camella Teoli, a figure in the 1912 strike of Lawrence mill workers. The story Herb Gutman told in a very brief but most powerful way in Paris became, ultimately, the hub of the position paper, and, indeed, the hub of this book. The account of Gutman, Cowan, and Teoli (with others) carried within it a number of issues and tensions that would define the work over the several years: the conduits among academic and public and official sites of history production; the complexity of the idea of "forgetting" and the dangers of knowledge; the power in silence; the catharsis of commemoration; the economy and politics of history; and the openings and closings of channels and reservoirs of knowledge of the past. A collection of accounts, with a latticework of commentary, was assembled into a position paper, "The Production of History," completed and circulated at the end of March 1986.[9]

The account of "the story of the story of the story" of the Lawrence strike, and of its memory and suppression among residents of Lawrence over a period of six decades, is taken up in chapter 1. The chapter sifts through Paul Cowan's account of recollections of Camella Teoli's daughter, who combed her mother's hair to cover a scar on her head, a suppression of the history of the scar which she would not decode until Paul Cowan visited Lawrence. The scar on her mother's head, she learned from the *Voice* reporter, was the result of an industrial accident. Camella Teoli's childhood injury in a Lawrence mill became a cause, a

---

position now steadily disseminated by the journal his program edits" ("Some Perceptions on the Writing of African History, 1948–92," *Itinerario* 16, 1 [1992]: 89).

9. The Fifth International Roundtable in Anthropology and History, convened in Paris, July 2–5, 1986, and was funded by the Maison des Sciences de l'Homme. This paper was written between September 1985 and March 1986. Titled "The Production of History," it is forthcoming in Gerald Sider and Gavin Smith, eds., *Between History and Histories* (Princeton, N.J.: Princeton University Press, 1994). The original paper has been widely

central event, in the textile mill strike in Lawrence, Massachusetts, in 1912; this combing metaphor was taken up as the title of an early draft of the 1985–86 position paper and has become the title of this book as the position paper has been revised, its examples multiplied, its discussion expanded.

The work on Lawrence interlaced with my own studies on the construction of history in western Kenya and Uganda that had been in progress for several years.[10] Such topics joined, and informed, other work in progress, including a study of the tensions between one scholar's construction of legal process within an African court and the programs of the litigants and witnesses within the court.[11] Chapter 2 builds on this treatment of litigation in a court in Busoga, Uganda, in the colonial period. The study of the contest between a woman and a man over a title to an office that held no formal authority in the Uganda Protectorate drew attention to the ways in which arguments in the courts of Busoga proceeded, the programs of testimony and questioning through which knowledge was invoked and withheld, the force of the agreements which the adversaries shared even in conflict, and the workings of discourses that operated beneath or outside the hearing of the court. The close reading of *Namuluta v. Kazibwe* opened an interest in the constitution and economy of debates and debates over the interpretation of the past—examples of which were presented in brief in the position paper. These discussions have expanded, and the examples multiplied, and they have been brought together as chapter 3, "The Economy of Debate."

An attention to "debate as production" developed, beginning in early 1987, around a concern to comprehend the extraordinary litigation over control of the remains of the distinguished Kenya lawyer S. M. Otieno. In recent years particularly illuminating debates over the disposition of relics of the dead have broken out in a number of settings, for example, the handling of skeletal remains of Native Americans held by the Smith-

---

circulated (and hundreds of copies are known to have been made since it was first distributed on March 31, 1986, to those invited to the Paris meeting).

10. David William Cohen and E. S. Atieno Odhiambo, *Siaya: A Historical Anthropology of an African Landscape* (London: James Currey; Nairobi: Heinemann Kenya; Athens: Ohio University Press, 1989); and also, David William Cohen and E. S. Atieno Odhiambo, "Ayany, Malo and Ogot: Historians in Search of a Luo Nation," *Cahiers d'Etudes Africaines* 27, 3–4, 107–8 (1987): 269–86.

David William Cohen, *Toward a Reconstructed Past: Historical Texts from Busoga, Uganda* (Oxford: Oxford University Press for the British Academy, 1986).

11. David William Cohen, "'A Case for the Basoga': Lloyd Fallers and the Construction of an African Legal System," in Kristin Mann and Richard Roberts, eds., *Law in Colonial Africa* (Portsmouth, N.H.: Heinemann, 1991), 239–54.

sonian Institution in Washington, the contention over the closing of the
skeletal display at Dickson Mounds, Illinois, and the controversy surrounding the display in a glass case of the remains of an African in a
museum in Banyoles near Barcelona. But where these conflicts stirred
sections of a population, the Otieno litigation shook a nation.

In Kenya, S. M. Otieno died suddenly in December 1986, on the eve
of the Christmas parties that he and his wife anticipated sharing with
friends and families at their residences in the Nairobi suburbs and in
town. Within days, S. M.'s widow, Wambui Otieno, and his brother, Joash
Ochieng' Ougo, had announced conflicting plans for S. M.'s burial on
Voice of Kenya radio. For 155 days, the body of S. M. Otieno would lie
in the Nairobi morgue as the widow and the brother, representing the
Umira Kager clan, fought through the highest courts of Kenya to establish who would gain control of the remains and where the remains
would be buried. First inquiries, and an early draft of a brief treatment
of the S. M. Otieno case,[12] were begun while the treatment of the law
case in Busoga was still being written. A productive and also connective
tension developed between the pull of each of these two legal conflicts.
The basic outlines of the S. M. Otieno case, presented here in chapter
4,[13] "Silences of the Living, Orations of the Dead," has grown into, more
recently, the publication—with E. S. Atieno Odhiambo as co-author—
of a work on the judicial and public conflicts over the lawyer's disputed remains.[14]

In the original position paper, several pages were devoted to claims
upon space, material things, and landscape, and more generally the
workings of metaphors of property in the production of history. The
original paper also addressed the sometimes unexpected ways in which
historical knowledge works its way through various channels. Chapter
5, "Pim's Doorway" takes up a number of examples of the unexpected
"properties" of historical knowledge and of the productions of history
in unexpected locations, focusing on the memory of pim. Pim is today
recalled as an old woman who would come into a Kenya Luo household

12. See the "Afterword," in David William Cohen and E. S. Atieno Odhiambo, *Siaya:
The Historical Anthropology of an African Landscape* (London: James Currey, 1989), 133–39, in
which a very brief account of the case is offered.

13. This specific chapter is a revision of a paper written for and presented to the Sixth
International Roundtable in Anthropology and History, Bellagio, Italy, August 31–
September 4, 1989. Gerald Sider and Gavin Smith hope to include it in their published
collection of papers presented at the Sixth Roundtable, which is going to press.

14. David William Cohen and E. S. Atieno Odhiambo, *Burying SM: The Politics of Knowledge and the Sociology of Power in Kenya* (Portsmouth, N.H.: Heinemann; London: James
Currey, 1992).

to nurse and nurture children, including teaching the young the histories of their households and lineages of which *pim* was not, typically, a member by birth.[15] S. M. Otieno's widow, Wambui Otieno, is herself recognized as a *pim*, within the Kenya courts the expert resource on the history of S. M.'s lineage, yet an individual who claimed no affinity with or interest in the world of his lineage. Chapter 5 also situates several other conflicts that have emerged over the standing of various forms of expertise and authority over the past: for example, over the deployment of an "historical map" within the galleries of the National Museum of African Art in Washington and outside of it in other contexts of presentation; and over the representation of the experience of Japanese-Americans interned in U.S. Government camps during the Second World War.

If there was a method in the construction of the original position paper, it was in examining individually, and side by side, a considerable array of events, incidents, and stories that "fell onto my desk" as the position paper was developing. As work on the story of Gutman, Cowan, and Teoli progressed through late 1985 and early 1986, I found an enormous bounty of material that augmented the Lawrence story and seemed likely to suggest to prospective participants in the Fifth Roundtable a broad range of "edges and dimensions in the production of history." A great deal of this material rotated around issues of authenticity and the public and scholarly judgments of the values and historicities of particular historical representations. These included public debates over the accuracy of historical representation in a beer commercial screened on American television, discussions concerning the elision of slavery in the replications at Williamsburg, struggles over the films *The Color Purple* and *Out of Africa*, and the "reading" of the murky narrative of Michael Cimino's 1980 film *Heaven's Gate*. These discussions are drawn together in chapter 6, "Ditmar's Revenge," which experiments with the rather digressive style which so marked and, for critics, blighted, Cimino's film treatment of the Wyoming cattle wars of the 1880s and 1890s.

A debative forum in Romania over the terms of commemoration of a revolt/uprising/revolution, presented in brief in the position paper, is taken up at some length in "The Economy of Debate" in chapter 3. But Katherine Verdery's intricate and illuminating exploration of the com-

---

15. And draws on research first published in David William Cohen, "Doing Social History from Pim's Doorway," in Olivier Zunz, ed., *Reliving the Past: The Worlds of Social History* (Chapel Hill: University of North Carolina Press, 1985), 191–235.

memoration of "Horea's Revolt" in Romania also became a stimulus to
make a close study of the hundredth anniversary commemoration in
June 1992 of the Johnson County cattle war in Wyoming, which was the
specific subject of *Heaven's Gate*. Chapter 7, "Tisdale Divide," treats a
number of representations of the cattle war, including the commemorative activities themselves, set among other histories of the war, including
Heaven's Gate.

The elucidation of expertise at unexpected sites in the past opens to
the examination, in chapter 8, of expertise in the relationship between a
local history text from eastern Uganda and an ethnography written by
a Cambridge-trained anthropologist.[16] The opportunity presented itself,
with the discovery of a previously unrecognized relationship between
the two texts, to explore the texture of a specific interstice between popular and academic programs of historical representation. An examination of the way one text is read in the production of another opens to
the ways in which a High Court judge in Kenya represents his readings
of authority, expertise, and knowledge in the representations of witnesses within the S. M. Otieno litigation.

A conclusion lays out some of the issues and arguments drawn from
the observations of "the combing of history" throughout the eight years
in which the research and papers drawn together here have developed.[17]

*

There is, in the presentation of the work here, a set of tactics. First, there
is an attempt to maintain an openness of text, in which pieces of material which "fall onto the desk" are entered into the text or notes and
allowed to provide augmentation, annotation, and also digression. Consequently, the "field" contrived here is neither Lawrence, Massachusetts,
nor Africa, nor anywhere else, but rather this field defined as "the production of history."

The nature of the material, and of the allowance of—indeed commitment to—digression lends itself to many and sometimes lengthy notes

16. David William Cohen, "La Fontaine and Wamimbi: The Anthropology of 'Time-
Present' as the Substructure of Historical Oration," in *Chronotypes: The Construction of Time*,
ed. John Bender and David Wellbery (Stanford: Stanford University Press, 1991), 5–24.

17. This "synthesis" builds in part on the "call for papers" that I drafted and sent to
prospective participants in the Sixth International Roundtable in Anthropology and History at Bellagio. It also draws from my notes of the Bellagio discussions and, additionally,
encompasses reflections from work outside and since the Roundtable. Gerald Sider and
Gavin Smith, who are editing the proceedings of the Sixth Roundtable, have asked to
include it in their collective volume a version of this "synthesis."

(which constitute something of a "para-text") and to the reproduction of considerable textual material as quotations. There is an attempt to keep in view multiple and laminate representations of the past—not every view surely—to preserve the folds and layers of production that join the past and the present. There is attention, here, to the practices of inscription of "text"—the sociology, politics, economy, and technology of production—including in a somewhat vain manner how certain trajectories of research, writing, and teaching were taken by the present author. Additionally, there is an attempt to maintain a conjoint vision of the past with the programs and practices of production of the past. While one may suggest that "this is keeping the 'text' with the 'context,'" there is an effort to maintain, as appropriate, the problematic and complex nature of "text" and "context" and, as well, to hold up to view the always ambiguous and always incomplete relationship among sites and moments of production of historical knowledge, the sites, events, and experiences represented in that knowledge, and the texts whereby those productions of knowledge become available to inspection.

Equally, throughout the text, there are surrenders to fiction and fantasy—working out within a written text a certain devotion to experimentation in analysis and exposition—as, for example, when "explanation" is sought for why a film's closing titles fail to match my phonetic transcriptions of a slurring actor's reading of the names on a death list; or the construction of a comparison of the uses of body in the readings of the court testimony of a professor of philosophy and of a gravedigger; or the juxtaposition of the conditions of capital on the nineteenth-century Wyoming prairie and the conditions of capital on a comparable late twentieth-century film set; or the comparative study of two texts on circumcision, one produced by a Cambridge-trained anthropologist, the other by a secondary school teacher; or the comparison of two other texts, one a section of a disappeared diary published in the *Chicago Herald* in April 1892, the other a scrap of paper handed from actor to actress to actor on a film set in Montana in 1979, and viewed for but one second in a feature-length film.

*

In 1983, the University of Pfilzing, in Bavaria, asked the brilliant young German historian Sonya Rosenberger to present a lecture on the occasion of commemoration of the fiftieth anniversary of Hitler's rise to power. Since a teenager, when she won a prize essay contest, she had been engaged in research in Pfilzing on the town, her home town, during the era of the Third Reich. Her research had originally been con-

ceived as an investigation of "how the town [especially the church] resisted the Nazis."

As she began her inquiries, even as a teenager unstudied in the modes
of historiography of the higher academy, Sonya Rosenberger was assuming the role of the historian, as Gabrielle Spiegel has recently defined,
or redefined it. Rosenberger was facing a common set of ethical constraints, and the problems of "knowing" much like any historian:

> How do we proceed ("behave") in order to "know" as historians;
> what is correct, true, "virtuous" even in our praxis; what, ulti-
> mately, legitimizes history as a disciplinary body of knowledge?
> For historians the ethical core of their professional commitment
> has always been a belief that their arduous, often tedious labour
> yields some authentic knowledge of the dead "other," a knowl-
> edge admittedly shaped by the historian's own perceptions and
> biases, but none the less retaining a degree of autonomy, in the
> sense that it cannot (putatively) be made entirely to bend to the
> historian's will. This belief . . . in the irreducible alterity of the past
> confers on history its proper function, which is to recover that
> alterity in as close an approximation of "how it actually was" as
> possible. In the interest of preserving this alterity, the historian
> practises modesty as a supreme ethical virtue, discreetly holding
> in abeyance his or her own beliefs, prejudices and presupposi-
> tions.[18]

As Rosenberger's research progressed, she uncovered the threads of
information about a "Brown Heinrich" who may have been involved,
she learned, with the murders of Father Schulte and a Jewish merchant.
As she asked the older people of the town about some of these details,
she found the town crash down on her head; she found the archives
closed to her research; files suddenly disappeared; her home was van-
dalized; she received multiple death threats; and she was told to stop
her research and get out of town. But she "soldiered on," extracting
pieces of information from various informants and getting court orders
to permit access to the archives (and even then she had to outsmart
those instructed to prevent her gaining full access to the particular files).

At the 1983 lecture at the university, Sonya Rosenberger denounced
"Brown Heinrich," identifying Professor Dr. Juckenack as the mysteri-
ous and bloody-handed director of Pfilzing's Nazi persecutions and
murders, raising an uproar and, at the same time, finding in the audi-

---

18. Gabrielle Spiegel, "History and Post-Modernism," *Past and Present* 135 (May 1992):
196. Spiegel was writing amidst a debate over the "linguistic turn" in the practice of
history.

ence one individual able and willing to speak in support of her denunciation. Professor Juckenack threatened legal action against her (having
earlier threatened to ruin her if she proceeded with her unpacking of
his early life), but she managed to defeat his action. Acknowledging her
contribution to the town, the city fathers of Pfilzing commissioned a
statue of her. A dedication ceremony was arranged, but at the moment
of unveiling, Rosenberger denounced the project of honoring her as a
means of silencing her voice. She walked out on the crowd that had
gathered to honor/silence her.

Sonya Rosenberger is "The Nasty Girl" (Das Schreckliche Mädchen),
the subject—and also title—of Michael Verhoeven's 1989 film which
was, according to a title in the opening of the film, "inspired by what
happened to Anya Rosmus in Passau . . . This story mixes fiction and
fact . . . and is pertinent to all towns in Germany." Of course, there is no
city or University of Pfilzing.

In the film, the director Michael Verhoeven has managed to provide
an important topography of "forgetting" in Pfilzing, in which knowledge is always and everywhere present, even where partial and conflictual, but almost never spoken. It is a knowledge which, on the one hand,
"does not exist" and, on the other, has the power to harm, even
kill. Remembering and forgetting in Pfilzing are not opposed and reciprocal programs; they are deeply intertwined. While there is no center
of power in the oppression, interest and power run through the entire
topography of "forgetting." "Forgetting" is not a process of disappearance; it is enhanced and nuanced by new conditions, for example, the
neo-Nazi "skinheads" who threaten and assault Sonya's family and
home.

As a very young historian Sonya naïvely and unknowingly falls into
this topography of "forgetting." Over the next years, as she deconstructs
the frameworks that regulate Pfilzing's history, she—and Verhoeven's
audiences—come to see the ways in which "forgetting" works as a powerful medium of historical production. Here, Rosenberger's experience
and her project complicate in important ways Gabrielle Spiegel's definition of the historian's purpose—"to recover that alterity in as close an
approximation of 'how it actually was' as possible"—by confronting the
challenge of the processes and programs of the production of "forgetting" that lie between her practice as a young historian and the "alterity."
The "forgetting" becomes, in a sense, the enlarged and refocused alterity.

Verhoeven's audience, of course, enters the cinema "knowing Pfilzing's secrets" in the sense of comprehending that Pfilzing's past could

not be what it purported to be at the outset of the film. As Sonya comes to share her audience's broader understanding, the audience comes to see how history in Pfilzing works—something not so easily understood or easily represented. The attention of the audience is drawn from the murders of the priest and the merchant—with which, some viewers might argue, they are not complicit—to the issues surrounding the programs of silence which have limited and regulated the comprehension of the past—programs with which they and we are, and will forever be, fully complicit.

On February 18–19, 1985, a group ONE
of historians and anthropologists
gathered at Johns Hopkins to The Production
explore recent directions in anthropology and history. At a lunch of History
break during this workshop, I
found myself sitting over Szechuan food with Rhys Isaac, Alf Lüdtke,
Hans Medick, and Gerald Sider discussing such issues as those Kundera
raised concerning memory and forgetting. As we moved from our soup
to main course, Hans, speaking for Alf and Rhys, opened a practical
discussion. They were proposing, Hans noted, that the planning for the
next Roundtable in Anthropology and History should shift to the
United States from Germany and France, where the four previous
roundtables had been organized,[1] and that Jerry Sider and I should assume responsibility for planning the next (fifth) roundtable.
The discussion shifted quickly to more difficult ground. Over the pre-

1. The first roundtable was organized in 1978 on "work processes." It was held at the
Max-Planck-Institut für Geschichte in Göttingen, Germany, with international participation which included Robert Berdahl, Eric Hobsbawm, and Edward P. Thompson. This first
roundtable was sponsored jointly by the Maison des Sciences de l'Homme and the Max-
Planck-Institut and led to the publication of *Klassen und Kultur. Sozialanthropologische Perspektiven in der Geschichtsschreibung* (Frankfurt, 1982), edited by Robert Berdahl et al.

The second roundtable, convened in Paris in 1980 under the sponsorship of the Maison
des Sciences de l'Homme, dealt with the "material and emotional aspects of family," and
sought to challenge the drift of work in kinship studies and family history in anthropology
and history, respectively. A call-for-papers was published by Hans Medick and David
Sabean in *Peasant Studies* 8 (1979). Fifteen papers prepared by scholars from the United
States, France, Germany, the United Kingdom, and Switzerland, presenting case studies
from different parts of the world, were published by Cambridge University Press in 1984
in *Interest and Emotion: Essays on the Study of Family and Kinship*, edited by Hans Medick
and David Sabean.

The third and fourth roundtables were concerned with the issue of "Domination/
Herrschaft" in historical and anthropological studies. The third roundtable, convened at
Bad Homburg in 1982 under the sponsorship of the Werner-Reimers-Stiftung, with assistance from the Max-Planck-Institut and the Maison des Sciences de l'Homme, was conceived as a "pre-conference" or planning workshop for the fourth roundtable. The fourth
roundtable, also convened at Bad Homburg, October 1983, through the generous hosting
of the Reimers-Stiftung, brought together historians and anthropologists from the United
States, France, Germany, the United Kingdom, Switzerland, Sweden, and Denmark. Eighteen papers on "Domination/Herrschaft as Social Practice" were tabled at the meeting. A
number of these, in revised form, plus additional contributions, have been published in
Alf Lüdtke, ed., *Herrschaft als soziale Praxis: Historische und sozial-anthropologische Studien*
(Göttingen: Vanderhoeck & Ruprecht, 1991).

Papers from the fifth and sixth roundtables, on "the production of history," are now
being edited for publication by Gerald Sider and Gavin Smith.

1

ceding months at the Max-Planck-Institut in Göttingen, Rhys, Alf, and Hans had exchanged ideas about the topics that future roundtables might pursue. There in Baltimore, they proposed that the roundtable group next look at "histories and historiographies." They expressed interest in my own work in rethinking the approach to history, knowledge, and memory in Africa; the paper I had just presented to the Hopkins workshop, "The Undefining of Oral Tradition,"[2] sought to free the discussion of oral materials from the excessively formalist epistemologies that marked and deformed the study of the precolonial past of Africa. They also saw an opportunity to examine new work and debates in central Europe concerning the memory and commemoration of the Fascist period and the Holocaust.

I did not find this an easy or attractive proposal. I raised questions concerning the shift in direction of the roundtables from earlier attentions to work, class, and domination. I did not feel inclined to enter anew the literatures on historiography: the theory of history, the philosophy of history, the varieties of history, historical imagination, the history of historical writing; these were and are thematic fields that I think of when I hear the word "historiography." To me at the time, and still today, the realm of historiography so construed is reserved for an arena of *scholarly* practice on the reconstruction of the past. As a field of *scholarly* activity, "historiography" privileges the written document and the learned and scholarly literatures on the past developing over the centuries. It omits, I asserted over lunch, the practices of history outside the academy.

We went back and forth, and I filled a placemat with notes and questions. Rhys spoke to an interest in "the practices of history, or historians, in handling data" and the "metaphorical structures" that find their way into historical prose. Alf spoke to the possible value of examining "different tempos of historicity" in different cultural and temporal settings and was interested in "the fate of expert knowledge." Jerry raised the issue of how "languages of power invade the discourses of professional historians."

Then Hans briefly drew out a contribution that Professor Herbert Gutman had made at the Second Roundtable in Anthropology and History, Family and Kinship: Material Interest and Emotion. Herb, Hans recalled, told the roundtable group of a woman who had in her youth experienced a dreadful and deforming injury in the workplace but had

2. Published in substantially the same form as "The Undefining of Oral Tradition," *Ethnohistory* 36, 1 (1989): 9–18; and, in longer form, as the introduction to David William

said not a word to her own daughter about her experience. The daughter had for years combed her mother's hair, carefully covering a scar on her head, but never learning the history that lay beneath the scar. For Hans, Herb was situating this story to remark on the complexity of the subject of memory and class consciousness: how does class consciousness evolve if the traumatic experiences of class are suppressed even within the households of those who directly experience them? Hans spoke of the practices of repression that mark and constrain history, including the "collective forgetting" of the Holocaust in central Europe.

I myself recalled Herb Gutman telling this story of the daughter combing her mother's hair across the scar that inscribed the history of work upon her scalp, but over lunch that February I asserted that I had heard the story differently, in the context of Gutman's presentation a few years earlier to the Atlantic Seminar at Hopkins, as a piece of his work in draft on the African-American family in the American past. A brief debate ensued with Alf Lüdtke expressing certainty that the context was a white working-class family in the North.

The lunch closed with a promise from Jerry and me that we would juggle with the proposal to develop a program for the Fifth Roundtable on "the experience, practice, production of history,"[3] and Hans promised to send me the protocols of the Second Roundtable which would, among other things, provide an opportunity to review the record of Gutman's intervention.

*

Between February and September 1985, I cleared away other work and puzzled over the subject of "history and historiographies." I talked to friends and colleagues, searched out essays, reviews, papers, and books and articles that sounded relevant and that I had never taken up. Among many individuals who offered suggestions, I remember well Nancy Struever directing me into some of the recent work of Hayden White and, playfully, into the novels of David Lodge.

In September 1985, I circulated a brief essay, "Discussion: The Production of History," to members of the roundtable and to colleagues and friends. This was intended as the beginning of a theoretical piece, a position paper, to serve as a call for papers for the next roundtable. It opened with some general remarks:

Cohen, *Towards a Reconstructed Past: Historical Texts from Busoga, Uganda* (Oxford: Oxford University Press for the British Academy, 1986), 1–20.
  3. Citing notes I jotted down on the placemat.

Work by historians and anthropologists has demonstrated the power of the processing of the past in societies and in historical settings all over the world. One might argue that in the cumulus of this work, historians and anthropologists have transcended the academic patter of what each discipline has done for, or taken from, the other. Historically minded anthropologists and anthropologically minded historians have, in one sense, shifted ground enormously. They have moved, or at least suggest now the potential of moving, from being audience to one another to being audience to the lively, critical telling, writing and using of history in settings and times outside the control of the crafts and guilds of historical disciplines. Historians and anthropologists together and separately are now comprehending what those outside the guild have long understood—or at least acted upon—that the control of voices on the past has been critical and remains critical in all sorts of settings. This processing of the past in societies and historical settings all over the world, and the struggles for control of voices and texts in innumerable settings which often animate the processing of the past, this we term the *production of history.*

A question central for historians, anthropologists, and others becomes "what is the fate of expert knowledge of the past as members of the crafts or guilds of the historical disciplines recognize, or are forced to recognize, the immense power created as people popularly process the past outside the work of the guild?"

After referring more directly to the production of popular texts on the past outside Europe in the twentieth century,[4] and then drawing out a loose and rather general agenda, the piece closed with some further reflection:

The recognition of this [popular] work frees the student of other societies and other pasts from narrow understandings about the nature of history, historical evidence, historical writing, and what should constitute history. One is presented with a far more spacious and challenging view of history—of the telling of the past—in which it is recognized that there are *multiple locations of historical knowledge.*

One is challenged to stretch comprehension to encompass clearly broad, yet sometimes largely unmapped, reservoirs of his-

4. "Within our agenda there is the recognition that in land after land beyond Europe there has been produced in this century a terrific tide of popular historical literature, produced locally, often in non-Western languages, by individuals and collectivities believing their past, and their histories which tell those pasts, have authority, significance, and meaning."

torical knowledge. Recognizing the spacious and uncharted reservoirs of historical knowledge in present and past societies, we can begin to think more clearly about the forms and directions of *historical knowledge* (which one of us has termed an "endlessly, constantly being woven tapestry of innumerably variegated patterns").[5] One can seek to recognize the play of central metaphors and paradigms, the process of literacy and the shapes of literary genres within the styles and levels of rhetoric, the locations and meanings of silences, the powers of hidden structures, and the forces and patterns of suppression.

In a still tentative way, we refer to these processes as the *production of history*. We mean this to encompass conventions and paradigms in the formation of historical knowledge and historical texts, the patterns and forces underlying interpretation, the contentions and struggles which evoke and produce texts, or particular glosses of tests along with sometimes powerfully nuanced vocabularies, as well as the structuring of frames of record-keeping.[6]

*

On the day that the preliminary position paper was circulated to several of the prospective participants in the fifth roundtable, I received in the mail a copy of a portion of the protocol of the Second Roundtable on Family and Kinship: Material Interest and Emotion.[7] It contained a report of Gutman's now much remarked Paris intervention. According to Herb, following here the skeletal presentation in the text of the protocol, a young woman, a young girl perhaps, had literally been scalped in an industrial accident in a textile mill in Lawrence, Massachusetts, shortly after she was employed at the mill. Soon after her accident—early in 1912—the mill where the girl was injured was shut down by a citywide strike of 20,000 workers. During the strike, which concerned both wages

---

5. Personal communication from Rhys Isaac.

6. In early October 1985, Gerald Sider circulated a parallel discussion piece, centering on "two stories," one concerning the contradictions involved in Native American efforts, through history, to gain federal recognition and registration. In his piece Jerry asked, "How do a people come to understand their own history, and how do such understandings participate in shaping social action? . . . What sorts of relations exist between variant forms of 'guild' histories and different kinds of ethnohistories—e.g., distant/intimate; antagonistic/collusive; borrowing/denying; etc.? . . . the concept 'the production of history' has a double meaning: how understandings of history are created and shaped, and how history itself is made."

7. Convened in Paris in June 1980; many of the papers appeared in a volume edited by Hans Medick and David Sabean, *Interest and Emotion: Essays on the Study of Family and Kinship* (Cambridge: Cambridge University Press, 1984).

and working conditions for the largely immigrant labor force, the girl went before a congressional committee in Washington and gave evidence on the working conditions in the mills, and how she had herself been hired by the mill while below the minimum age.

Continuing, Herb recounted how, some sixty or so years later, a New York reporter went to Lawrence collecting information about electoral politics. While there he learned about the strike of 1912 and about the testimony of the young girl before Congress. He discovered that the girl had married and had a family and that her children were still living in the Lawrence area. He found a daughter and arranged for an interview. What the reporter learned, according to Herb's account, was that the woman, the daughter of the young worker who had courageously gone before Congress, knew nothing of the strike or of her mother's testimony before Congress. To the reporter, the daughter recalled that for years and years she had combed her mother's hair and saw the scar or bald spot on her head; indeed, she combed the hair to cover the scar. It had become, from the daughter's perspective, an everyday ritual, an important moment with her mother in which they could talk about many intimate things. But the mother never once told her daughter of the cause of the injury, of the strike, of her testimony before Congress.[8] It was only through a series of coincidences that sixty-five years later the daughter was to learn—from a reporter from New York City—of her mother's early labor movement activities and of her mother's accident at the mill.

For those who recalled the 1980 roundtable in Paris, Gutman's account was a story powerfully told, deftly placed upon the table to raise in a striking way the question of the fate of worker consciousness. According to the protocol, Herb's discussion began with the observation that there is a mystification about the role of the family in industrial society, that in fact we need to understand what passed between generations as history, even within single families. The story of two women, mother and daughter, was a story of the repressive mechanisms which destroy historical memory. The suppression of history is, in a sense, commented Herb, the suppression of experience, the suppression of dissent and resistance. How does class consciousness evolve, asked Herb rhetorically, if the experience of class action is suppressed even within the house-

---

8. Of course, as I was looking over these notes once again in 1991 and 1992, the question arose as to whether Anita Hill was offering up her recent testimony before Congress in the same room as this young girl—whose name was Camella Teoli. Where the structure of Anita Hill's testimony built upon a *silence broken*, the testimony of Camella Teoli was, as we shall see below, substantially effaced by a *silence constructed*.

holds of the participants? And how does such suppression, and the consequent distortion of class consciousness, occur? Should we recognize that history and memory are as much about repression and suppression as they are about creation and recollection?

While those present recognized that Herb's story, offered extemporaneously, came to the table second or third hand, the story—as participants later related—hung over the group as if the roundtable participants had themselves witnessed an intensely powerful experience.[9] Herb's narrative was taken down into the minutes of the second roundtable; as a text, as intervention, it surfaced again at the third roundtable; and again at the fourth, Herrschaft: Domination as Social Practice;[10] and then again at the planning meeting in Baltimore in February 1985. The story, the experience of hearing it told, in 1980, formed a central piece in the thinking of all those involved in the planning of the fifth and sixth roundtables.

The power of Gutman's intervention only increased when word of his death on July 21, 1985, circulated among a far-flung planning group, and, for some in late 1985, Herb seemed in 1980 to have constructed out of this story an interpretative and critical space for considering the extraordinary moment, five years later and just two months before his death, when a furious debate broke out around the plans for President Ronald Reagan to visit the German military cemetery at Bitburg.[11]

*

Late in August 1985, just a few weeks after Herb Gutman's death, and several years after his presentation of the story at the second roundtable,

9. I participated in the fourth, fifth, and sixth meetings. At these sessions, and in several planning meetings I observed the way in which stories well told could frame a significant segment of the discussions, supplanting abstract and theoretical discussion with exemplary and well-grounded narratives. Greg Dening, Karen Hausen, Utz Jeggle, Pete Linebaugh, Vanessa Maher, Sidney Mintz, Renato Rosaldo, Peter Schneider, Regina Schulte, Gerald Sider, and Michel-Rolph Trouillot were among the participants at roundtable meetings at which I was present who told such stories, and entered them quite brilliantly into the discussions. Was this cohort—over a series of meetings across much of the 1980s—collectively, yet without an organized program, constituting narrative as theoretical intervention?

10. Papers from the fourth roundtable have appeared in Alf Lüdtke, ed., *Herrschaft als soziale Praxis* (Göttingen: Vandenhoeck & Ruprecht, 1991).

11. On Sunday, May 8, 1985. In attempting to explain away the embarrassment of having asserted that the German soldiers, including SS members, buried at Bitburg and those killed by the Nazi machine and buried at Bergen-Belsen concentration camp were together "victims," the president noted that "the German people have very few alive that remember even the war, and certainly none that were adults and participating in any way." For a

a small memorial service was organized in Göttingen. Pete Linebaugh commented at the service that "Herb must have gotten the story from the *Village Voice.*" Later, Pete sent a photocopy of the story, by Paul Cowan, "A City Comes Alive: Lawrence, Massachusetts, 1980," *Village Voice,* July 9–15, 1980, to Hans Medick, one of the organizers of the fifth and sixth roundtables, and so Cowan's 1980 article circulated among the other organizers.

What Pete Linebaugh did not recognize was that the Cowan piece was published four weeks after Herb Gutman presented his account of the Lawrence story at the Paris roundtable. In situating his 1980 Paris intervention around the account of a New York reporter, Herb was recalling the earlier Cowan article published in the *Village Voice,* April 2, 1979, entitled "Whose America Is This?" He had perhaps also seen the galleys, or published book, *Lawrence, 1912: The Bread and Roses Strike,*[12] which had an introduction by Paul Cowan. Clearly, Herb knew far more about Cowan's research on the story than his skeletal, yet moving, account to the roundtable suggested. Indeed, in 1980, he published a brief discussion of Cowan's reportage in an introduction to *Working Lives: The "Southern Exposure" History of Labor in the South.*[13] And Herb may have heard about Cowan's research in Lawrence as early as 1976 or 1977, perhaps through chats with Moe Foner of District 1199's Bread and Roses Project or from David Schneiderman of the *Village Voice.* Steve Brier of the American Labor History Project at the City University of New York recalls that he and Herb had used the Cowan research in a summer labor education seminar in the late 1970s.[14]

*

Cowan's 1980 article is a thick presentation of the story Herb told to the roundtable. And it is also an eloquent presentation of his own discovery of Lawrence and of the "climate of economic and psychological repression in Lawrence which made it an act of courage simply to remember." In the 1980 piece, Cowan traces his own (from a reading of the article, at least three) visits to Lawrence:

(i) The first, in 1976, in which he was researching an "article about the legacy of the events of 1912." This is when he found and met

reading of the debate that developed over the months after the Bitburg debacle, see chap. 3.

12. William Cahn (New York: Pilgrim Press, 1980).

13. Edited by Mark S. Miller (New York: Pantheon, 1980).

14. Personal communication, December 1985.

Josephine Catalano, whose mother, Camella Teoli, had "lost her scalp in the mill" and had testified before the U.S. Congress, and this was when Josephine, or Josie, discovered her mother's role in the strike 64 years earlier and also discovered the source of the scar on her mother's head.

(ii) In 1979, when he returned to do some more research in conjunction with an introduction that he had been asked to write for the *Lawrence, 1912* book. During this visit Cowan was witness to what he describes in his 1980 article as a sudden awakening of consciousness about the 1912 strike throughout the city of Lawrence.

(iii) In the spring of 1980, when he was in Lawrence for Bread and Roses Day, a celebration of the city's "labor and ethnic past that it [the city] had buried for more than fifty years." On this day, Camella Teoli's testimony before Congress was reenacted by a twelve-year-old girl from Lawrence and a path in the Lawrence commons was named Camella Teoli Walkway.

In his 1980 article, Paul Cowan provides some precious insight into the nature of suppression of the knowledge of the past following the "settlement" of the 1912 strike and then through to the mid-1970s, including both larger and smaller dimensions of the process of suppression in Lawrence. "Nationally, the [mill] owners began to lobby for restrictive immigrant legislation, and, locally, they sought to make participation in the strike seem like a stigma rather than a badge of honor." In October 1912, Father James O'Reilly organized a mass demonstration against "radical and atheistic protest." Fifty thousand people, including those who had earlier struck the mill, demonstrated "For God, For Country." By the end of the year, reports Cowan,

> most of the strike organizers and most of the journalists had left town. Local people, abandoned by the outsiders, were forced to choose between the IWW [the International Workers of the World] and God, between being regarded as patriots or as un-Americans. And suddenly, the insurgents, not the conditions in the mills, were the main issue in Lawrence.

Camella's daughter Josie told Cowan that as a child "she had heard a few hints about her mother's role" in the strike but that every time Josie's grandmother brought up the subject of the strike or

> would mention a trip to the "big house" in Washington . . . Camella would silence her mother with a curt nod of the head. So Josephine knew nothing at all about the sensational impact her moth-

er's words had made on America's consciousness [through the
news of her testimony before Congress].

And yet, "Almost every morning Josephine had combed Camella's hair
into a bun, to disguise the spot . . . a six inch bald spot on the back of
her head."

There was also the story of Camella's father, who had been arrested
after the accident for forging the papers that got her into the mill when
she was still under age. And "though he was released immediately he
didn't like to discuss the incident." There was also the story of Camella's
son, Frankie Palumbo. Frankie recalled for Cowan that he too had
worked in the mills, along with his mother, and he remembered that the
mill supervisors had "always treated her badly." Frankie remembers his
mother as

> an obedient, uncomplaining woman . . . her bosses often repri-
> manded her. Instead of promoting her to a job where she'd receive
> an hourly wage, they kept her on piecework until she retired.
> They'd give her "bad work" for days at a time . . . weak bolts of
> fabric that sometimes fell apart after they'd run through the ma-
> chine. Every fifteen minutes or so, she'd have to stand up and retie
> the fabric. At the end of the day, when workers weighed in with
> their pieces, her bundle was often lighter than the others: as a re-
> sult, she earned less. Everyone knew that "bad work" was a form
> of punishment.

But until Paul Cowan visited him in 1976, Frankie Palumbo too did not
know why his mother was punished with "bad work." "My mother
didn't talk about her past because she thought it might get all of us in
trouble," Cowan quoted Frankie.

> We were afraid to speak our minds in the mills. Our parents
> worked there, our aunts worked in there, our cousins worked
> there. They'd fire all the relatives if anyone spoke out. Sometimes
> they even threatened to fire all the Italians and replace us with
> Poles or with Syrians. So we didn't want them to think we were
> agitators.

Frankie himself had experienced such punishment. Cowan noted that

> some days the bun that Josephine had combed in the morning
> would fall apart, exposing Camella's scar. Frankie, who oiled ma-
> chines, would have to leave his workplace to fix his mother's hair.
> The supervisors regarded that act of filial loyalty as a form of in-

subordination. As punishment, they'd send him to another part of the mill to work.

A feature of the suppressive process—larger than irony—was that Frankie could not know that in risking his situation in the mill to cover his mother's scar he was suppressing one small piece of the articulation of the history of the strike in the mill workplace.

Cowan himself commented that

> The act of going to Washington must have been the most exciting in Camella Teoli's life. But the mother her children knew, Camella Teoli Palumbo, was just a mill hand with an odd bald spot, a sweet silent lady who bought and cooked the traditional eels on Christmas Eve, who rarely missed a Sunday Mass. She concealed her past to protect her young from reprisals—to help them achieve the kind of upward mobility in America that the 1912 strike, a victorious mass action, had helped make possible.

Cowan produced other illustrations of the processes of constricting and suppressing the memory of the past in Lawrence. Josie, in 1976, spoke of the meaning for her of discovering her mother's history, but did not want her name used in the story.[15] And only in 1979 or 1980 did a few of Cowan's informants in Lawrence allow him to use their real names. Most wanted to preserve their anonymity as they presented their stories of their experience of the strike six and a half decades earlier. One man told how his father had gone underground to avoid being deported and the "son still feared [in 1976] that if he was publicly associated with the strike his business would be boycotted." Another man was afraid that he would be fired from his city hall job, even in 1976. "You have to understand," he told Cowan, "I'm a very popular kid around town. I don't want to go around giving away the city's secrets." Another thought Cowan might be an FBI agent.

There were both general and intimate forces of suppression which removed the strike of 1912 from public discussion and from the discourse between generations within families in Lawrence. One recognizes immediately the central place of conflict in the production of historical knowledge, and the hegemony of those who controlled the Lawrence mills. One can also see that the suppression is not made actual by edict alone. The people of Lawrence—the mill workers, those who struck, even one who bravely spoke before Congress about the exploita-

15. In Cowan's 1979 *Village Voice* story, Josie was referred to as Mathilda.

tion of the mill system—organized, and carried the burden of, the suppression of their past.

*

In a study completed in 1981, the anthropologist Eva Hauser has taken
up a similar problem of suppression of memory in an immigrant community in a different New England mill town.[16]

> During the field investigation . . . it became apparent that these mil-
> itant ex-peasants from Galicia did, in fact, participate in the labor
> movement of the 1930s, but that the traces of their past involved
> with the labor struggle have been carefully concealed . . . instead
> of [asking] *why*, I asked my data *how* the militant past was con-
> cealed. I ask *how* this group concealed certain militant working-
> class features of its past in order to try to understand *why* this
> was so.[17]

What Hauser's research revealed was that in this setting "the ethnic
story consciously conceals class conflict and any evidence of past class
struggles."[18] And, "Ethnicity seems to function as part of the repertory
of avoidance strategies though earlier it had nurtured class solidarity."[19]
She notes that "In my analysis of the oral histories and direct communication with members of the group about their past the traces of the
pattern of concealment emerge, sometimes in the content, sometimes in
the distortion, and sometimes in the anxious laughter or rapid speech
of the informant."[20] One is given a sense that, as in Lawrence, the mute
character of "public memory" involves an active process of production
and suppression of history of participation in the labor struggles and
strikes.[21]

The social historian Ardis Cameron, who has worked on the events

16. "Ethnicity and Class Consciousness in a Polish American Community" (Ph.D. diss.,
Johns Hopkins University, 1981).

17. Ibid., 3.

18. Ibid., 340.

19. Ibid., 333.

20. Ibid., 341.

21. In a personal communication Richard Rathbone has pointed out, among his numerous helpful responses to a draft of "The Production of History" position paper, the case
of the "arriviste" ethnicity of the "new Welsh" who have returned to Wales, and to Welsh
tradition, from, for example, London. He notes that "Command of the language and bris-
tling indignation [concerning Welsh tradition and Welsh rights] are the passports to ca-
reers in the Welsh media, the civil service, and so forth. The honed memories, the stories
of stories of stories, are part of a qualification as pertinent as muscle in a labourer or
math in a programmer." Rathbone sees an active and creative production of history, and

in Lawrence of 1912 and especially their prelude, as opposed to the suppression of memory of the Lawrence strike, has brought attention to the "varied and at times radicalized forms of women's consciousness formed below the surface of official scrutiny, in the convoluted yet ordinary web of female daily life" in Lawrence. Cameron takes this formation as the prime basis of the militancy and class consciousness which in 1912 shook the manufacturing system in Lawrence.[22]

The immense significance of the terrains of intimate association of Camella and daughter Josie are underlined. Intimate and social domains become one. The reader of Cowan's articles might imagine—even if one has not been told—that each time that Josie combed her mother's hair, Camella confronted her own historical memory privately, actively, consciously, while closing off her daughter from inquiry into the events of her working and insurgent childhood. In a comment on a draft of the roundtable position paper, Ruth Behar remarked, in respect to the story of Camella Teoli and her daughter, "You can't draw a line between the personal and social domains in this case; it is as if the two domains become translations of each other."[23]

One may also see that this experience of suppression was not self-willed; it was enforced, and continuously enforced, by the supervisors' punishment of Camella and the disciplining of her son Frankie. Yet this hegemony was clearly not entire. Cowan has noted that Josie remembered that, "as a child, she had heard a few hints about her mother's role [in the strike] . . . Once in a while, her grandmother would mention a trip to the 'big house' in Washington—the White House—and describe some sort of meeting with the President." Frankie recognized that his mother's work was an unexplained punishment. Another resident of Lawrence, Ignatius Piscitello, while in high school, discovered in the Lawrence public library Camella Teoli's testimony in a two-volume memoir of the 1912 congressional hearing. The memoir had been published by the congressional printer after the hearing. Cowan himself discovered that Piscitello, raging over his own mother's long, painful

---

manipulation of history, in this case ethnic, in the strategies of the upwardly mobile, extending the attention of the Cowan story upon the working class of Lawrence. It is perhaps production, and simultaneously it is also "production as suppression," of earlier or alternate expressions concerning the past.

22. "Bread and Roses Revisited: Women's Culture and Working-Class Activism in the Lawrence Strike of 1912," in Ruth Milkman, ed., *Women, Work and Protest: A Century of Women's Labor History* (Boston: Routledge & Kegan Paul, 1985), 42–61. Kathy Peiss kindly brought Ardis Cameron's research to my attention.

23. Personal communication, 1986.

dying (from 1974 through 1976) after what he remembered as her awful life at the mills, "became obsessed with a desire to vindicate her difficult, obscure life. Since then, he'd been fighting his own lonely battle to revive the memory of the 1912 strike." And others had kept the memory alive within their own hearts and minds.[24] During his 1979 visit, Cowan participated with Piscitello in a radio call-in program. Cowan recounts that

> old-timers called in, and reminisced about Big Bill Haywood's speeches on the [Lawrence] Commons, about the soup kitchens, which were organized by nationality groups, about the Harvard students, who had gotten academic credit for serving as militia men, or about the experience of working in the mills.

One of the more powerful aspects of Cowan's discussion of the lifting of the veil of public silence from the memory of the strike concerns the young mayor of Lawrence, Lawrence Lefebre, who was eating lunch "casually listening" to the radio call-in show which, Cowan noted, so animated the people of the city to tell their own stories of the strike, the repression, and their work in the mills. According to Cowan, Mayor Lefebre himself

> tried to phone the show, but all the lines were jammed. When he finally got through, he said he'd never been exposed to the positive version of Lawrence's history that he was hearing on the radio that day. The stories the callers told were thrilling . . . He urged all Lawrence citizens to share their reminiscences of the Bread and Rose[s] strike with Piscitello, [Ralph] Fasanella [whose series of paintings of the strike had just gone on display at the town library] and me [Cowan].

The evidence presented suggests that Mayor Lefebre experienced a catharsis during that lunch hour. One interpretation of that day in October 1979, and of the subsequent months culminating in the Bread and Roses celebration the following spring, is that the energy of history production in Lawrence was moved from the unveiling of memory by many individuals in and around the city to the unveiling of a walkway by the city corporation. One might observe that as the mayor listened to the stories

---

24. Paul Cowan's articles do not mention some fairly well organized oral history projects in Lawrence. Some preliminary inquiries into this research have suggested that these projects were organized to capture information about events and experiences in the past of Lawrence but have not addressed themselves to the experience of suppression of memory and of public expression of history. Some of Cowan's sources have interview testimonies preserved in the Lawrence oral history archives.

told on the radio and as he dialed the radio station again and again he was moving himself to the front of a popular "uprising" of history production. Cowan reports,

> The night before "Bread and Roses Day" [spring 1980], Mayor Lefebre attended a dinner dance for a local alderman. The audience of 1000 was mostly composed of policemen and firemen. When the Mayor got up to speak, he held a copy of *Lawrence 1912: The Bread and Roses Strike* above his head, pointed to the Fasanella picture of militia men marching towards a picket line of striking workers on the cover, and predicted that soon, "Lawrence will take its place next to Lexington and Concord in the forefront of American history."

Might one be excused for recalling Father O'Reilly's mass demonstration in Lawrence on Columbus Day 1912, in which a different intervention forced order and control upon a disordered and creative insurgency?

Mayor Lefebre's linkage—Lawrence, Lexington, and Concord—of the reawakening of the past in Lawrence in 1979 and 1980 with the broader production of history in the nation is a telling transformation. On the one hand, Mayor Lefebre had taken it upon himself to transform the enthusiasm of individuals telling their own stories in public, reclaiming and proclaiming their past, into a formal and corporate celebration and memorial. In placing Lawrence beside Lexington and Concord, he was further transforming the experience of the past, of the suppression and repression, and of the reawakening, into a larger story in which the process of producing history at one level is closed and at a broader level is opened. In holding above his head the 1979 book, and in directing the eye toward the 1979 paintings by Fasanella, Mayor Lefebre was essentially calling for—indeed producing—a closure of public and private production of the individual, personal stories of the strike which had begun to be told openly only after the printing of the book and only after the paintings had been shown in Lawrence.

*

There is another plane to the story of the reawakening of the story of history telling in Lawrence—the story of the story—and this is in studying the role of Paul Cowan from 1976 to 1980 in the transformation of historical processes in Lawrence. According to his own presentation, Cowan was able to grasp and to articulate the meaning of suppression of the memory of the past in Lawrence from his first visit in 1976. An indication of the power of the outsider in the Lawrence story, and in the

story of the story, is that it was Cowan who linked Ignatius Piscitello's
reading of the testimony of Camella Teoli before Congress, which Piscitello found in a Lawrence public library, to Josie's curiosity, or absence
of knowing, about the causes of the scar on her mother's head.

Cowan's role in the Lawrence story was larger than this, for Cowan
was clearly part of a wider collection of individuals interested in the
struggle for control of historical memory in Lawrence. Indeed, Cowan
lets the reader know that at least a handful of individuals and their
organizations, mostly based outside the city and mostly in New York,
were heavily engaged in the organization of the reawakening of historical memory in Lawrence. By 1979, the Pilgrim Press of New York was
bringing out the *Lawrence, 1912* volume (a new edition of a work originally titled *Mill Town*) and Moe Foner of the District 1199 Bread and
Roses project was assisting with the distribution of the book.

Following his visit to Lawrence in 1979 (the time of the call-in program), Cowan returned to New York and

> described the enthusiasm I'd encountered to the editors of Pilgrim
> Press, to officials of the United Church of Christ, Pilgrim Press's
> parent organization, and to Moe Foner of District 1199's Bread and
> Roses program . . . They wanted to co-sponsor the event [Mayor
> Lefebre's planned celebration] . . . So, in mid-November, the New
> Yorkers and the Lawrence political leaders met to plan a "Bread
> and Roses Day" on the [Lawrence] Commons. They agreed that
> the walkway would be named after Camella Teoli . . . Moe Foner
> had commissioned a song for the occasion—"The Ballad of Ca-
> mella Teoli," composed by Nicholas Scarem.

And a film strip for the Lawrence schools was commissioned by Moe
Foner's project.

When Cowan describes those dignitaries or celebrities present for the
1980 Bread and Roses Day commemoration—

> Congressman James Shannon; Peter Yarrow and Mary Travers of
> Peter, Paul and Mary; Marge Tabankin, the head of VISTA; repre-
> sentatives of the White House and the Department of Labor;
> Ralph Fasanella . . . ; Moe Foner . . . ; and Howard Spragg of the
> United Church of Christ . . . along with dozens of newspapers and
> television reporters . . .

—it is almost as if Cowan wants the reader to draw a parallel with those
who came to Lawrence to witness, and join forces with, the strikers of
1912. Cowan, remarking on the 1912 enthusiasm, notes the arrival in
Lawrence of

> an all-star cast of activists came to town, including Big Bill Hay-
> wood, the cool-headed Elizabeth Gurley Flynn, the poet and orga-
> nizer Arturo Giovanitti, IWW organizer Joseph Ettor, and a young
> socialist named Margaret Sanger whose advocacy of birth control
> methods would soon . . .

Later the journalists Lincoln Steffens and Ray Stannard Baker came "to
investigate working conditions in the mills, living conditions in the tene-
ments." And Mrs. William Howard Taft, Cowan records, "journeyed to
Lawrence herself."

The publication, the paintings, the mayor's intervention, the ceremony,
the planning committees in New York and Lawrence, did not, however,
close off the energy of history production in Lawrence in 1980. Beyond
the reportage of the local newspaper and the regional cable television
station,

> scores of people . . . have begun to boast about a father or mother
> who worked in the mills. Sometimes they bring old books, family
> pictures, strike posters, workman's tools over to the library, for the
> whole town to see . . . and children from every school in the city
> will tape-record interviews with their grandparents and other
> elderly people in town, and discuss the stories they've heard
> with their classmates.

*

Considerable freedom has been taken here[25] with Paul Cowan's excellent
story, taking it apart and putting it together again in several different
ways. It is as compelling a story, or story of a story, today as it must have
been for Herb Gutman when he first came across it and for those present
when Herb told the story at the Paris roundtable.

In the fall of 1985, as I considered how to construct a position paper
out of the first discussion draft, the effect on my roundtable colleagues
of Gutman's intervention in Paris claimed a central position: the story of
Camella Teoli's accident in the Lawrence mill, the Bread and Roses strike
of 1912, the girl's testimony before Congress, the daughter combing her
mother's hair to cover the scar, the silence between mother and daughter, the New York reporter reconnecting the woman to her mother's experience in the mill. These were the essential pieces of Herb's question
concerning memory, the fate of experience, and class consciousness. But
as I sifted through the various texts and reports—the roundtable protocol, the various remembrances of Herb's intervention, the reports of the

25. And, similarly, in the original position paper completed in 1986.

August 1985 memorial service in Göttingen, the articles by Paul Cowan in the *Village Voice*, the testimonies of Lawrence residents recorded by Cowan, and other materials—additional questions and data came to be adjoined to Herb Gutman's original query.

One cluster of questions surrounded the author Paul Cowan himself from 1976 to 1980. Paul, who died four years ago, was the *Village Voice* reporter who went to Lawrence to look at the state of working-class America. In a personal communication, Paul told me that one of his main interests in exploring Lawrence was a lingering concern with the George Wallace phenomenon in working-class American communities.[26] As I traipsed around the Lawrence stories, I came to see Cowan as in one sense the *Grenzgenger* (border-crosser), the stranger, the outsider who ignited public and private catharses of history and memory in Lawrence, and in another sense the organic intellectual able to grasp and articulate the meaning of suppression of the memory of the past in Lawrence from his first visit in 1976. He clearly was *making* the account in numerous senses of the word, and his connections to labor organizations and progressive publishers in New York determined that the events which transpired in Lawrence following his visits there would be enjoined to, reconstituted by, individuals and organizations outside Lawrence.

Another array of questions and observations surrounded the processes of memory in Lawrence. The ignorance of Camella Teoli's daughter—and others in Lawrence—in 1976 was not a consequence of a forgetting, a loss of knowledge, but rather of powerful and continuous acts of control in both public and intimate spaces. Such control was organized not only by the firm but by the descendants of the 1912 strikers who even in 1976 still feared that word of their parents' participation in the strike would result in their deportation to Italy. And, in an important sense, it was unknowingly organized by Camella's son Frankie as he left his work station in the mill to fix his mother's hair after the bun that covered the scar fell apart.

And there are observations and questions concerning the removal of the veil of public silence from the memory of the strike. During 1979, there was a dramatic opening toward the telling of long silenced histories and memories that surrounded a radio call-in show in Lawrence

---

26. On March 14, 1986, in a discussion at the Graduate Center, City University of New York, of a draft of the roundtable position paper, Cowan related that he was drawn into the Camella Teoli story for several additional reasons. (1) He was seeking a way of discussing the "cultural chaos" he saw within the *Village Voice* office in New York City in the early 1970s. Cowan was intrigued by the paradox that the radical intellectuals were abandoning the culture of families, marriage, children while family life and marriage

in which Cowan was participating. From that day through elaborate commemorative exercises the next spring the energy of history production in Lawrence was moved from the unveiling of memory by many individuals in and around the city toward the corporate unveiling of a public walkway honoring Camella Teoli, giving the history of the strike, finally, an official status within the city of Lawrence.

And one may seek to understand better Herb Gutman's engagement with Paul Cowan's writings on Lawrence. From Ira Berlin's recent compilation and editing of Gutman's unpublished essays, we learn that Herb in 1982 wrote out his own rendering of the Camella Teoli story in a paper entitled "Historical Consciousness in Contemporary America,"[27] given as an address to the Organization of American Historians the same year. While the text of Herb's address was not known to participants in the Paris roundtable or to those organizing the Fifth Roundtable, it is clear that by 1982 Herb had read closely all of Paul Cowan's articles in the *Village Voice*, for he quotes from them liberally in constructing his account of the experience of memory in Lawrence. But between the 1980 intervention and the 1982 essay, Herb appears to have somewhat reframed the arguments surrounding his retelling the story. While in 1980, his intervention concerned "simply" class consciousness, by 1982 he was intrigued by the way in which the contemporaneous evocation of African-American experience through the celebration of *Roots*—both the book and the television series—contrasted with the absence of attention to the reawakening of memory concerning the Lawrence strike of 1912. He wrote, "The devices [Alex] Haley used to humanize slaves—his achievement ideology, which pitted the individual against society—ironically reinforced the same American possessive individualism which allowed no place for Camella Teoli and her daughter."[28] In his 1982 essay, Gutman sought to elaborate an argument on, for America, the distinctions and tensions among individual and collective memory and consciousness.

As an aside, one might note that, whatever the inherent power or fate

---

were, evidently, essential elements of working-class lives. (2) He was intrigued by the continuing primacy of the "melting pot" thesis of American immigrant history, even as so much experience reflected the social and political vitality of ethnic continuities from the strands of European homelands. And, (3) Camella was captivating because his own family's past had never been disclosed to him. Only later did I discover, through my son Ben Cohen, Cowan's book *An Orphan in History: One Man's Triumphant Search for His Roots* (New York: Doubleday, 1982). In this book Cowan discussed his Lawrence research in brief, pages 207–11.

27. Herbert G. Gutman, *Power and Culture: Essays on the American Working Class*, ed. Ira Berlin (New York: Pantheon, 1987), 395–412.

28. Ibid., 404.

of the story of Camella Teoli, it seems to be readily told and retold. In his long introduction to the Gutman essays, Berlin tells it still again,[29] though in a still more economical form than either here or in Gutman's written rendition.

*

When Herb Gutman introduced the essential elements of the Lawrence story to the Paris roundtable, he was seeking to exemplify the—for him—core question of worker consciousness, but as one unlocks the history of the "story," or the "story" of the "story," one recognizes a far more complex frame of reference extending from the editorial office of the *Village Voice* to the site of Camella Teoli's accident. Gutman's intervention and the response to it—attempting to read some coherent meaning from the story—seemed to tap into what was then a prevalent, and still persisting, fascination with cultural interpretation exemplified by Clifford Geertz, most notably his reading of a Balinese cockfight.[30]

In a discussion of the shifting attentions of anthropologists from a concern with structure to an interest in the way in which events unfold—such as the daughter's unknowing participation in her mother's suppression of her own history or Herb Gutman telling a story in Paris—Sally Falk Moore has argued forcefully against the kind of reification of essential cultural system that she saw in the Geertzian approach, and with a skepticism about the value of such readings of "events":

> An event is not necessarily best understood as the exemplification of an extant symbolic or social order. Events may equally be evidence of the ongoing dismantling of structures or of attempts to create new ones. Events may show a multiplicity of social contestations and the voicing of competing cultural claims. Events may reveal substantial areas of normative indeterminacy.[31]

Without saying as much, the concept of "event" comes apart[32] as Moore develops her critique of assumptions of coherent meanings and norma-

29. Ibid., 65–66.

30. "Deep Play: Notes on the Balinese Cockfight," *Daedalus* 101 (1972): 1–37. Also published in Clifford Geertz, *The Interpretation of Cultures: Selected Essays* (New York: Basic Books, 1973), 412–53.

31. Sally Falk Moore, "Explaining the Present: Theoretical Dilemmas in Processual Ethnography," *American Ethnologist* 14, 1 (1987): 729.

32. Moore does not surrender the "event" as the appropriate focus of the processual approaches she calls for, nor does she intend to let the concept of "event" come apart as one notes the multiplicities and complexities of source and effect; indeed, she sees partic-

tive determinacy. "It is difficult to find in any society universal sub-
scriptions to the overarching ideological totalism that the Geertzian
search suggests. To say the obvious, the making of history is taking
place in many connected locales at once."[33]

*

We may also pause, perhaps, to think more broadly about the manner,
and the manners, of interpretation. The structure of the presentation
here, in speaking of Gutman, Cowan, Lefebre, Camella, Josie, Lawrence,
and the mill, we are clearly not looking at a story but rather at a skeletal
account of stories of stories. The *laminate* quality of this reading of history production has several effects. The terrains of Camella, Josie, and
Frankie are joined to the terrains of Mayor Lefebre, Paul Cowan, and
the New York labor committees, and to the terrains of Herb Gutman
and those of us working on the subject of the production of history,
and those who pick up these accounts and thereby constitute a specific
audience in addition to the audiences we imagine. Many historians
work, knowingly and unknowingly, on the representation and presentation of a story of a story of a story. Sometimes they/we lose sight and
sound of those we study telling their own stories, sometimes those
voices are made to sound clearly in our minds and in our words as we
of the guild proceed with our professional production of history.[34] One
challenge is to distill the processes through which these stories develop.
Another is to recognize the edges of our stories and of the stories being
told to us from the past, to work toward comprehending the forces
emergent at these edges.[35]

In his life history of a cane worker, Sidney Mintz locates such a site,
the figure of his subject Taso. Mintz allows Taso his own voice; for example, Taso speaks,

---

ular "kinds of events" as "a preferred form of raw data," which she refers to as "diagnostic
events." To this reader, this specific part of her formulation seems stiff, brittle, and theoret-
ically unproductive.

33. *American Ethnologist* 14:730.

34. Renato Rosaldo has remarked that "Doing oral history involves telling stories about
stories people tell about themselves. Method in this discipline should therefore attend to
'our' stories, 'their' stories, and the connections between them. The process of reconstructing the past, in other words, requires a double vision that focuses at once on historians' modes of composition and their subjects' ways of conceiving the past" ("Doing Oral
History," *Social Analysis* 4 [September 1980]: 89–99).

35. For an important example of this approach, see Carolyn Hamilton, "A Positional
Gambit: Shaka Zulu and the Conflict in South Africa," *Radical History Review* 41 (Spring
1989): 5–31.

I ... suffered an infection in my hand, which was the result of the prick of a fish spine ... And that day ... they came by selling fish and we bought some for the house. And as Elisabeth [Taso's wife] was ironing, I set about cleaning the fish. It happened that as I passed the knife to scale them a spine pricked my finger. I thought it would be a trivial thing, and I only undertook to squeeze a few drops of blood out of the finger and left it that way. And later on I went again to serve in the store, and I attribute what happened to putting my hand in a barrel of salt pork (*tocino*). It formerly came in barrels, with water and everything. And I believe I got the infection from that. When night came, well, the hand hurt, and during the night it bothered me a lot.[36]

Taso is allowed to compose, and to convey, his meaningful environment and experience, to explicate pain, to relate his moments, to depict the matter of his own relationships to work, kin, his body, and friends; in a sense, Taso has seized the opportunity to define the meaning of experience that Clifford Geertz appropriated in establishing his authority over the reading of the Balinese cockfight. It is also clear that Taso produced his own history inside of Sid Mintz's intentionalities. At the same time, Sidney Mintz's "life history" is permitted to give space to Taso to relocate in our consciousness the *tocino*, to produce history, in ways not permitted Camella Teoli.

Taso and Camella suggest how much more skill must be acquired to handle the meanings of forgetting and remembering. Camella's knowledge of self was suppressed, not forgotten, and the processes were active, conflictual. There was, clearly, remembering in the "forgetting." If there is an operative expression, it is not "history lost." For Taso, remembering the past was a medium of crystallization of elements to which he himself appropriated significance, combing essential pieces from masses of detailed memories. To tell the story of his injury, he had to clear to the side, to "forget," much of the experience—a "forgetting" in the "remembering."[37]

The story of the story of the story of Camella and Lawrence's strike is continuous transformation of past, as history, into present experience, not only in 1976 or 1979 or 1980 but also within the routine of the daughter's combing her mother's hair or Frankie troubling himself to cover his mother's scar. History, in this sense, is not only the proof or the prod-

36. Sidney W. Mintz, *Worker in the Cane: A Puerto Rican Life History* (New Haven, Conn.: Yale University Press, 1960; New York: W. W. Norton, 1974), 166.

37. I am grateful to Ruth Behar for her assistance in the comparison of the Camella and Taso stories.

uct—Mayor Lefebre's commemorative activities—but also the stuff of the process of production. And while History may be "the artefact of cultural systems,"[38] it may also be, as in Lawrence, the tissue and the force of the cultural and social processes of work, consociation, and family. In approaching the "production of history." one is also approaching "history as production."

38. In a presentation, "A Poetic of History," tabled at, and circulated well before, the Fifth Roundtable in Anthropology and History in July 1986, Greg Dening wrote: "It is unimaginable that someone—'primitive' or 'civilized'—has no past: it is unimaginable that someone does not know some part of that past. 'Memory' is our everyday word for knowledge of the past, but memory suggests some personal or institutional immediacy in the connection between the past and those who experienced it. We need a word that includes memory but embraces all the other ways of knowing a past that has not been experienced. We do not have such a word, but in this poetics of history let me declare that word to be history. History is public knowledge of the past. That I should describe history with the adjective 'public' will alert an audience familiar with Clifford Geertz's writings to the fact that I consider history in this sense to be *the artefact of cultural systems* [emphasis added], to be expressed in communicative exchanges, to have forms specific to social occasions. History is a human universal."

TWO
Namuluta v. Kazibwe

The close reading of the story of the story of the Lawrence strike suspends attention upon the "events" themselves—the strike of 1912 and the Bread and Roses Day of 1980—and draws one to the "middle period" in which history suppression and history production were alive and powerful in Lawrence. Such a reading of the Lawrence stories recovers, rather than elides, the boundaries or membranes which both separate and join the several readings of the past. This laminate reading of the stories of the stories may be reckoned a most cumbersome contraption; for example, in just simply attempting to understand how Herb Gutman came to learn about "the story" and how his iterations of the account changed over time.

The form of presentation sought or rendered here is rather different from the "clean text" around which notations, exterior and interior readings, and other source material are filtered to the periphery. And, as well, some elements of the process of production of the text and preceding texts are intentionally introduced into the presentation, where in another version of the account—as in Herb Gutman's and Ira Berlin's published versions—the sociology of discovery and the mode of reconstitution of the story are left to the side, as if, perhaps, they never happened. These boundaries, between the story told (as with Gutman, Berlin, Cowan, and myself) and the story not told (as with Camella Teoli and her daughter), are enraveled with authorities and power, immersed in the concise narrative form of the historian's account, saturated by the powerful silences constructed around the combing of Camella's hair.

In a different, though not unrelated examination of the circumstances of "authorial" authority, the photographer Richard Avedon complicates his audience's "reading" of his photographs by unveiling his perspective on the contingencies of power that lie between photographer and subject in the interstice marked by the clicking of the shutter and the changing of plates of film.

> What happens as we observe one another . . . involves manipulations, submission . . . assumptions are reached and acted upon that could seldom be made with impunity in ordinary life. The subject imagined . . . must be discovered in someone else willing to take part in a fiction he cannot possibly know about. My concerns are not his. We have separate ambitions for the image. His need to plead his case probably goes as deep as my need to plead mine, but the control is with me.[1]

1. Foreword to *In the American West* (New York: Abrams, 1985).

Unknowingly, Avedon has captured an image—not photographic this time, but nevertheless powerful—of the historian at work.

Such an exposition *of*, and at the same time *on*, power is offered in an extraordinarily similar if also disorienting voice by James Clifford when he establishes his position within the observation and representation of the Mashpee trial in Massachusetts in 1978:

> It should be clear from what follows that I am portraying primarily the trial, not the complex lives of Indians and other ethnic groups in Mashpee. Still, in the process I make strong gestures toward truths missed by the dominant categories and stories in the courtroom. Thus I invoke as an absence the reality of Mashpee and particularly of its Indian lives. I do this to maintain the historical and ethnographic seriousness of the account, a seriousness I wish both to assert and to limit . . . I accept the fact that my version of the trial, its witnesses, and its stories may offend people on several sides of the issue. Many individual positions are more complex than I have been able to show. My account may be objectionable to Native Americans for whom culture and tradition are continuities, not inventions, who feel stronger, less compromised ties to aboriginal sources than my analysis allows. For them this version of "identity in Mashpee" may be about rootless people like me, not them . . . When I report on witnesses at the trial, the impressions are mine . . . I offer vignettes of persons and events in the courtroom that are obviously composed and condensed. Testimony evoked in a page or two may run to hundreds of pages in the transcript . . . Overall, if the witnesses seem flat and somewhat elusive, the effect is intentional. Using the usual rhetorical techniques, I could have given a more intimate sense of peoples' personalities or of what they were really trying to express; but I have preferred to keep my distance. A courtroom is more like a theater than a confessional. Mistrustful of transparent accounts, I want mine to manifest some of its frames and angles, its wavelengths.[2]

Clifford allows his subjects to speak, and of course conveys their words to us, his audience. In doing so, however, he assigns himself a self-consciously conceived and manifested power to control the relations of speakers in the courtroom and readers of his book.

One is invited to examine this authorial claim more closely[3] and an opportunity lies in opening to view a photograph taken in the 1920s

2. James Clifford, "Identity in Mashpee," in James Clifford, *The Predicament of Culture: Twentieth-Century Ethnography, Literature, and Art* (Cambridge, Mass.: Harvard University Press, 1988), 290–91.
3. Is there a word that has the opposite meaning to "disclaimer"? This seems the word that Clifford seeks.

of and by Herr Theo Gaudig. In his close study of photography in and on German work processes, accidents, and discipline in the German machine tool and heavy industries between the 1890s and the 1930s, Alf Lüdtke has sought to understand the complex "fields-of-force" between management ideals and worker resistance and worker collusion in the workplace. In his examinations of works albums, illustrated management journals, and the use of photographs in labor journals and newspapers, Lüdtke has developed critical profiles of found photographs taken and printed by works photographers which seem to be staged and framed to reflect the image of the worker at his machine, images that works management believed in and sought to foster through the use of industrial photography. Management sought not only to celebrate the ideal worker but to deflect labor from careless and indolent practices that resulted in accidents in the workplace and defective manufacture.

One such photograph of a Hanomag turner presented the worker at his metal lathe, perfectly focused, dedicated to his tasks, in control of his machine, his materials, and his effort. In his research Lüdtke came across a nearly identical photograph of a turner at his lathe published in a trade union journal and taken, apparently, by a worker interested in photography. The image seems formulaic, and the photograph reflects the mastery of the industrial photographer producing an image for management. Lüdtke has sought to interrogate the consonance of a management image and the representation of a Krupp turner selected for a cover of a critical labor review.[4]

Later, Lüdtke found the person who appears in the photograph, Theo Gaudig, who was the photographer himself. Herr Gaudig recalled that the photograph was taken in 1928. His family had wanted him to use his photographic skills to take a picture of himself at work, a picture that could be placed among the valued portraits of family members. Such photography being against the rules of the factory, Gaudig went into the plant at night, ostensibly on another mission, set up his lights in an empty workshop, and took the picture without management or guards knowing that he had done so, and framing the self-portrait in a way that he felt his family would cherish.[5]

4. The version of this photograph—focusing only on the worker—graced the cover of *Arbeiter-Illustrierte-Zeitung* in February 1928, a journal whose editors, Lüdtke relates, "explicitly understood photography as a 'weapon' in class struggle." Within a few weeks, the complete photograph was published in the *Arbeiter-Fotograf*, the journal of the Vereinigung der Arbeiter Fotografen, the society of worker photographers, whose membership numbered about 2,400 in 1931.
5. This account of Alf Lüdtke's research on the Hanomag photographs and on the Krupp turner Theo Gaudig's "self-portrait" is drawn from notes taken at a seminar at

In a sense, by violating the rules against unauthorized use of photographic equipment inside the plant, Herr Gaudig had stolen time and opportunity to produce an image of himself for his family, an image almost identical to the one plant management itself fostered through its own regular use of a professional photographer. In nighttime, he had smuggled into the plant not only his bulky equipment but his sense of his family's sense of himself. And through considerable ingenuity, if not also courage, Gaudig had portrayed himself to his family exactly as the firm would have portrayed him: not as the thief of time and opportunity, but as the earnest, dedicated, and loyal worker knowing his machine and his materials. By stealth, he confirmed the management's image of the ideal worker, and perhaps simultaneously suppressed alternative images which the opportunity he had created for himself would have allowed.

How far removed from Theo Gaudig's photographic gambit was Frankie Palumbo's risking his position in the mill by leaving his post to cover his mother's scar, thereby in the breaking of plant discipline suppressing one small piece of an alternative vision of work and of factory?[6]

As the Gaudig story suggests, and the Lawrence story reveals, hegemony is a present condition in the production of historical knowledge, but we are also drawn toward a recognition of the incomplete nature of dialectics, the reality that outcomes are neither known nor assured. We see that hegemony does not fully enclose the processes of production of history but lies within the contexts that produce, reproduce, change historical knowledge. The public discussion of the 1912 strike had been suppressed and repressed for six and a half decades but the silence had multiple edges; witness the tremendous force of the silence within the familial relations of Camella, the daughter, and Frankie.[7]

Against Clifford's view of the power of the observer, ethnographer,

---

Johns Hopkins University in the mid-1980s. He is now preparing for publication a full treatment of this research: "Industrie bilder—Bilder der Industriearbeit? Zur Industrie- und Arbeitfotografie ca. 1890–1940," *Historische Anthropologie: Kulture-Gesellschaft-Alltag* 3 (1993). See also, "Zu den Chancen einer 'visuellen Geschichte,'" *Journal für Geschichte* 3 (1986): 25–31.

6. The ultimate power of Alf Lüdtke's work on photography of the work process in German heavy industry lies in its immediate recognition that for those involved—like Theo Gaudig and like the editors of the worker journals—images did not neatly resolve themselves into dominant and alternative versions. Lüdtke has been seeking ways of establishing a far more sensitive and complex reading than is suggested, in brief, here.

7. One might think of Walter Benjamin's salutation that "only that historian will have the gift of fanning the spark of hope in the past who is firmly convinced that even the dead will not be safe from the enemy if he [the enemy] wins. And this enemy has not

within the moment of representation, Avedon sees his subjects active in the process of production of his own representation:

> The subject must become familiar with the fact that, during the sitting, he cannot shift his weight, can hardly move at all, without going out of focus or changing his position in the space. He had to learn to relate to me and the lens as if we were one and the same and to accept the degree of discipline and concentration involved. As the sitting goes on, he begins to understand what I am responding to in him and finds his own way of dealing with that knowledge.

If Avedon—in the section previously quoted—mastered the essential nature of the guild historian at work, here he brilliantly comprehends colonialism as a process, and helps those who are still attempting to understand colonialism in Africa with a fresh opening to the subject.

*

In 1950, a woman, Saida Namuluta, stood before the chief of Sabagabo *ggombolola* (subcounty), Butembe-Bunya County in Busoga, a district in the Uganda Protectorate, and declared:

> I accuse Varantini Kazibwe for claiming my hereditary *mutala* (village) which belonged to my grandfather Gumula. When Gumula died it was taken over by Mwegambi; when Mwegambi died it was taken by Kyemba; after Kyemba's death Babaire took it; after Babaire's death Kagoma took it; after Kagoma the *mitala* [villages, plural form] remained vacant and became uninhabited. The defendant is charged with having claimed the mutala Nakati which is Namuluta's *mutala*.

So began nearly a year of litigation over the claims of a woman Saida Namuluta and a man Valantini Kazibwe for recognition as holder or owner (*ow'omutala*) of a section of land close by an Indian-owned sugar estate, a title which the last court of appeal in Uganda, the High Court, in its final order, described as involving:

---

ceased to be victorious" ("Theses on the Philosophy of History," in Hannah Arendt, ed., *Illuminations*, trans. Harry Zohn (New York: Schocken, 1969), 255. But perhaps Benjamin is too bleak and hegemonic, if not simply messianic, for it is a perspective that ignores or misses the potential intensities and significances of silences, as well as the production in the suppression, and the possibly marginal role of the historian in "fanning the spark of hope in the past." Perhaps one should remake Benjamin's remark and suggest that "only at great risk will the historian ignore the power in the ashes."

not land, nor rights over land, nor the right to receive profits from land, nor the right to exact services or tribute from living on land, but merely the right to be known as Mutala chief, a right which carries with it, so far as I can see, only a few ill defined and partially recognized executive duties and a certain standing in the community.

The case passed through four courts before Saida Namuluta "lost her claim" against Kazibwe.

A close reading of *Namuluta v. Kazibwe*[8] provides another opportunity to see the power that resides and is constructed in the boundaries or membranes that separate—again in laminate fashion—differing and contending claims on the world, including, in respect to this case, the discordant and nonreciprocal claims and defenses relating to the multiple definitions of what resources and physical terrains were seen to be at dispute by the litigants; distinctive readings of the dispute by court authorities at each level of appeal; jointly enacted silences in the positions and arguments projected by the disputing parties; the differences between an instituted and evolved system of justice (the colonial courts of Busoga) and a sociology of participation of litigants; the definition of a "case" from the perspective of court authorities and such researchers as Lloyd Fallers and the definitions of "a case" for litigants and witnesses; the tensions between the work of research concerned with the evaluation and improvement of overlying judicial practice and the "silencing" or "distancing" into categories of irrelevance the underlying field of articulation of claims, interests, and histories.

In evaluating the claims of the litigants, the courts of Uganda were

---

8. David William Cohen, "'A Case for the Basoga': Lloyd Fallers and the Construction of an African Legal System," in *Law in Colonial Africa*, ed. Kristin Mann and Richard Roberts (Portsmouth, NH: Heinemann; London: James Currey, 1991), 238–54. This reading of *Namuluta v. Kazibwe* was originally prepared for an Emory University–Stanford University joint conference on law in colonial Africa sponsored by the Social Science Research Council, held at Stanford in April 1988. In discussion, conference participants stimulated a good deal of further thinking on colonial litigation. Then at Johns Hopkins, George Martin provided extensive and valuable assistance in developing an approach to the subject, a method of reading Fallers, and a way of giving a fresh perspective to the reading of *Namuluta v. Kazibwe*. Ashraf Ghani, Alf Lüdtke, Hans Medick, and Gabrielle Spiegel provided sounding boards during the development of the project. The John Simon Guggenheim Foundation and the dean of the College of Arts and Sciences at Johns Hopkins made possible a second year of field work in Busoga in 1971–72, which in turn made possible this present reading of litigation in Busoga. Students in my African History Seminar at Hopkins in the second semester, 1988, contributed in important ways to my thinking on "customary" and colonial law.

working within an economy of judicial practice that resembled rather closely the practices of Taso: the crystallization of elements to which he himself appropriated significance, combing essential pieces from masses of detailed memories. On the other hand, the litigants, like Avedon's subjects, were, to paraphrase Avedon, becoming knowledgeable as to the procedures and interests of the court authorities, recognizing the control that lay with understanding the demands of court procedures, learning to relate to the court and the court authorities as if they were "one and the same," accepting the degree of discipline involved ("consent"), understanding how the court responses to the presentations of litigants, and finding their "own way of dealing with that knowledge."

*

In 1969, Lloyd A. Fallers published his *Law without Precedent: Legal Ideas in Action in the Courts of Colonial Busoga,* based on fieldwork in Uganda between 1950 and 1953. In introducing his work, Fallers located his study of law in Busoga in a broad, comparative tradition of studies of "the historically recurrent phenomenon to which the term 'customary law' has usually been attached."[9]

Seeking to free his inquiry of African law from a notion of a natural jural order, Fallers defined "customary law" generally, and particularly in respect to Busoga, as

> not so much a kind of law as a kind of legal situation which develops in imperial or quasi-imperial contexts, contexts in which dominant legal systems recognize and support the local law of politically subordinate communities . . . customary law is folk law in the process of reception.[10]

Fallers's method in *Law without Precedent* was to apply a case method to the study of the courts of colonial Busoga. He ordered a large number of case records into a series of fields of civil litigation: marriage, divorce, adultery; landholding; inheritance and succession; and tenancy.[11] Focusing on these fields, Fallers examined the social wells of litigation in Bu-

9. Fallers, *Law without Precedence* (Chicago: 1969), 3.
10. Ibid.
11. In selecting cases for his study, Fallers eliminated a large number of proceedings that individuals brought against their chiefs and headmen (dereliction of duty and abuse of office) as well as cases that the government brought against common people (for tax avoidance and disobedience).

soga, the nature of argumentation, the work of the courts in fact-finding and recording witnesses, and the patterns of decision, resolution, and appeal. His definitive achievement lies probably not so much in his larger interest in the "process of reception" of local concepts and practices of law by a dominant colonial legal system but rather in detailing "the courtroom encounter" through the recording, presentation, and analysis of a group of distinctive cases which he read or observed during his fieldwork in Busoga.

Fallers began his research in Busoga at a time when the relations between chiefs and local officials of the Protectorate were generally cordial and constructive. The Busoga chiefs had been effective in the immediate postwar period in checking unrest among peasant farmers and laborers; the Europeans in the Protectorate service held a more informed and positive view of the capabilities of African chiefs. On both sides, greater training and experience were reflected in the work of the Protectorate civil service, both African and European. Fallers was in Busoga at a time when African chiefs were toning down their rhetoric, and their rhetorical claims to domination, as a means of establishing stronger associations with those groups actively opposing colonial rule.

This particular, and short-lived, context may be part of an explanation of Fallers's construction of a harmonic world in Busoga in 1950–53. But there is certainly a larger context for Fallers's work, and this is in his formation as a scholar. In a 1973 essay, Fallers reflected on his training under Marion J. Levy, Edward Shils, and William Lloyd Warner at the University of Chicago and of the catharsis he experienced in the field in Busoga in the early 1950s, when he discovered that what he had learned about classes and strata did not work.[12] Instead, Max Weber was encountered.

> One of the first things I discovered was that in the African kingdoms the hierarchy of chiefs, despite their great wealth and authority vis-à-vis their people, and despite the elaborate deference granted them, was very fluid. Except for the kings and a few princes, most persons in authority were "socially mobile": they were not in hereditary positions but instead were appointed by rulers on the basis of ability and personal loyalty. I had read Max Weber and I thought: Aha! I had found "patrimonial authority" in the flesh.[13]

12. Lloyd A. Fallers, *Inequality: Social Stratification Reconsidered* (Chicago: University of Chicago Press, 1973), 3–29.
13. Ibid., 4.

In his subsequent work on Busoga and also on Buganda,[14] Fallers was concerned to demonstrate the ways in which status and wealth differentiation were mediated and a working polity organized through such mediation. In *Bantu Bureaucracy,* Fallers showed how chiefs mediated the tensions that surrounded and defined their multiple responsibilities: to their administrative overseers, to their kin, and to their clients and subjects.

Beyond this, Fallers sought to evaluate how these new political roles and practices, shaped through the mediation of tensions and conflicts, were being integrated into the larger political systems of the "new states"; indeed, he demonstrated how the observations of smaller political units in practice could reveal process in the larger units. Fallers saw the Busoga courts as the locus and means of important integration between "traditional ideas and practices" and the larger overlay of regional administration and national state. This was, in simpler terms, the study of the modernization of traditional and neotraditional political institutions in colonial and postcolonial institutions and was reflected, for Fallers, in the very hierarchy of justice in the Uganda Protectorate. The officially recognized subcounty (*ggombolola*) in Busoga stood above informal and continuing local "courts" unrecognized by the colonial administration. Appeals from the subcounty courts traveled to the county (*ssaza*) court, then to the Busoga *Lukiiko,* the recognized district council of senior chiefs, then to the magistrate's court in Jinja, and finally to the High Court of Uganda, the latter two the only courts, at the time of Fallers's research, in which Europeans served as judges.

In *Law without Precedent,* Fallers joined the study of this integrative process to the close examination of the "case" in Busoga practice. Fallers defined a "case for the Basoga" as

> a proceeding to decide whether or not a particular set of "facts" falls within the reach of one particular concept of wrong. All sorts of other issues may be raised in argument but only those relevant to the reach of the particular concept of wrong enter into the decision; and the latter is delivered quite unilaterally, with little attempt to elicit consent.[15]

---

14. For Busoga, *Bantu Bureaucracy: A Century of Political Evolution among the Basoga of Uganda* (Chicago: University of Chicago Press, 1965), first published in Cambridge, U.K., in 1956; and for Buganda, Lloyd A. Fallers, ed., *The King's Men: Leadership and Status in Buganda on the Eve of Independence* (London: Oxford University Press for the East African Institute of Social Research, 1964).

15. *Law without Precedent,* 327.

Fallers's definition of "a case for the Busoga" matches perfectly his own intellectual formation, of a modeling of local ideas and practices in a process of integration and, in some respects, unification, within an expanding "modern", state apparatus. For Fallers, this state was itself marked by "patrimonial tendencies" incorporated within the administration of justice in the formal apparatus of the courts.

Fallers's definition is extraordinarily arresting and invites closer scrutiny. The passage captures Lloyd Fallers's method precisely and offers at least three critical entry points to the examination of Fallers's work, and to the work of others who have deployed a similarly constructed case method in the study of colonial African law.

I. *"All Sorts of Other Issues . . ."*

In declaiming that "All sorts of other issues may be raised in argument but only those relevant to the reach of the particular concept of wrong enter into the decision . . . " Fallers indicated that litigants raise a broader range of arguments and "facts" than those which will enter into the court's decision. What is implied is that there is a remarkable distinction between what the courts see as appropriate, relevant, and correct facts and arguments and what the litigants see as appropriate, relevant, and correct.

By the time Fallers began his studies in Busoga in 1950, the colonial courts had been in operation for about half a century. The distinction observed here between two forms of discourse in the same location, the colonial court, clearly, has its own long history. Still, Fallers did not himself invite his readers to attach significance to this observation of the distinctive discursive intentions and activities among the "players" in the Busoga court setting. If this is the meaning of "a case for the Basoga" as Fallers argued, how does one explain the persistence of broader, alternative, and "irrelevant" discourses within the proceedings of the Soga courts?

II. *"Only Those Relevant to the Reach . . ."*

Fallers suggested here a legal grid through which "issues raised in argument" are sifted. One may ask what sort of mechanism of authority drives this process of selection, determining relevance, limiting what information and what arguments are to enter into "the decision"? What are the frames of knowledge and what are the litigants' expectations concerning the nature of information and argument that will enter into the decision? Do litigants share a vision of what enters into a decision

that is different from the vision of the judges? How do litigants perceive
the relation of the information and argumentation they bring with respect to the decisions the court produces? What is the relationship between anticipation and result?

III. *"With Little Attempt to Elicit Consent."*

What is the form and effect of court decisions and opinions with respect
to the consent of litigants and observers? How do litigants perceive the
form and voice of the court as it produces its decisions and opinions?
What is the motor of consent in the processes of litigation in a colonial
setting such as Busoga?

*

When one looks within *Law without Precedent* for answers to these questions, one notes that Fallers closed off the possibility of making certain
fresh observations from his text. Fallers systematically used ellipses in
his presentation of court testimony, omitting from the reader's view
some of the "facts" and arguments presented to the court. Most critically, Fallers deleted, by using ellipses, all testimony he viewed as not
relevant to the "reach of the particular concept of wrong" or which did
not "enter into the decision," thereby producing, in the end, a record of
the nature of "what the court heard." Fallers's compact representation
of case records resembles the abstracted and abbreviated documented
records of other courts in which an administrative routine, or a technology, of full transcription is not available. So, in closing off from view
"that which was presented" as opposed to "what the court heard," Fallers positioned himself, and his own act of discerning relevant and appropriate argumentation, between the setting of the court and a possible
audience's intention to read directly and closely the litigants' presentations to the court.

*

In their introduction to *The Disputing Process: Law in Ten Societies*, Laura
Nader and Harry F. Todd, Jr., argue for a recognition of the significance
of alternative and multiple intentions in a courtroom.

> There is a special importance to be derived from treating the parti-
> cipants in the disputing process as deserving of equal sociological
> attention. People who write about the judicial process and the judi-
> cial decision as if the outcome were solely the product of a third

party, a judge, miss the sociological relevance of the courtroom as
an interactive arena.[16]

The practices of elision in the recording and reporting of court testimony, whether from Fallers's emphasis on the receptive mode of the
colonial court or from imperfect or selective practices of court reportage,
have the power to close off from inspection these alternative agendas
and complex intentions to which Nader and Todd have drawn attention.
The questions raised concerning Fallers's definition of "a case for the
Basoga" may also suggest the incomplete nature of colonial judicial
practice in Busoga, where there may indeed have been alternative
agendas and complex interactions operating beneath the dominant and
recorded official practice of the court. These alternative practices may
have constituted, on the one hand, resistance to further "integration"
and, on the other, they may have established facts and modes of domination, extending and refining the receptive process even where the receptive mode (in its practice and in its scholarly examination) closed off
access to these alternative, but thoroughly involved, "voices."
   Through the close reading of a single piece of litigation, one may examine more closely the field of difference between a case as it is heard
by a colonial court (in Fallers's receptive mode) and recorded imper-
fectly or selectively (in the manner of many court records) and the case
as it is presented by the litigants, informed here both by a close reading
of the case record and by material drawn from the neighborhood in
which the case, *Namuluta v. Kazibwe*, originated. The case selected for a
close examination here comes from the period of Fallers's fieldwork
(though he does not refer to it in his books) so as to illuminate better
the risks and opportunities associated with the narrow and broad con-
ceptualizations of "a case for the Basoga" which one might choose to
implement.

*

When, in the April 1950 hearing before the *ggombolola* court of Butembe-
Bunya County in Busoga, the woman Saida Namuluta completed her
charge against Varantini Kazibwe, the chief turned to Varantini and
asked, "Do you agree to the charge or have you got something to say to
defend yourself?"
   Varantini responded,

16. *The Disputing Process* (New York: Columbia University Press, 1978), 22.

I am not guilty of the charge for the following reasons: The *mutala* Namasiga which she claims is mine, it is hereditary. As to the *mutala* Nakati which she says that I claim I have never claimed such a *mutala* for Nakati is only a *kisoko* [subvillage] within my *mutala* Namasiga; and that same *kisoko* is called Itala, but Nakati which she is talking about is neither a *mutala* nor a *kisoko* but only a well. This *mutala* Namasiga was given by my grandfather, Bamba, to Kirimuta Nkoma who was his assistant. Magaya Mulema and Magaya Alabike first settled at Namasiga and it is where they were buried. After their death Bamba Musumba, their son, changed his home (official residence) and built it at Kasozi, Bugaya, and he gave the *mutala* to Kirimuta Nkoma. In 1928, on August 26th the *mutala* Namasiga was given to me and I was confirmed in it by Kitawo Biwero. Musumba Biwero son of Nawaguma gave me his son Munaba to escort me to the *mutala* Namasiga together with the following emissaries: (i) Kasia Kasiba, representative of the *gombolola* chief; (ii) Bakonte was representative of the *muluka* [parish] chief. There were other representatives too.

The following are the people who ruled Namasiga: (i) Kirimuta Nkoma; (ii) Nkoma; (iii) Mulyansime; (iv) Ikanka; (v) Ikanka Kisibo; (vi) myself, V. Kazibwe, the present ruler. I have ruled the *mutala* for 22 years now. To prove that the *mutala* Namasiga is definitely mine Nsaiga the clan head of Namuluta's clan accused Biwero in 1922 and he (Bandi) lost the case in the *gombolola* court at Bugaya, and in the *saza* court at Kiyunga in the same year. Then in 1929, Namuluta's kinsman, Enosi Byansi, accused me; he called my *mutala* Namasiga another name, Bukasa. He lost the case in the *gombolola* court at Bugaya before L. Muwanika who was the *gombolola* chief. The case was left at that. In 1940 Aloni Kanyika accused me; he claimed my *mutala* Namasiga and he called it Bulondo. He lost the case in the court at Bugaya when Eria Waiswa was the *gombolola* chief. On the other three occasions Bandi and Bakikuya gave evidence in 1929 and in 1940 but they lost the case. From that Namuluta accuses me that I claim her *mutala* Nakati whereas my *mutala* is Namasiga but not Nakati as she says and Nakati which she is talking about is merely a well; and the *mutala* which Namuluta says that it was ruled by six ancestors of hers, those people have never ruled Namasiga.[17]

---

17. The case record of *Namuluta v. Kazibwe* is a handwritten translation of the proceedings, which were rendered from the original Luganda or Lusoga transcriptions when they were readied for presentation to the Jinja magistrate in the next to last court of appeal. The orthography has been left in the form written. There are companion records for the county (*ssaza*) and district (*lukiiko*) proceedings, though not for the magistrate's and High Court pleadings. However, the rulings are available from all five courts. *Namuluta v. Kazi-*

Following several questions to clarify Varantini's statement, the *ggom-bolola* chief then turned to "The Plaintiff, Namuluta," who was given the opportunity to restate her claim:

I accuse Valantini because of claiming my hereditary *mutala* Na-kati which belonged to my grandfather Gumula. After Gumula's death, Mwegambi took the *mutala*; after Mwegambi's death Ky-emba took it and the following ruled in that *mutala* in succession: Babaire, Kagoma Mpalageni, Mugimba; after Mugimba the *mutala* remained without a ruler. At that time I was taken out of Busoga by my husband; then I came back to settle in my *mitala* [plural]. On my arrival I accused the clan leader and he sent me to higher powers to accuse V. Kazibwe who claims my *mutala* Nakati. There is a boundary between Nakati and Bugaya and also a hill called Luwuga on the upper side. The baiseMagaya who, he said, gave him the *mutala*, used to stop in [settle up to the edge of] the boundary between Bugaya and Nakati, but I am claiming my *mutala* Nakati. His statement that I claimed three *mitala:* Nakati, Namasiga, and Ntala is untrue, the clerk made a mistake. The name Namasiga is a misnomer and the boundary between Nakati and Bugaya passes through that *mutala*. That *mutala* belonged to my uncle Nsaiga Kibwa and Kibwa gave it to my father Gumula.

Following Saida's statement, the chief then directed a series of clarify-ing questions to her. After completing the examination of the testimony of Saida and her witnesses, the chief rendered his ruling. In his judg-ment, April 4, 1950, the *ggombolola* chief stated,

The defendant, Varantini Kazibwe, has lost the case, for he claimed the *mutala* Nakati, calling it a *kisoko* or the boundary of Namasiga; he made it a part of Namasiga. That *mutala* Nakati be-longed to the forefathers of Namuluta. Nsaiga Kibwa gave it to Gu-mula son of Nsaiga; on Gumula's death Kyemba took it and it was ruled by other rulers in succession until people evacuated on ac-count of sleeping sickness. But the defendant says that there is no *mutala* called Nakati, that Nakati is merely a well, but in that part the *kisoko* is called Ntala. He says that Namasiga is his hereditary *mutala*; his grandfather Bamba Musumba gave it to him. The wit-nesses of the plaintiff have given evidence proving that Nakati is a *mutala* and it belongs to Namuluta, it belonged to her grandfather Gumula son of Nsaiga; in the end it became uninhabited, at that time Varantini took it. The witnesses of Varantini said that they do

---

bwe was selected from notes, microfilms, and xeroxes of some twenty cases collected in Busoga in 1971 and 1972.

not know the *mutala* Nakati; they know Namasiga which is Varantini's *mutala;* but the plaintiff does not claim Namasiga; therefore
the *mutala* has been given to Namuluta and Varantini will pay
sh[illing]s 10/- court fee.

So Saida won her case in the *ggombolola* court, but then Valantini appealed and the decision for Saida was reversed in the County (*ssaza*)
Court. Saida appealed and won in the Busoga District (*lukiiko*) Court.
Valantini again appealed and won in the Magistrate's Court, Jinja. Saida
then appealed to the High Court of Uganda, the last court of appeal in
the Protectorate, which dismissed her claim. The High Court declared,

> Here is a woman who for half a life time has been absent from her
> place of origin, returned to claim not land, nor rights over land,
> nor the right to receive profits from land, nor the right to exact ser-
> vices or tribute from persons living on land, but merely the right
> to be known as *Mutala* chief, a right which carries with it, so far as
> I can see, only a few ill defined and partially recognized executive
> duties and a certain standing in the community.
>
> This scarcely seems a claim triable by court of law. If however I
> must adjudicate in the matter I would say that the decision of the
> *Saza* Court and of the Magistrate seems preferable to that of the
> Central Native Court [Busoga *Lukiiko*]. If the *Mutalla* of Nakati
> ever existed, the community ruled by the petitioners' ancestors
> had disappeared. There has been no continuity of rule. Part of the
> land where the old community lived has been peopled by a fresh
> group of families who have acknowledged the respondent's rule
> for many years. The petitioner does not claim the land on which
> they live as her land—she cannot do so, they do not hold the land
> from her. If her claim is granted she cannot eject them. There
> seems absurdity in saying that they must at this stage in history
> fall under her rule because long ago an earlier community in the
> same spot was ruled by her ancestors.
>
> Though I avoid the term "Prescriptive Right" used by the Magis-
> trate I think the long settled order of things should not be broken
> upon by this lady with her contentions of a pre-existing *mutalla* in
> this area. If one went back in history the whole map of *mutalas*
> and *kisokos* [subvillages] could no doubt be disrupted and a com-
> plete re-deal of these headmanships could be effected. I make no
> order, and the decision of the Magistrate will stand.

And so the case of "Saidi Namuluta, Petitioner, versus Valantini Kazibwe, Respondent" concluded. Saida Namuluta had lost her claim.

Namuluta v. Kazibwe was a familiar case in the courts of Busoga and
Uganda. In its ruling specific to this case, the High Court does not reiter-

ate what it had declared in an earlier order concerning "these tiresome
Busoga headmanship cases." Fallers himself discussed seven such cases
among the fifty-one cases cited in *Law without Precedent*. Fallers's citations developed the central issues in each of these cases as they were
introduced in the court; he then reported the decisions of the courts and
the rationale in each; and he finally discussed that logic of the rulings
which was seen to straddle the several cases within this category of
"possession of subvillage or village." Fallers was concerned to show the
ways in which considerations of persisting concepts of sovereignty in
Busoga—the capacity of existing authorities and executives to continue
to command authority over such rights and offices as subvillages and
villages—was supported by, or in conflict with, the concerns, interests,
and existing policies of Protectorate administration.

*

How does one read a series of texts, so incomplete in the sense discussed earlier, within a single judicial case? Do we, as Fallers has done,
examine the testimony, arguments, and facts to see what constitutes relevant matter for the judges in making their rulings as a way of understanding the process of reception of local ideas and practices by the
overlying judicial administration? Here, immediately, we face a conun-
drum created by the very different readings of the litigation by the two
judges whose rulings are presented above (not to speak of the three
intervening judgments). What, in this sense, is "a case for the Basoga"?
    In discussing his method, Fallers noted that he fell short of his own
objectives in broadening his knowledge of each case.

> The case records provide, I believe, excellent data on what takes
> place in Soga courtrooms, and my ethnographic inquiries make it
> possible to relate these data to their general sociocultural setting.
> But for far too many cases, I know only what the case records tell
> and what I can infer from my knowledge of the society. In too few
> cases do I know what happened before and after and I have too
> few interviews with judges and litigants about particular cases
> and about law in general. More of such material would have made
> possible a richer analysis of Soga legal culture and of the relation-
> ship between the legal institution and society than I am able to
> provide.[18]

The agenda here is to explore but one case, not so much to discern
the relationship "between the legal institution and society" but rather

18. *Law without Precedent*, 38.

to examine the broader range and deeper meanings of the voices of individuals in the practice of litigation. The several texts produced within *Namuluta v. Kazibwe* in this one court proceeding at the *ggombolola* level could themselves be read in a number of different ways; the direction taken here is to look at the *silences, allusions,* and *indirections* in the light of a much thicker body of material relating to the dispute than that which the parties articulated within the courts; and, finally and briefly, to discuss the implications in recognizing the distinctions among (a) what the judges chose to hear; (b) what the litigants chose to say; and (c) what broader knowledge the court players held concerning the material detail of the dispute.[19]

*

In Varantini's rejoinder to Saida's first statement of claim the very logic of Saida's claim is not recognized. Where she asserted a claim to a *mutala* which she called Nakati, Valantini responded with a defense of his title to a *mutala* which he called Namasiga. And far from implying that this is one place or one office or one title, with two different names, Valantini insisted that Nakati is not a *mutala* at all but a well. And he noted that the place she claimed as Nakati is a *kisoko* (subvillage) known as Itala and that this lies within the *mutala* Namasiga which he owned. He thus multiply confounded Saida's claim through the implication that he was holding expert knowledge of the essential meaning of the name Nakati (a "well") and of the materiality of the place which Saida claimed (the *kisoko* Itala), as well as concerning his own authority (over Namasiga).

In recording Saida's first statement, the clerk of the *ggombolola* court noted that "after Kagoma the *mitala* remained vacant, and became uninhabited." The clerk used the plural form, that is, "villages," giving the implication that Saida was concerned with more than one *mutala*. In her second statement, Saida attempted to correct what she remarked was an error in the record of previous court testimony, an error which she attributed to the clerk: the notion that she was claiming "three *mitala:* Nakati, Namasiga, and Ntala." It is possible that this "error" was introduced to the record by a clerk who did not readily recognize the incongruity of the claim and the response: Saida claiming Nakati from Varan-

19. This broader knowledge comes from records of examination of witnesses, plaintiff, and respondent in the *ggombolola, ssaza,* and district courts; from research by the present author on this area of Busoga, done before the case record was discovered; from the records of interviews done by the author in 1966–67 and 1971–72 with a number of the parties to the case, also before the physical record of the case was found; and from the records of a survey of *mitala* and *bisoko* histories done by the author in 1971–72.

tini and Varantini defending Namasiga, of which he claimed "Ntala" or "Itala" as a part, from Saida. But there is possibly another edge to the question of the number of *mitala* under discussion, for Saida's lineage forebears were recognized to be the "owners" of two other *mitala* in the area. To succeed in the case against Varantini would have made three.

Elsewhere in the court testimony, Saida argued, under questioning from the chief, that "Namasiga is not a *mutala* but only the name of a spirit [*musambwa*]," though Varantini responded, "Namasiga is a *mutala* and it is where the spirit is."

In giving his ruling, the *ggombolola* chief worked within the *logic* of an asymmetrical debate: "the plaintiff does not claim Namasiga; therefore the *mutala* Nakati has been given to Namuluta and Varantini will pay sh[illing]s 10/- court fee." He left open, however, the critical question: if Saida can be given Nakati and Varantini can be left with Namasiga, then what were the essential grounds for Saida's original claim against Valantini? Indeed, from a very distant perspective Varantini could have looked upon the chief's decision as the fourth occasion upon which a court vindicated his ownership of Namasiga. But if this was so, why did Varantini appeal his case to the next level court? What is suggested is that both Saida and Valantini recognized that a claim for Nakati was a claim for Namasiga, but perhaps Saida recognized that this direct assault on Varantini's title would not work, as it had not worked when members of her lineage brought cases against Varantini earlier. For Saida to assail Varantini's control over Namasiga was for Saida to assault a well-defended turf, so she perhaps consequently moved forward into the litigation by *indirection*. The *ggombolola* chief saw an opportunity for a resolution not in adjudicating the actual material claims of the two parties but through moving into the spaces opened in their incongruent discourse.

In the ruling of the judge in the High Court of Uganda, the issue was much simplified into a debate between two parties to a single title, office, *mutala*. It is as if Saida's claim and Varantini's response are, essentially, reciprocal, predictable, commonplace, and reducible to the statement of a principle (the judge's reference to "prescriptive right"). In looking at the presentations Saida and Varantini made to the court, one might say that they agreed, and in a powerful way, on the primacy of factual detail in settling differences, rather than on the basis of which party held the stronger claim to an acknowledged principle. Indeed, they agreed on the larger principles which the High Court judge found objectionable: that these headships mattered and that one's rights in them could be substantiated by fact and force of argument. For the two litigants, a facility to control the outcome of the litigation lay in their control of distinct sets of "facts" concerning, of a first order: grants, appointments, and legacies; and of a second order: the names, locations, and meanings of places. If the grammar of each of the rulings of the *ggombolola* court and the High Court of Uganda were distinctive, so also was the grammar of presentation of argument to the *ggombolola* court different from that of each of the rulings. What was offered to the courts was substantially different from what was received by them.

*

In his presentation to the court, Varantini brought attention to what he alleged to have been a series of prior cases developed by members of Saida's lineage forebears against his ownership of Namasiga *mutala*. Beyond giving further depth to his gambit of opposing Saida's claim to Nakati by defending his ownership of Namasiga, his testimony suggests an implication that Saida's claim against Varantini for Nakati was simply a further invention, E. Byansi having "called my *mutala* Namasiga another name, Bukasa" and A. Kanyika having "claimed my *mutala* Namasiga and he called it Bulondo." Moreover, in *alluding* to these cases, Valantini evidently sought to establish a long judicial record behind his defense of Namasiga, extending back twenty-eight years to 1922.

Varantini went one step further. In reviewing what he presented as a series of vindicating cases he was at the same time appropriating status and authority to two individuals whom he would later call as witnesses to his ownership of Namasiga: Lameka Muwanika and Eria Waiswa, who had long periods of service in different parts of Busoga as *ggombolola* chiefs, eventually leaving government service in good standing. Later, Saida's witnesses challenged the status of Muwanika's and Waiswa's knowledge of such local details, saying that they were not in the area long enough to know the details concerning ownership of *mitala*. Saida's witnesses, with Saida, were, in this countertestimony, alluding to general understandings concerning the effects of practices of frequent rotation in the African civil service in Busoga, that responsible office did not necessarily translate into authoritative knowledge. In his statement, Varantini impugned the testimony of one of Saida's initial three witnesses, Bakikuya, by stating that Bakikuya had been the losing party in cases in which he gave evidence in 1929 and 1940. Before Bakikuya even testified, Varantini was suggesting that, if his evidence were not to be believed ten and twenty years before, how could it be credible in 1950?

Saida, in turn, introduced in her second statement two new issues: one in the admission of an explanation of the delay in her initiating her claim to Nakati *mutala;* and a second in bringing attention to a "boundary between Bugaya and Nakati." In the first, she was anticipating what would become a major concern of the High Court judge in his ruling, in a sense predicting the judicial reasoning of an appellate court four courts removed from the one in which she was testifying.

In the second *allusion,* Saida placed before the court the concept of a "Bugaya" as a territorial entity sharing a boundary with Nakati. Though Varantini mentioned Bugaya at three points in his formal presentations to the *ggombolola* court, it was his adversary, Saida, who sought to place Varantini's claims and rights within a history of the small Bugaya state in southwest Busoga, a state ruled in precolonial times by a lineage of the abaiseMagaya. The implication of Saida's reference to "boundary" was that there was, historically, a limit to the authority of the old Bugaya state and therefore of its capacity to turn over estates (*bisoko* and *mitala*), such as Nakati, to clients and kin of the members of the ruling house of Bugaya, the authority of which in this area was still recognizable through the 1960s.[20]

Saida's reference to boundaries in her second statement carried an additional power in the debate before the court, for just previously Varantini and two of his witnesses had admitted that they could not find or discover, and did not mark, boundaries when they first were sent to set up Varantini as head of Namasiga. In an important sense the coteries or networks of witnesses on both sides actually represented the present (1950) form of old territorial expansionist and defensive practices of the ruling houses, and their clienteles, of the *ancien* Soga states, still extant in some significant respects in the mid-twentieth century.

In her second statement to the *ggombolola* court, Saida *alluded* to still another development: "I came back to settle in my *mitala.* On my arrival I accused the clan leader and he sent me to higher powers to accuse V. Kazibwe who claims my *mutala* Nakati." Saida here was giving her own claims a special legitimacy, that they exceeded other claims to Nakati, or against Kazibwe, which had long been festering in her lineage; and also that she appeared in court with the blessing of the leader of the clan. Here we see the first indication of what is later revealed through

---

20. Following the reasoning implied in Saida's *allusion,* if Bugaya, through which Varantini traced his claims to title-holding, shared a boundary with Nakati, then Nakati existed, could not be part of Bugaya, and thus Varantini could enjoy no claim over it.

questions posed to Saida and her witnesses that there was a struggle within her own lineage and clan for precedence in going forward with a case against Kazibwe. This was the little case before the big one.

Relatively few of the *allusive* gambits of either party were recognized in the rulings of the *ggombolola* court and the High Court. They were, however, recognizable because again and again the transcripts of the proceedings show the witnesses checking and counterchecking on such points and they show the very standing of the witnesses in the court rising and falling with the play of allusion within the testimony presented to the court.

If the testimony of *indirection* was about the valorization of "factuality" as opposed to principles, the *allusions* in the testimony were about the character and values of participants in the case and, in turn, about the credence to be given to particular claims of fact.

*

There are critical silences and suppressions to be found throughout the formal statements to the court given by Saida and Varantini. In his statement, Varantini mentioned Kirimuta Nkoma as preceding him as "owner" of the *mutala* of Namasiga. He gave Kirimuta's name as part of a "genealogy" of recognized office-holders. But under questioning, Varantini revealed first that Kirimuta Nkoma was removed from the Namasiga post by the local government for, we learn, incompetence. The opening of this oyster produced a succession of difficulties requiring Varantini's explanations. Did he receive the title to Namasiga from the local government, that is from the representatives of the district administration, or from the hereditary "rulers" of the neighborhood in which Namasiga was located? Who then actually appointed him to his title or office and what was that person's standing at the time? Under further questioning, Varantini and his witnesses were pressed to reveal that Kirimuta Nkoma actually held Namasiga not as *ow'omutala* ("owner") but rather as the representative or surrogate of another *ow'o-mutala*. When therefore, if ever, did that *ow'omutala* turn over ownership of the *mutala* to Varantini? In the county (*ssaza*) court proceedings we find two of Varantini's expanded array of witnesses claiming that Varantini did not hold the title of *ow'omutala* but was himself a surrogate or representative of the actual owner who was recognized to be a member of the royal house of Bugaya.

A second suppression is a jointly enacted one (though it is slightly breached by Saida in her second statement). This concerns the evocation in court of the expansionist programs of two old and residual political corporations: neighboring Bukasa and Bugaya in southwest Busoga. Saida and her lineage were closely affiliated with the ruling house of Bukasa while Varantini was part of the "ruling" establishment of the Bugaya state. The suppression of argument based on the legacies of the small states drew on a recognition that the courts, from top to bottom in Busoga, were considerably suspicious of claims that came explicitly out of the ancient political and social histories of states in the district. It was anachronistic to establish or support claims on grounds, on histories, that were not supported by the colonial state. And so Saida and Varantini and their witnesses contended over boundaries to polities which did not, in their constructions of the court's "mind," exist; yet the ebb and flow of state expansion in the neighborhood in the nineteenth and early twentieth century, and indeed in the cases before the local courts, constituted the very motor of the dispute between Saida and Varantini.

A third suppression or *silence* is opened slightly when, in her second statement, Saida mentioned that she "accused the clan leader and he sent me to higher powers." This is a most important element in the development of the case, for, as the record of responses to questions placed by the *ggombolola* chief indicates, Saida had to establish her claim to Nakati within her own clan against the prior claims of several individuals. This is tender ground, for Saida would not have wanted to make too evident the embattled nature and, therefore, fragility of her claims to Nakati. Yet at the same time the critical evidence which she would have wanted to bring before the court lay within these struggles within her clan for rights to the Nakati title, the "little case before the big case." For Saida to build a picture for the court of her success in struggles among her peers and kin was to introduce discordant voices and disputed evidence from within her own family.

On the other side, for Varantini the history of the struggles within Saida's lineage for control of the rights to Nakati contained both opportunities and risks; he had already claimed to have defeated three members of her lineage—Bandi, E. Byansi, and A. Kanyika—in previous legal assaults on his title. To make too much of a sustained claim by a single lineage would possibly have jeopardized his own history of his title. And, again, to raise this history of litigation in its fullest and roundest way would, possibly, have given status to the notion of Nakati as a *mutala*, something which was obviously not in his interest to do.

Through the silences and suppressions, small and large, both parties, their witnesses, and other court players were identifying issues for which there were substantial risks in bringing forward in too great detail, or at all—risks for both the case at hand and for broader concerns. The court players were, through considerable selectivity in argumentation and fact-bringing, gathering control over what it was that the court should know, even in a setting in which the procedures of the court were such that the judge could delve into practically any matter through his own examination of plaintiff, respondent, and witnesses.

*

Namuluta v. Kazibwe was a narrow thread of organized dispute within a broad lattice of contention concerning the ownership of titles, offices, and estates in the neighborhood of Namasiga/Nakati. There was, in 1950, a long history in and of the various contentions which inflected this single case, and the contentions spread out through the various coteries of witnesses and supporters on both sides. The very form and meaning of the contest—as the reproduction of an old pattern of territorial aggression across an indistinct political boundary between the remnants of the Bukasa and Bugaya polities—was withheld from the view of the court.

In each of the rulings which have been examined here—the lowest and highest courts of the organized Protectorate judiciary—the judges picked through what was placed before them for a handle on a complex case. The *ggombolola* chief saw the possibility of preserving both claims, and in the process he ignored the meaningful interests being asserted and defended by the two parties. The High Court judge simply saw the case as one in which a new party was attempting to swipe the office of an old one. Neither opinion articulated the older, historic issue at the base of the dispute.

What is finally revealed in this discordance between the "case" as presented by the litigants in all its indirections, allusions, and silences, and the "case" as it was heard by the judges? Here we may begin to see some of the distinctions between an approach to litigation and legal ideas in colonial Africa oriented around the "receptive mode" of a developing colonial judicial system and an approach which brings into focus the ways in which facts, arguments, practices, and ideas are offered by those participating in the courts.

*

The close reading of this one case suggests that there are two rather different discourses or programs present in the setting of the colonial court in Busoga. In the program of the judiciary there was an economy of practice, a selectivity in hearing the participants. As noted earlier,

Fallers argued that "a case for the Basoga . . . [is] a proceeding to decide whether or not a particular set of 'facts' falls within a particular concept of wrong."[21] Reading *Namuluta v. Kazibwe*, one would turn the emphasis from the "whether or not" to the question of particularization: how judges heard certain "facts" from a broad webbing of fact-bringing and argument and how judges particularized a specific "concept of wrong" from the dispute context constituted by the "facts" heard.

In the second program or discourse, the litigants and witnesses worked on their own criteria of what "facts" and arguments were to be voiced, and how strongly they were to be voiced. They were not simply attempting to make "their best case": bringing forward all the facts and arguments that would empower their claims and defenses. They were evaluating the risks of bringing certain information before the court and the dangers of opening certain points too broadly. They were introducing material, by allusion, which held the power to depose the adversary's witnesses and arguments. They were, through silences, constituting argument, containing risks, and gathering control over what the courts should learn.

The litigants and witnesses were, as well, attempting to predict what material might be 'heard' and be effective among the broad arrays of knowledge which they had the capacity to muster. In *Namuluta v. Kazibwe*, the litigants appeared to agree that there were certain boundaries in producing testimony across which one should not venture. There is in this an indication of some undefined, unvoiced rules which were evolved by litigants as they experienced the practice of courts and which, at times, were confirmed by subsequent judicial rulings. Yet, as we compare the readings of the rulings of the judges to the readings of the testimony brought before the judges, we recognize immediately that the litigants nevertheless brought substantial evidence and argument before the court that would, subsequently, hold no interest for the judges producing their rulings.

These "discordant voices," which Fallers has removed from his renderings of cases through the use of ellipses, have or—as we are referring to the colonial period—*had* several important resonances. First, such discordant testimony was epiphenomenal to broader, continuing, and often irresolvable tensions outside the courts; it also gave sustenance to particular claims and rights even where courts had ruled against them (witness the series of claims brought by members of Saida's lineage against Kazibwe). Second, the presentation of discordant testimony

---

21. *Law without Precedent*, 327.

within a formalized court setting, as opposed to a market, a bar, or a feast, accorded status to particular speech and to particular issues. An argument over an ancient boundary between two small precolonial states in a court in 1950, even where embarrassment kept the litigants from explicating the historical dimensions of the boundary issue, provided a means of reproduction of ideas of perduring local sovereignties and statuses unrecognized by the colonial authority. Third, and following on these first two points, discordant testimony of such kind was the means of establishing consent. Where Fallers looked for consent in the rulings of the court and did not find it, we might look for the motors of consent in the very patterns of introducing discordant voices—the stuff that Fallers has elided. The litigants and witnesses were, through their voices, discordant and otherwise, establishing the very facts and modes of domination, consenting to the administrative and judicial functions of the courts while organizing therein the reproduction and defense of an underlying system of domination. Fourth, and still more speculatively, the discordant voices—the far broader realms of testimony brought to the courts than that which the judges "heard"—may have induced the formation, in the practice of the courts, of an economy of judgment in which judges were distanced from the deep contours of facts and argumentation and were pressed into patterns of narrow and specious judgment, simply to get on with the system of governing.

*

This approach to the study of litigation in colonial Africa reveals a critical arena of tension and discord between an instituted, evolved system of justice—the colonial courts of Busoga—and a sociology of participation. These overlying and underlying fields of litigation practice are inextricably involved, each operating in the context of the other, and yet critical aspects of each field are undisclosed to the other.

Most studies of African colonial law have focused on the overlying field of litigation practice. Such an orientation of legal research in Africa may be explained, variously, by the relatively privileged survival of documentation in the overlying field, by applied concerns of many researchers with evaluation and improvement of overlying judicial practice, and through the political silencing of the underlying field in the more general "work" of authority formation of judges, jurists, and administrators operating in the overlying field.

*

Lloyd Fallers, like many observers of African and colonial legal systems, used the case method. He drew his material from courtroom observations and court and appellate proceedings. While his observations of litigation were brilliantly contextualized in the anthropological study of Soga society and culture, his perspective of law as the work of courts subordinated, and effectively closed off from view, the broader and elongated aspects of ideas and action relating to specific disputes and conflicts. Fallers's definition of "a case for the Basoga" was likewise quite restrictive; and the manner in which he operationalized this definition in his presentation of testimony worked to suppress discordant voices in his reports on the practices of litigation.

Fallers's concentration on the work within the courts, his suppression of discordant voices through the use of ellipses in the presentation of testimony, and his search for the integrative mechanism in colonial litigation lead us away from a comprehension of the discursive intentions of the "players" in the Busoga court setting and from an understanding of the constructive power located in such discursive practices. In a certain way, Fallers has become part of the process of elaboration of a distanced and selective authority in the colonial courts of Busoga, establishing in our domain of study further rules of what is "heard" and how meaning is to be attached to what is "heard."

THREE

The Economy
of Debate

In spring 1990, a committee of the Department of History at North-western University was tidying up a document that would propose to the department as a whole a revised graduate curriculum. One of the committee members recommended the establishment of a series of "historiography" seminars, one in each of the three or four recognized areas of the department's portfolio of specializations. There was some discussion about what such a seminar would look like, and eventually the consensus shifted toward the view that it would be better to have a unified historiography seminar for the department's first-year graduate students as a means of simultaneously introducing a shared intellectual framework and providing an opportunity for socialization of new students to a departmental culture. Yet there remained on the table an interest in having some element, perhaps a general field seminar, emerge within each of the department's specializations.

The planning discussion shifted back to what a general field seminar might look like if developed for each of the three or four recognized departmental areas. One suggestion was to organize readings of recent and important works in the field. Another was to survey historically the evolution of historical literature: a history of historical writing.

As a member of the committee, I was intrigued by the possibility and challenge of undertaking the development of a seminar on the history of African historical prose. Various scholars and practitioners had, over the years, wondered—perhaps for both self-serving and communitarian reasons—whether historians of the "profession" would get around to recording the career histories of "founders" of the "schools" of African historiography in the twentieth century, or take up the study of their professional and personal papers while these "founders" were still living. During a long walk on the streets of New York in the mid-1980s, Martha Gephart, then program officer of the Joint Committee of African Studies,[1] offered that this was such an obvious project that it demanded explanation why no one had taken up the challenge.

Of course, Bogumil Jewsiewicki and David Newbury had, in 1986, published a set of papers entitled *African Historiographies*, which might be said to have imagined an architecture of the project that Gephart proposed. The collection was a more expansive, but perhaps a less inter-

1. Of the American Council of Learned Societies and the Social Science Research Council.

esting and certainly less polemical exercise than *Historians and Africanist History*, the 1981 critique of "liberal" historiography by Arnold Temu and Bonaventure Swai. There have been, as well, numerous essays and reviews which engage, define, and criticize a particular section of writing on the African past, many of the scope and form of those included in the Jewsiewicki and Newbury volume.[2] There has been, however, no work on the writing of the African past that approaches the broad and sturdy historical treatment of a field such as Gerald Graff has produced for the field of American literary studies (*Professing Literature: An Institutional History*).

In spring 1991, when I was asked to take on the responsibility for the 1991–92 iteration of the newly devised General Field Seminar in African History—and for some reason accepted the charge—the speculations on the possibilities of the seminar shifted toward more practical questions of how one might organize the work of the seminar over the ten or twelve weeks of the quarter. I was then involved in drafting the guiding text for the 1992–93 Institute for Advanced Study and Research in the African Humanities titled "The Constitution of Knowledge: The Production of History and Culture"—for which I had been selected as preceptor—and the coincidence of possible work seemed at the time most engaging.

Some obvious possibilities presented themselves as means of organizing a seminar: (a) "great books"—but then who wants to authorize a new canon, and the expected question "what makes a work of history 'great'?" would demand the opening of a large and complex ground concerning authority, reading, audience, sociology, and epistemology, the examination of which would squeeze the time available to read and discuss the "great books"; (b) the reading and discussion of a series of texts such as the Temu and Swai volume or the Jewsiewicki and Newbury collection which, with assorted reviews and essays, would provide critical perspectives on some of the lines of work on the African past— but a great deal of this feels, on second or third reading, to be rather ungrounded, and a quarter's worth of readings seemed an exhausting and dissociative venture, separating the reader from the social experience of writing history; (c) a "brilliantly selected" sequence of exem-

2. Jan Vansina, "Some Perceptions on the Writing of African History, 1948–1992," *Itinerario* 16, 1 (1992), has staked a position in the writing of this history of African history, yet in just the first lines (77) Vansina locates the historiographical field as the academic guild alone, with a denotation of a specific context (the School of Oriental and African Studies) and a specific date (1948). One might well ask what is the value—other than economy— of so restricted a view of the writing of African history.

plars of prose historiography over several centuries or more, allowing one to note the appearance of certain tropes and paradigms, the moments of epistemological and methodological shift, the emergence of certain schools and programs of historiography, and the mapping of various interpretative and critical positions; this was a most attractive vision, but it was also one that seemed, as I worked upon it, to involve completing a Graff-like volume before drawing out a syllabus.

As various approaches surfaced and challenged one another, the "economy" of historical production began to establish itself as an issue. "Africa" is, after all, an immense quantity and subject, in some respects—as Valentine Mudimbe and others have noted—invented and still being invented. A recent experience in working with the planners of two conferences on national historiographies is revealing: the planning groups include scholars working on, separately, China, India, and Japan ("Cohen would 'represent' Africa"; "We need to find someone working on Latin America") and so on, in which the modes and means by which certain branches of scholarship enter global discourse as "branches" or "arenas" or "fields" are only marginally discussed. Equally—and obviously—the very form of handling the subject of history within the frame of a seminar develops through an economy of a kind. There are sessions, hours, weeks, participants, opportunities, constraints, as well as production and consumption.

An attention to a sense of "economy" in the practice of producing a seminar opened to further thoughts on the "economy" of history production more broadly. How far can one represent the work of reconstructing and representing the past in terms of an "economy," of "production" and "consumption," of the imparting of "value," of the construction of cultural and intellectual "capital"? Here, *debate*, contests over the reconstruction, interpretation, and representation of the African past, drew attention as a means of maintaining a sense of "economy" (What works? How does value attach to a work or idea? How is production organized and revised and reorganized?) while examining the production of history. One might argue (debate?) that *debates* are moments and contexts in which "production" and "consumption" occur simultaneously (as well as reciprocally and conflictually) "within a common space," moments and contexts in which "value" is negotiated through a social as well as through an intellectual process.

As anxiety began to develop as to whether or not this seminar would have any form or structure whatsoever, the notion of situating *debate* as the centerpiece in a seminar on African historiography seemed increasingly attractive, for it held the promise not only of positioning research and writing on the African past within an impassioned and potentially powerful discursive field but also provided an opportunity to examine more closely the idea, form, modality, structure, and genre of "debate."[3] In my paper on the study of legal conflict in Busoga, Uganda,[4] I explored debate within a 1950 law case in Busoga, Uganda. In discerning the allusions, indirections, and silences through which the litigants' arguments were organized, one could see that

> the court players, litigants and witnesses, were identifying issues for which there were substantial risks in bringing . . . forward in too great detail, or at all—risks for both the case at hand and for broader concerns. They were, through considerable selectivity in argumentation and fact-bringing, gathering control over what it was that the court should know . . . They were, through silences, constituting argument, containing risks, and gathering control over what the courts should learn. They were . . . attempting to predict what material might be "heard" and be effective among the broad arrays of knowledge which they had the capacity to muster . . . the litigants appeared to agree that there were certain boundaries in producing testimony across which one should not venture. There is in this an indication of some undefined, unvoiced rules evolved by litigants as they experience the practice of courts. (Pp. 251–52)[5]

3. In his opening essay to the recent *Debating P.C.: The Controversy over Political Correctness on College Campuses* (New York: Dell, 1992), Paul Berman adopts, finally, the position of "The literary critic Gerald Graff [who] has argued . . . that the best possible response to the crisis in the universities is to 'teach the conflict'—to make a study of the debate itself" (p. 26). This view has informed and influenced my recent work, for in several different forums, I have sought to bring attention to the sociology and politics of the so-called debate over multiculturalism which seemed for some time to be something more akin to an assault than a debate. The American press seemed too ready to characterize the attacks as a "debate" through a considerable period when the "other side" seemed to exist only in the imagination of the critics of multiculturalism. For me, questions were raised about how critical work qualifies as "debate" and how such reception and adjudication of the language and terms of criticism are adjudicated in a larger sphere. If Graff had at one time sought to maintain a critical distance from the "debate" in order to study it, by September 1991, he had become one of the principal organizers of Teachers for a Democratic Culture, the aim of which was to answer the attacks from the "Right" (and specifically from the National Association of Scholars) on proponents of multicultural education and campus diversity. Gerald Graff has now written his "text" for teaching "the conflict": *Beyond the Culture Wars: How Teaching the Conflicts Can Revitalize American Education* (New York: W. W. Norton, 1992).

4. "'A Case for the Basoga': Lloyd Fallers and the Construction of an African Legal System," in Kristin Mann and Richard Roberts, eds., *Law in Colonial Africa* (Portsmouth, NH: Heinemann, 1991), 239–54, reproduced in part here as chap. 2.

5. See chap. 2, above.

While the judicial authorities of colonial courts may have seen themselves as creating a specific and controlled context for the settlement of disputes (and the orchestration of consent to colonial authority), one might well ask about the relationship between the form of debates within such courts and the form of debate outside them. Not all debates take place before a "higher authority" such as a colonial court. But when one compares debates over history and culture *within* a judicial process with those *unadjudicated* by such authority, questions are raised concerning *what makes possible* contests and debates. Where one may readily seek to know the locations and causes of certain types of conflicts, debates, disputes, and contests, one may also go further and attempt to define what agreements—over knowledge, language, relevance, polarity, closure—constitute requisites for debate.[6]

The conventional American curriculum in history is full of examples of workbooks that set up the basic ground of debate over interpretations of the past. These most commonly assume a neutral or middle position between two polar positions. The politics and sociology of such historiographical debate are fully elided; nothing is usually remarked concerning the employment of power and professional influence in constituting an authoritative position; there is typically little regard for the historical process of naturalization of a bipolar or dyadic contest; nor are the logical terms and determinative force of the enabling questions exposed to challenge.[7] The student is encouraged to see the strengths of alternative and symmetrical positions and to consider the relative virtues of the two positions or the possibility of constructing, within a blue book exam essay, some middle position. The asymmetries of discourse in lived experience do not enter such workbooks or assignments.

In shifting the address to the interpretation and representation of the African past, one may be able to recognize—across a great body of work since the earliest prose historiography on Africa—a comparable bipolar structure in the discourse of historians—a framing of all sorts of work around seemingly incompatible and reciprocally opposed ideas:

(i)   that Africa's past has its own meaning or that it is located on the periphery of the world system; that Africa can only be understood

6. A very simplistic and recent example is that of the "canon debates" at Stanford in their 1988 phase; vocal participants on both sides of a great political divide agreed that a recognized, standard curriculum should serve "to provide Americans what they need to know" (paraphrase).

7. One could, equally, note the approach of Ted Koppel, the now perpetual host of the American program *Nightline*. Koppel presents a "specific" issue on each program and then sets the structure of the discussion in terms of an opposition between two alterna-

by examining "interior processes" or that it can only be understood by measuring the impact of "external forces"

(ii) that Africa is to be understood in terms of its deep cultural base and deep structure and its enduring institutions or that it is to be understood in terms of continuous transformation; and

(iii) that Africa has been marked by the force of powerful states and political and economic forces or that it is marked by continuous opening of space for the composition of culture and society through the action of people as opposed to states.

Such a limited set of paradigmatic oppositions defines—not totally but quite substantially—the terrains of professional and academic interpretation and representation of the African past. There may be more and the above might be better defined,[8] but one may ask how such basic oppositions become seated within the operations of a range of different debates that have developed around the writing of African history. One may readily compare such a perduring set of oppositions to the persistence of the "objectivity question" in professional historical discourse in America[9] and ask how far such oppositions carry from one field or arena of historical practice to another.[10]

In situating *debate* as an opening to the inspection of the production of texts on the African past, one may well ask at the outset: how far does *debate* give force, spirit, voice, and direction to historical research and writing? If one chooses to investigate debates over the interpretation and representation of the African past, one is of course immediately selecting those sections of historical production and reception which are directly affected by contest. How, on the other hand, does one imagine historical research and writing outside the contours of dissent, resistance, revision, and conflict?

---

tives, represented by found advocates or authorities. It is perhaps appropriate to note that Koppel's program was created as a supplemental news program during the Iran hostage crisis, in which the complexity of events was dissolved into a bipolar struggle between what were represented as American and Islamic standards of behavior in the world.

8. Though hardly better defined, a somewhat more developed discussion along these lines is offered in David William Cohen, "Doing Social History from *Pim's* Doorway," in Olivier Zunz, ed., *Reliving the Past: The Worlds of Social History* (Chapel Hill: University of North Carolina Press, 1985), 224–28.

9. See Peter Novick, *That Noble Dream: The "Objectivity Question" and the American Historical Profession* (New York: Cambridge University Press, 1988).

10. One could ask, for example, if within debates over the African past such argumentation over politics (in the dress of "objectivity" and "science"—by Novick's treatment) takes such a disguise, where so much other ground is available to enable or disable a political position.

*

In opening a study of *debate* over the African past, how does one proceed? It would, for example, be useful to have, or construct, an inventory of significant or exemplary debates over interpretation and representation of the African past (and to have the basic bibliographical material on hand). At the same time, one might wish to keep open the possibility that a comprehension of the nature of debate might require the examination of contests over the past in "eccentric" domains, such as theater, film, *shabeens*, buses, taxis, newspapers, music, and so forth, along with courtrooms and academic seminars.

From all appearances, debates over the African past have their own temporality and temporicity.[11] We can look at current debates, such as the "*mfecane* debate" in southern African historiography,[12] and we can also look at examples of debates that seem to recur periodically and at innumerable sites, such as the "nationalist historiography" debate exemplified so well in the early postcolonial writing centered at Dar es Salaam.[13] We can also look at "disappeared debates," ones that flourished briefly at specific local sites and within local literatures and for which a comprehension of the passion and form of the debate would or will require close reconstruction of the context in which the debate occurred.

One may seek to comprehend specific moments or contexts of historical debate in Africa, perhaps in parallel to Katherine Verdery's remarkable analysis of the debate over "Horea's Revolt" in eighteenth-century

11. Though such might be elided by participants in the debates, by redactors or editors of collected papers, and by essayists, who might focus on the "fundamental issues" as the combatants set them forth rather than the sociologies of discourse through which various positional deployments are rendered public.

12. Carolyn Hamilton, one of the active participants in these Mfecane discussions in South Africa, was visiting Northwestern at the time the seminar for which this position paper was prepared was meeting and kindly led a discussion on the "*mfecane* debate." Over several decades, *Mfecane* had became a currency for representing the process, episode, or epoch defined by what some twentieth century historians saw as the explosive movements and dispersals of southern African peoples consequent on the expansion of the Zulu kingdom at the close of the 18th and opening of the 19th centuries. Julian Cobbing, as noted in the present chapter, has played a major role in showing how the *mfecane* rubric was an artifice, a historian's fiction or ruse that came to be uncritically accepted by a generation of southern African historians.

13. Quite serendipitously, Professor Isaria Kimambo, long chair of the Department of History, University of Dar es Salaam, and a father of Tanzanian historiography, brought an important paper to Northwestern during the period in which the seminar was meeting; the paper explored three decades of history production at Dar, including the nationalist historiography debate in the early 1970s.

Transylvania, observed on its two hundredth anniversary commemoration in then socialist Romania.[14] In recording and analyzing the events of the Horea commemoration, Verdery has produced an enormously valuable sociology of the struggle for interpretive power. And this was no simply defined contest between state interests and intellectuals. While the author has admitted "an interest in the extent to which historiography 'legitimates' or promotes the power of these [eastern European] states," she has located this promotion of state power as "the result less of coercive impositions of new meanings than of the way oppositional intellectuals may actively participate in sustaining an ideological discourse, through historical research and debate."[15]

In studying the commemoration of the "revolt," Verdery found that competing grammars and vocabularies of representation of the history of the revolt among state and party officials, archivists, and historians—how, for example, it was reconstituted by some as an "uprising" and by

14. Katherine Verdery made available to me an early version of her work on historical production in the commemoration of "Horea's Revolt" during the months when I was drafting the "Production of History" position paper. Verdery's investigation of the commemoration of the "revolt" had a considerable influence on the position paper, and also on this volume as it developed from the original paper. Verdery's research on the Horea commemoration was also a stimulus for me to study the commemoration of the Johnson County War in Buffalo, Wyoming, in June 1992 (see chaps. 6 and 7 below). "Horea's Revolt" has had an interesting publication history. The circumstances surrounding the protection of informants and commemoration participants initially led the author to disguise not only her own identity and the identities of informants and commemoration participants, but also the name of the country in which the commemoration was observed. A revised paper was then published under the pseudonym E. M. Simmonds-Duke ("Was the Peasant Uprising a Revolution? The Meanings of a Struggle over the Past," *Eastern European Politics and Societies* 1, no. 2 [1987]: 187–224), and all the names of participants in the commemoration remained encoded, while the country—Romania—was identified. The changes in Romania in late 1989, when Verdery's *National Ideology under Socialism: Identity and Cultural Politics in Ceauşescu's Romania* (Berkeley: University of California Press, 1991), 215–55, was being completed, led to a relaxation of protection of the identities of the author and of some of her informants, as well as a further revision of the discussion of the "revolt." While the issues of protection were deadly serious ones at the time, there was some humor in the ways these texts could confound readers. In the 1987 version, Simmonds-Duke was identified in the journal as the author of a nonexistent book and as "currently interested in post-modernism as anti-esthetic . . . Professor Simmonds-Duke lectures in social sciences at various universities under an assumed name." In the article, Simmonds-Duke cited the previously published work of Verdery as well as a forthcoming work—the 1991 book—which would be the one published with Katherine Verdery as its author. At a seminar where I, though not she, was present, one participant denounced the 1987 article for being "poorly researched" and argued that "Simmonds-Duke could not really have read Verdery [her study of Transylvania]."

15. "Was the Peasant Uprising a Revolution?" p. 189.

others as a "revolution"[16]—opened to, and drew upon, broader tensions
and issues over national identity and international politics, the values
of specific intellectual traditions and disciplines, and the relative statuses of the various institutions in Romania that saw the production of
history as their métier.

In her treatment, Verdery has provided a detailed account of the
events of commemoration, focusing attention on the two-day commemorative conference in Transylvania in which a number of experts presented views of the history of the "revolt." Verdery was not attempting
a "true account" of the 1784 events, but rather was situating each historical presentation through a close reading of its explicit and implicit referents and allusions. Having access to written texts prepared for oral presentation, as well as her notes on the lectures, Verdery has been able to
discern significant shifts in language within the public proceedings, as
the presenters participated in a performative and contentious sociology.
And she was able to look at the specific commemorative conference
within the broader context of national discussions of the "revolt," as
well as diverse representations in fiction, opera, theater, and film across
the year of commemorative activity.[17]

Verdery's treatment of the commemoration of the "revolt" has also
addressed the workings of the Romania state as the practices and authority of intellectuals and experts were mediated by a wide range of
state-saturated interests and conditions.[18] But more than seeing the commemoration as a way of "reading the state" in the performances of state-
sponsored expertise, the author sees the commemoration as *constitutive*
of the power of an essentially weak state.

> The commemorative festivities engraved into people's neurons
> both the power of the state that subjected them and the historical
> notion of identity that was the occasion for it . . . the festivities . . .

16. These words were, Verdery notes, much more than differences in terminological
taste. Each marked out ideological and political difference, and each carried with it a
substantial history and conceptual and theoretical framework regarding the reconstruction and representation of the Romanian past.

17. Verdery recorded one voice at a Horea symposium muttering "I'm sick to death of
Horea"; "Horea's Revolt and the Production of History," in *National Ideology under Socialism*, 228.

18. Verdery shows the way the bicentennial commemoration of "Horea's Revolt" was
elaborated through "various people's efforts to build and feather their own nests or pursue their own individual and institutional objectives at state expense" ("Horea's Revolt,"
236). And, she notes, "the persons most anxious to colonize Horea were bureaucrats and
intellectuals, including Party activists in institutions, the groups in Romania most likely
to turn nationalism and national history to their own uses" ("Horea's Revolt," 237).

showed the state's control over Time, not only through displaying its power to control the past (and therefore the present) by parading a redefinition of history, but also through proving its capacity to expropriate the time and effort of others. The occasion was a magnificent display of the state's ability to gather up Time from living persons and redistribute it to the dead . . . Horea's celebration both displayed and further constituted power, by dramatizing subjection. Horea was a godsend to Romania's weak state; he [Horea] provided an excellent pretext for projecting an image of strength, offering the populace a visceral experience of their subordination and building up their belief in the regime's power—which, of course, strengthened it in fact. Through commemorations like Horea's Romanians gradually came to believe they had no alternative.[19]

In 1987, Katherine Verdery, in the guise of E. M. Simmonds-Duke, underlined programmatically this concern to decode the constitutive practices and "events" within the commemoration. She defined her interpretative project as very different from Clifford Geertz's interpretative treatment of the Balinese cockfight.[20] Although she, like Geertz with the cockfight, saw herself attempting to read thickly a single event or set of events,

unlike Geertz . . . I hope not just to explicate the event as a "text" but to show how texts such as this are themselves "written"—how they are produced and processed by intellectuals and politicians. This makes the exegesis of Horea's bicentennial a fairly complex matter. It will take us through a number of subjects: the events themselves, who produced them, what concerns of Marxist-Leninist or Romanian nationalist ideology they betray, the internal and international audiences for debate about Horea, the nature of the socialist state, and the structural sources of weakness that make productions such as Horea's celebration indispensible for the Romanian party . . . [but] it may be helpful to keep in mind the overall objective: how historical debates perpetuate Romanian historical consciousness and history as ideology, and how these results bear upon the matter of "legitimacy" and state power.[21]

*

Perhaps more overtly, questions concerning "legitimacy" and state power seem to have given energy and form to the extraordinary debates

19. "Horea's Revolt," 242–43.
20. "Deep Play: Notes on the Balinese Cockfight," *Daedalus* 101 (1972): 1–37.
21. "Was the Peasant Uprising a Revolution?" 189.

in Kenya over the meaning and proprietorship of the history of Mau Mau. These debates have continued from the early 1960s to the present day and are now, certainly, into their "nth" phase. Was the Mau Mau experience an insurgency, a peasant revolt, an uprising, a revolution? Did it fail or succeed? What happened to its actors, apostles, and spokesmen? Was it an authentic expression of nationalism and thus the property of all Kenyans or a distinctive expression of the landless and powerless? Was it a Kikuyu rising or the rising of a particular section of Kikuyu society?

Since the midst of the Mau Mau experience of the 1950s, what Mau Mau was, what it means, how it was individually and collectively experienced, whether its ideals and objectives were abandoned or carried on, and by whom for what ends have been the most captivating questions in Kenyan political life, theater, and literature. In the early 1980s, the debates had reached the point where lawsuits were being filed among combative Kenyan historians. By the 1990s it had become clear that the question of "whether or not Mau Mau was betrayed" has since the 1950s been the core motor of production of Kenya historiography, joining questions of social justice with debates arising from the inspection of fresh layers of material from archives and memoirs.

The shifting architecture of these debates over the status of Mau Mau and the alleged betrayal of its "cause" is most complex, mediated by accessible contests over the proper definition of ideology and the appropriate categorization of different forms of social, economic, and political protest. In a recent essay, E. S. Atieno Odhiambo has argued that the betrayal thesis has persisted even without concrete empirical or theoretical grounding, resting rather on a "legitimate passion," a search for a different and more radical Kenya than the one its national leaders constructed.[22]

But there was never a possibility that the debates on Mau Mau would become the "property" of the scholars. In the late 1970s, Ngugi wa Thiong'o's play *The Trial of Dedan Kimathi*, an historical dramatization of the British prosecution and execution of a Mau Mau leader, was playing to packed audiences throughout the central Kenya countryside, and the young European architect who played the hanging judge in the piece had to be rescued from audiences turned angry mobs at the end of every performance. This was not the first dramatization of the struggles and prosecution of Dedan Kimathi. Indeed, it is held that Ngugi wrote his play, with his co-author Micere Mugo, immediately after the opening

---

22. "Kenyatta and Mau Mau," *Transition* 53 (1991): 147–52.

of, and in angry reaction to, Kenneth Watene's play *Dedan Kimathi,* first produced in Nairobi in 1974. The Ngugi-Mugo treatment of Kimathi has less of the complex psychological dimension than the Watene original. The Ngugi-Mugo play is a far more explicit demand for struggle against continuing exploitation in postcolonial Kenya. David Cook and Michael Okenimkpe, reviewing the Ngugi-Mugo dramatization, have written,

> Mythologizing is not falsification. Selected images, events, speeches and individuals embody certain needs of a people. Myths draw upon history. But writers who develop national myths are using history as part of a continuing process which can help determine and shape the future by encouraging certain possibilities in society and perhaps discouraging others. To such writers history is not static, but is material out of which social and economic realities have created the present, providing various openings for the future. The historical Kimathi is important to Ngugi and Micere Mugo as a man whose work must be projected into the future. So their play selects facts of his life-story which can inspire an audience to action in the present.[23]

And the academic sphere of debate has been no "ivory tower." In 1985, combative Kenya historians closed ranks to defend one of their most caustic (and previously argued libelous) critics from intimidation by the state for the expression of radical views, and, in the following months, they were challenged by the Mau Mau generals who attempted to seize the responsibility for writing the history of Mau Mau from the professional historians.

> In [1985 and 1986] the Mau Mau generals have set up two research phalanxes from amongst themselves. The first research phalanx is led by Field Marshall Mbaria Kaniu and politician Waruru Kanja (with a two million shilling public gift from the President [Daniel arap Moi]). It is going to document, write plays, and make movies about Mau Mau. The second phalanx met in Nyeri in February this year and, while denouncing Kaniu's group as "ignorant" (one does not know on what criterion), said it would undertake the same activities.[24]

23. David Cook and Michael Okenimkpe, *Ngugi wa Thiong'o: An Exploration of His Writings* (London: Longman, 1983), 161.
24. E. S. Atieno Odhiambo, "The Production of History: The Mau Mau Debate," prepared for the Fifth International Roundtable in Anthropology and History, Paris, July 2–5, 1986, 5.

The historians of Kenya also found themselves standing with considerable and unpredictable solidarity against what was viewed as interventionist interpretations of the meaning of Mau Mau by non-Kenyan historians. Here the question of the competence and manners of the *report* of expert discourse and debate may matter as much as the dispute itself. On February 13, 1986, the Baltimore *Sun* reported a conference of scholars in Kenya under the headline:

> Kenyans, seeking identity, haggle over their history.

Hal Piper, a *Sun* correspondent reported

> A scholarly conference on Kenyan history fractured in bitterness recently on the issue of whether the Mau Mau movement was a heroic inspiration or an embarrassment to Kenya . . . Officially, the Mau Mau are regarded as revolutionary freedom-fighters and architects of the Kenyan nation . . . Even the debunkers could not agree, however, on whether the Mau Mau, predominantly drawn from the Kikuyu tribe, were waging something like a civil war, or whether the disparate activities of farm workers in one area and squatters in another were simply too amorphous to be packaged under a single category as "The Mau Mau War" . . . a researcher from Cambridge University argued that Dedan Kimathi, regarded as a Mau Mau hero, was simply a warlord with no coherent ideology or intention to lead a national movement:[25] . . . As father of a nation . . . Kimathi was "a real embarrassment" . . . He was hotly rebutted by William Ochieng[26] . . . who suggested that belittling the heroes of the struggle for independence was a way of attacking the present government. Then Dr. Ochieng professed embar-

25. One might juxtapose this 1986 association of the "warlord" label with the absence of a coherent ideology, in Piper's report, with the representation of African National Congress (ANC) "warlords" in South Africa in *The Economist*, August 8, 1992, 32.

26. E. S. Atieno Odhiambo chaired the session that Hal Piper reported in *The Washington Post*. He has recorded ("The Production of History in Kenya: The Mau Mau Debate," 1) the event in this way: "It all started with a mimeo from John Lonsdale, the historian of Kenya's colonial period, embodying his own reflections on the Mau Mau war/revolution/revolt. There was a crucial sentence in his test: 'However one approaches the subject, Mau Mau is an embarrassment.' Kenya's local gadfly, William Ochieng' (he once labelled David Livingstone as a 'hippy and a spy') captured that sentence as the Lonsdale paper was being read out by the presenter David Throup. As soon as it was question time, Ochieng' pitched in: 'Yes, Mau Mau is an embarrassment to all of us, particularly because the present Kikuyu elites want to appropriate it as an exclusively Kikuyu movement, so as to exclude every other Kenyan from the fruits of independence, which in their opinion must only be eaten by those who physically fought for *Uhuru*—freedom.' A clear enough exposition. But the journalists chose the punch line: '"Mau Mau is an embarrassment" says Professor Ochieng',' blazoned the headlines of the following days."

rassment at what he said was the way current Kenyan politicians and some scholars try to wrap themselves in the memory of the Mau Mau to claim personal advantage.[27]

The controversy did not end with the closing of the conference. E. S. Atieno Odhiambo has noted that

> the Mau Mau veterans convened their own Conference in Nyeri in February [1986], where they dubbed the now very subdued and muted Professor Ochieng' as an ignorant youth, and there they resolved to write their own "truth" about Mau Mau. The tentative reflections of the Cambridge don (Lonsdale), presumably scribbled in the gas-lit chambers of Trinity College, Cambridge, have found a reverberating echo on the foothills facing Mount Kenya.[28]

As in the commemoration discussions of "Horea's revolt" in Romania, there were conferences in Kenya where different parties debated interpretations of Mau Mau;[29] and there were also fundamental questions of terminology.

> the guild historians [in Kenya] themselves queered the pitch . . . for they began discussing Mau Mau in the *Kenya Historical Review* (1977) using the semantics that the humanities and social sciences deployed in the 1960s and 1970s: was it a *nationalist* movement? a *tribal* civil war? a *revolution?* In doing this they were calling for a baptismal name for a movement they had only heard of, but not yet studied.

One might also wish to examine debates in which the "debate" seems so asymmetrical that one side appears in a state of "absence" or as an

27. Piper concluded with some commentary of his own: "Kenyans evidently are having difficulty deciding who they are. One reason is that there is not a long record to draw from. Considering that the oldest human bones on earth have been found here by Richard Leakey and dated to about three million years ago, Kenya does not have much history." One may choose to read Piper on the historians of Kenya not as authority on the debates in Kenya, but as an example of how complex discourse in one place can be translated into "news" in another, with considerable contention flattened to generalization.

28. "The Production of History in Kenya: The Mau Mau Debate," 2.

29. In the paper tabled at the 1986 Paris roundtable, Atieno Odhiambo reflected more broadly on the multiplicity of interpretations, remarking, "Truly, nobody knows it all, nor do the audiences expect to hear it all from one source. There would be no point to the story if it were [told in] unison." One might compare Atieno Odhiambo's observation here to the continuing search for a unified and officially inscribed account of the assassination of John F. Kennedy. For an exhaustive attempt at the production of a coherent account of the history of Mau Mau, see Bruce Berman and John Lonsdale, *Unhappy Valley* (London: James Currey, 1992).

"absent subject," as in an earlier stage of the so-called multicultural debate in the United States in 1990 and 1991, or in such censoring programs as surrounded the Nazi "examination" of "degenerate art" or the French judicial "criminalization" of Flaubert's *Madame Bovary* in 1857.

*

Another remarkable example is the debate that developed in the Federal Republic of Germany in 1986 around the publication of Ernst Nolte's "The Past that will not go away."[30] Nolte was calling for a program of historical revisionism to correct what he argued was a misrepresentation of the German past during the Third Reich. Nolte's article ranged across a broad front of issues, but focussed upon what he suggested was an orchestrated persistence of the "final solution" issue as framing the representation of Germany in this period. Nolte was prepared to argue that historians had to understand the ways in which the "deed" was not at all unique in the twentieth century, but that it was a comprehensible response to what was then seen as justifiable fear of Bolshevism in the Soviet Union in the 1930s. Nolte also suggested that the inability of Germany to achieve a normalization of past was the result of a most interested promotion of the "final solution" paradigm.

Whatever the virtues, or lack thereof, of his logical or empirical ground, Nolte's arguments were seconded by other "revisionists." Nolte also tapped into and found support from sections of German society who saw no value in tracing their collective past back into the Third Reich.

Five weeks after *FAZ* published Nolte's blast, *Die Zeit* published a response by Jürgen Habermas to Ernst Nolte and to other "revisionists."[31] Habermas configured his response to the "revisionists" around the issues of historical and moral relativism, situating then recent examples in Germany of ceremonies and memorials that evaded or effaced the distinctions between "victims and culprits" in the Second World War and under the Third Reich. Such an evasion was considered the issue at hand with the May 8, 1985, plans of President Ronald Reagan to lay a wreath at the Bitburg military cemetery, which included the graves of

---

30. "Vergangenheit die nicht vergehen will," *Frankfürter Allgemeine Zeitung,* June 6, 1986. The debate—referred to as the "Historikerstreit"—involved a great section of the German historical profession. A valuable treatment of the debate—one of the strongest treatments of any historiographical controversy I know—is to be found in *New German Critique* 44 (1988), edited by Anson Rabinbach.

31. "A Kind of Settlement of Damages (Apologetic Tendencies)," July 11, 1986. Reprinted and translated in *New German Critique* 44 (1988): 25–39.

SS corpsmen, an act of "normalization" of German relations with its former enemies that created a storm across Germany and Europe as well as in the United States (and which seemed beyond the capacity of the American president to comprehend). Habermas argued,

> One cannot employ a moral abstraction and at the same time seriously insist on concrete historical analysis. Whoever still insists on mourning collective fates, without distinguishing between culprits and victims, obviously has something else up his sleeve. Whoever does Bergen-Belsen in the morning and in the afternoon arranges a meeting of war veterans in Bitburg has a different conception of things—one which did not simply form the background to the eighth of May events yesterday, but is also the inspiration today for the planning of new memorials and new museum buildings: the intention is that a Federal Republic firmly anchored in the Atlantic community of values should regain national self-confidence through an identification with a past which can be agreed upon, without getting onto the fast track of the neutral nation state.[32]

In raising as a problem this trend toward the collectivization of mourning, with its effacement of boundaries between victimhood and responsibility, Habermas was entering a complex and important ground. While noting that "if it was really a question of simply remembering the *individual* dead, no one would be so presumptuous as to try and sort out the unspeakable pain of children, women and men, or to divide up their—for mortal eyes—impenetrable suffering according to characteristics of culprits and victims,"[33] Habermas recognized the absolute necessity of distinguishing the issues both hidden and overt involved in the remembrance of the collective dead. In his "Gettysburg Address," November 19, 1863, Abraham Lincoln dedicated the new military cemetery at Gettysburg. In preparing his "remarks," Abraham Lincoln recognized what Habermas was arguing in 1986, that one could turn a re-reading and un-reading of the details of a specific historical experience, the Gettysburg battle and its still then unburied dead, to a far more substantial end: the transformation of the United States Constitution through the reestablishment of the precepts of the Declaration of Independence and the ordering thereby of a different American nation than existed one day earlier on November 18, 1863.[34] Would an 1860s Habermas have railed against Lincoln's attempt to resurrect a new con-

32. "A Kind of Settlement," 27.
33. Ibid., 26.
34. This is the argument of Garry Wills, *Lincoln at Gettysburg: The Words That Remade America* (New York: Simon & Schuster, 1992), particularly 36–40, where Wills sets out his

ception of nation on the graves of dead soldiers? Or would he have recognized, as our contemporary Habermas has argued, that the constitution—as opposed to the celebration of patrimony—is the basis of the nation and that the underpinnings of this commitment to a constitution are located in the engagement, rather than the effacement of, a horrible "deed"?

In challenging what he saw as the core arguments of Nolte and the other "revisionists," Habermas unlocked what he took to be the key to the dilemma of revisionism:

> The ideology planners [the revisionists] want to construct a consensus about the revitalization of national consciousness, but at the same time, they have to banish the enemy images of the nation state from the sphere of NATO. Nolte's theory offers a great advantage to this strategy of manipulation by killing two birds with one stone: the Nazi crimes lose their singularity by being made at least comprehensible as an answer to Bolshevist threats of destruction which persist today. Auschwitz shrinks to the level of a technical innovation and is explained by reference to the "Asiatic" threat of an enemy who is still standing at our gates.[35]

Habermas himself called for an alternative program of historiography, one that acknowledges the values of a "pluralism of interpretations." In an important sense, this is for Habermas unavoidable as he asserted that "the sharpened methodological consciousness of recent years means the end of every image of history which is closed or indeed ordained by government historians."[36] In responding to the national interest and foreign policy segments of the arguments of the "revisionists," Habermas pointed out that as far as the NATO countries are concerned, the standing of Germany in the West rests on a

> commitment to universalistic constitutional principles which is anchored by conviction and [which] has only been able to develop in the German *Kulturnation* since—and because of—Auschwitz. Whoever wishes to exorcise the shame surrounding this fact . . . , whoever wishes to call Germans back to a conventional form of national identity, is destroying the only reliable basis of our link with the West.[37]

---

essential thesis concerning what he calls "one of the most daring acts of open-air sleight-of-hand ever witnessed by the unsuspecting" (38).

35. "A Kind of Settlement," 36.

36. Ibid., 38.

37. Ibid., 39.

In terms of the practice of historians, Habermas regards a commitment to a "pluralism of interpretations" as allowing opportunities for a full examination of "our own identity-forming traditions in all their ambivalence."[38]

In examining the *Historikerstreit*, or "historians' debate," that began with Ernst Nolte's June 1986 article—if not with Reagan's Bitburg ceremony—which engaged the attentions of historians and publics across Germany[39] for months following, one notes the tensions between the polarity of emerging positions and the asymmetry of the structure of argument on the two sides. While on both sides participants in the debate were confident in their answering one-by-one the arguments of the other side, their essential positions were not simply reciprocal or bipolar. The "revisionists" saw their project as the reclaiming of national pride through the constitution of a refreshed, revitalized, and corrected *national* history. Those like Habermas who stood their ground against the "revisionists" saw their own responsibility as one of maintaining sight of the powers and dangers of such a "national vision." They saw this "national vision" as an "old stench," as producing—in the decades before and after 1933—the very "moral catastrophe" which the "revisionists" would like to forget.

There are other edges to the *Historikerstreit*. It was a debate among professional historians but was made accessible to broad publics through two major papers, which themselves stood in opposition to one another through the debates—and played impresario to the protagonists. The historians' debate touched many other public controversies in Germany of the day (or decade), including the discussions developing around Edgar Reitz's *Heimat* program on German television in 1984,[40] as well as films[41] and literature, and the debates across Europe, Israel, and North America around the attempts to cleanse Kurt Waldheim's war record. Local historians, radical historians, and public historians—many associated with the history workshop movement—were through the

38. In "A Kind of Settlement," 39, Habermas reads as positive signs the widely observed (and well measured through polling) tentative, resistant, negative, and alienated responses to national symbols and national pride among Germans of "younger generations," seeing a hopeful "development of a post-conventional identity."

39. See Judith Miller, "Erasing the Past: Europe's Amnesia about the Holocaust," *New York Times Magazine*, November 16, 1986, 30–40, 109–11, for a general discussion of the *Historikerstreit* and its public reception in Europe more broadly and among victims of the Holocaust outside Germany.

40. For a critical treatment of *Heimat*, see the special number of *Geschichtswerkstatt* 6 (May, 1985), "Schwierigkeiten beim Entdecken der Heimat."

41. Including Michael Verhoeven's *The Nasty Girl*. See Preface of this present volume.

1970s and 1980s reopening the closets of local events during the Third Reich, seeing their work as importantly "revisionist";[42] it was, perhaps, such work—and the growth of a young generation of involved and critical historians—that gave Habermas and others challenging Nolte and his colleagues a confidence that "a return to a conventional form of national identity" would not be easily achieved.[43]

As well, the *Historikerstreit* seems at one look to have an inaugural moment—the publication of Nolte's article or the Bitburg ceremony— and at another to contain the threads of issues long powerful, and continuing to have power today,[44] among historians and publics in Germany and Europe more broadly including

(i)   the never settled priority of the so-called Jewish Question versus the so-called German Question, which reaches back through the discussions regarding German reunification to Bitburg and to debates over reparations, to the Nuremburg trials, and to the promotion of "Reichskristallnacht" and "the final solution" and to the rise of the Third Reich;

(ii) the challenge of reconstructing and representing the experience of genocide—the impossibility of comprehension—whether public, professional, or official;

(iii) the problems facing historians, publics, and others—including archivists, state veterans' departments, and war crimes tribunals— in evaluating the complicity and responsibility of soldiers in war, and in wartime occupation;

(iv) the responsibilities and obligations that descend upon states and populations from the acts of earlier generations; and

(v)   the ambiguities of support, consent, and acceptance, which appear

42. For an overview of some of this work in the "history workshop" mode, in the light of the historians' debate, see Mary Nolan, "The *Historikerstreit* and Social History," *New German Critique* 44 (Spring–Summer 1988): 51–80.

43. Of course, the struggle to unpack the history of the "moral catastrophe" and to comprehend its capacity to create silences and to mold the practice of history to the Western strategic demands of a post–World War II era, has been the most central impulse through the several Roundtables in Anthropology and History; as noted earlier, Herb Gutman's 1980 intervention anticipated the tumult that came with Bitburg as the February 1985 discussions in Baltimore, concerning the planning of the Fifth Roundtable, anticipated the *Historikerstreit*.

44. The attention to some of these issues has been heightened by the process of integration of West and East in Germany since fall 1989 (it might be remarked that the critical moment in this process was the fiftieth anniversary of "Reichskristallnacht" or the "November pogrom"), which introduced within one state and nation—the "new Germany"— two very distinct protocols of remembrance of the Holocaust nurtured by distinct state

between the programs of totalitarian regimes on the one hand and "everyday life" on the other.

These issues are powerful not only because they define the moral ground of the practice of history (in its broadest sense) in Germany, but also because they reach through all those professionals and publics outside Germany who would measure, weigh, and judge the actions of Germans both remembering, and refusing to remember, their past(s).

One is further intrigued by the locations of "publics" within, and also as audience to, the historians' debate in Germany. The debate was, as noted, carried out within—and in some respects orchestrated by—major newspapers. Professional historians argued the practices and responsibilities of their craft in public view, with their various "publics" as, in a sense, judges as well as readers. But the debate was also about the appropriate forms of history to be held, revered, or known by a national public; if the major adversaries in the debate could agree on nothing else, they could, it seems, agree that professional historians held the responsibility of defining how that history should be practiced. In an unpublished paper presented to the Sixth Roundtable in Anthropology and History in 1989, the Tübingen folklorist Utz Jeggle entered this issue with an important, and perhaps still little recognized, intervention. Jeggle, who has been studying the workings of memory and silence in the Wurttemburg village of Baisingen, has argued that

> scholarly reconstruction of what happened in this [the Nazi] era has mostly ended up by rendering obsolete the private experiences preserved in written records or handed down by word of mouth inside families, or residential areas, or communities. The reason for this is the discrepancy between the invisible structure of Nazi terror and the reach of personal experience—a discrepancy that necessarily palliates the full enormity of the reality even when it avoids the trap of embellishing it.[45]

Jeggle observed that professional historians have created a boundary between what they regard as significant and "the day-to-day banalities of private remembered experience," which they leave over to the local and nonprofessional historians. Jeggle's approach to such material—which he sees left behind by both sides in the *Historikerstreit*—is to en-

---

policies in the Federal Republic and the Democratic Republic from 1950. Alf Lüdtke has been studying the history of war commemoration and victims' memorials in the East.

45. Utz Jeggle, "Recollecting State Terror: Local Memories of the Persecution of the Jews in the So-called 'Reichskristallnacht,'" paper presented to the Sixth International Roundtable in Anthropology and History, Bellagio, Italy, August 31–September 4, 1989.

gage the "memory of experience" worked through and over by various personal, intimate, and communal forces of suppression and revision. Jeggle's work is, in an important sense, a micro-historical one, looking at history production and historical revisionism under a very close lens; at the same time it is a consciously interventionist one, retrieving a local past to challenge the forces and programs of repression of history within the community. Jeggle's work is not simply on life in the Third Reich— getting at truths beneath the veneer of *Heimat*[46]—but also examining the "work" of postwar German "audiences" in the production of a history. And Jeggle's overall approach is hardly "local" at all:

> In my opinion, any attempt at a historical treatment—by Germans at least—of the Nazi era that neglects to scrutinize the personal motives of the post-war German audience it is addressed to is, in my opinion, likely to summon up deep-seated anxieties, so that questions that are actually intended to probe the structural makeup of man are countered—in typical smokescreening fashion—with assertions about the structural nature of history.[47]

While holding attention on the experience of the Third Reich, Jeggle is attempting to enlarge the field of engagement of the historian to include the various "programs" of memory and suppression that stand between the events themselves and the present, much as Sonya Rosenberger did with her campaign to write a history of Pfilzing in the Third Reich.[48]

*

In the late 1980s, a vigorous debate developed among historians in South Africa concerning the representation of late eighteenth- and early nineteenth-century Zulu influence upon the peopling of southern Africa. Various participants in the debate have signaled its inauguration in the publication of Julian Cobbing's "The Mfecane as Alibi: Thoughts on Dithakong and Mbolompo,"[49] in which Cobbing, a historian at

---

46. In his *Ordinary Men: Reserve Police Battalion 101 and the Final Solution in Poland* (New York: HarperCollins, 1992), Christopher R. Browning has brilliantly opened *Heimat* to intense inspection, and also judgment, showing that approaches to the study of "everyday life" of ordinary people need not evade the ways in which criminality and terror permeated the activities of the everyday among the German occupiers of eastern Europe. "As the story of Reserve Police Battalion 101 demonstrates, mass murder and routine had become one. Normality itself had become exceedingly abnormal" (xix).

47. "Recollecting State Terror," 3.

48. In Michael Verhoeven's 1989 film *The Nasty Girl*, discussed in the Preface of this volume.

49. *Journal of African History* 29, 4 (1988): 487–519.

Rhodes University, brought to a wider audience his intense skepticism concerning the "Zulucentric" explanation for the distribution of peoples, cultures, and societies across southern Africa. This explanation, constructed around what Cobbing has identified in this and subsequent papers as an invention, "the *mfecane*," had found a foothold throughout southern African historiography, in textbooks, and in recent constructions by Zulu nationalists of their own past. *Mfecane*, for years, held currency among historians as an appropriate, serviceable structure for representing the complex of migrations of peoples across southern Africa in the late eighteenth and early nineteenth centuries, set in motion, it was averred, by the rise and expansion of the Zulu kingdom. The *mfecane* was seen as a series of events and processes of immense human scale and significance that lay beyond the frontier of European expansion in southern Africa, yet set the stage for the encounters that would develop between Europeans and African societies across the region. The *mfecane* model would firmly plant Zulu agency, as well as Zulu culture and politics, as the explanatory core of preindustrial southern African historiography.

Julian Cobbing has unmasked the *mfecane* model as a contrivance. For Cobbing, the mythification of Zulu influence—with its accompanying glorification and demonization of the Zulu ruler Shaka—as an explanatory structure for the history of preindustrial southern Africa was a disarming cover for European plunder, including the Portuguese slave trade and demands for servile labor in the Cape Colony. One target of Cobbing's revisionism may have been the early nineteenth-century liberals who documented conditions on the "frontier," but the effective quarry has been a lineage of historians descending into the present who have, according to Cobbing, bought into "the myth of *mfecane*" and even embellished it.[50]

In linking at least five significant elements—the invention of *mfecane* as a process-model, the late eighteenth- and early nineteenth-century demands for African labor, the hypocrisy of early Cape liberals, the duplicity and naïveté of twentieth-century historians of South Africa, and the mythification of the Zulu past—Cobbing himself has taken on a number of interested parties, who have reacted sometimes in kind even though they may agree in part with the thrust of his revision of southern African history from 1790 to 1820. The debate has itself "motored" a complex process of conferences and publications, including a three-day

50. An important answer to Cobbing's deconstruction of the European demonization of Shaka is to be found in Carolyn A. Hamilton, "'The Character and Objects of Chaka':

program called The *"Mfecane"* Aftermath at the University of the Witwatersrand.[51] The debate has set off and been accompanied by (but in a
sense also been sparked by) a great deal of new research on slaving
and the slave trade in southern Africa and a revitalization of interest in
preindustrial southern African historiography.[52]

The debate or debates developing with the publication of Cobbing's
articles are continuing, and the debates present themselves for observation[53] and study, not only because of the strident quality of the discourse
but also because of the timing of these exchanges. While southern African historians have been calling one another to reexamine the sources
on the late eighteenth and early nineteenth century, the "new South
Africa" is fitfully and violently emerging within a virtual and metaphorical stone's throw of the John Moffat Building on the East Campus of
the University of the Witwatersrand, where The *"Mfecane"* Aftermath
conference was convened. The site of debate is not insignificant; note,
by comparison, the role of the leading newspapers of Germany in her-
alding the *Historikerstreit;* note the site of Reagan laying a wreath (or
was it a "bomb") on Helmut Kohl's program of normalization of the
past at the Bitburg cemetery; note the literal *reconstitution* of America at
Gettysburg; note the debates in the highest courts of Kenya over the
meanings of "custom" and "modernity" and the force of Luo "tradition"
in the struggle for the body of S. M. Otieno.

The *mfecane* debate absorbs into it a powerful double paradox. On
the one hand, those who see Cobbing reducing Africans to victims of

---

A Reconsideration of the Making of Shaka as 'Mfecane' Motor," *Journal of African History*
33, 1 (1992): 37–63.

51. September 6–8, 1991, with something like twenty new papers and a special section
of the *South African Historical Journal* (vol. 25, November 1991).

52. When Carolyn Hamilton, who convened the University of the Witwatersrand conference, invited me to participate or attend—and at minimum to circulate information
about it in our Northwestern newspaper *PAS News and Events*—I wondered out loud how
she would find enough scholars interested in preindustrial and precolonial southern African historiography to fill a conference panel. The visible weight of recent historiography
of South Africa and neighboring regions has been channeled into post-1880 experience
surrounding capital formation, industrial labor questions, urbanization, and so forth. In
respect to American-based scholarship on southern Africa, one staff member of the Social
Science Research Council observed to me in 1989 that it had been a very long time since
SSRC's Africa Program had received a conference or research proposal on precolonial or
preindustrial southern Africa.

53. In the aftermath of The *"Mfecane"* Aftermath conference at the University of the
Witwatersrand, Stephen Taylor published a succinct account of that forum, and the longer-
running debate, in *The Times Higher Education Supplement,* under the title "Zulu History
Rewritten and Rerun."

European interests and their complex intrigue wonder about the implications of Africans denied a history of their own, as European actions come to monopolize the whole of the historical stage. Those who see the oppression of Africans in southern Africa as deeply vested in nineteenth- and twentieth-century European ideas concerning the absence of African possibility and agency in the region must wonder how the historians who bring powerful criticism to early European exploitation in the region should come to approximately the same conclusion as those European actors they are criticizing: the absence of significant African agency. One is reminded of the programmatic calls by anthropologists to make the concept of "culture" disappear from contemporary anthropological discourse which have come at the very moment that peoples long studied by anthropologists as "cultures" have broken the anthropologists' monopoly of inscription of that construct. At the moment that Africans in southern Africa may be looking to their pasts to seek tools for construction of the future, experts on their pasts are asserting that whatever they thought their capacity for initiative may have been, it is pretty much a pack of lies. Only the Europeans had interests, initiatives, and agency.

Caught in progress, amidst the paradoxes and contradictions of some of the core positions, the *mfecane* debate reveals some of the ways complex situations become polarized into simple oppositions. For example, in response to Elizabeth Eldredge's attempt to reconceptualize the *mfecane*,[54] tabled at the University of the Witwatersrand conference, Julian Cobbing argued,

> I have reiterated what "the mfecane" was—historically and historiographically; and believe that Eldredge was insufficiently conversant with this. Her changing of "mfecane" from the Zulucentric construct that it is into "generalised time of troubles" (with "Alibi" [Cobbing's critical article] an "interpretation of the *mfecane*") is an impermissible step, redolent with confusion. She should reexamine her critique and decide whether "the mfecane" lives or not. "Alibi" was an "anti-mfecane"; its job was negative. The two tasks

54. "Sources of Conflict in Southern Africa, ca. 1800–1830: The 'Mfecane' Reconsidered," *Journal of African History* 33, 1 (1992): 1–35. Eldredge offers a far more complex vision of southern African history than that bequeathed by the historians that Cobbing originally targeted as the inventors of *mfecane*. Her essential brief in so far as Cobbing goes is that "Historians working throughout Africa have spent the last three decades challenging the racist assumption of exclusive European agency in African historical change and demonstrating the complexity of internally generated change over time in Africa. It is a step backwards to depict African history in South Africa again as a wholly reactive process and to deny to Africans their own history" (p. 35).

of removing "the mfecane" and researching the new history that is necessary, though closely related, should nevertheless be firmly and consciously separated. Redefining "the mfecane" as Eldredge has done, whether intentionally or not, will produce endless confusion and give longer life to the old "mfecane" in the places where it most matters; South Africa's school text books.[55]

While Cobbing and colleagues, and their adversaries, are arguing over the values and interpretations of particular early sources, and later readings of those sources, they are also arguing the fate of implicit social theory concerning the role of ethnicity in the formation of African communities; the value of core and periphery models in the historicization of early capitalism in southern Africa; and the relationship between past, as constituted in historical texts, and the present.[56] Yet the debate appears to have constructed a wall of professionalization around itself, leaving an overhang of questions:

(i)   What are the implications of the "de-ethnicization" of historical explanation for those across southern Africa who have found themselves for decades bound and suppressed by state adjudication of identity but who also see value and possibility through revisiting and reasserting their own histories, languages, and cultures?

(ii) What are the implications of a destabilization of Zulu history and identity—through the problematization of heroic history—for women and men nurtured in this identity and history? And how will a revisionist and deheroized "Zulu history" be taught—or learned? And what, indeed, will it be called?

(iii) Given that the intricate revisionist historiography, such as Cobbing's writings exemplify, rests on the deployment of ethnic group

55. Julian Cobbing, "Overturning 'The Mfecane': A Reply to Elizabeth Eldredge," paper presented to the Colloquium on the *Mfecane* Aftermath, University of the Witwatersrand, September 6–9, 1991, 36.

56. In a study of the *Historikerstreit*, John Torpey, "Introduction: Habermas and the Historians," *New German Critique* 44 (Spring–Summer, 1988): 6, notes that the historians' debate is "in fact more political than historiographical, is principally concerned with the way in which the understanding of history shapes contemporary popular discourse. In the German case, the very framework of postwar democracy rests on a certain minimal consensus about the past: namely, that German nationalism and illiberalism were in no small part responsible for 1933." One could ask, in relation to the *mfecane* debate in South Africa, whether part of its salience and power isn't that Cobbing's "rereading" of the sources and textbooks has destabilized one of the few bits of consensus about the past which could enable a discussion across diverse positions and interests about "a new South Africa."

nomenclature—"who" was where when?—how far has this de-
ethnicization gone and how far has it, in a surreptitious way,
simply reinforced the deep consensus among scholars and observers that "tribe" was the essential unit of social action in the precolonial or preindustrial era?

(iv) How far does the *mfecane* debate reproduce the older "modes of
production" schema which held that Africans—a relatively un-
questioned unit of analysis—were simply victims of, and not
agents in and of, their experience?

As the *mfecane* debate continues, one may wish to look more closely
at the ethnography, or the economy, of this debate. How does the debate
reproduce older lines of discussion in new language? How do positions
within the debate assert, or connect with, representations of the past
held more widely, and also outside this particular conflict? What are
the evidenced and possible passageways between academic and public
discourse? What are the agreements among adversaries that make this
debate possible? What are the processes in this debate that suggest a
next stage, or after-stage?

*

In "reading" debate, significant tensions develop between the possibility of an infinite (or at least an exhaustive) array of conceivable interpretative positions and representational outcomes and the reduced, and
often bipolar, set of positions constructed or evolved through the course
of the debate. How does such a reduction proceed as a simultaneously
intellectual, political, and social project? How does this reduction work
as an economy, in the production of value and capital? How do proponents of distinct and sometimes opposed positions achieve coherence
and how does such a project of consolidation produce a reduced and
clearer opposition? How are nonreciprocal and dissonant interests sustained within a contest of reduced structure and complexity?

And how do adversaries achieve, through conflict, agreements over
the language and terms of debate: a common question or a reduced set
of overlapping questions; a consent to interact within a common forum
(conference, seminar, journal, courtroom, parliament); agreements on
certain timing of disquisition; shared understanding of the possible and
limited forms of closure? How do combatants in one site of debate produce silences and suppressions in other potential sites?

One may also seek to understand the contingencies of the material
ground of debate on the African past (perhaps somewhat parallel to

Sally Falk Moore's analysis of the material constraints on the operations of precedent in Tanzanian legal practice).[57] The very matter of debate— for example, the sources of nationalism, the meaning of resistance— may have opened and closed opportunities for extended discussion and publication. The collapse of publication across much of Africa in the 1970s may have altered the form of—and even produced closure in re- spect to—particular debates in Africa, reducing the opportunity struc- ture for participants based on the continent. The precarious role of intel- lectuals in a number of African settings may have also limited the form and force of certain debates. The search for generalization—and also the quest of many intellectuals for a postcolonial ground broader than the nation—may have induced a specific economy of practice into re- cent historiography. And the current transformation of the African uni- versity toward the model of a teacher-training institute may today be bringing shifts in the possibilities of academic debate within Africa. Moreover, with the attention to Afrocentric discourses in the New World (or diaspora), there may be something of a reorganization of the geogra- phy of prime debate on the African past, moving certain debates right outside the continent itself.

With respect to African historical writing—and likewise, or compara- tively, for other areas of the world—how does one detail a debate, pro- duce an ethnography of debate, and weigh the import of such debate on the production of historical research and historical texts? How does one note the ways in which specific "productions of history"—official investigations, litigation, commemorations, museum exhibits, confer- ences, seminars, workshops, collective books—reorganize debates into distinctive form? And, reiterating the concerns of Katherine Verdery, how do debates construct as well as reflect culture, society, and nation? Studying the S. M. Otieno case in Kenya—in which the claims of the widow's and the clan's rights in the subject's body were fought over in courts, streets, and seminars across Kenya for a good part of 1986–87— is one venture in this direction.[58] The court litigation over Otieno's corpse is saturated by debate over history, culture, and nation: the life of S. M., of his family, and of his marriage; and the meaning of asserted or alleged customs in regard to burial appropriate to a Luo individual, and the meaning of "tradition" and "modernity" to a nation.

57. *Social Facts and Fabrications: Customary Law on Kilimanjaro, 1880–1980* (Cambridge: Cambridge University Press, 1986).

58. See the next chapter. Also see David William Cohen and E. S. Atieno Odhiambo, *Burying SM: The Politics of Knowledge and the Sociology of Power in Africa* (Portsmouth, N.H.: Heinemann, 1992).

In addressing debates over the representation of the African past, one invariably confronts the verge or boundary between academic and non-academic discourses. The contest over the virtues of "nationalist historiography" in East Africa were situated at the crossroads of local and national curriculum development, state projects, and new ventures in historical research and writing. Long and complex debates over the demography of the slave trade or the "effect of the slave trade on Africa" or of the nature of "precolonial modes of production" or the "Bantu migrations" seem to have offered little scope for popular enthusiasm and dynamic, yet emerged during far broader and not altogether academic discussions of underdevelopment, national liberation, and Pan-Africanism. How have certain passageways between academic and non-academic arenas opened and closed within particular debates over the past? How have academic debates over the form of early revolts and revolutions—Uthman dan Fodio and Chimurenga, for example—drawn from and entered discourses outside the fold of academic research? Recent debates across the globe developing around the care of the remains of the dead have been especially provocative examples of confrontations over both the authority to control human remains and the authority to regulate the interpretation of such remains.

FOUR On February 22, 1986, National
Public Radio reported the emer-
Silences of the Living, gence of a fiery debate between
Native Americans and curators at
Orations of the Dead the Smithsonian Institutions. The
debate had developed around the
disposition of Native American skeletal remains from prehistoric sites,
remains stored in the laboratories and storerooms of the Smithsonian.
The debate, which has continued into the early 1990s, was early on la-
beled the "reburial controversy."

According to the radio report, the Native Americans wanted to "re-
bury" the remains. Authorities at the Smithsonian resisted on the
grounds that the bones came from populations and periods that preceded European settlements in the Americas and therefore "scientists
are not able to establish which Indian tribe the bones come from."[1] On
the other side, Native Americans were arguing that "these are their ancestors" and were insisting on retrieving the remains for burial. The
Smithsonian officials noted that they would consider turning the bones
over if particular remains could be established to be related to a particular Native American tribe. Indeed, the radio report noted, the Smithsonian was shortly to return human remains originating in Peru to authorities in that country.

The Smithsonian officials were arguing that the skeletal remains were
needed by scientists for study of health, disease, stature, life expectancy,
and nutrition. They argued that the studies of Native American material
have been important in the enhancement of scientific analysis of remains
from a number of world populations. But the representative of interested Native American groups remarked that "We Native Americans do
not like to think of our ancestors buried in cardboard boxes in storerooms and laboratories in Washington."

Earlier, the radio program noted, Native Americans had complained
about the "sacred remains of the ancestors" being mounted on walls
and in cases in the Smithsonian's Museum of Natural History. The
Smithsonian officials had conceded this issue and removed the remains
from displays.

National Public Radio reported Smithsonian spokesmen claiming that
Native Americans

> do not realize the scientific importance of the skeletal remains and
> they do not understand the degree of knowledge of Indians that

1. From a tape recording provided by National Public Radio.

> Smithsonian scientists and other scientists have gathered through
> skeletal and bone studies . . . Native Americans often do not under-
> stand that scientists know more than they do about the history of
> their precontact ancestors.

On the other hand, the Native Americans were insisting that their ancestors should have proper burials according to Native American tradition.

The reburial controversy—as it was set out in one of the earliest reports on national radio and television—has been more than a simple
contest over the remains of the ancestors. For the participants—and for
observers—it is a piece of a continuous struggle for control over the
history of Native Americans. It has been, as well, clearly a battlefield
over the authority of claims to expert knowledge. Indeed, in the contest
over the Native American remains, one may note a transformation from
the category of struggles over whose historical knowledge is more expert, more scientific, more correct, more factual, to a rhetorical conflict
between, on the one hand, powerful statements of expertise and, on the
other, powerful statements of emotion. In the Smithsonian battle, the
scientists not only controlled the remains, and the interpretation of
the remains, but they also controlled the terms of resolution: determining that the issue would only be settled by expert or scientific knowledge (proof that the remains "belong" to specific Native American
groups).

If one reads the debate closely, and looks at the multitude of contests
between Native Americans and American civil authorities, one recognizes that the reburial controversy has become the present version of
older debates over such questions as Who speaks for Native Americans?
Who commands authority over, and what evidence holds power within,
the authenticization processes of legal challenges by Native Americans
concerning their status, their lands, and their autonomy in the United
States? Who is empowered to tell the history of Native Americans? In
American civil life, who determines the definition of who is or is not a
"Native American"?[2]

There is another edge to the current discussion of reburials and it
involves the growing apprehension concerning the exhumation and examination of prehistoric and historic human remains in other regions of
the world. This was first raised for me at a workshop on Caribbean

2. In *The Predicament of Culture: Twentieth-Century Ethnography, Literature, and Art* (Cambridge, Mass.: Harvard University Press, 1988), James Clifford surveys at close range the
judicial conflict over the legalities of Mashpee claims to Native American identity. See
also the forthcoming study by Gerald Sider of parallel Lumbe identity claims.

anthropology and ethnoarchaeology at Johns Hopkins University, February 22, 1986, during a discussion of an "agenda for future research" in archaeology. One participant, Dr. Jerome Handler, said that the examination of slave cemeteries and burial grounds and the scientific analysis of the remains should have a high priority in research, for such research would have the potential of revealing, as did his own study of a slave burial ground in Barbados, abundant evidence about status, nutrition, health, disease, toxicities, and so forth. Other participants remarked that current debates about the scientific examination of skeletal remains in the United States—reported for the first time, coincidentally, on National Public Radio later the same afternoon—made such work unlikely in the future and that governments of other countries would be sensitized to the ethical issues involved in exhumation and would ban such research, no matter what its use might be.

A bit later in the workshop discussions, Handler returned to the discussion of the study of slave burial grounds and noted that a few years earlier the government of Barbados gave official recognition to the Cropover Festival, a celebration marking the end of the sugar season in the slavery era. In 1985, on Cropover Day, officials from the government and Barbados television came to the slave burial ground that Handler's team had been studying. In special ceremonies, they joined the exhumations to the cropover celebration. The organizers and celebrants of Cropover Day in Barbados—and other public authorities who had earlier honored the exhumation research by organizing lectures and exhibits— evidently saw the exhumations and analyses of slave skeletal remains as worthy of recognition rather than censorship. That the remains were relocated in laboratories in Illinois was viewed as a part of the worthy reconstruction of the slave era and as consonant with the public revaluation of the Barbados slaves, not as a desecration of slave ancestors.

As the overthrow of expertise and expert knowledge in regard to the Native American remains was underway in North America, and as "experts" in archaeology were consequently moving away from the touchy issue of handling the remains of historic and prehistoric populations, archaeologists of the slave burial grounds in Barbados were being encouraged by popular consciousness concerning the exhumation and examination of the slave remains. Curiously, one of the findings of the Handler team was that in at least one case Barbados slaves had interred one of their number in a manner distinct from the burial patterns both of other slaves and of masters and others in the community; the interpretation derived was that the slaves had put their own imprint upon the status and meaning of this individual rather than acknowledging the master's "hand."[3] In a sense, in slavery they had managed to command the procedures of burial, to mark their own interpretation and valuation upon the deceased person, an authority over the deceased among them which was for years out of reach of the Native Americans in respect to the "ancestral" and "prehistoric" skeletal remains housed in the Smithsonian.[4]

*

In early November 1991, I traveled to St. Louis with a friend who was going to screen a program of films at a college there. I was visiting Washington University to encourage some cooperation between Northwestern and Washington University. At my friend's suggestion, we took a long-about and back road to St. Louis via, among other stops, Dickson Mounds, located above the Spoon River a few miles northwest of Havana, Illinois. At Dickson Mounds is located a State of Illinois Archaeological Museum that sits on the site of excavations begun in the first decades of the twentieth century by Marion H. and Don F. Dickson, residents of the area who, like other farmers, had stumbled across significant remains of Native American culture surviving from pre-European settlement of the Mississippi Valley. The Dicksons found and began to uncover a Native American burial mound. By the late 1920s, Dickson Mounds was an important stop on the midwestern itineraries of a new motoring public that, summers and weekends, sought out unusual archaeological, geological, and historical sites, along with other spectacles, as destinations for a new culture of touring by motorcar.

Charging fees to view the skeletal remains which were contained first under tenting and later within a building constructed over the site, the Dicksons straddled amateur and professional traditions in archaeology. Their site not only earned them cash from the curiosity-seeking motoring crowd, but also became well known to professional archaeologists; from the Depression, the University of Chicago archaeological

3. A presentation of early findings from the study of the slave burial ground in Barbados is to be found in Jerome S. Handler and Robert S. Corrucini, "Plantation Slave Life in Barbados: A Physical Anthropological Analysis," *Journal of Interdisciplinary History* 14, 1 (Summer 1983): 65–90.

4. For a review of a large range of contests over the disposition of human skeletal remains, see Douglas H. Ubelaker and Lauryn Guttenplan Grant, "Human Skeletal Remains: Preservation or Reburial?" *Yearbook of Physical Anthropology* 32 (1989): 249–87. At the time of the publication, the authors were employees of the Smithsonian Institution. See also Glen W. Davidson, "Human Remains: Contemporary Issues," *Death Studies* 14 (1990): 491–502.

programs fastened on to Dickson Mounds as a research and training laboratory. In 1954, the State of Illinois bought the Dickson museum and site from the Dickson family and, by 1972, had opened a substantial museum building that housed research laboratories and an exhibit hall and also enclosed the burial remains. The entrance to the "burial room" is on the second floor of the museum and in November 1991, one passed through elaborate displays presenting information about Native American history and culture before one reached the entrance to the stairs that took one down two flights of stairs to the dimly lit burial exhibit. On the third floor of the museum was a very effective exhibit on the history and practice of American archaeology.

The burial site enclosed within the building is some ten by twenty meters. Under Dickson family command, approximately ninety graves were opened and the remains of approximately 250 individuals were uncovered. The graves included various material goods, many specifically associated with the individual remains of the Native Americans. In November 1991 a visual presentation on the wall above the burial site drew attention to various details within the overall grouping of remains and related some of the findings on diet, nutrition, health, size, and demography, findings from some fifty years of intensive analysis of the remains.[5]

For months, newspapers had carried stories of demonstrations by Native Americans seeking to close the museum; there were no demonstrators present that day—had there been, would I have crossed their picket line?—but there was a sign in the "burial room" warning visitors that anyone who entered the exhibit itself would be prosecuted for criminal trespass and more.

At one corner of the burial site I noticed some signs of fresh earth spewed across a very small part of the exhibit area. At the main entrance to the museum, I asked the guard on duty about the disturbed earth in the exhibit. He reported that, in recent weeks, there had just been a great deal of agitation from Native Americans who wanted to close the burial ground. Guards had had to drag away several demonstrators who had entered the exhibit (by climbing over the wall that separates the burial mound from the visitors' observation walk) and dug up some of the earth, trying to cover the graves. He remarked in a depressed voice on recent stories in the press concerning the likelihood that Governor Jim

---

5. It has now been recognized that some remains were moved, early on, from other burial sites to the exhibition space, raising questions concerning the analysis of the Dickson Mound remains as a "population."

Edgar would "reverse positions" and close the burial site.[6] Dickson Mounds had been a campaign issue in 1990: Republican candidate Edgar edged toward what seemed a more neutral position—or was it a less decisive one?—than either his Republican predecessor, Jim Thompson, who had after months of pondering decided in August 1990 that the burial mound should be left open to the public, or Neil Hartigan, who had more explicitly committed himself to keeping it open. In November 1991 the guard at the museum voiced what was probably the essence of the various possibilities of political positioning on the issue, but also an initial argument of the Smithsonian scientists. "None of these Indians are from around here anyway. And the people demonstrating are not even descendants of the people buried down there [looking in the direction of the "burial room"]." The guard was also concerned about jobs, and he thought that if the governor ordered the closing of the "burial room," he might as well doom the whole museum to closing because "who would come if they couldn't see the bones?"

Within two weeks of my November 1991 visit, Governor Edgar announced that the "burial mound" would be closed and sealed to public view effective April 3, 1992,[7] but that the museum would remain open and that there would be funds for developing other attractions to maintain public interest. Over a longer period—were there to be sufficient funds—the burial mound would be permanently sealed, so that it could not be simply reopened with the turn of a key if the political winds changed. But the issues of engineering the sealing of the mound within the structure of the existing building would require a special state government appropriation for technical and engineering study.

One view of the extraordinary tension around the Dickson Mounds site centered on its being the "last significant open burial remain" in the United States. To Native American activists, this made Dickson Mounds an especially opportune target for political work and the open burial

6. At the time, and still today, Governor Edgar's positions are enmeshed in ambiguity and complexity. The deeper institutional situation seems to have been that before Governor Jim Thompson began to study the issue (eventually deciding to keep it open as an educational medium), the senior staff of the State of Illinois Museum in Springfield had already decided to close the skeletal exhibit and had drawn up a plan of how to close it, but a leak of the plan caught Governor Thompson off guard and he was, evidently, embarrassed into a "re-study" of the plan to close.

7. Sean Noble of *The State Journal-Register* (Springfield, Illinois) reported that Edgar—at the November 25, 1991, press conference when he announced the closing—"deftly sidestepped questions about the politics of his change of heart . . . 'If you look at my comments during the [1990] campaign, I said we should not close Dickson Mounds . . . We are not closing Dickson Mounds, only its Burial exhibit.' When reminded that the skeletal display

exhibit rose to near the top of the long register of Native American grievances developing from the 1960s onwards. But its reputation as the "last site" only reinforced the interest of many people within sur-rounding Fulton County—who *do* vote on such "local" issues with great passion—and others who found some rationale or other for sustaining public access to the site. They, with others outside Fulton County, argued that the mounds protected a unique set of remains, and it was here at Dickson Mounds that there had been a sustained commitment to the preservation of Native American culture across a century in which Na-tive American culture was being destroyed right across North America. Dickson Mounds was for them the "last site" of *protection* of the ancient cultures of Native Americans on the continent.[8]

Some of those who sought to keep the "burial room" open introduced quantitative evidence to the debate: it was only from 1990 that the State of Illinois Museum received any significant numbers of complaints con-cerning the morality or legality of maintaining an open Native Ameri-can burial site; from the time of the opening of the new museum build-ing until 1990, only a handful of complaints were received; and the latest surge of complaints looked thoroughly orchestrated. On the other side, a survey of ZIP codes of letters on both sides of the issue from 1990 indicated that the expression of "for" or "against" closing varied in di-rect relationship with the geographical distance from the site itself. As one moved away from the site, and from Fulton County, support for maintaining an open site fell off steadily, and there were more and more negative opinions about the State of Illinois maintaining an open site at greater remove from the mounds. (All the mail from overseas was for closing the mounds). At the press conference in Springfield, where he announced the closing, Governor Edgar

> conceded that the national mood . . . played a part in his decision. The National Geographic Society this fall dropped Dickson from a map of Indian historical sites. Plus, Edgar noted, federal grants have been put in jeopardy by the lingering closure questions.[9]

---

was the museum's sole source of controversy, Edgar replied, 'You can view it [the semantic involved] any way you want'" (*Journal-Register,* November 26, 1991, p. 3).

8. An outstanding treatment of the issue of the open burial exhibit at Dickson Mounds is to be found in James Krohe, Jr., "Skeletons in Our Closet," *The Reader: Chicago's Free Weekly,* Friday, February 14, 1992, pp. 1–26. A subtitle projects the essential thrust of Krohe's exposition: "'Who were they?' is a question always asked by visitors to the burial display at Dickson Mounds. Now the bones force us to confront a deeper question: Who are we?"

9. *The State Register-Journal,* November 26, 1991, p. 1.

On the other hand, Michael Haney, a leader of the United Indian Nations,

> lauded the reversal of Edgar's gubernatorial campaign support for
> keeping the exhibit open. "This is a first step . . ." [said Haney]. He
> indicated Native Americans intend to use the closure as a building
> block toward eliminating other parts of popular culture they
> find offensive, such as the University of Illinois' mascot, Chief
> Illiniwek.[10]

One of the significant arguments for maintaining an "open site" was the Fulton Countians' claims to affinity with the site and with the remains. In interviews cited in the Illinois newspapers, and at greater length in a seminar at the Institute for Advanced Study and Research in the African Humanities at Northwestern, James Brown, chairperson of the Anthropology Department at Northwestern and president of the Illinois Archaeology Survey, related the history of the relationship of the people of Fulton County to the Dickson site and to the remains.[11] The people of Fulton County and the surrounding area see these remains as

> part of nature, part of their environment. They see a direct con-
> nection between themselves as living and these remains as part of

10. Ibid. The University of Illinois mascot, Chief Illiniwek, had just weeks before stirred protests during Homecoming Week activities at the University of Iowa in Iowa City (which preceded the Iowa-Illinois football game), in which the Homecoming planning committee acted quickly to remove a series of offending exhibits from shop windows across Iowa City and produced agreements to ban representations of Native Americans from all Homecoming displays and from the Friday night parade, annually one of the major events in the state of Iowa. The uproar in Iowa City over the Illinois mascot led the University of Illinois adminstration to ban Chief Illiniwek from traveling outside the state. I am grateful to Rich O'Connor, then a student at Iowa active in removing the exhibits, for providing an account of the events in Iowa City.

11. The institute was host for ten days to a group of archaeologists and museum officials from Africa, who were touring several programs and sites in the United States. In planning programs in the Chicago area for the group, it was decided to place some of the documentation on the Dickson Mounds controversy before the group—with James Brown agreeing to convene the seminar—with the objective of opening discussions concerning the comparable issues being faced by the archaeologists and museologists working in African contexts. Some of the visitors from Africa spoke of experiences with conflicts over access to human remains for archaeological research; one spoke of the controversies his museum had faced in developing a plan to mark the atrocities in Uganda during President Amin's regime; curiously, none spoke of the "search for early man" which has emerged as "big science" in the world of archaeology and paleontology and which has, for years, absorbed vast funding for archaeology in Africa, including funds from the postcard solicitation mounted by the Louis Leakey Foundation in Pasadena, California, noted in the next chapter.

their environment. They don't hold the skeletal remains to belong to some disappeared or distant population with whom they have no contact or relationship. Rather, they see their own pasts, and, indeed, their own fates through these remains.

While conveying an informed respect for such claims to affinity, Brown was not prepared to translate these observations into an argument for keeping the mounds open.[12]

*

In August 1991 the federal government ordered a halt to construction of a $276 million federal office building on a block of lower Manhattan bounded by Broadway and Duane, Reade, and Elk streets. Remains of a previously unmapped eighteenth-century burial ground had been found twenty feet below street level in the earliest stages of preparation of the site and adjoining land for construction of the thirty-four-story skyscraper. By the end of December 1991 more than a hundred skeletons had been discovered at the site immediately north of City Hall. From documentation of the day, it was learned that this site, known as the "Negro Burial Ground," was located outside the early colonial city, and apart from the church cemeteries in early Manhattan, which barred blacks—both slave and free—from being buried in their grounds.[13]

In December 1991 the *New York Times* reported Mayor David N. Dinkins's first visit to the burial site. Dinkins was reported as remarking, "My God, how things have changed. Here I stood the first African-American mayor of the City of New York, examining the place where I would have had to have been buried. I couldn't have been buried in the

12. And in the seminar at Northwestern, James Brown saw no special validity to any claim from science that the remains should be kept open to public viewing. Brown appeared to reckon the power of Native American feelings on the issue and seemed to acknowledge that ultimately and universally human skeletal remains should be returned from scientific laboratories and museums to the ground. He also helped the seminar group navigate the complex terrain of litigation and federal legislation which, ultimately, would close all such public exhibitions of skeletal remains, except on Native American reservations where Native American authorities might choose to exercise the power to maintain open archaeological sites and museum exhibits. Brown also noted that not all Native Americans or Native American authorities were pushing such issues as hard as those Native American organizations and leaders who had targeted Dickson Mounds for closing.

13. Garrey Dennie, of the Department of History, St. Mary's College, St. Mary's City, Maryland, has been studying the early segregation of the dead in the burial politics of late nineteenth- and early twentieth-century South Africa.

city" as it was then defined. The excavation of the Negro Burial Ground has not been without controversy, including the predictable pressures from construction planners seeking to accelerate the project and seal the site for construction. On December 6, 1991, the *Times* reported that federal government officials were attempting to speed up the archaeological investigations at the site. A letter from Steven Wilf, published in the *Times* on December 26, 1991, argues:

> It appears that, once again, blacks will have to fight to protect their burial places. By calling for less careful work by archeologists, Federal officials do more than risk losing vital information that might be added to our fragmentary knowledge of eighteenth-century African-American life. They are demonstrating a lack of respect for those early blacks who struggled to establish a community of both the living and the dead.

In his letter, Wilf sketched a history of African-American burial controversies in New York from the 1780s, when free blacks in New York campaigned to protect their cemetery from "grave robbers who provided cadavers for New York's anatomists." Wilf provided a text of "a 1788 black petition" that surgeons

> under the cover of night, and in the most wanton sallies of excess . . . dig up the bodies of the deceased, friends and relatives of the petitioners, carry them away without respect to age or sex, mangle their flesh out of wanton curiosity and then expose it to beasts and birds.

Wilf recorded that the petition translated into the Anatomy Act of 1789 of New York, which "marked the first time that an American black proposal was transformed into law."

By early August 1992, 415 human skeletons had been disinterred and studied. Some of those working on the site estimated that the excavation might uncover as many as a thousand individual remains, but that the original burial ground, covering approximately five present city blocks, probably contained the graves of 20,000 persons in 1790.

The reports of the excavations and the studies of the skeletal remains, according to a long article in the *New York Times*, have

> revealed much about life in the eighteenth century. From the number of skeletons of children, for instance, experts have estimated that 50 percent of the black population died at birth or in the first

few years of life. The remains are also raising questions about
burial customs and whether they were transported from Africa or
borrowed from Europeans.[14]

An earlier report in the *Times* noted that while numbers of those buried at the site suffered from a range of disease, including rickets, arthri-
tis and syphilis, there was little evidence of individuals dying of violence. And there was, as of December 1991, nothing found in the
excavations that would connect those buried in the ground to the dozens
of blacks burned and hanged by white New Yorkers in the 1741 "Negro
Plot," where white residents of the city "imagined a conspiracy among
the slaves."[15] The director of urban archaeology for New York City,
Daniel N. Pagano noted the absence of mass burials. In spite of yellow
fever and cholera epidemics, "each individual is carefully placed in the
ground and with great respect."[16] The *Times* report of August 9, 1992,
noted that "some individuals were buried with coins in their hands or
over their eyes. One was buried with a shell next to the head . . . [another
man] was buried in a British marine officer's uniform." According to
Pagano, "There's just an incredible wealth of information on daily life
on individuals not written about in the history books. We're not going
to find it anywhere else."

The *Times* report also noted, in August 1992, the great excitement that
was developing around the site, and around the recovery of historical
knowledge from the archaeological, anthropological, and biological
analysis of the site and the remains. "The construction site has become
a place of pilgrimage for students, for politicians, even for actors who
starred in the television miniseries that is credited with renewing interest in African-American history, 'Roots.'"

The *Times* noted the effect the site has had on Noel Pointer, a jazz
musician and singer, who was reported as readying himself for participation in a twenty-six-hour remembrance vigil at the site, beginning at
noon on Sunday, August 9, 1992.

> I cried. You hear all about these archaeological and scientific terms
> and you say to yourself, "This is very interesting." But until you
> get down there and you see what the bodies look like—you see

14. E. R. Shipp, "Black Burial Ground Is Revealing Significant Glimpses of Lives of
Slaves," *New York Times*, August 9, 1992.
15. David W. Dunlap, "Near Mayor's Door, Slaves Were Once Buried," *New York Times*,
December 26, 1991.
16. Quotes here are from the *New York Times*, August 9, 1992, p. 19.

the skeletons of the children laying in the earth—then you realize
that these are people.

One of those working on the project, Michael Blakey, an anthropologist on the faculty of Howard University, saw the possibility of linking
the remains in New York with specific areas of Africa, through examination of genetic material, dietary evidence, and burial practices. Blakey
felt that the experts "can determine what the social and economic positions were for these ancestors . . . and [get] a better handle on exactly
where folks came from." With its story, the *Times* printed a photograph
(by Edward Keating) of a man standing in the middle of the site under
a protective canopy with an office building in the background. The
caption reads: "Chief Algaba Egunfemi, of the Bronx, a priest of the
African-based Yoruba religion, anointing a grave yesterday in a ceremony preceding the closing of the old grave site in lower Manhattan."
    While it was clear from late 1991 that public pressure would succeed
in producing dramatic changes in the federal construction program in
order to conserve the remains and mark the Negro Burial Ground, public and official discourse produced a renaming of the site. It would
henceforth be called "the African Burial Ground."
    The *New York Times* noted that, with Mayor Dinkins's leadership, plan-
ning was under way to alter the plans for the federal building and the
adjacent pavilion, to include a museum on the site. However, according
to the *Times,* some people did not want the site opened at all, arguing
that "a people who received no justice in life were receiving no peace
in death." The *Times* quoted Alton H. Maddox, a lawyer and community
leader: "So many people were willing to forgo challenging the system
in the present life just simply to have a decent afterlife. So many of our
people, because they've been so mistreated in life, really want to rest in
peace." On the other hand, the Howard University professor, Michael
Blakey, responded that "to learn from archeological sites constitutes another form of respect for our ancestors. It has special importance because so much of African-American history has been lost."
    Under immense public pressure, and as a consequence of the inter-
vention of the chair of the Subcommittee on Public Buildings and
Grounds of the United States House of Representatives, the construction
of the federal building was halted in July. In October 1992, President
George Bush signed a bill protecting the burial ground and appropriating $3,000,000 for the construction of a museum that would record and
preserve the history of people of African descent in New York. And the
General Services Administration (of the federal government) estab-

lished an advisory committee to develop and coordinate plans for "reburial of the remains, an African Burial Ground memorial, a burial
ground exhibition in the office tower, and a museum of African and
African-American History in New York City."[17]

*

In 1987, I was invited to present a public lecture at the National Museum
of African Art in Washington, in an inaugural series that was to survey
different branches of scholarship in African studies. I was asked to
speak on "the use of oral tradition in the reconstruction of the African
past." As I worked on the lecture,[18] I searched for an example of how
an historical datum might come "down" from the past in unexpected
ways, through unanticipated channels, an example that might indicate
to the audience the power of knowledge to reproduce itself in the absence of written documentation, archives, and so forth. I recalled one
particularly evocative piece, one that seemed at the time to play off
neatly against Milan Kundera's accounting of the disappearance of
Clementis from Czech memory, but not of his hat sitting atop Gottwald's head.[19]

Between 1966 and 1968 I was on the trail of the origins and migrations, perhaps five hundred to fifteen hundred years ago, of a parent
lineage of the Lungfish clan of the northern Lake Victoria region in eastern Africa. This was the clan whose leaders in Buganda (the kingdom

17. Spencer P. M. Harrington, "Bones and Bureaucrats," *Archaeology* 46, 2 (March-April
1993): 38. I am grateful to Dr. Jerome Handler for bringing attention to the Harrington
article, which provides an overview of the events following the uncovering of the Negro
Burial Ground in 1991. Handler, the archaeologist who had led the research on the slave
burials in Barbados noted earlier, has been appointed a member of the General Service
Administration's advisory committee on the burial ground in Manhattan.

18. The lecture—"Words Spoken Become History: Memory, Oral Tradition, and the
Reconstruction of the African Past"—was given at the National Museum on February 9,
1988. While some in the audience, and also on the museum staff, wondered why I had
not brought slides or other visuals to enhance the lecture, others indicated by their questions and comments afterwards that they had been successfully transported into the intended "zone" of contemplation of the possibilities, and also pleasures, of attempting to
write history from "words spoken." While I also relished the joy of lecturing for the first
time in an audience that included my father and my sister, I was not so enthralled by the
critique of my arguments concerning the value of oral tradition in historical construction—and also of my failure to bring visuals—which came at me from a written text
contained within a fortune cookie which I broke open at a meal at a Mongolian restaurant
in Washington immediately following the museum talk. The text read, "Believe all that
you see and half of what you hear."

19. See the opening discussion in the Preface of this volume.

which developed over several centuries around the northern shores of the lake) included the hereditary Admiral of the Fleet, an office with which Henry Morton Stanley became acquainted during his travels in Buganda in 1875–76. This search involved the collection and sifting of a considerable range of information from explicit clan and lineage traditions of migration to a multilingual etymology of the word *Bumogera*, the name which the historians of the core Lungfish lineages in Buganda associated with their origins.

One story recorded by a Ganda writer some years ago relates that the son of Mubiru, one of the heralded founders of the clan of the Lungfish and a blacksmith and fisherman, lost his axe in the lake and his people therefore and thence decided to climb into their canoes and leave that place. Through the application of a pool of evidence, an association seemed to emerge between the Bumogera of such accounts and Lolui Island with its adjacent mainland on the eastern side of Lake Victoria. Lolui Island had been in this century several times abandoned because of sleeping sickness but there were fishermen on the northern shore of the lake who reported that the original inhabitants of Lolui included people who, among other things, customarily removed one lower incisor tooth. Now many groups around the northeastern coast of the lake have in the past been known to remove "as custom" (and at different ages) two or four teeth.

The Baganda, of whom the Lungfish people have long identified themselves as part, have considered such evulsions barbaric and no Muganda—one has heard and read over and over again—would have a tooth removed for reasons "of custom." But, in 1967, I discovered an unpublished account written by a Ganda historian who recorded that about one year after the death of a Gabunga, the Admiral of the Fleet, two men from the Lungfish clan would go at night to the grave of Gabunga (some ninety miles of open water from Lolui Island), exhume the remains, and remove Gabunga's jawbone (an act not unknown in Buganda burial and unburial practice), and then remove one lower incisor.

One is brought face to face with Marx's oft-quoted remark that the "dead generations weigh like a nightmare on the brain of the living," the power in the "silences of the living, orations of the dead."[20]

20. This phrase, from which the title of this chapter is taken, was first suggested by Gabrielle Spiegel in mid-1988, as she read my early book proposal on the S. M. Otieno litigation in Kenya, 1986–87; more recently, Spiegel asked "permission to have it back" for the title of a talk: "Orations of the Dead/Silences of the Living: The Sociology of the Linguistic Turn," in which she proposed that Derrida and deconstructionism be historically examined "as a Post-Holocaust phenomenon . . ." [personal communication].

*

On November 20, 1991, the Spanish newspaper *El Pais* reported that a controversy had broken out around an exhibit in the Museo Municipal Darder of Banyoles (Gerona) not far from Barcelona. Alfonso Arcelin, a Haitian practicing medicine in Spain, had started a campaign to remove "the stuffed black man from Banyoles" from a glass case in the museum. Arcelin was threatening to call African nations to boycott Banyoles, which was to be the site of the rowing events in the 1992 Olympics in Barcelona.

The museum was reported to have identified the figure in the case as a "bechuanas" [Tswana]. The Barcelona naturalist Francisco de A. Darder, who opened the museum in 1888, had acquired the figure from a Frenchman, Edward Verraux, who had stolen the corpse of a purported Tswana chief at midnight following the chief's burial in southern Africa. A museum text relates,

> [the acquisition of the corpse] is owed to the audacity of his [the corpse's] preparer, the Frenchman Verraux ... [who] in one of his many trips that he frequently took in the search for notable models which have enriched many European museums, attended the burial of a tribal chief which was being celebrated with great pomp in those remote territories.

The Haitian doctor Arcelin, however, was surprised to face stiff opposition to his call for removal of the display.[21] According to *El Pais*

> Many citizens of Banyoles are opposed to the removal of the stuffed man, something they have seen in the museum all their lives. In addition, they have merchandized several products related to the preserved man and have begun a campaign to keep him with stickers and pins with the logo "We love you. Stay." The

---

21. While Dr. Arcelin was attempting to remove the "African" from the Banyoles Museum, the Wounded Knee Survivors Association were attempting to repatriate relics and remains of Native Americans massacred at Wounded Knee in 1890. According to a *New York Times* report (February 19, 1993), the remains, including scalps, a buckskin doll, a doll's cradle, clothing, and more than a hundred other items were stripped from Native Americans by "a contractor in charge of clearing the killing field where hundreds of Indians' bodies were tossed into mass graves" and sold to Frank Root, who donated them to the museum in Barre, Massachusetts, where they have been for a hundred years. The *Times* also reports that the association which operates the library and the museum are not prepared to hand them over directly to the survivors' association and is looking for a compromise. The *Times* notes that Tim Giago, publisher of *Indian Country Today,* has pointed out, "When someone steals something from you, what is there to compromise? You return it."

municipal government . . . agreed unanimously to support the museum council, which considers it indispensable to keep the black
man in the exhibition . . . [agreeing] that this type of museum represents a *fin de siècle* scientific conception which should be respected as history and serve a pedagogical function.

Two months later, the *New York Times* reported the controversy over
El Negro, as the figure was called. The *Times*[22] quoted a member of the
Banyoles City Council, Carles Abella, "El Negro is our property. It's nobody else's business. And all of this talk about racism is absurd. Human
rights only extend to living people, not dead."[23] And the mayor of Banyoles, Joan Solana, argued that "We have mummies and skulls and even
human skins on display in the museum. What is the difference between
those things and a stuffed African."

The *Times* also reported that *Jeune Afrique* had called for an African
boycott of the Olympics and that a member of the Nigerian Embassy
had traveled from Madrid to investigate the controversy. But the rowing
congress's general secretary was quoted as saying "This is well and truly
outside the realm of our [rowers'] experience. I've never heard of anything like it." At the same time an Ethiopian official with the International Olympic Committee reported that "There exists nothing worth
boycotting over [this] on the part of the African nations. I don't find
anything humiliating about the existence of this black man."[24]

22. While *El Pais* treated the story as news, placing it in its news pages, the *New York
Times* treated it as sports, placing the story in its sports pages as an Olympic update.

23. The *New York Times,* February 5, 1992. The articles in *El Pais* and the *Times* were
reprinted (the Spanish text appeared in English translation) in *Passages* 3 (1992): 16. I am
grateful to Richard L. Kagan for bringing the first article to my attention, and to John B.
Godfrey for his translation.

24. The *New York Times*, February 5, 1992. At the same time that the *Times* was reporting
Dr. Arcelin's efforts to remove the mummified body of the purported Tswana chief from
the glass case in Banyoles, Spain, Ethiopian workers digging under the office of former
President Mengistu Haile Mariam in the Grand Palace in Addis Ababa found the remains
of Emperor Haile Selassie and removed them to a laboratory for forensic examination.
According to the *Chicago Tribune*, February 18, 1992, p. 8, the new government of President
Meles Zenawi, whose army had overrun Mengistu's defenders of Addis Ababa, exhumed
the remains so that some determination of the cause of death might be made and the
remains could be returned to his family for reburial on July 23, 1992, the hundredth anniversary of the emperor's birth. Ethiopian radio reported that Haile Selassie's body was
secretly buried on August 27, 1975, and "The reason why Mengistu chose this site [under
his office] was to see that the body did not rise from the dead." The reports from Addis
also noted the exhumation of the remains of sixty-two officials of Haile Selassie's government from a mass grave at Addis's main prison, along with the bodies of twelve generals
executed after a failed coup in May 1989.

*

On Saturday, December 20, 1986, Silvanus Melea Otieno, a prominent Nairobi lawyer, age 55, fell ill at his farm at Ngong near Nairobi. At 6 P.M., he was declared dead at Nairobi Hospital. Within a few days, Voice of Kenya radio carried the widow's announcement that the body of S. M. Otieno would be buried at their Ngong farm on Saturday, January 3, 1987. But on the same day, VOK carried S. M. Otieno's brother's message that the burial would take place on January 3, 1987, at Nyamila village, in Siaya District, western Kenya. Nyamila, Otieno's birthplace, and Ngong, his residence for a number of years, are some four hundred kilometers apart.[25]

The *Daily Nation* of Nairobi quickly reported that a dispute had developed over the plans for removing Otieno's body from the City Mortuary, for a public viewing, and for the burial. The dispute pitted the widow, Virginia Wambui Waiyaki Otieno, whom the press conventionally referred to as a "Kikuyu lady" (her brother is Dr. Munyua Waiyaki, a former minister of foreign affairs), against Joash Ochieng' Ougo, the deceased's brother, and Omolo Siranga, head of the Umira Kager clan. The Umira Kager (more properly the incorporated clan organization) joined Joash in claiming the corpse of their Luo kinsman as one of their own and their rightful property. On December 29, the *Daily Nation* reported that announcements of plans for Otieno's burial had been halted by the Voice of Kenya. In the days which followed, court orders and injunctions blocked the plans of the widow and the brother for their respective January 3, 1987, ceremonies.[26]

The contest for control of the remains of S. M.—as his friends knew

25. This discussion of the Otieno litigation in Kenya is based on a paper first presented to the seminar at Johns Hopkins University, October 24, 1988; in a slightly different form as a talk at Northwestern University, November 21, 1988; as a paper presented at the Institute for Commonwealth Studies, London, December 19, 1988; with some expansion, to the PARSS Seminar at the University of Pennsylvania, April 27, 1989, and then to the Sixth International Roundtable in Anthropology and History entitled The Production of History: Silences and Commemorations, at Bellagio, Italy, August 29–September 2, 1989. I am grateful to those who participated in these discussions, providing suggestions as to "what the case was about" and "how the story should be told." As this paper was developing through the several iterations, E. S. Atieno Odhiambo joined the writing project and the paper eventually grew into our jointly authored book *Burying SM: The Politics of Knowledge and the Sociology of Power in Africa* (Portsmouth, NH: Heinemann, 1992).

26. As more attention is given by scholars to the unfolding of the case for S. M. Otieno's body, so new layers of dispute will develop over the intentions of the actors, the meanings of action and rhetoric, and the very "facts" of the case. There is already disagreement over the rendering of certain fundamental details, for example, whether it was Wambui

him during his life and at death—moved through seven legal settings over the next months. The struggles within the court were accompanied by large demonstrations in the streets of Nairobi, calls by one side and the other to take the body by force from the City Mortuary, as well as by an avalanche of correspondence and commentary in the national press. The legal struggle for S. M.'s remains was also widely reported in the overseas press, which tended to view the litigation as either a struggle between "tribes" (Wambui, the Kikuyu widow, versus Ochieng', the Luo brother) or as a struggle between "modernism" and "traditionalism" (occasionally, read "tribalism"), missing the crucial role of the courtroom contest in the very constitution of ideas concerning the "modern" and the "traditional" in Kenyan life.[27]

The fate of S. M. Otieno's body, the rights of the disputants, and the prospective reverberations of the various possible outcomes became subjects for serious comment at funerals held throughout the country during the litigation. While the president of Kenya, Daniel Arap Moi, did not speak publicly on the case during the period in which it was before the courts, a number of his ministers, members of Parliament, and important public figures positioned themselves on one side or the other. The struggle was concluded only by a final judgment for Joash Ochieng' handed down by the Court of Appeal, Kenya's highest court. S. M. Otieno was finally buried by court order not on his Ngong farm in the Nairobi suburbs but rather in the land of his kinsmen at Nyamila village in Siaya on May 23, 1987, just a few days more than five months after his death.

From the end of December through May, the question of who would bury the body of S. M. Otieno, and where that burial would be, produced an immense public debate in Kenya—within the courts, in the streets, in clubs and bars, and in scholarly seminars—concerning the risks and liabilities of "intermarriage between tribes"; the nature of the body as material property; the appropriate authority of "custom" and "tradition"; the relative standing of statutory, customary, and common law; the meaning and force of bonds of intimacy between husband and wife; the worth and legitimacy of "modern" social practice; the rights of women within marriage, as widows, and before the law; the

---

Otieno who brought the initial action against the clan before Justice Shields of the High Court or the clan who initiated the legal contest by completing the legal paperwork to collect the body from the mortuary. See, for example, Patricia Stamp, "Burying Otieno: The Politics of Gender and Ethnicity in Kenya," *Signs* 16, 4 (1991): 808–45.

27. See the *New York Times*, February 25, 1987, and the *Washington Post*, February 14, 1987. During the trial, the Kenya press at times reflected this same reading of the case as

meaning of death and the purposes of interment; and the idea of "home" as the only appropriate site of burial of a Luo individual. Within the struggles for S. M.'s body, powerful texts on Luo and Kenya culture and past were produced and invoked by witnesses, jurists, and the public. Political networks were realigned amidst public valorizations of "tradition" and the "modern marriage." Ideas about culture and the past were openly debated as to their veracity, appropriateness, and meaning. History and anthropology, as largely scholarly ventures in knowing and representing past and culture, were convened as open fields defined now through deeply interested debate within the examination of witnesses and the arguments of jurists. And much of this argumentation revolved around representations of S. M.'s life, of his interests, of his intentions: the *orations* of the dead.

While some observers of the Otieno case would hardly imagine that there could have been any *silences* constituted or sustained within and around the case, there were "silences" of great significance, including the exclusion from the judicial case itself of Wambui's political agenda, the place of wealth and privilege in the dispute, and the complex ways in which "tradition" and "custom" were handled within and outside the courtroom.

That the contest for S. M.'s body became the site and the moment for a great national debate over the meaning of culture, and over the place of national and customary law within the intimate lives of Kenyans, is not to assert that this was the first such struggle, the first such vigorous national experience centering on a corpse. The sudden deaths by apparent assassination of Pio Pinto, of Tom Mboya, of J. M. Kariuki, unleashed enormous public demonstrations centered on the funerals of the victims, anticipating the mass and heavily politicized funerals of fallen revolutionaries in South Africa in the 1980s.[28] Moreover, this is clearly not a phenomenon of twentieth-century Africa, for we know that across precolonial Africa, the funerals of kings were moments of immense contestation over the past and future of a kingdom. And hardly a day goes by when one cannot find a prominent news story relating a struggle over a dead body, from the contest in the state of Washington among several parties to establish authority over the ashes of the late transsexual jazz pianist Billy Tipton to the threat by Imelda Marcos to spread her husband's ashes across the Hawaiian landscape if his then

---

a reconvening of old, persisting struggles between Luo and Kikuyu in Kenya national life, misreading the complex interests and intentions on both sides of the case.

28. One looks forward to the research on "the politics of funerals in South Africa" being undertaken by Garrey Dennie.

still living body were not permitted to be returned to Manila, from the debates surrounding the movement of Kwame Nkrumah's remains from his family home to a monumental grave-site in the center of the Ghanaian capital, Accra, to the initiatives to remove Lenin's remains to a normal grave and the celebration of reburial of the heroes of the 1956 uprising in Hungary. And since February 1990 through 1991 and well into 1992, Kenyans have participated once again in agonizing debates over a dead body, this one the mutilated corpse of Minister of Foreign Affairs and International Co-operation Robert Ouko which was discovered on February 16, 1990, near his western Kenya home.[29]

*

The living S. M. Otieno was widely recognized as one of Kenya's leading legal practitioners. He had been called to serve on a number of national boards and commissions and maintained a substantial private practice until his death. Remarkably, he left his survivors no written instructions concerning the disposition of his remains. However, during his last years, S. M. had, according to an astonishing number of witnesses, given considerable voice to the question of his own burial. He had, as the record of litigation reveals, communicated to a number of associates and family members a clear sense of his intentions and desires, only he had given distinctly different "instructions" to various relatives and acquaintances.

The question of S. M.'s intentions, and of the import of his alleged instructions, constituted the first layer of the open courtroom struggle over the control of his remains. The statements of but three witnesses, among a considerable parade of witnesses, suggest the rhetorical and dramaturgical range of these recollected/alleged instructions. On the one side, in testimony before the High Court of Kenya, Wambui, the widow, recalled that her husband had once announced, in her presence, that "If I died and you pass Westlands (in Nairobi) on the way to Nyamila, I will kick the coffin open, come out and beat up all those in the convoy and go back into my coffin."[30]

The Nairobi advocate Timan Njugi was presented as a witness before

29. E. S. Atieno Odhiambo and the present writer are examining the Robert Ouko case, with specific attention on the tensions between public and official knowledge throughout the investigative process since the discovery of Ouko's corpse.

30. The court transcripts are provided in Sean Egan, ed., *S. M. Otieno: Kenya's Unique Burial Saga* (Nairobi: Nation Newspapers, c. 1987). The quote from Wambui Otieno is found on page 22. The Egan volume presents the case record with a number of additional reports from the *Daily Nation*, Nairobi. Catherine Gicheru and Paul Muhoho are credited

the same High Court proceeding. Mr. Njugi recalled that, as counsel
to the Miller Commission of Inquiry into the conduct of former attorney
general of Kenya, Charles Njonjo, he had worked closely with S. M.
Otieno, who was serving as a consultant to the commission. Njugi recalled a day in early 1984, when he and several others were seated in a
Nairobi office awaiting Mr. Otieno's arrival. S. M. Otieno entered the
office, greeted his friends, and, according to Njugi, announced, "Mussaj-
jah, I've bought a piece of land in Kiserian (Ngong [a short distance to
the west of Nairobi]) . . . I shall be buried at Kiserian and I have made
this plainly clear to all parties that might be interested in my funeral. I
shall be buried at Kiserian."[31]

On the other side, the High Court of Kenya heard from Mr. Albert
Ong'ang'o, an elderly gravedigger and mason from Siaya District,[32] that
a few years earlier—when he was completing the preparation of a grave
at Nyamila in Siaya—Mr. S. M. Otieno, the distinguished Nairobi criminal lawyer, had stooped down over the edge of the grave and called
down to him: "Albert, Albert, you have prepared my brother's grave. In
case I die, you will also prepare mine next to my father's."[33]

These simple gambits concerning S. M.'s intentions opened into a far
larger and more complex struggle over the essential nature of Otieno's
entire life, as if the character of his life, as constructed through witnesses
and examination, held its own declaration of S. M.'s intent. For the
widow, a considerable number of witnesses—including Wambui Otieno
herself—offered stories, episodes, which presented S. M. as a "modern"
individual, a devout Christian, a person of the city rather than of the
countryside, oblivious to the activities of his clan, hardly ever attending
funerals in the Siaya. His life was accounted by the books he was said
to have read, the conversations he was said to have had, the friends he
kept. Piece by piece, an image of a person almost whole was constructed

as reporters for the entire publication. The case was discussed at a special seminar organized by the Faculty of Law of the University of Nairobi, July 18, 1987. A number of
papers were presented to this seminar. The daily and weekly Kenya press contains an
extraordinary reservoir of correspondence and commentary on the case. And there has
been a wealth of personal expositions of the case that have come to my attention, including some from several members of an audience at the African Studies Association 1990
annual meeting in Baltimore who spoke of their own experiences in Kenya during the
time the case was being fought.

31. Ibid., p. 40.

32. The court removed itself to Westlands Cottage Hospital, Nairobi, for the purpose
of taking testimony from Mr. Ong'ang'o, who lay in hospital following surgery.

33. Egan, 83. Mr. Ong'ang'o reported that the grave in Nyamila was being dug for the
remains of Mr. Simon (Simeon) Odhiambo, who had died in Nairobi Hosptial. Simon was

through day after day of witnesses, examination, cross-examination, and summary argument.

For the brother and the clan, their witnesses presented an alternative perspective. S. M. could not, according to their construction of the man, throw off the traditions, responsibilities, and laws of his birthright. Though he had married not a Luo but a Kikuyu, though he had not built himself a *dala* (a residence) in the countryside, his home was at Nyamila, where his placenta had been buried at the time of his birth.[34] The witnesses and counsel for the brother and the clan argued that because S. M. had not asked his father to perform the rites which would have established for him a home at a site other than his birthplace, that while he had houses and property elsewhere, his home, and his place to be buried, was nowhere else than Nyamila in Siaya.

It is in the tension, within statements and cross-examination, over the simple and fundamental words "home" and "house" that one sees most clearly the *work* of counsel upon the production of texts in the litigation.[35] In cross-examination, John Khaminwa, lawyer for Wambui Otieno, appears to have sought to force a slip, an admission, even inadvertent, on the part of one of his adversary's witnesses, that S. M. Otieno's residence in Nairobi was *his,* or even *a,* "home." Likewise, Richard Kwach, counsel for the brother and the clan, appears to have made his witnesses exceedingly sensitive to this tactic. This constructed and imposed tension is further reminder of the particular quality of a court transcript, in which composed and tactical speech is rendered more powerful by such naturalization. The point here is not that court testimony is thereby unreliable by means of its extensive "scripting" but that there is a process of production of text—court testimony and other— which may be unraveled and comprehended.

Subtleties lay within the various testimony on S. M. Otieno's life, and the arguments of counsel and witnesses were in considerable disagreement over the meanings and intentions of a vast number of things which S. M. was reported to have said and done during his life. For example, counsel for the widow Wambui asserted that Albert Ong'ang'o, the gravedigger, had simply lied about the incident or, being elderly and

---

a brother of S. M. For a fuller discussion of Albert Ong'ang'o's testimony, see chap. 9 below. For a further "reading" of the Ong'ang'o testimony, see chap. 8 below.

34. For a discussion of the significance of the burial of the placenta, see David William Cohen and E. S. Atieno Odhiambo, "Ayany, Malo and Ogot: Historians in Search of a Luo Nation," *Cahiers d'Etudes Africaines* 27, 3–4, 107–8 (1987): 269–86; see also *Siaya,* chap. 2.

35. The Kenyan linguist Duncan Okoth-Okombo has explored the semantics of the court discussion of "house" and "home." See his "Semantic Issues," in J. B. Ojwang and

also well down in the grave from where S. M. spoke, did not hear S. M. correctly, given that S. M. had made clear to so many of his Nairobi friends and to members of his immediate family that he wished to be buried at his Ngong residence.

But counsel for the brother and the clan said that the point of S. M.'s statement at the graveside was not that he wanted to have his body buried at Nyamila—there could not have even been in S. M.'s mind any alternative to Nyamila—but that he simply wanted Ong'ang'o to know that he should be the one to prepare the grave. And, for the brother's counsel, S. M.'s alleged declarations to his friends, children, and his wife were either the fabrications of the witnesses or just the kind of joking about things which goes on in everyday conversation among friends.

Around the events in the courts there was occasional discussion of whether S. M. was a party to the case or the subject. At the conclusion of the litigation, toward the end of May 1987, the law correspondent of the *Nation* newspaper in Nairobi noted that S. M. had died before letting the Law Society of Kenya know what paper, if any, he was to present in response to their invitation for a paper to go before their 1987 annual meeting. The journalist wrote,

> Did S. M. probably wish to write a paper like "Of the laws of
> Kenya and burials and all that?" We do not know. What we do
> know . . . is that it is no simple topic to discuss . . . In his death
> and during the hearing of the dispute, in the final submissions by
> counsel and in the judgment of the honourable judge, S. M. has
> written his paper worth reading and analysing.[36]

Through the contests over the accuracy and meaning of practically every detail offered up concerning S. M.'s life, an extraordinarily con- flicted person—or is it a "transcript" of a life?—was resurrected from the body lying in a fully embalmed state in the Nairobi City Mortuary. One is alerted, through the episodes related by witnesses and their cross-examination, to the simultaneous fragility and power of memory; the struggle was, at one level, over the very nature of the person who could be resurrected or constituted in testimony and through memory, but also—at another level—over the authority to inscribe S. M. Otieno's "transcript." As each side attempted to anticipate and also establish the logic through which the justices would hear and read their argumenta- tion, one sees memory shaped and organized into testimony.

J. N. K. Mugambi, eds., *The S. M. Otieno Case: Death and Burial in Modern Kenya* (Nairobi: Nairobi University Press, 1989), 89–97.

36. Egan, 183.

The key to the power of the body of S. M. Otieno in this struggle for the remains was that he, S. M. Otieno, was both party to and absent from the litigation. A whole life was created in the court proceedings. Meanings and emotions could be attached to the body in death, and associated with it, retrospectively, in life. His interests and intentions could be located, cited, and relayed through the attributions, inferences, and declarations appropriated to his corpse, "the orations of the dead"; as the title of this chapter conveys, S. M.'s life, with its multiple voices and intentions, could be thickly and conflictually inscribed in death in ways that it could not in life.

The immense public notice of the case throughout Kenya provides another challenge in the comprehension and dissonance between the courts of Kenya, with their self-confirming authority, and their meaning and reception by Kenyans at large. The work of Carlo Ginzburg on the formulations and reformulations produced and articulated by the miller Menocchio[37] invites a close examinination of the ground lying between a formal and self-presented legal system and all its apparatus on the one side and its popularly received and reformulated constitution as constructed in public discourse on the other.

*

The case for S. M.'s body brought into an organized dispute setting the entire moral ground of Luo beliefs about death and Luo funeral practices. Witnesses for the brother and clan were brought into the court to unveil the meanings of death and the purposes of burial for the Luo. Under cross-examination by John Khaminwa, the chief counsel to widow Wambui, Mrs. Idalia Awino Odongo put forward the view that

> If Luo adults die and are buried outside Luoland, everybody in his family, including children, will be in problems . . . evil spirits will follow even us who are married. The whole family will be affected . . . Even in the Bible, there is a parable of the demons which descended upon swines and they went and drowned in the river.[38]

For the brother and the clan, countryside burial sustained ancient and core values of being Luo and sustained the Luo person in life and also in death. The funerals of S. M.'s forebears among many other of Luo "rich and famous" were recalled as substantiation of the countryside

---

37. *The Cheese and the Worms: The Cosmos of a Sixteenth-Century Miller* (Baltimore: Johns Hopkins University Press, 1980).
38. Egan, 76–77.

burial tradition. In his summation, the counsel for the brother and clan, Richard Otieno Kwach argued,

> it is my submission that my clients are not a group of cannibals. They want to carry out a time-honoured custom which we believe in. The witnesses called have testified about these customs. Their belief in them and what would happen if they did not carry them out. Professor Oruka has told us that if a child named after a person who has died falls sick, *manyasi* is prepared to cure him or her. This consists of some soil from the grave of the person who the child is named after. My lord, it would be a long distance from Siaya to Upper Matasia if there is a need to save a life in this manner . . . My lord, my learned friend asked you to strike down as repugnant some Luo customs. That would be a draconian measure and will offend the tribe. My lord, you need evidence of atrocity before you can strike them down as being repugnant to justice and morality.[39]

Witnesses and counsel for the widow brought attention to the numerous burials of Luo corpses, including some of S. M.'s own late kin, which had occurred far from countryside homes. And they sought to present Luo funeral practices as archaic and outside the fold of Christian belief. In his summation, John Khaminwa, for the widow, argued that

> It has been emphasised to your lordship that Luos are never buried outside Luoland so that Umira Kager clan can have an opportunity to exercise these rituals to remove fears of being haunted because death can destroy them. My lord, this is not what a court of law should enforce. It is contrary to public policy and Christian beliefs. Your lordship is fully aware that whoever causes death by witchcraft must face the consequences. Witchcraft is no defence. The fact that the Umira Kager clan believes in ghosts, spirits and demons and that they fear that their son will kill them or that their wives will be unable to give birth is not sufficient to warrant this court to give them the body of S. M. Otieno for burial. It is neither here nor there. In my submission, it would be outrageous that such myths should be given a legal basis in our courts.[40]

Within the litigation, an ethnography of Luo death beliefs and rituals was constituted through the statements of counsel and witnesses. Yet also, in testimony, through cross-examination, and by summary argu-

---

39. Egan, 97. Professor Oruka is the philosopher and Nairobi University professor Henry Odera Oruka. His testimony is discussed at some length in chap. 8, below.
40. Egan, 88.

ment, Luo burial practices were deconstructed. Luo core values were problematized. Implicit and hidden meanings were exposed and challenged. Concepts of "modern," "tradition," and "Christianity" were constituted within the examination and cross-examination of witnesses.

Expert witnesses were invited to the court by both sides to participate in this intensive scrutiny of Luo culture;[41] and seventy published authorities were referenced in argument.[42] The cross-examination of experts as well as the challenging of expert texts, and the juxtaposition of expert and non-expert testimony, raised questions for the jurists and for observers concerning the relevance and authority of "modern" academic expertise in the representation and reproduction of "traditional" cultural practice. Expertise—ethnographic, historical, and legal—was continuously invoked, yet also continuously challenged. Indeed, in their final opinion the judges of the Court of Appeal admonished John Khaminwa, the widow's counsel, who, they said,

> confessed before us that he did not really understand the Luo customary law. Needless to say, it was his professional duty to carefully study and understand the Luo customary law and, if he thought it was in the appellant's interest, to call evidence.[43]

The layering of assertions and arguments concerning expert knowledge opened to view some of the complexity of cultural debate within and around the Otieno case. For example, juridical practice, and the social

41. At the same time one must note that an extraordinary number of experts on Luo history and culture were *not* called. See *Burying SM*, 78–79, for a discussion of this absence.

42. The Bible was quoted as authority by both sides throughout the court proceedings.

43. Egan, 178. Curiously, two days after the judges of the Court of Appeal of Kenya issued the final ruling on the fate of S. M. Otieno's body, with its admonishment of Mr. Khaminwa, Mr. Robert Stevens, then president of Haverford College in Pennsylvania, presented a degree of Doctor of Laws, *honoris causa*, to (in the words of Mr. Stephen G. Cary, who presented Mr. Khaminwa for the degree): "John Mugalasinga Khaminwa . . . Distinguished lawyer, spokesman for human rights, articulate scholar educated on three continents, you have come far indeed from your modest Quaker roots in rural Kenya. In your achievements, you do honor to your parents and your teachers, who gave you knowledge, and through their example, illumined the values that now guide your life." The honorary degree was awarded without reference to Mr. Khaminwa's role as Wambui Otieno's counsel, but was intended to bring attention to Khaminwa's courage during seventeen months of detention without trial in Kenya and to Human Rights concerns in Kenya more generally. I am grateful to Professor Linda Gerstein, Haverford College, and especially to Mr. Hogie Hansen, secretary of the college, for assistance on this point. On March 19, 1988, President Moi of Kenya raised the subject of the Haverford degree with a visiting group of Kenyan scholars: "I cannot understand some people instead of rewarding someone like Mr. Kwach who has defended our culture I hear that they have now honored the other person." The president shortly thereafter rewarded Richard Kwach by appointing him to

constitution of argument among people in the streets, clubs, bars, law chambers, and court rooms, unearthed and mediated and also silenced the discussion of certain critical conflicts. The court contest appears to have constructed a grand silence around lowly voiced, yet heavily conflicted ideas concerning community and equity among Kenyan Luo.[44] Neither side appeared interested in disclosing and centering the explosive tension emergent in Kenya between relatively wealthy urban residents and their poorer urban and rural affines and kin. Wambui Otieno's counsel clearly saw no value in an argument concerning the importance to many urban citizens, like the Otienos, of protecting their hard-won wealth from the claims of country cousins.[45] One could and did speak of the morality of immense expenditures on funerals in Kenya but the counsels of neither side chose to consider such an expenditure as essentially a transaction between those of wealth and those of poverty nor did either counsel bring into view the lowly voiced ambivalences among many Luo between the prioritization of programs of collective and private expenditure in education, development, and business and the great cultural project of countryside burial.

A further silence concerned the history of Luo burial practices. The counsel for the brother and clan, with witnesses, tried to define Luo

---

the High Court. The field of relations developing in Kenya between lawyers and the state is treated in *Burying SM,* 75–87.

44. There appears to have been an effort, beginning with leaders of the Umira Kager clan but also extending out among other Luo leaders, to silence the voice and opinion of Oginga Odinga at gatherings, meetings, and funerals in which support for the brother and clan's position in the litigation was developing. Odinga, the great patriot if not living patriarch of the "Luo nation" of Kenya, expressed strong support for long-time comrade Wambui Otieno in her ordeal. See further discussion in text, below. For a discussion of the tensions around notions of community and equity in Luo thought and practice, see *Siaya,* chap. 6, particularly pp. 119–20: "Some rural people have sought to mediate some of the tension that has emerged because of this differentiation by reiterating the essential humanity of all beings; the sense of this is presented in the Voice of Kenya song [the signature tune from the Luo broadcasting service—"A person is a person, however mean he looks, his being is being, he will always have a place wherein to be buried"] . . . It is a refrain that reaches out for moral equity in circumstances where economic equity is not be dreamt of."

45. Some observers of, and participants in, the litigation saw the struggle as being one over the inheritance of S. M. Otieno's property and have variously interpreted different positions taken as gambits to grasp control of his property. For example, the datum that Wambui locked the gates to their farm immediately upon word of S. M.'s death is read as a ploy to give her time to remove some of his property from the range of access and view of visitors and, in one variant, to give herself time to find and destroy his will so that she could, in the intestate situation, impose her will upon the disposition of his remains and personal property.

beliefs concerning death and practices of burial as ancient, perduring, and authentic. In so doing they produced an ethnography both normative and static. The counsel for Wambui portrayed such Luo beliefs and practices as antiquated, out of touch with the realities of the "modern Kenya nation."[46] The static and normative portrayal of "Luo custom" was jointly enacted, and this ethnography from the court excluded knowledge of substantial change in burial and belief in this century, from a baseline source of 1905 which observed that Luo corpses were buried in a sitting up position within their houses, to a later practice that Luo were buried in a reclining position with head facing in a specific direction, to the growing use of coffins more recently and the early reaction to coffins that "they tended to suffocate the ghosts of our people." The counsel for the brother and clan saw it in their interest to present Luo beliefs and practices as relatively unchanging, of having value and power because of their antiquity. The counsel for Wambui would find no value in revealing to the court that Luo death beliefs and burial practices were flexibly changing to new circumstances.[47]

While substantial portions of witnesses' testimony concerning the nature of Luo burial rites read as normative and static, the trial transcripts are also thickly illustrated with detailed information on the social organization of funeral practices, the ways in which individuals, families, clans, and associations undertake the practical arrangements of transport, mourning, and burial. One recognizes that the entire ritual of Luo death and burial rests profoundly upon carefully organized and orchestrated activities—activities in, also, a conflicted field—and that the cultural architecture of a funeral is not handed-down or simply given tradi-

46. John Khaminwa, Wambui's counsel, used anthropological monographs in a curious way. He argued that these monographs—during the trials he referred specifically to quite a number of works including ones by Leakey, Wagner, Hobley, Ochola-Ayayo, Snell, Hollis, Peristiany, Kipkorir, Welbourn, and Massam—presented a passing way of life not chosen or shared by S. M. Otieno:

"The Luos cannot continue with customs that tend to isolate them from the rest of the country. There are a lot of books written by people—anthropologists—on burials. In respect to these books, they refer to a society of the old order and do not refer to contemporary society at all. Some of the things said in these books—we are living in a modern Kenya—and we would find them unacceptable and not in keeping with us . . . The literature by anthropologists is no longer applicable in contemporary Kenya" (Egan, 89).

47. This is not to claim that there was an organized suppression of knowledge on the part of counsel and witnesses. It may be that they actually were poorly informed on earlier Luo practices and beliefs. Needless to say, the model of "unchanging African tradition"—whether accorded great value or subjected to intense criticism—holds great power in Kenya and elsewhere, even when everyday knowledge and common sense provide alternative perspectives on the past and on change.

tion but rather a complex social construction. One sees in the Otieno case resonances with Clifford Geertz's 1959 treatment of a Javanese funeral,[48] in which he attempted to situate a heavily conflicted burial rite between what was held to be the mode of burial correct by Javanese tradition and what was held to be possible given the specific form of the political and social field in which the funeral was worked out as rite.

*

The Kenya courts were only slightly exposed to the deep contests and struggles located within the Luo political community of Kenya and of the play of this case as an effort to restore unity to the Luo house. Oginga Odinga, the Luo and Kenya leader of the left, whose writings on the core values of Kenya Luo culture were clearly a centerpiece in the production of a case for countryside burial, was notably absent from the proceedings in court.[49] Odinga was heard to have said in a number of settings that "it was only since the 1940s that all this attention to burial in the countryside began . . . that before 1940 people were buried pretty much where they died . . . that somehow the present Luo interest in funerals is related to the accumulation of wealth in the cities,"[50] and that it is only with the legal capacity and financial enthusiasm of Luo for the purchase of property that the issue of where to bury a corpse would arise. That the leader of the great chronicle of Luo movements in the twentieth century and supreme authority on Luo political values was to be separated from this movement introduced a range of contradictions into the political agenda of the Umira Kager clan. The fate of Odinga's voice leads one to consider how the battle for Otieno's body broke across old, well-established boundaries of solidarity and established a significant new ground for the constitution and invocation of broader political and social thought concerning both local and national culture and both given and produced history.[51]

48. "Ritual and Social Change: A Javanese Example," *American Anthropologist* 61 (1959): 991–1012; also reprinted in Clifford Geertz, *The Interpretation of Cultures: Selected Essays* (New York: Basic Books, 1973), 142–69.

49. And, as indicated in note above, he was excluded from a range of public functions in which support for the brother and clan were being encouraged.

50. From personal communication, E. S. Atieno Odhiambo.

51. Atieno Odhiambo reports that Oginga Odinga explained his situation to a friend, Odinga Odera, in these terms: "There is no need for the Luo to be struggling for the body of S. M. Otieno. Otieno was lost a long time ago—*nene olal choon!* So you people are trying to rehabilitate a lost cause." Some guides to the evidently broader resonance of the Otieno case in Kenya are to be drawn from work underway by E. S. Atieno Odhiambo, Bruce Berman, and John Lonsdale on the debates—both popular and expert—concerning the

The case, and the debates around it, have been seen by some as a next phase in the elaboration of an idea of a strong Luo nation within the Kenya nation, advancing its interests into every sector of life while defending itself against the oppressions and inequalities of a larger society. That the contest for S. M.'s body was also a contest between a Luo clan and a "Kikuyu lady" was somehow confirmation to many observers, and particularly to the foreign press, that once again ethnic or tribal conflict had lifted its ugly head in Africa.

But the case, with Luo witnesses on both sides, and its subtleties, which the foreign press failed to capture, has the potential of revealing much about the various "republics of free discourse" within the "Luo nation." Great silences concerning wealth and privilege among Luo families, about the leveling yet also impoverishing functions of vast expenditures on funerals, and on the source and purposes of extraordinary pressures upon successful Luo in Kenya "to build a *dala*" [residence] in the countryside—these great silences themselves actually illuminate the differences in condition, status, opportunity, and interest among Luo in Kenya, whether in the city or the countryside. Was the Umira Kager clan's case for S. M.'s body empowered by these differences while various parties struggled for interpretive power among several possible positions? Or did its source and power lie in the recurrent experiences of ethnic consolidation, where the signs of the various and conflicting "republics of free discourse" are suppressed?

It is quite clear that "Luo ethnicity" was centrally involved in this case, but the unveiling of this move within the contest over S. M.'s body reveals a great deal of complexity within Luo ethnic politics. One approach might be to see the problem of S. M.'s body as, initially, a problem for the Umira Kager clan, of which S. M. was member number 18, and then only secondarily as a problem for the entire Luo speech community, of which the Umira Kager clan was but one corporate entity among

nature and meaning of Mau Mau in Kenya and in the academic guilds more generally; from a most important paper by E. M. Simmonds-Duke, "Was the Peasant Uprising a Revolution? The Meanings of a Struggle over the Past," *Eastern European Politics and Societies* 1, 2 (1987): 187–224 (see chap. 3, above) in which the expositions of several historians are peeled away layer by layer to reveal critical silences and hidden and low-voiced argument along with the broad forces and resonances which surround the productions of history within and alongside the academy; and from the important work on the production of history in South Africa—most particularly, the work of Carolyn Hamilton on the struggles for control and meaning of history, culture, and politics in the production and reception of the Shaka Zulu television series, for which see her long exposition: "A Positional Gambit: Shaka Zulu and the Conflict in South Africa," *Radical History Review* 41 (Spring 1989): 5–31.

many which served Luo constituencies in Nairobi and Mombasa. But there was more to this than one clan or lineage among many: the Umira Kager clan, in its experience over the past hundred years, has most clearly exemplified a subhegemonic process in western Kenya of continuous expansion into and increasing control over once Bantu-speaking areas along the Luo-Luhya speech boundary. Umira Kager carried a heightened sense (as against other Luo congeries) of ethnic solidarity and considerable experience in operationalizing it, and this was extended to the neighborhoods of Nairobi as large numbers of Luo speakers traveled and settled in Kenya's capital.

In the growing tension between the voiced positions of Umira Kager and those of Oginga Odinga, one may see a paradox in which the informed historical sensibility brings Odinga to an inflexible position at odds with his own historical and political community while the experience of extraordinary change, coupled with an ahistorical discourse, promotes a more flexible interpretation of history and culture on the part of Umira Kager and drives the formation of a new political constituency, far broader than the clan. In this shift the Luo were for the first time "liberated" from the working-class ethos and radical agenda of Odinga, and thereby became more acceptable to the core of power in Kenya constituted in the power of the president's office and the person of Daniel Arap Moi and in the interests and resources of a national bourgeoisie (and thus more accessible to the entitlements of cooperation than ever were the legions and rabble of Odinga).

*

Still another powerful layer of debate rose to the surface amidst the open discussion of the moral ground of Luo burial and this concerned the rights of women within marriage in Kenya and within the Kenya nation. For some Luo women, Wambui Otieno's case offered a chance for their assertion as individuals and as spouses.[52] But for others, Wambui's claim was perceived as ultimately threatening to the woman's fragile security in her countryside household. The various voiced positions of Wambui, the widow, seen moving along a continuum, reveal much about the chal-

---

52. On the day the manuscript of *Burying SM* was completed, and as a copy was being made for Heinemann, the publisher, I received a call from a Kenyan woman resident in the United States and living in the Chicago suburbs. She wanted a copy of the manuscript to use in an American court to demonstrate the liabilities of her position as a woman were her current divorce proceeding to be ordered to be moved to Kenya, as her estranged husband, also a Kenyan, evidently wished.

lenges faced by women within litigation in Kenya.[53] Wambui first announced that she was burying her husband at their farm. When this was
blocked, she—or her counsel before the court—asserted that she was
following her husband's wish to be buried at the farm. Again, when
this simple position was answered, she and her counsel were forced to
reposition their case in terms of a more complex argument—but one
which at first appeared not so difficult to mount—that her husband had
lived outside the locus of operation of Luo customary law. Challenges
to this led Wambui and her counsel and her witnesses to develop an
elaborate argument that the Otienos lived and raised a family within a
"modern marriage" which gave her absolute rights to her husband's
property, including his physical remains, both within Kenya statutory
law and in broader English common law (which has continued to have
some standing in Kenya courts since independence). The day after the
Court of Appeal had made its final decision, Wambui, the widow,
moved her position again, angrily announcing that she and her children
would not attend the burial in Siaya.

> As far as I am concerned, that is the end of the road. I have now
> discovered that women are discriminated against in Kenya. There
> is discrimination in Kenya, contrary to the United Nations Con-
> vention for the Elimination of the Discrimination against Women
> which Kenya ratified in 1984 . . . The judgement was very bad. I
> have been denied the right to bury my husband. I will take the
> matter to the International Court abroad.[54]

Wambui's positions, constituting a continuum, suggest an "economy
of constraint" which confronts women before the law in Kenya, as well
as within marriage.[55] Most profoundly, neither counsel saw it functional

53. For a fuller discussion, see *Burying SM*, 43–58; and Patricia Stamp, "Burying Otieno:
The Politics of Gender and Ethnicity in Kenya," *Signs* 16, 4 (1991): 808–45.

54. Egan, 181. In the event, she may not have actually done so. Wambui did become a
"reborn Christian" immediately after her defeat in court; this is not necessarily to be read
as a retreat from the politics of women in Kenya, for the new churches of "reborn Chris-
tians" in Kenya are now seen as an important arena for the expression of opposition to
some state policies in a setting in which free expression is felt to be impossible.

55. For a discussion of the risks and difficulties of generating a feminist debate or
organizing debates around women's issues in Kenya, see Lynn M. Thomas, "Contestation,
Construction, and Reconstitution: Public Debates over Marriage Law and Women's Status
in Kenya, 1964–1979" (M.A. thesis, Johns Hopkins University, Baltimore, 1989). From a
more polemical feminist position, Patricia Stamp, of York University, studied the Otieno
case, focusing on the embattled nature of Wambui Otieno's situation within the case, before the law, and in Kenyan political life. See her "Burying Otieno: The Politics of Gender
and Ethnicity in Kenya," *Signs* 16, 4 (1991): 808–45. Stamp's perspective in many ways

to relate that Wambui Otieno was respected as one of the leaders among Kenyan women—through the National Council of the Women of Kenya—as well as one who carried the credentials of a vigorous and radical fighter for national independence in the 1950s, nor did they relate that her marriage to S. M. Otieno had the stuff of national mythology, with a record of participation in protest movements and union organization, of having served a year of detention in Lamu Prison, having left prison in January 1961 to marry S. M. shortly thereafter. Wambui campaigned for Parliament, served as treasurer of the International Women's Conference just two years before the Otieno litigation, was active in national women's organizations in Kenya for a number of years, and maintained close ties with prominent feminists in other countries. All this personal history was excluded from the litigation. Whereas Wambui left prison and married Otieno, Kenyatta left prison to negotiate Kenya self-government and independence—a divergence of experience and consequence which may elaborate its own further meanings. Eight years before Otieno's death, Wambui related her thoughts on her own "intermarriage" to Chelagat Mutai, a reporter for *Viva* magazine (April 1979, 10–12):

> I was not bothered by his tribe, though this very issue was to cost me much in later life. I cared only for an assurance from him that I was free to continue my public activities. He has given me, as he did then, wonderful love and support and I do not mind telling you that in the 1969 election he spent ten thousand pounds on my bid for the Langata seat . . . I had not realized at first that inter-tribal marriages are so detested, especially ones between a Kikuyu and a Luo. It amazed me because this was the only thing that made me lose the 1960 election. In 1974 I knew the score; I had not divorced my husband, so I could expect nothing from the electors . . . If two people have a basic affection, and a willingness to understand each other's shortcomings and the patience to work out solutions, any marriage can work, be it inter-racial or intertribal. Personally I do not stand many ceremonies of my husband's people which I regard as archaic, but apart from that our attitudes are the same . . . Kenyans must practice what they preach: that we are all united as one people, that we are above petty belief in tribe and custom, that we shall give leadership to those of ability. I should dearly love to see such a Kenya.[56]

joins—indeed, extends—the view taken here of the structural, political, juridical, and rhetorical constraints on the constitution of a feminist position in Kenya in the 1980s, thus complementing Lynn Thomas's work on the period immediately before.

56. I am grateful to Lynn Thomas for bringing this interview to my attention.

Both within and outside the litigation and for the duration of the case, the personal and intimate relations of S. M. and Wambui within their marriage were exposed to public view, as one side sought to impugn Wambui as a witness and the other sought to enhance Wambui's status as a "modern wife" duty-bound to organize the rites as her husband (or she herself) would have wanted.[57] As the contest spread out from the courtroom to streets, bars, clubs, and residences, a "whole" family history was exposed to the public and became centered in public debate, including discussions of Wambui's sexuality.

Her social and political capital nil, Wambui came to recognize the complexity of organizing, as a woman and in respect to the rights of women, a position within legal contests in Kenya.[58] The silencing of the "transcript" of Wambui, the disappearance of her person behind the litigation—accompanying the constitution of the person of S. M. Otieno out of his corpse in the Nairobi City Mortuary—was, it could be argued, jointly transacted by both parties to the case, their counsels, and witnesses. Within the production of the case, Wambui was immobilized by the very positions which the anticipated juridical discourse (the good wife, the good husband, the good marriage, the modern family) imposed upon the practices of counsel and witnesses. As her husband's dead body was invested with life, so Wambui in pressing her claim for his remains became socially dead.

57. Patricia Stamp details this assault on Wambui Otieno's credit during and after the litigation in her article "Burying Otieno."

58. One might imagine that Wambui Otieno, symmetrically, could draw on Kikuyu hordes to support her position, and also women across Kenya. At one point in the public remonstrations concerning the body of her husband, she said that she could bring out her legions just as Umira Kager were bringing out theirs. In fact, Wambui Otieno largely failed. Politicians like Grace Ogot, novelist and an elected member of Parliament, moved away from early support of Wambui based on the expression of women's solidarity toward a position more in consonance with her (Grace Ogot's) Luo constituency in Gem in Siaya. After the Court of Appeal ruling in May 1987, a number of Kenyan women went to court and, arguing from the Otieno precedent, got judges to enjoin their husbands by "traditional marriage" from taking new wives by civil marriage, hardly the outcome of the modernizing agenda that Wambui and her counsel sought within the litigation.

FIVE

Pim's Doorway

The appearance of historical knowledge in unexpected locations was well noted in the transcripts of the S. M. Otieno proceedings within the High Court of Kenya in 1987. During his examination of Wambui Otieno, S. M. Otieno's widow, Wambui's lawyer, John Khaminwa, asked, "When you were married to Mr. Otieno did you consider him as a Luo?" Wambui replied, "No. I did not consider even whether he was a leper, a poor man or whatever. All I know is that we were young people who had met and fallen in love."[1] But in reading their final judgment on the Otieno case, Justice Nyarangi intoned, "Otieno was born and bred a Luo and as such under Luo customary law his wife on marriage became part and parcel of her husband's household as well as a member of her husband's clan."[2]

The contrast between Wambui's representation of herself and of her marriage, spoken with emotion and conviction, could not have been more thoroughly opposed to the cold, judicial, and consequential representation of that identity by the Court of Appeal. Yet Wambui's portrait of her husband and of her marriage, in which she attempted to position the S. M. Otieno household as distant from, and uninvolved in, the world of the Umira Kager, was itself in stark contrast to Wambui's keen intelligence on the subject of S. M.'s patrilineage. It was Wambui, in both Khaminwa's examination and (for the clan) Richard Kwach's cross-examination, who provided the court with a detailed and annotated map of the social world of Jairo Ougo—the father of her late husband and of her court adversary Joash Ochieng'. In and out of court, Wambui constituted herself as widow of a man who had long ago ceased to be Luo, but in exercising her expertise on this issue she substantially constituted herself as a Luo citizen. When John Khaminwa asked, "Is it true that S. M. was one of the three sons of the late Jairo Ougo and his wife Salome Anyango as stated in affidavit?" Wambui replied, "No. My late father-in-law had five sons . . . There was Isaya Ougo, Simeon Odhiambo Ougo, Silvano Melea Otieno, Joash Ochieng' Ougo and another one who died when Mr. Otieno was still young."[3]

Wambui's evidence in court revealed that at age fifty-one, she, a grandmother, had, in essence, become a Luo *pim.* Everyone associated with the Umira Kager position reckoned that Wambui had achieved such a status, that, while as S. M.'s widow she would not be remarried, she would be given *ndawa,* tobacco or a cigarette to graduate—in Profes-

1. Egan, 34.

sor Odera Oruka's words—into clan widowhood, which aligns with the old category of *pim*.

Luo familiarly recall *pim*, the woman who imparted history, wisdom, knowledge to the children of the *dala*.[4] *Pim* is remembered as a figure, a woman who came into the household from a social and sometimes geographical distance. Often an outsider, *pim's* entry into the household as a widow, or new bride, offered protection, food, friendship, a renewed position in life. In some instances, she came from an "enemy lineage" and thus the designation *nyar wasigu*, daughter of the enemy. But in time, *pim* learned the lore of her new household while bringing the intelligence of the wider world to her new folk.

In preparing for the responsibility for care, nurture, and instruction of the younger children and maturing girls, the *pim* accumulated knowledge about the family, the clan lands, lineage disputes, uterine jealousies (*nyiego*), the heroic past, and fields of silence, fear, and anxiety of everyday importance to the lineage. Her role and her knowledge protected her from social death, from neglect and starvation because of infirmity.[5] As the respected older woman of the household, "graduated" to the station of *dayo*, *pim* assumed the role of teacher, passing on to the children broad sections of this corpus of knowledge, interlaced with folk stories and songs, as the children fell to sleep in the *siwindhe* (dormitory). In *Not Yet Uhuru*, Oginga Odinga described his early years within the *siwindhe*:

> At about nine o'clock, after hearing the elders, we went to bed, leaving the elders talking among themselves. Young boys and girls slept together in their grandmothers' houses [*siwindhe*], and we were told stories of the past. The older boys went to sleep in the *simba*, a dormitory built near the gates by the grown-up boys who were yet unmarried. Boys grown too big to live in the houses of the old women stayed in the dormitory house and there became acquainted with girls from other villages, and had dances at night.[6]

The *siwindhe* was usually indistinguishable from other domiciles in the compound; however, the interior of the *siwindhe* is recalled as a

2. Ibid., 177.

3. Ibid., 27.

4. See Cohen and Odhiambo, *Siaya: The Historical Anthropology of an African Landscape* (London: James Currey, 1989), 92–93.

5. For a comparable role in another Kenya setting, see Peter D. Little, "Woman as Ol Pa'yian [Elder]: The Status of Widows among the Il Chamus (Njemps) of Kenya," *Ethnos* 52, 1/2 (1987): 81–102.

6. Oginga Odinga, *Not Yet Uhuru: An Autobiography* (New York: Hill & Wang, 1969), 10.

structure of transition from infancy to maturity. It was within the *siwindhe* that much of the essential social intelligence of the Luo world has been imparted by *pim* to those with little experience or knowledge of that world.

Children learned about the past from *pim*. They drew upon her wisdom. They learned about the people, the groups, and the settlements around them. They learned a geography of succor and a geography of danger. They learned about sexuality and about childbirth. Using her wide-ranging social knowledge *pim* both broadened and delimited fields of possible and optimal marriages. From *pim*, children learned about health, illness, misfortune, and death. They learned about interest, opportunity, and obligation that would both open and restrict their lives. As *pim* nurtured and instructed her charges, joined them to the mature world, the material she brought from outside the enclosure neighborhood and from outside the patri-group provided the young with an array of referents extending far beyond the patrilineage and gave the young the elements of an intimate understanding of a complex and physically remote social universe.

In 1979, the late Elijah Oduor Ogutu wrote briefly on *pim*.

> The *pim* instructed the girls concerning their sexuality. *Pim* taught the girls to be tolerant of their future spouses and in-laws during domestic problems. She taught them about responsibilities of the adult woman and she taught them about the respect due husbands in marriage. *Pim* instructed the girls to refrain from sexual relations outside marriage. A successful union was perceived as being marked from the beginning when a young woman was found to be a virgin, *"en kod ringre."* The girls were taught never to eat at a boyfriend's house. Secret visitations, *wuowo*, with boyfriends were undertaken at night and girls were instructed to be back before dawn. Such visitations were only known to *pim* and the girls of the *siwindhe*, not to their parents. They were instructed not to visit their boyfriends during menstruation, *dhi boke*. *Pim* taught the girls to offer persistent boyfriends an experience of lovemaking, but without penetration, through the skilful use of the thighs while making love.[7]

In a broad sense, in taking up the care of her first charges, *pim* embraced a pattern of nurturing which is held to have descended from far

---

7. Elijah Oduor Ogutu, then an employee of the National Museums of Kenya who, during leave, worked with me in Siaya as a research assistant. Ogutu conducted interviews with elderly women who had been brought up by a *pim*. There has been little research published on *pim* and the *siwindhe*, but see A. B. C. Ocholla-Ayayo, *Traditional*

in the past. *Pim* learned her critical role within the *siwindhe* of her own childhood; yet *pim* was assuming a new role which called upon all her experience beyond the *siwindhe:* in marrying, in gathering valuable domestic materials, wild foodstuffs, and condiments from the field margins and scrubland, in organizing the cultivation of foods, in cooking and serving, in treating illness, in producing and marketing ceramic and fiber wares, in handling childbirth and young children, in visiting and helping friends and relations, in coping with dangerous conditions and forces, in identifying and securing refuges in times of war, famine, and epidemic, in caring for the ancestors, and in discovering pleasures and interests. And in taking possession of her new role as *pim*, the elderly Luo woman also protected herself from a "social death." She would neither be abandoned to starve admist a famine nor be left without companionship and protection.[8]

It was this sometimes helpless and dependent figure whose knowledge and experience pierced the fences of the enclosure and the walls of the *siwindhe* and transformed the social intelligence of the young from that of the enclosure and the immediate patri-group to that of marriage and adulthood and the many associations, alliances, dangers, and opportunities lying beyond the enclosure. The circulation of social knowledge from *pim* through the *siwindhe* literally extended the horizon of young Luo speakers and made it possible to meet various contingencies, whether in an area twenty kilometers away or over much greater distances in Kampala, Nairobi, and Mombasa.

*

It appears not to have been the intention of any party to the S. M. Otieno litigation to construct Wambui as an authority—in the tradition of *pim*— on the lineage of Jairo Ougo, S. M.'s late father, but that is exactly what the evidence of Wambui herself, and of other witnesses, amounted to.

Ideology and Ethics among the Southern Luo (Uppsala: Scandinavian Institute of African Studies, 1976), 73–74; also, David William Cohen, "*Pim's* Work: Some Thoughts on the Construction of Relations and Groups—the Luo of Western Kenya," paper presented to the Conference on the History of the Family in Africa, School of Oriental and African Studies, London, September 1981; and Asenath B. Odaga, "Some Aspects of the Luo Traditional Education Transmitted through the Oral Narratives—*sigendini*," UNESCO Seminar on Oral Traditions, Past Growth and Future Development in East Africa, Kisumu, Kenya, April 1979, pp. 4–7. Ocholla-Ayayo and Odaga view the *siwindhe* as an important setting for the transmission of oral narratives, *sigendini*, in the past, under the tutelage of *pim*.

8. Some older Luo have related that widows without protection were occasionally seized and sacrificed to assure the wellbeing of a new Lake Victoria transport or fishing craft.

It was Wambui who revealed to Ochieng' knowledge of a brother who had died in Tanganyika in 1941 and was buried there. It was Wambui who told the court of the earlier marriage of S. M.'s stepmother, Magdalene, and about the latter's subsequent widowhood and remarriage to Jairo in 1944. It was Wambui who brought knowledge to the court about the division of family land in Nyalgunga by the patriach Jairo to his sons. Wambui likewise unraveled material exchanges, signals of familyhood, between S. M. and his brothers extending back to 1956. And it was Wambui who detailed acts of generosity between her late husband and his young nephew, the other "S. M.," son to S. M.'s stepsister, Felgona Akinyi.

Wambui brought to court knowledge of the Jairo Ougo family spanning nearly half a century, though she had been married to S. M. for only half that period. Within the court testimony alone, Wambui provided detailed information on twenty-three individuals in the Jairo Ougo lineage of the Umira Kager clan.[9] The knowledge she presented may have challenged the foundations of her, or her counsel's, overall argument. Could S. M. Otieno have been all that distanced from the world of Nyalgunga if Wambui were repository to all this intelligence? But the revelation that Wambui had acquired over many years a unique and extensive knowledge of Nyalgunga would hardly have been useful to Kwach's side either. Wambui could not be a "rebel"—the clan's lawyer's word—and still take an interest in the detailed workings of the Jairo Ougo family. In this sense, the valediction of the justices of the Court of Appeal rings true in a double sense. Having married a Luo, Wambui "became part and parcel of her husband's household as well as a member of her husband's clan."[10] And, in time, she became a special resource in the transmission of Umira Kager history and culture to another generation of Kenyans. She was, in this sense, *pim*, constituted through the elaboration of extraordinary expertise and experience some four to five decades after what many Luo regard nostalgically as the time in which *pim* disappeared from their world.[11]

Before 1930, there may have been thousands of *siwindhe* in western Kenya. But after 1930, there were few. Kisumu, Nairobi, and Mombasa, along with both rural and town schools, promised greater opportunities

9. For a fuller accounting—from her court testimony—of Wambui Otieno's knowledge of the history of her husband's Umira Kager lineage, see Cohen and Odhiambo, *Burying SM*, 57–58.

10. Egan, 177.

11. This treatment of *pim* draws, essentially, on David William Cohen, "Doing Social History from *Pim*'s Doorway," in Olivier Zunz, ed., *Reliving the Past: The Worlds of Social*

for nurturing the young, while the changing shape of the rural household economy made the feeding of an elderly and dependent woman coming from outside the home more problematic. When in the late 1960s and early 1970s, a sociolinguist, Ben G. Blount, did research on the acquisition of language of Luo children in western Kenya, he found that a "young girl . . . of five or six may become the principal caretaker for a young sibling, assuming the responsibility for feeding the child, protecting him from harm and danger, and catering in general to his needs."[12] Without access to the memory of *pim* and to the material on the evident transformation of childhood socialization in this century Blount accepted this absence of adult supervision as "characteristic of the Luo and closely related Nilotic groups." One is reminded of how easy it is to accept the present and observed social world as given and traditional.

Pim's nurturing was an almost invisible crucible of Luo culture and society, and, consequently, its critical activity has been missed, as anthropologists and historians have attended to the form and play of "larger," and in a sense more "masculine," structures and processes in Luo society.

*

The camp where my research in Siaya in western Kenya and on *pim* was based was used as an archaeological camp from time to time, and during different periods of my stay, trays of artifacts—pieces of pottery and stone tools—were pulled out of storage by members of my staff who had also worked on the excavations. Fragments and shards were examined and columns of data were entered in a registry book. Pieces were handled and discussed, and I received an education on the Late Stone Age and Early Iron Age activity in the vicinity of our camp. At the time, it occurred to me that the material on *pim* and her work could be seen as a fragment or shard from which projections of the complete object or social complex might be made, projections that would in turn illuminate a much wider social process. Indeed, the identification of an arena of social production where knowledge from outside the patri-group residence reorganized knowledge within it provided a means to comprehend the formation of Luo society.[13]

The case of *pim* and the *siwindhe* of the late nineteenth and early twen-

History (Chapel Hill: University of North Carolina Press, 1985), 191–232; and David William Cohen and E. S. Atieno Odhiambo, *Siaya*, 92–95.

12. Ben G. Blount, "Aspects of Luo Socialization," *Language and Society* 1 (1979): 247–48.

13. David William Cohen, "*Pim's* Work."

tieth century makes one wish to have access to still deeper layers of learning and socialization such as have been revealed in Françoise Zonabend's study of childhood in Burgundy. Unlike the *siwindhe*, where an "outsider" was often brought in to nurture and educate, in Minot "throughout childhood and even beyond it, the grandparents played a leading part in the process of socialization, a part that was long unsuspected as it was on the sidelines, in the shadow."[14]

The point here is not to introduce a comparative analysis of fostering in Agulu—where one well-known *pim* resided—and Minot, though there is an implication that a contextually far broader, social intelligence may have been brought into the lives of the children of the *siwindhe* than into those of Minot. The point is that there are critical areas in the shadows, critical silences in the social worlds we study. They are there not because we are few in number and sources are recondite, but because the attentions of anthropologists and historians tend to follow the visible wake of the past, ignoring the quiet eddies of potentially critical material that form at the same time.

Pim's work may also remind us that for *pim* and her children, knowledge began not with a remote world-system but with the vista seen just beyond the doorway of the *siwindhe*. *Pim* and her charges may encourage us in our quest for a composition not to lose sight of each tiny multiple-edged fragment that constitutes knowledge of the African past, nor to ignore the yet to be studied areas of silence. The unearthing of *pim*'s work has a didactic function but doubly so, for we can recognize the possibility not only that the inconsequential can have significance in the construction of society but also that it can illuminate our understanding of it. A former colleague has argued, "prominence and visibility no longer constitute a *prima-facie* case of historical significance. On the contrary, the value of every subject depends entirely upon how much it reveals about larger historical processes."[15]

Returning to the *siwindhe*, one might see that *pim*'s work is socially and culturally centered as a locus in the social and cultural education of children, in the formation of marriage linkages, in the elaboration of broader affinal networks, in the formation as knowledge of a still broader social geography. If in the study of the African past, one rushes too quickly toward an agenda that deals with the relations of larger processes, big social structures, and whole populations—the "big

14. Françoise Zonabend, "Childhood in a French Village," *International Social Science Journal*, 31 (1979), 492–507, esp. 498.

15. Jack P. Greene, "The New History: From Top to Bottom," *The New York Times*, June 8, 1975, 37.

changes"[16]—there is a risk of losing sight of the intimate areas of social life where real contradictions are managed and actual structures are enraveled and of falling into a falsely placed confidence that these contradictions have been managed through the elaborations of the academy's own discourse.

*

A few years ago, the Louis Leakey Foundation sent me a reproduction of a 1930s photograph. It came as a postcard, and it was an invitation to upgrade my small financial contribution to paleontology. The postcard shows Louis Leakey sitting at the wheel of his long roadster, his automobile packed tightly with equipment, one gun on his lap, another strapped to the side of the vehicle. The reverse of the card suggests he is saying "Wish you were here," while it looks like he might be saying, "Do you think I should take another gun?" There are two African men in the picture, one to the front of the car, one to the back—packers, presumably, perhaps the sons of porters—and in the shadow of one of these men, and right up against the left border of the photograph, there is a European woman. She appears to be well dressed, and while Louis looks like he has just been to Banana Republic, the woman's hat and dress suggest she may have been to Bloomingdale's. From the look of the packing job, she was not to accompany Louis on this trip; at least she would not have found a seat in Louis's car as represented in this photograph.

There is certainly a story here—the woman, Louis, the two African men—which the Louis Leakey Foundation chooses not to relate. But there is still another story, and that is that this card perched on my office mantel for some six weeks before a friend pointed out that there was a woman in the picture. I did not see the woman in the photograph for 42 days. Was this elision the consequence of my "skill" in separating

---

16. This argument was developed as a challenge, from within the collective work on social history edited by Olivier Zunz, *Reliving the Past: The Worlds of Social History* to the historical sociologist Charles Tilly and others who have called for a social history that begins with the "big changes," with the processes of "capitalism and statemaking" constructing and enclosing other arenas of human activity. Charles Tilly, *As Sociology Meets History* (New York: Academic Press, 1981), 46, in presenting an agenda for sociological history, uses the phrases "the analysis of power, of participation, or rebellion as historical problems, ultimately (linked) to the expansion of capitalism and the growth of systems of national states ... Capitalism and statemaking provide the context for a historically grounded analysis of collective action—of the ways in which people act together in pursuit of shared interests." See also, Charles Tilly, "Retrieving European Lives," in Zunz, ed., *Reliving the Past*, 11–52, particularly, 11–17, 31–32.

"Wish you were here" is the message of Louis Leakey in this vintage convertible as he sets off on roadless plains through barren territory to Olduvai Gorge in the 1930's. "The Darwin of Pre-History" went on to make discoveries that were to change our ideas about human evolution.

L.S.B. LEAKEY FOUNDATION, FOUNDATION CENTER 1-7, PASADENA, CA 91125

her from the image of Louis Leakey at the center? Or was it the consequence of the photographer's art and skill in placing her in the photograph but at its very margins?

My friend observed the woman in the picture immediately, marked her marginalization in the picture, but more profoundly for me, observed my own marginalizing and silencing reading of the card. Where I could say that what struck me were the differences between the departure of Louis Leakey "into the field" in the 1930s and my own departures three or four decades later, what was surely true was that I had read this card, this source, precisely as the Louis Leakey Foundation chose me to read it, silencing all else but the project of Louis Leakey, researcher (except that I did see the small paradox in that my last and only gift to the foundation was my own car, and it was empty).

In the days and weeks beyond this moment of confrontation between not seeing and seeing, I have thought about this postcard and the very different readings which just two individuals can bring to a rather commonplace source. I thought about the problematics of singular readings, and the power of multiple readings in which powers of observation and interpretation drew upon the distinctions between one "seeing" and another. I came to see the other reading, the observation of the picture and simultaneously a critique of how it had previously been read—by me— as the more powerful and creative one, for it transformed a simple photograph, and a charitable promotional device, into a significant query and produced a critique which would challenge another's way of reading and thinking.

This other, now attractive, reading of the picture appeared to resonate with some of the things which I had tried in some of my work, looking at those without writing, studying those at the edge of things—the power of edges, margins, borderlands, studied not as margins for all time, but sites of quiet, unheralded construction of culture, society, and the state, yet at the same time studied in the contexts of how others, of both the academy and not, had seen them or overlooked them. Yet for all this attention to the margins, I had not noticed the woman at the edge of the photograph.

The program of reading the so-called margins is not conveyed here as a program of displacement, a revolution against some notional "mainstream," of "bottom-up" versus "top-down," or a reification and celebration of "history from below" but rather an approach to the contextual complexities of historical production, what might be called the

Louis S. B. Leakey, 1903–72, a postcard.

incomplete dialectics of experience. The challenge here is to discern and mobilize the interpretive, explanatory, and representational powers that are located *between* first and second "readings," or that develop among multiple and sometimes disconnected and nonreciprocal readings of the past.

In an August 2, 1992, meeting at the Center for Cultural Studies in Chicago, the Hong Kong literary scholar Akhbar Abbas sought to apply the concept of *arbitrage* to literary analysis, in which the differences and disorientations between signs or between objects constitute something like interpretive capital or a force which permits one to "negotiate the mixed space that is post-coloniality." The power of interpretation would be located then not in the next and better reading but in the comprehension of the difference and disjuncture between the first and second readings. In the case of the postcard, the recognition of the woman in the image might in one interpretive mode simply displace and replace the older and "imperfect" reading in which the woman is not recognized. But the story of the postcard here has a different plot: the juxtaposed and partially conflicting readings draw into the foreground the distinct reading tactics and abilities of differently positioned observers without losing sight of the questions that the second reading introduces to the first: What is the woman doing in the photograph? Who is she? What is her relationship to Louis Leakey and his project? What was the photographer's program in rendering the picture so? What was the other observer's (my own) program in eliding the woman in the image?

*

In late 1985, as I was preparing an early draft of "The Production of History" position paper, I received my copy of the November-December issue of the *Wisconsin Alumnus Magazine*. When I eventually opened the magazine, I noticed a photograph on page 19, under the heading "The Way We Were–24." The photograph shows a number of students, women and men—in this photograph, women were at the center, men at the edges—in a scene unlike anything I had seen or heard about while a student at the University of Wisconsin, Madison, in the early 1960s. Well-dressed women were walking in file between two lines of men, at least one of whom had a clipboard and pencil, or pen, at the ready. The men seemed to be examining the women as they passed between their two lines. A caption published under the picture noted that

> This rite was known as the Call-Out. Immediately after women
> went through sorority pledging ceremonies they went out on the

The Way We Were–24 from *The Wisconsin Alumnus,* November/December, 1985, 19.

front lawn to pass between waiting lines of fraternity men. (Does anyone know if the procedure was ever reversed?) There are no records to show when the custom began or ended: it was big after World War II, but a sorority housemother who's been on campus for more than a decade never heard of it. This picture appeared in the 1951 *Badger,* the ladies are Kappa pledges, and a vintage caller-outer has tentatively identified the two in front as Helen Heuston and Jean Becker.

I was intrigued by the photograph, but more intrigued by the "fact" of incomprehensibility. What was this all about? What was its history? What did it signify? How did it come to disappear? And, as noted in the caption, it was also incomprehensible to the staff of the *Wisconsin Alumnus,* who asked their readership for interpretative assistance.

I decided to write to the editor of *Wisconsin Alumnus* to see what more could be discovered from the magazine, or readers' responses, or the university archives. I was interested in the problem of "memory" here: the status of remembrances of those appearing in the photograph and of others who had been witnesses to, or had participated in, such "events." In a letter January 16, 1986, I reported that I was interested in "the memory of things that seem retrospectively to be out of place or unfathomable." I posed a series of questions and was quite pleased to find, shortly, a long letter from Thomas H. Murphy, editor of the *Wisconsin Alumnus,* who identified himself as a 1949 graduate of the university and as "the writer of the photo caption." Murphy wrote,

> As I recall, sorority pledging was much more structured than was that of fraternities (as was all female living on the campus: strict hours, housemothers, etc.), and after spring and fall rushing, those accepted were pledged all on the same day at the various houses. Thus, up and down Langdon Street, there were the official teas, with the women dressed to the nines to be welcomed into the various clubs. The males, on the other hand, were just out-and-around, coming from class or going to a part-time job or whatever, and dressed accordingly. I have a hunch the "call-out" just growed—the men knew the sororities were having their receptions and, not illogically, made it a point to see which groups had inducted the best-looking women. So groups of men moved from sorority house to sorority house, stood outside in two lines and made enough noise so that the women got the message, whereupon they came out to be viewed. (Not one of them had to be dragged out, if I recall those years and if I may be permitted to editorialize).[17]

In my letter to the editor, I expressed an interest in learning in particular what the one man with the clipboard might have been doing in the way of creating a record of the "event." There seemed to be a story *within* the rite, as one notes the eyes of both female and male students focused, apparently, upon this young man with the clipboard. What was his status? What was he writing, or was he reading from notes previously prepared? Why the attention to him by virtually all those caught by the camera? Was this a rite within the rite? Focusing on the man, Murphy suggested that

> [this student] isn't a reporter, nor is he from some University office. Chances are strong, I think, that he was some wag who was pretending to rate the women as they passed—to write down phone numbers or whatever—and that he had either said something or done something that focussed crowd attention on him just as the picture was snapped.

Murphy reported that he had not yet received any replies from readers (other than my own inquiry), but that he had—on his own—been able to identify one woman in the picture, a member of Kappa Kappa Gamma sorority. Murphy still expected responses but also suggested

17. Letter dated January 28, 1986.

that I might send a letter quickly to be published in the next issue of the magazine (which I did, and it was, but my letter elicited only one reply). Murphy noted, with ironic disappointment, the absence of response to the call for information on the photograph, "since this situation personified male chauvinism at its zenith, I fully expected several irate women readers to tell me so. But, as I say, there has been nothing."

Murphy's letter was helpful in explaining "the Call-Out," but it was necessarily only a partial response to my request, because I was also interested in how participants and witnesses "read" the photograph out of their memories of the experience. Had time (even just three and a half decades) closed this experience to such a passing and, admittedly, nominal explication as I, and also the *Wisconsin Alumnus*, sought? Was the regime of relations between women and men exemplified in the photo so exotic by 1985, or so objectionable and embarrassing, that no one cared to involve themselves in revisiting this campus ritual?

For a few months I saw this photograph, and the challenge of constituting a substantial understanding of its content and of the history of the ritual it recorded, as worth further investigation. Here was an historical text—a thirty-five-year-old photograph of a scene on the Madison campus, an "experience near" in both location and time—recording some organized activity involving, from the demography of the photograph, some twenty-five women and men aged perhaps 18–23 at the time and perhaps no older than fifty-five or sixty when the photograph was republished in 1985. What did this population—represented by those in the photograph—know of this rite as they participated in it, produced it, or observed it? How was it organized and how well did those participating know the manner of its organization, with men and women having to organize themselves to appear at a common site at one moment? How did the rite mark gender relations and how was it marked by prior relations between young women and men? What meanings did individuals derive from their presence, or impart to the proceedings, by their gestures, postures, and, what we cannot see, their words and other utterances, and by their silences? In what ways was status marked by the order of procession and the arrangement of individuals in the male lines? How did this activity relate to other sections of social life on the campus and, perhaps, with social activities and social rites outside the university? How much significant and evocative matter lies outside the records of officials, reawakened in chance remarks or in occasional publications or "unseemly" revelations?

These questions emerged in late 1985 and early 1986 as I thought about the photograph, which sat among piles of other materials as the position paper for the Fifth Roundtable developed. The questions I had were not composed as a questionnaire for those who were present at these rites some thirty-five or more years ago. Their value was seen to lie in restraining the propensity to project interpretation and meaning into the "reading" of the photograph or the rite itself, and to underline how little experts know, and how little experts are actually capable of imputing, or recovering, of their/our own social worlds.[18]

After a few months, I had learned nothing more from the correspondence with the *Wisconsin Alumnus* and from the readers, who were asked once again for help in "reading" the "call-out" photograph. I did not consider this venture in "detection" worth further effort, nor did I consider—at least until 1992—that it would be something I would write on further, the "deadline" for the position paper having passed in March 1986.

But then, in 1992, the "Tailhook incident" came to be reported in newspapers, magazines, and on television, throwing the United States Navy into deep distress. At the center of the Tailhook scandal have been the revelations concerning the behavior of Navy airmen at an annual meeting held at the Hilton Hotel in Las Vegas, Nevada. In a practiced and ritualized way, the Navy airmen formed a gauntlet and both physically and verbally abused and assaulted women who were pressed into the mouth of the gauntlet and forced to pass through it. The gauntlet was formed by two lines of aviators arranging themselves along a Hilton hallway. The nature of its formation (along with various reports in the papers) suggests that the Navy gauntlet was a regular piece of business at this convention, or at parallel conventions, that the architecture of the gauntlet was the result of knowledge passed down over the years, along with the coordination of spatial and temporal elements organized

18. I have to admit that the interest in the photograph was impelled by a skepticism of the vogue-ish interpretative ("interpretive") mode of cultural and historical analysis that had been spreading from Clifford Geertz's authoritative "reading" position at a Balinese cockfight ("Deep Play: Notes on the Balinese Cockfight," *Daedalus* 1 (1972): 1–37) through the humanities and the social sciences after the mid-1970s. For me such a trend reached its zenith at a recent conference at the University of California, Santa Cruz, where one participant saw—in studying the riots that resulted from the Rodney King beating in Los Angeles in April and May 1992—the smashing of glass of refrigerator cases in 7-11 stores by "looters," rather than simply opening the unlocked doors and extracting their booty, as "an act of deconstructing the fetishization of display." For an interesting look at the interpretive vogue among historians in the United States in the 1970s, see Peter Novick, *That Noble Dream: The 'Objectivity Question' and the American Historical Profession* (Cambridge: Cambridge University Press, 1988), chaps. 15 and 16.

through some social program. As more was revealed about the Tailhook Convention, the behaviors located within the gauntlet seemed actually not to be so eccentric but rather they drew on values and practices radiating through the entire convention, and the Navy more generally. Did the Navy gauntlet condense into a ritualized and concrete event values and practices broadly grounded in the wider American society? And did the revelations, and prosecution of official investigations, of the Tailhook gauntlet effect a closure of attention to the passageways between the broader society and the Hilton hallway?

While one would not—without further information—want to constitute one of these "gantlets" as consonant with—or derived from—the other, they both and together raise questions concerning the ways in which social values, and notions of gender, condense into specific rituals and repetitive experiences, "creating" programs or events in the past that are, on the one hand, passed down over time as a form of "tradition" both defensible and indefensible and, on the other, dissembled into unknowing. Is this the Geertzian possibility of restoring the condensed values and practices into larger understandings and meanings? In July 1992, as more information surfaced about the Tailhook incidents, it was learned that photographs and videotapes provided further witness to the atrocities in the Hilton hallway at the Tailhook Convention. I wondered, and continue to wonder, what further secrets these pictures and tapes held, images that hid while also revealing, much like the photograph of the "call-out"—"The Way We Were–24."

*

In his "re-enactment" of a session in which a group of men in western Kenya constructed a genealogy, the sociolinguist Ben G. Blount recorded that

> Okumu asked "Who was Alego's mother?" in response to Nyanjom's directive "All right, write down the mother of Alego." Nyanjom's answer was "Just the mother of Alego," but, interestingly, he referred to her grinding stone (for maize), which still exists in Alego's Location: "The stone for grinding is still there." In addition, Nyanjom asked another elder, Ochondo, to verify the existence of the stone. Ochondo did, marking the first instance of a practice to be repeated time and time again in the discussion. This practice consists of reference to an object or entity whose physical existence serves to establish the validity of the point made in reference to it. Phenomena outside the realm of descent and filiation

can be used to establish the validity of the genealogical claim. Ochondo's response to Nyanjom, in full, was *"I understand that the grinding-stone is there. The mother of Alego was a person."*[19]

The investment of historical meaning in material objects is clearly a well-known and much-worked ground. There are, however, important tensions in how this conveyance is implemented. W. G. Hoskins, in *Fieldwork in Local History,* explained how he came to learn to "read" the English landscape over a forty-year period of education.[20] Initially, he found that poring over histories from the libraries did not help him resolve the mysteries in his youthful apprehension of the English countryside. He began to find his answers walking through the countryside, picking up patterns, observing breaks in and exceptions to these patterns; and he began to grasp the meaning, the historical stories captured, within "farmsteads and field-patterns; of hedgebanks, boundaries and lanes; of church and earth-work; of manor-house and woodlands."[21] In a later work Hoskins remarked,

> Fifty years ago I used to spend my holidays in a then remote, and still beautiful, bit of Devon. There was no village, only the squire's house . . . the church and the smithy and the school, and beyond that a landscape of scattered farmsteads, shining in the sun in their green combes for they were mostly built of cob and then whitewashed. The lanes wandered between high hedgebanks, turning abrupt corners and just wide enough for one cart; the fields varied in size and shape but usually made very irregular patterns. Even then I felt that everything I was looking at was saying something to me if only I could recognise the language. It was a landscape written in a kind of code.[22]

Hoskins related that "using various kinds of evidence and not least that of my own eyes (and conversations with farmers on the spot), I have answered some of the questions I used to ask in vain of other books."[23]

Hoskins's program contains several voices: one is the voice of the landscape itself in all its elements, muted, disguised, suppressed; an-

19. Ben G. Blount, "Agreeing to Agree on Genealogy: A Luo Sociology of Knowledge," in Mary Sanches and Ben G. Blount, eds., *Sociocultural Dimensions of Language Use* (New York: Academic Press, 1975), 125 (emphasis added).

20. W. G. Hoskins, *Fieldwork in Local History* (London: Faber & Faber, 1967). Also, *The Making of the English Landscape* (Baltimore: Penguin Books, 1955).

21. *Fieldwork,* 17.

22. W. G. Hoskins, *English Landscapes* (London: British Broadcasting Corporation, 1973), 5.

23. *Fieldwork,* 18.

other is the voice of the farmer who presumably uses the land and knows the land in ways which Hoskins yet fails to make clear; and the third is the voice of the expert who has trained himself to comprehend the language of the landscape. There are other presumed voices: those "parent" to the farmers of Hoskins's research days who passed on information about the terrain, the environment of the farm, to their children, their laborers, and others; those who counseled others in the maintenance of usable elements of the landscape; those adults and children who played with the landscape as a kind of recreation and whose activities had the capacity of remaking the knowledge in the landscape; and there are those voices which evoke the features which confirm ownership, status, control.

There are similar tensions and ambiguities in the realization of elements of the landscape as symbols and monuments—a critical tension between a readiness on the part of a present observer to read what appears to him or her (the outsider) as important symbolic materials in the landscape and a patience to listen to the meanings and significances attached by those experiencing within the context. In his *Transformation of Virginia*, Rhys Isaac points out that

> A society necessarily leaves marks of use upon the terrain it occupies. These marks are meaningful signs not only of the particular relations of a people to environment but also of the distribution and control of access to essential resources. Incised upon a society's living space appears a text for the inhabitants—which he who runs may read—of social relations in their world. Moving more slowly, anthropologists for present societies, and historical ethnographers for past ones, must seek to interpret such texts—both to understand the relations of production inscribed upon the land and to decipher as much as they can of the meanings that such relations assumed for those who were part of them.[24]

With Hoskins and with Isaac, the key is to be able to grasp the distinctions between, on the one hand, the meanings which people make out of, and impose upon, their landscapes and, on the other, the additional meanings which only distance (an apartness from intimacy) or expertise or science, and a search for organizing symbols and materials will constitute.[25] Is this the potential interpretive power of *arbitrage* which

24. Rhys Isaac, *The Transformation of Virginia, 1740–1790* (Chapel Hill: University of North Carolina Press, 1982), 19.

25. In *The Past Is a Foreign Country* (Cambridge: Cambridge University Press, 1985), David Lowenthal attempts to make sense of the "relics of the past" through the study of architecture, buildings, gardens, landscape designs, and other artifacts produced in the

Akhbar Abbas has mooted? The term "forests" holds distinctive meanings for Kenya scientists and Kenyan claimants to the history of Mau
Mau, and still further meanings for those involved in Professor Wangari
Maathai's *greenbelt movement,* the pragmatic environmental resource
campaign, with a solid democraticization edge, spreading from Kenya
to other countries on the African continent.[26] For the projects of Hoskins
and Isaac—and in order to seize the value of the *arbitrage* moment—it
seems critical to maintain the boundary of distinction between interpretation, marked by specific claims to expertise, on the one hand, and the
knowing and intimate perspectives of the people who find themselves
the subjects of such interpretative programs, on the other.

It is also worth noting that most lives are not lived out in the Kenya
"forests" and that, as Richard Rathbone notes, "most people do not live
in events but through them. There is a dulled texture about most
people's lives . . . so much of the drama in the lives of individuals is in
their minds and not in their streets."[27] Much of this drama is not explicitly revealed and historians face a large challenge in attempting to dis-
close these intimate dramas.

*

In Rea Tajiri's 1991 video, *History and Memory: For Akiko and Takashige,*
the narrator, the videomaker herself, relates

---

past. While rich in examples—particularly from the United Kingdom—Lowenthal's treatment ultimately and also utterly fails to introduce issues of interest and conflict over the
holdings of knowlege, and over interpretation and interpretive authority, coming down
from the past. One finds in Lowenthal's treatment a homely sensibility and a portrait of
an organic world in which interests do not attach themselves to the values and readings
of "things." Beyond muddling concepts of "history" and of "past," Lowenthal burdens his
text with an indefinite and consensual use of "us" and "we" in ways that effectively efface
the distinctions in attentions that develop among "audiences" to the materials Lowenthal
interprets. On page 187, Lowenthal presents his essential argument, and the essential
mode of its operation: "The fact that the past is no longer present clouds knowledge of it
with uncertainty. Assigned varying durations, insecurely linked with the present, its very
existence unproven, the past often seems disconcertingly tenuous." In an astonishing way,
Lowenthal misses the very points that Hoskins and Isaac have made. He misses as well
the force of the past in such constructions of silence as enjoined Camella Teoli and her
daughter Josie.

26. And one may discover rich and complex worlds within the forests of Wole Soyinka's
imaginative writings, including his autobiographical *Ake: The Years of Childhood* (New
York: Aventura Vintage, 1981).

27. Private communication from Dr. Richard R. Rathbone in response to an early draft
of "The Production of History" position paper.

> My Mom used to have this bird, this little wooden carved bird that
> was inside her jewelry box. I used to ask her if I could play with
> it and she kept saying, "No, no, no. Grandma gave me that. Put it
> back." Twenty-five years later I was sitting inside a room in the Na-
> tional Archives, going through a box that contained hundreds of
> pictures. Suddenly, I came across a picture of my grandmother
> seated in a classroom taken while she was in camp [the Japanese-
> American internment camp at Poston, Arizona]. I turned it over
> and the caption read, "Bird-carving class, Camp 2, 1942." I began
> searching for a history, my own history.

On March 18, 1992, the American videomaker and installation artist
Rea Tajiri spoke at Northwestern University. She provided views of her
theory of practice as she researched and constructed her half-hour video
History and Memory: For Akiko and Takashige. Her goal was to to reconstruct and represent her mother's experience within a Japanese-
American internment camp during the Second World War, but more
particularly to examine and reconstruct her mother's memory of the experience. In terms of the operation of her own practice, Rea Tajiri made
a resolute distinction between the internment, as it might be represented
in innumerable ways, and her mother's memory of internment.

During the seminar,[28] Tajiri discussed her juxtapositions of her own
images with scenes from wartime propaganda films which the U.S. government used to rationalize or justify the internments and to restage
the internments as something acceptable and comfortable to Japanese-
Americans who, within a few hours, were taken from their homes and,
with a minimum of possessions, transported to such confinements in
the desert as Poston, Arizona, "offered" her mother and grandmother.

Rea Tajiri's video provides an accounting of the internment experience
radically different from, and opposed to, the representations of the internments produced by the American government. But her film is far
more complex, going well beyond a revisionist statement of a next and
also critical generation. Tajiri organized her argument as much around
the meanings and processes of memory as around the "content." Her
method involves juxtaposing different visual sources, including photographs and amateur film and other found "archival" material. Her finished product, *History and Memory,* includes a new reading of the film

28. Tajiri was in Chicago the week that marked the fiftieth anniversary of the deportation of Japanese-Americans to the internment camps that were quickly opened in isolated
areas throughout the West. Northwestern University and the Randolph Street Gallery
cooperated in bringing the videomaker and her video to Chicago.

Bad Day at Black Rock, in which the absence, the orchestrated disappearance, of knowledge of the Japanese-American farmer Komoko, is set against the disappearance of the experience of the internment camp at Poston from her mother's memory.

In the juxtapositional mode Tajiri has gone still further, introducing within her video a critique of Alan Parker's treatment of the Japanese-American internment, *Come See the Paradise,* which presents a detailed and emplotted account of a family's deportation and suffering.[29] To Tajiri, Parker's film erased the centrality and complexity of memory, of silences, of suppressions within the experience of internment: between state and victim, but also within families and between generations. In Parker's film, one finds absent the complexities of knowing, but also not knowing, or of knowing but having no way of speaking, which are richly explored in *History and Memory.*[30] In confronting the challenge of her own search for an understanding of her mother's memory of the internment, Tajiri grasps the force of silence, rather as Herbert G. Gutman and Paul Cowan had grasped the force in Camella Teoli's silence as her daughter combed her mother's hair every day to cover her scar from the industrial accident.

In reconstructing her mother's memory of the Poston camp, Tajiri told the seminar she was herself "taking on a memory of the camp." Tajiri spent days in the National Archives in Washington going through boxes of photographs of the period. She found photograph after photograph which Alan Parker clearly used in constructing his sets and his scenes, the dress of various internees, the postures and groupings of individuals and families being loaded onto trains, in exacting replications of the photographs produced in the period, reminding this listener of the program at the Department of Interior laboratory at Harper's Ferry in which photographs were being assembled and used to construct a perfected replication of Booker T. Washington's study at Tuskegee. In an indirect way, *History and Memory* draws attention to Parker's appropriation of these images.

---

29. To push the critique of the Alan Parker film, Tajiri uses the spoken text of a review of *Come See the Paradise,* written by a high school student, a relative of hers, and published in the *Chicago Tribune* while she was doing research for the video. The student review marks the film as stifling, reducing people to cardboard characters, and, in conclusion, renames the film *Come See the Parasites.*

30. In the video, the narrator/filmmaker remarks on her mother's "memory" of Poston: "She tells the story of what she does not remember. But remembers one thing: why she forgot to remember."

In her essays *On Photography* Susan Sontag has worked her way back
and forth across the questions that Rea Tajiri contemplated in her remarks to the seminar. Sontag has pointed out that

> Photography has always been fascinated by social heights and
> lower depths. Documentarists (as distinct from courtiers with cam-
> eras) prefer the latter. For more than a century, photographers have
> been hovering about the oppressed, in attendance at scenes of vio-
> lence—with a spectacularly good conscience. Social misery has
> inspired the comfortably-off with the urge to take pictures, the
> gentlest of predations, in order to document a hidden reality,
> that is, a reality hidden from them.[31]

Sontag, like Richard Avedon in his discussion of method,[32] also explored
the relationship of power that enveloped the photographer and his or
her subject. In speaking of Diane Arbus's use of the the frontal pose,
with "subjects looking straight into the camera," Sontag notes that

> In the normal rhetoric of the photographic portrait, facing the cam-
> era signifies solemnity, frankness, the disclosure of the subject's es-
> sence . . . What makes Arbus's use of the frontal pose so arresting
> is that her subjects are often people one would not expect to sur-
> render themselves so amiably and ingenuously to the camera.
> Thus, in Arbus's photographs, frontality also implies in the most
> vivid way the subject's cooperation. To get these people to pose,
> the photographer has had to gain their confidence, has had to be-
> come "friends" with them.[33]

It is in response to the implication of "cooperation" that Rea Tajiri's
questions concerning the documentary photograph take on immediacy
and power; her approach is dramatically noted in her reconstitution of
the core visual image of her mother, portrayed only momentarily from
the front but more fully from the side and back, over the shoulder. *History and Memory* works from an image of a Japanese-American woman
catching a few precious drops of water falling from a water tank. The
camera captures the woman from the back, and the viewer looks over
her shoulder as she takes the water into her cupped hand and lifts it to
her face. In *History and Memory,* the image of the woman (actually played

---

31. *On Photography,* (New York: Anchor Doubleday, 1989), 55. First published in *The
New York Review of Books* between 1973 and 1977.
32. *In the American West.* See discussion of Avedon early in chap. 2, above.
33. *On Photography,* 37–38.

by the videomaker herself) with her face hardly disclosed, is the starting point of the unraveling of the mystery of Tajiri's mother's memory.[34]

In studying photographs of Japanese-Americans in the 1930s and 1940s, as she sought to reconstruct her mother's memory of internment, Tajiri found herself looking at practices of subjection, discipline, efface-ment, and disappearance as she read them across the boundaries of deportation and confinement. In the Northwestern seminar, Tajiri spoke of a sense in which such films as Parker's *Paradise* were, by their method, already scripted before the filmmaker arrived,[35] constructed through those images which earlier filmmakers, documentarians, and photogra-phers—including those working for the Army Signal Corps—had long ago produced, and which filled countless boxes in the National Ar-chives. She began to think about the violence and victimization of the subjects of these documentarians, even those heralded radical and pro-gressive conservators of America's dark recesses (was she thinking of Edward Curtis, Walker Evans, Dorothea Lange, Jacob Riis, Paul Strand?).[36] She reflected on the abuse, or misreading, of such photo-graphs in the search for authority and authenticity in the representation of the American past—for example, in seeking the look of authentic-

---

34. It is also at such a water tank as Tajiri represents that the investigator in *Bad Day at Black Rock*, played by Spencer Tracy, begins to unravel the mystery of Komoko.

35. As I listened to Tajiri's argument here, I thought about the logic and power of this premise of pre-scripting; a "parallel" came to mind—and found its way into my notes at the seminar—the pre-constitution, in anticipation, of the "barbarians," in John Coetzee's novel *Waiting for the Barbarians*, and of ethnographers' and travelers' texts in which the inscription of "culture" is, in an essential sense, already pre-scripted. One notes the "rec-ipe books" on ethnographic reporting that missionaries and administrators carried to the colonies; and the "rules of the game" which such ethnographic film projects as "Disap-pearing World" disseminate to interested anthropologists. See *Passages*, iv (fall, 1992). Such pre-scripting is discussed in a number of different writing contexts in Mary Louise Pratt, *Imperial Eyes: Travel Writing and Transculturation* (London: Routledge, 1992), esp. chaps. 3 and 9. Also, more generally, Edward Said, *Orientalism* (New York: Vintage, 1979), and, for Africa, Christopher L. Miller, *Blank Darkness: Africanist Discourse in French* (Chi-cago: University of Chicago Press, 1985), esp. chap. 1.

36. In the notes prepared for the 1992 exhibition at the Whitney Museum of American Art in New York, of the photography of Paul Strand from 1915 to 1976, there is a discus-sion of Strand's 1953 portraits of people in Luzzara, Italy. "For the first time in his career, Strand saw portraits of people as the heart of his statement . . . he wanted these works to transcend time, distilling all the events and relationships that combined to form the char-acter of his subject and revealing 'the core of their humanness.'" The exhibition also in-cluded his very early work in New York, conceived and executed in an entirely different way. Strand concocted a trick lens that would allow him to take pictures from what would appear to be an angle, so that he could take the photographs of people (typically frontal "portraits") without their noticing it and, one may construe, without their consent or

ity in *Paradise*—but also in the victimization of the posed subject, in which the experience of the act of documentation is extinguished with the clicking of the shutter. One might guess that Tajiri would hardly share Sontag's view of the photography of the "documentarists" as "the gentlest of predations."

The Sowetan photographer Santu Mofokeng has further complicated this discussion by examining side by side the workings of the international market in photographic images from South Africa and the readings that some of his Soweto subjects bring to his practice. At a seminar at Northwestern in March 1992, Mofokeng, who was on a study visit to the United States, spoke of the two orbits of his professional practice. On the one hand, there was an unending demand outside South Africa for his photographs of violence, conflict, desolation, and want, but neither Sowetans nor the wider South African public were interested in such photography, recognizing the glut of these images and of the settings, events, and experiences recorded. On the other hand, Sowetans valued his family portraits and, as subjects, insisted that these conform to the subjects' idea of what a "proper" and "natural" representation of a family grouping was, seeking a century-old mode of domestic and family portraiture.

What are the implications for documentary method, as the subjects of photographs, portraiture, video, and film write and speak about and question the modes of representation? While in recent years there have been notable examples of those "peoples" long documented through film and photography finally obtaining in their own hands the means of representation—cameras and video equipment, for example[37]—one may ask in what ways the seizing of these technologies opens interrogations of the modes of representation, such as Tajiri and Mofokeng have begun, and in what ways these projects essentially reproduce the authority of photographer, filmmaker, and videomaker over the subject.

*

In the summer of 1991, as the planning of this book was developing, it was expected that a reproduction of a map hanging on the wall of the

---

"involvement" . . . in contrast to the photographer-subject protocols of Arbus, Avedon, the Army Signal Corps documentarians, and, presumably, the later Strand.

37. One may note here such projects as Video Sewa, the video production and distribution unit of the Self-Employed Women's Association, in India, which has as its goal the production of videos portraying Indian life "from the bottom up," with particular attention to the articulation of interests of working women whose voices have been little heard in the higher chambers of state and nation.

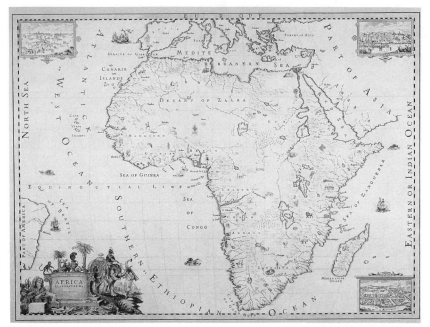

The Map of Africa, from the National Museum of African Art, Washington, D.C.

National Museum of African Art, a Smithsonian institution, in Washington would be located as a visual in the text, with its associated caption attached. It was thought that such a visual might demonstrate both the power and contingency of representation. There, at the National Museum of African Art, the search for modes of positive and elegant representation of African masterworks and African culture found partial embodiment in a map that conflated European geographical knowledge from the fifteenth through the nineteenth centuries into a flat composite, historical yet ahistorical, rendering of the African continent's geographical past. Acquiring a copy of this map was not as simple as expected.[38]

Every day hundreds of visitors to the National Museum of African Art in Washington, D.C., pass through the gallery displaying materials from Benin. They may notice and inspect a large map of Africa located just to the left of the entranceway. Indeed, the architecture of the area around the entrance to the the Benin gallery, along with the large scale of the map, encourages a viewing of the map from a considerable distance.

38. This account draws upon a narrative of these discussions which I published in *Passages* 2 (1991): 1–4, and *Passages* 3 (1992): 8.

The display area, *The Map of Africa,* from the National Museum of African Art, Washington, D.C.

From such a distance the map appears to be a reproduction and en-largement of a seventeenth- or eighteenth-century map of Africa. As one moves closer and examines the detail, one is jarred by the possibility— or certainty—that the maker of this map played with considerable li-cense in deploying names and illustrations onto the map from different periods. The observer may be bemused, or confused, by the conflation of diverse historical elements within one geographical illustration. One's sense of the African past is engaged and challenged by the inter-mingling of an intense historicizing image—that Africa has a past and there is one geographical representation of that past—with the deforma-tion and reconstitution of historical "knowledge" through the anachro-nistic and ahistorical textual elements imposed on the map's surface. The late twentieth-century map designer has creatively reintroduced the imagery of different eras into a map contemporary both by its date of creation and by its possibility of incorporating multiple themes and ideas in a composition both historicizing and ahistorical.

In early 1988, during my first visit to the museum, I noticed the map in its prominent location at the entrance to the Benin exhibit space. Then, after some moments of captivation and confusion, I found an ex-planatory caption in small print mounted next to it on the wall. That evening, I asked one of the educational staff for a copy of the caption, which I received in the mail a few weeks later. Until December 1993, I understood that the text I had in hand was the one I had seen on the wall in 1988. When I visited the museum in 1991, I took note of what appeared to be a new version of the text, with small changes seeming to have entered the text at a number of points:

> This map is a composite rendering of maps of Africa that were drawn between the 15th and 19th centuries. During that period, the real geography of the interior of the continent was largely unknown. The map captures some of the excitement and unintentional whimsy of early representations of the "mysterious" continent. The coastline, the first area explored, is relatively accurate, but the inland sources of the rivers remain somewhat fanciful. The sources of the Nile, for example, are shown farther south than the river's actual headwaters. Animals vary in appearance from the fantastic to the scientifically accurate. Many of the mountain ranges are imaginary. Art objects from a number of early traditions are illustrated, although most were not known to European travelers.

In a first published discussion of the map and its caption, I compared the text received from the museum in 1988 with the "revised" text that I had noted during my 1991 museum visit.[39] I was intrigued by the several small modifications in the text, observed in comparing the two versions of the caption, which suggested the continuing interest of museum staff in getting right the supportive explanation for this whimsical cartographic treatment. But as this book was going to press, with a presentation of the comparison of the two caption texts in galleys, I learned that a member of the museum staff had in 1992 alerted senior museum staff that I had notably erred in my first publication of this material, that what was provided to me as "the first caption" had never actually hung on the wall, and that the only element of the caption that was altered between the museum's opening on September 28, 1987, and April, 1992, when my discussion was published, was the deletion of two sentences: "The ships allude to the triangular trade between Europe, Africa, and the Americas. An active partner in this trade was the Benin Kingdom, whose art is exhibited in the adjacent gallery."

But in late August 1991, I had neither a photographic copy of the map for closer inspection nor a copy of what I thought was the revised caption text. I wrote to the National Museum of African Art to request, first,

39. *Passages* 3 (1992): 8–9.

a photographic print of the map and, second, the present version of the adjoining caption, the two pieces to be published together without extensive comment in a forthcoming number of *Passages*. A first response, September 9, 1991, was that an 8-by-10-inch photograph of the map was available and could be provided for $10, and that an inquiry would still have to be made in regard to the availability of the present caption text and also as to the method of payment.

On September 10, 1991, the situation changed. A curator at the National Museum of African Art wrote, via fax, that "As it turns out, the map was done strictly for in-house exhibition use and we have never had it published. Therefore we will not be able to provide you with a photograph of the map."

A further inquiry in regard to the availability of the caption text was made the same day by return fax. This request elicited a call from another curator at the museum who reported that the reason the map and caption could not be provided was that "They [the map and text] were intended for this specific installation . . . and it is felt that to publish them would be to take them out of the context for which they were created."

On September 15, 1991, a further letter of request was sent to Mrs. Sylvia Williams, director of the National Museum of African Art, along with information about the field of interest of *Passages*. The letter noted that

> I am able to visit the Museum periodically, as are thousands of others who pass by the map into your exhibition hall. But I would very much like to publish a photograph of the map and the related caption text/s in our new *Passages: A Chronicle of the Humanities*, published twice a year by the Program of African Studies, Northwestern. *Passages* is circulated free to three thousand addresses, including five hundred on the African continent. It is mailed to many who will never be able to visit the Museum and, therefore, who will never have an opportunity to be challenged by the issues that the map raises concerning the presentation and representation of the African past.

Receiving no response to this "appeal to higher authority," I made a further request to Mrs. Williams by mail on October 7, 1991. The next day, October 8, she responded by telephone that her staff was "in full agreement that the map is part of an installation . . . it was done for this specific purpose . . . and the staff did not want to see it published outside of this context."

During the telephone conversation, Mrs. Williams posed a series of questions: What was the interest in this particular map as opposed to other maps displayed in the museum and otherwise available? Why were we not interested in an authentic map from an original historical source such as the museum staff members drew upon to produce this rendering? What could be the interest of the readership of the publication in this map that does not pretend to be accurate? What possibility might there be in some future collaboration of an interdisciplinary kind in which historians of Africa would be invited to assist in the redevelopment of this particular exhibit? Had I ever myself worked in a museum and seen the problem of exhibiting for the public from the museum staff's perspective?[40]

An opening to the manner of construction of the African past by the National Museum of African Art through the creation of a "composite rendering of maps of Africa" drawn over several centuries passes into a second domain in which the museum, by its policies, attempts to control the place, time, and manner in which the map will be read. Perhaps the most frequently viewed and inspected map of Africa in the Washington area is withheld from view by broader and more distant audiences with an interest in the ways different authors and audiences construct—through imagination, composition, and reconstruction—images of Africa and representations of its past.

The notion of context—that the map and its caption were intended for a specific installation and therefore should not be carried to a remove from that context—draws attention to the very role of the National Museum of African Art, and other institutions with related projects, which—as their essential project—collect, draw upon, document, and display materials created for a specific and *other* context or function, materials which find themselves displaced or transplanted into museums distant from these contexts of origin.[41]

A third issue concerns the different permutations of the notions of "public." The museum, a federal installation supported by public funds, seeks to engage a public through encouraging visitors to pass through its doors—without charge—day after day through a range of publica-

---

40. Some of these queries appear in approximately the same form in a letter of October 11, 1991, from Mrs. Williams, which again turns down the request for the map, though establishing prior review procedures for, possibly, obtaining the map.

41. For a most valuable treatment of such practices of exhibition in museums, see Sally Price, *Primitive Art in Civilized Places* (Chicago: University of Chicago Press, 1989). And for a still more elaborate exploration of the questions raised within and around museums by reason of their exhibitions of the objects of the "Other," see Ivan Karp and Steven A.

tions, activities, special shows, lectures, educational projects, public relations programs, and a well-organized and popular museum shop. Yet
at the same time the museum seeks to regulate how "the public" will
view its exhibits, experience its activities, and understand its project
through, as noted in the experience of obtaining an 8-by-10-inch photo
of a map, controls placed upon the communication of images from
within its galleries into other interpretive spaces.[42]

Following "appeals to higher authority"—the associate secretary for
museums of the Smithsonian, and also the secretary—on November 8,
1991, Sylvia Williams, the director of the museum, and Roy Sieber, associate director, provided a photograph of the map, along with a copy of
the text of its present caption, but also photographs of three additional
maps which, according to the letter "are used to place the Benin Kingdom in historical perspective" within the context of the museum's exhibition, Royal Benin Art in the Collection of the National Museum of
African Art. Permission to publish the photographs of the map was
granted for *Passages* and for this book. According to the museum's letter,
the maps were designed in 1987, with credit to the artist David Ravitch
and photographer Jeffrey Ploskonka and James Young. The maps, accompanying captions (original and revised), and a brief accompanying
discussion, were published in *Passages,* iii (1992): 8–9.

With the map of Africa at the museum, the past is presented in a
1987 production, designed out of the styles of European cartography
developing from the fifteenth through the nineteenth century, presented
as history, with history made to stand still.

In an extraordinary critical discussion of cartography, "Deconstructing the Map," published in 1989,[43] the late geographer J. B. Harley
opened the consideration of the "quest for the map" in still another way.
Harley, whose death in December 1991, was reported in *The New York
Times* as I was readying the dossier of the "quest" to send to him for
comment, set a challenge to what he saw as the prevailing view that
cartographers, or mappers, "engage in an unquestionably 'scientific' or
'objective' form of knowledge production."[44] In his critique, Harley

---

Lavine, eds., *Exhibiting Cultures: The Poetics and Politics of Museum Display* (Washington,
D.C.: Smithsonian Institution Press, 1991).

42. A range of important papers dealing with the complex ideas about what museums
are, or should be, and what their audiences are, or should be, is contained in Ivan Karp,
Christine Muller Kreamer, and Steven D. Lavine, eds., *Museums and Communities: The Politics of Public Culture* (Washington, D.C.: Smithsonian Institution Press, 1992).

43. *Cartographica* v, 26, 2 (Spring 1989): 1–20; reprinted in *Passages* 3 (1992): 10–13.

44. "Deconstructing the Map," *Passages* 3 (1992): 10.

questioned these assumptions and unmasked the ways in which social values, cultural norms, and particular interests come to be naturalized within the map as text, as well as the ways in which these forces have been hidden from view of those who read and use maps.

Harley seized "deconstruction" as his method, seeking to read the margins and

> through its tropes to discover the silences and contradictions that challenge the apparent honesty of the image. We begin to learn that cartographic facts are only facts within a specific cultural perspective. We start to understand how maps, like art, far from being "a transparent opening to the world" are but "a particular human way of looking at the world."[45]

Harley also has gone on to discuss how maps come to work, "to be so convincing" as to supplant or suppress other forms of reason and other realms of knowledge.[46] In examining the ways in which "the rules of society and the rules of measurement are mutually reinforcing," Harley noted that

> much like "the rule of ethnocentrism," [the] hierarchicalization of space is not a conscious act of cartographic representation. Rather it is taken for granted in a society that the place of the king is more important than the place of a lesser baron, that a castle is more important than a peasant's house . . . Cartography deploys its vocabulary accordingly so that it embodies a systematic social inequality. The distinctions of class and power are engineered, reified and legitimated in the map by means of cartographic signs. The rule seems to be "the more powerful, the more prominent" . . . Much of the power of the map, as a representation of social geography, is that it operates behind a mask of seemingly neutral science. It hides and denies it social dimensions at the same time as it legitimates . . . The [rules of society] have ensured that maps are at least as much an image of the social order as they are a measurement of the phenomenal world of objects.[47]

Finally, Harley moves the reader into a third area: the effect, or power, of maps upon those who use them. It is not that maps produce knowl-

45. Ibid., 10. Harley was quoting here from H. G. Blocker, *Philosophy and Art* (New York: Charles Scribner's Sons, 1979), 43.

46. These issues are taken up in a valuable essay by Thomas Richards, "Archive and Utopia," *Representations* 37 (Winter 1992), 104–35, though it does not give any notice to Harley's seminal paper.

47. "Deconstructing the Map," 11.

edge, and thus shape and determine the way the world is known, they also "manufacture power." Building on a reading of Michel Foucault and Roland Barthes, Harley has argued that "to map" is to catalogue the world and to catalogue the world is to appropriate it

> so that all these technical processes represent acts of control over its image which extend beyond the professed uses of cartography. The world is disciplined. The world is normalized. We are prisoners in its social matrix . . . It is a local knowledge which at the same time is universal. It usually passes unnoticed. The map is a silent arbiter of power.[48]

What is extraordinary about the map in the National Museum of African Art is that it is associated with a caption that unmasks its own mode of construction, signaling the map as *a* representation. That its curators sought to regulate and limit its viewing, and also, evidently, that they sought to inhibit the critical discussion of it as a representation and as an installation, doubly complicates the challenge that Harley brilliantly set in the path of those who "read," display, and produce maps.

*

In early 1992, the Maryland Historical Society, in collaboration with the Contemporary,[49] opened a new exhibition "Mining the Museum" on the third floor of the Maryland Historical Society building in downtown Baltimore. The exhibition was designed by installation artist Fred Wilson, who wanted, through the "re-exhibition" of pieces in the Maryland Historical Society collections, to demonstrate the ways in which assumptions, manipulations, silences, and racism are naturalized within the project of museum exhibition. Landscape and architectural paintings from Maryland's plantation era are relit and relabelled to bring attention to the black figures who are shown at work in the fields and marshes. Period chairs are regrouped and set in rows before a whipping post found in the museum's storage area. Chains and whips are positioned more visibly, along with domestic materials from slave villages and from early African manufacture. Cigar store Indians are displayed

---

48. Ibid., 12.

49. A new entity established in Baltimore that exalts its unsitedness and transiency in a unique way, by its own announcement the Contemporary presents "the art of our time in the most unexpected places. We tranform unexpected urban sites into unique settings for meeting new artists, new genres of the visual arts, and new ideas." By its "unconstructedness," it implicitly deconstructs the sited-ness of "traditional" museums and galleries.

so that one first sees their backs, rather than their fronts. There is a series of pedestals with heads or busts absent or disappeared. A child figured in a painting is heard to speak through a tape playing over and over again: "Where did I go?" The scientific writings of the eighteenth-century black genius Benjamin Banneker are redisplayed in computerized form. Fred Wilson's project was intended to raise questions for the museum, for the historical society, and for its public, working within the "text" of what was available in the cellars of the museum.

In one of the "minimalist" program notes associated with the exhibition, Chief Curator Jennifer Goldsborough, of the Maryland Historical Society, has commented on Fred Wilson's mining of her collections:

> Each object, new or old, inspires a multitude of questions about the lives of those who made it, used it, owned it, chose it, saved it, discarded it, exhibited it. By putting objects together in different ways the questions are enhanced and multiplied. As a curator working with an extraordinary collection of art and a vast accumulation of historical artifacts, I am excited by what the manipulation of these objects in exhibitions asks. My role is to encourage others to question. The search is expanded by every interaction.

Lisa Corrin, of the Contemporary, spoke of how much she and others working with Fred Wilson learned from the project.

> We learned how museums and museum professionals are not immune to stereotyping. We learned the importance of "re-siting" the museum as a place of debate, not one of absolute judgements.[50] We feel indebted to Fred Wilson for galvanizing a line of self-questioning which will ensure that our institutions can go forward with a continued sense of purpose and relevance.

As one completes the tour of "Mining the Museum" and enters the elevator to descend to the lobby of the Maryland Historical Society—to recognize once again the museum in its old dress, still unaffected by the critical and reinterpretive art of Fred Wilson, one finds on the elevator a sheaf of hand-outs. Under the heading "Mining the Museum," a list is presented:

50. In remarks published in *The Smithsonian*, April, 1992, pages 13–14, Robert McC. Adams, secretary of the Smithsonian, echoes these remarks: "Why not let our audiences in on the controversies and uncertainties of science and scholarship? Why not recognize that there really is no such thing as complete neutrality with regard to either facts or values? . . . let us by all means avoid parading the finality of our present knowledge, and still less our certainty as to the superiority of our own moral positions."

The exterior doors to the *Burial Room,* Dickson Mounds, Illinois, April 1992.

What is it?
Where is it? Why?
What is it saying?
How is it used?
For whom was it created?
For whom does it exist?
Who is represented?
How are they represented?
Who is doing the telling? The hearing?
What do you see?
What do you hear?
What can you touch?
What do you feel?
What do you think?
Where are you?

*

In *History and Memory,* Rea Tajiri opens the video with juxtapositions of different representations of the Japanese attack on Pearl Harbor. The narrator's voice intones the videomaker's essential position:

There are things which have happened in the world while there were cameras watching, things which we have images for.

There are other things which have happened while there were no cameras watching which we restage in front of cameras to have images of.

There are things which have happened for which the only images that exist are in the minds of the observers present at the time.

While there are things which have happened for which there have been no observers, except for the spirits of the dead.

*

On Saturday, April 18, 1992, as I was leaving the display areas of the museum at the Dickson Mounds State Archaeological Site,[51] I looked for a sign on the second floor at the entrance to the burial mound exhibit that would indicate that the display was closed by order of the governor of Illinois. There was no sign or notice. I refused to touch or test the doors, but a colleague on the trip to the mounds did try the handle of the double glass door through which, in November 1991, I had descended to the enclosure which held the remains. Appropriately, and fortunately, it was locked. I went outside and looked at the double doors through which I had, months before, exited the "burial room"—clean doors, in steel frames set into the plain concrete wall, without hardware, signaling no access, and also no indication of where they led. Again, there was no notice, sign, or explanation, though there were the remains of two pieces of tape on the double doors, which suggests that some notice was removed from the doors.[52] And nowhere on the museum grounds was there any notice which indicated that one stood near, or above, what had been for some eight decades an opened Native American burial site, a tourist spectacle, a hallowed ground, and a scientific research site all in one. The stark exterior doors echoed both the immense silence in regard to those buried there centuries before and the complete disappearance of the intense debate which, finally "won," sealed not only the burial site but also public acknowledgment at the site that a controversy had ever occurred.

51. See discussion, chap. 4, above.

52. The presence of the tape on the exit doors was only later discovered in examining a photograph I took of the doors and the adjoining bare walls. During the April 1992 visit to the Dickson Mounds Museum, a staff member reported that, were the Illinois legislature to appropriate funds for the purpose, a filmstrip or video would be prepared in the future that might include some mention of the controversy.

On October 25, 1985, the Baltimore
Sun published an article in its
sports pages by Bill Carter, the paper's television critic:

SIX

Ditmar's Revenge

The very first commercial in the first inning of the ABC coverage
of the World Series summoned a nostalgic image from a bygone
baseball era.

Twenty-five years ago, the unforgettable matchup of the mighty
Yankees and the upstart Pittsburgh Pirates: 1960, Game Seven,
with everything on the line, score tied, Bill Mazeroski at the plate,
bottom of the ninth.

The commercial captured in a series of scenes the nation as it
was then, people huddled around radios at midafternoon listening
to the thrilling finish of the game, as called [on radio] by Baltimore's own Chuck Thompson. The sponsor was Budweiser,
though the beer's name appeared only at the end of the message
establishing a link between the beer and baseball's storied past.

Carter's presentation of the commercial is an effective one. One could
add that the commercial attempts—through something of a montage—
to capture an era and a moment in less than a minute of air time. While
Carter remarks that "the commercial captures in a series of scenes the
nation as it was then," one could also note—pedantically—that it is *but
one* reconstruction or reconstitution of the "nation as it was then." It is
certainly not a documentary treatment in the sense of editing actual
films from the period, but rather a carefully worked theatrical reconstitution of home, tavern, farm, and factory. It is history produced by television and by Madison Avenue in one of its most creative and powerful
forms, the beer commercial. The commercial purveys authenticity.
Carter writes on,

There was only one problem with this sweet memory—it had one
part of the drama all wrong. As Thompson called the inning . . .
he set up the dramatic final pitch by describing how Yankees
righthander Art Ditmar got ready to deliver . . .

But Art Ditmar never pitched in the game. Ralph Terry was on
the mound then. He threw the famed pitch that Bill Mazeroski hit
over the left-field ivy in Forbes Field. Terry was the man who
lived with that moment in baseball history as an albatross around
an otherwise distinguished career.

How could a commercial made with such loving care contain
such a colossal blunder?

Easy. The blunder . . . was made right then and there, on the air.

> Budweiser had merely repeated the error because the commercial
> uses Chuck Thompson's actual call of the play, which he made for
> NBC radio that afternoon in 1960.

In the same article, Carter reports a Budweiser spokesman explaining "such a glaring misstatement." "We were just unaware of it. We were simply going for authenticity." Carter comments, "What Budweiser got was an authentic blunder, magnified by history, national exposure and the technically pure sound of the commercial's production." And Carter reports the Budweiser spokesman's remarks that it was "certainly possible" that they would pull the commercial from the air.

There were other reactions to the commercial, and to the revelation of the error transported from the original radio broadcast to the television commercial. Chuck Thompson, the original broadcaster, remarked that

> he has never been "at all bothered" at that miscall, putting [it]
> down to one of those things that happens to announcers in the
> heat of the moment. "It had been a weird Series all around," he
> said. In fact, he pointed out, if you listen carefully, you can hear
> him make a second mistake on the tape used in the commercial.
> "After the home run, I have the Pirates winning 10–0 instead of
> 10–9."

Thompson also indicated that he had told the producers of the advertisement that the tape contained the error about Ditmar.

Three days later, Carter reported in the *Sun* that the "mistake" in the commercial was being reported in the New York press as well as in Baltimore and that Anheuser-Busch, the maker of Budweiser and owner of one of the teams in the 1985 series, was "getting calls from fans— 'hundreds of them'—who said they loved the commercial, but the guy had the pitcher wrong." Carter reported an Anheuser-Busch vice-president saying, "We decided that if there were a number of fans getting distracted from the good feeling in the ad, maybe we better change it." While in his story of October 22, Carter reported that the Budweiser people disclaimed prior knowledge of the error in the radio broadcast, in the article of October 25, he records the Budweiser vice-president acknowledging that "the filmmakers who had decided to leave the error in argued that it was an interesting bit of baseball trivia. 'But they didn't have to answer the phones.'"

One solution that the Budweiser people worked on was to add a short piece at the end which would note that "There was a little mistake in that commercial you just saw." But they abandoned this proposal when they estimated the cost of the additional segment. The correction they did make was to add some crowd noise to mute the reference to the pitcher's name, a change that cost "Maybe a couple hundred bucks. All it involved was a little technical work on the soundtrack." And the commercial was aired again on television during the succeeding games.

It is a trivial experience, though the fans who were animated by their recognition of the "error" did not necessarily take it lightly. Budweiser paid millions for the production and airing of the advertisement and they, along with their filmmakers, along with ABC television sports, were drawn into a crisis for which they were unprepared.[1] For other observers of the experience, it is an accessible contest over the meaning of authenticity, accuracy, and historical truth. The Budweiser producers believed that their confected presentation of the nation at the side of the radio in 1960 was a reach for authenticity. A collection of critics, newspaper writers, and viewers saw the more authentic version in getting the radio broadcast right, while the filmmakers themselves appear to have seen Thompson's error as imparting that bit more of realism to the film. For others it was another artful or not so artful beer commercial on American television.

The episode is one example of audiences and subjects participating in the production of their history—arguing over details on the past and arguing over the meaning of realism. Here, these had become matters of contest even in the most trivial of settings. While a 1985 television audience apparently accepted the partial and confected vision of their American past, circa 1960, a vision contrived to sell beer by the soft method (where were the freedom marches, the presidential election with the Kennedy-Nixon debates, Eisenhower's increasing impatience with what he saw as the military-industrial complex, the Cuban Revolution, Berlin, economic recession?), there was a startling reaction to the "glaring misidentification of the pitcher who threw the famous pitch" to Bill Mazeroski.

1. I gave this passage the title "Ditmar's Revenge" in December 1985, the implication being that Ditmar would get his "revenge" through the heady discussion of the Budweiser commercial 25 years after he was implicated in the broadcast of the Mazeroski game-winner. As this passage in the Fifth Roundtable position paper was about to be photocopied, my son Benjamin Cohen discovered a story in *Sports Illustrated*, March 24, 1986, 10, which he had just received. The story notes, "Art Ditmar has never thought the call was wonderful . . . and he didn't appreciate Budweiser's dredging it up. Ditmar, 56, who works as the recreation director in Brook Park, Ohio, has filed a lawsuit in U.S. District Court in Cleveland against Anheuser-Busch and the agency that produced the ad, Needham, Harper Worldwide of Chicago. Ditmar's suit makes no mention of [Chuck] Thompson's bum call, but claims merely, 'The Budweiser commercial's reference to plaintiff was false, because plaintiff did not throw the pitch which cost the Yankees the 1960 World Series.'

"Ditmar's Revenge" provides a curious backdrop in which to observe the silencing of the past in the Clarence Thomas and Anita Hill interrogations in the recent Senate Judiciary Committee hearings in Washington in 1991 and 1992. On the one hand, questions from members of the Judiciary Committee seemed posed to determine—against all odds— exactly what happened in both private and public spaces years before. While the history of events—truth, true accounts, accuracy, credibility— were at the center of the inquiries, virtually no one on any side sought to place the alleged events/non-events in the contexts of known public events and debates of the time.[2] Was this absence of "history" in the very search for "historical truth"[3] a silence somehow enacted by parties on both sides? And while there has been a great deal of writing about the "Hill-Thomas hearings" since their conclusion,[4] one still awaits an "ethnography of the moment" which would explore the social and political worlds of Washington in the early 1980s, in which the personal and intimate, and also working, lives of Anita Hill and Clarence Thomas intersected.

*

Peering into the work of historical replication at Colonial Williamsburg allows one to view a sociology of practice of historical replication in which an "absence" is carefully crafted within (or, better, away from) the construction of replications of the past. Colonial Williamsburg exists in our time and refers to the eighteenth-century colonial capital: Williamsburg, Virginia. Colonial Williamsburg is a "living museum" and at the same time the working laboratory of efforts at reconstructing society

---

Ditmar says his reputation has been tarnished and is asking $500,000 in compensatory and punitive damages."

The case was eventually dismissed by the court without an award of damages or a declaration of wrong.

2. Of course Anita Hill attempted to contextualize her anxieties in the period when President Reagan was exercising the idea of trimming out the United States Department of Education.

3. Curiously—or significantly—this discrepancy between the interrogation of truth and the reconstruction of the past may mark the challenge of historical practice; consider the work of Carlo Ginzburg, *The Cheese and the Worms: The Cosmos of a Sixteenth-Century Miller* (Baltimore: Johns Hopkins University Press, 1980), in which Ginzburg's task is to wrest a comprehension of Menocchio's intellectual development from the effort of a court of the Inquisition to establish through close investigation and interrogation the *truth* of that development.

4. See, for example, the diverse essays in Toni Morrison, ed., *Race-ing, Justice, Engendering Power: Essays on Anita Hill, Clarence Thomas, and the Construction of Social Reality* (New York: Pantheon, 1992).

and culture in seventeenth-, eighteenth-, and early nineteenth-century North America. Within the laboratories, researchers create and maintain among the most comprehensive inventories of data anywhere available on ceramics, papers, paints, furnishings, clothing, gardens, architecture, and lifeways in the Americas. Outside the laboratories, Colonial Williamsburg has attempted to replicate with "historical precision" the look, feel, smell, sounds, and order of Williamsburg in the eighteenth century.

More than a million people visit Colonial Williamsburg each year, many of them searching out the inner recesses of meticulous authenticity in the twentieth-century replication of a disappeared world, which is what the staff of Colonial Williamsburg reaches for.[5] Other visitors may seek an imagined and idealized preindustrial world, seen as a budding point for the American constitutional system. Others may look for ideas for the redecoration of their own homes and gardens.[6]

Expert knowledge has been deeply involved in this project of historical replication.[7] There are problems of how sources are to be read, of gaps in the sources, of how such elements as eighteenth-century wall-

5. In 1985, 1,075,000 tickets were sold for Colonial Williamsburg. This does not include visitors to the Carter's Grove Plantation nearby, which the foundation operates. The foundation estimates that three and a half million visitors ate meals in the immediate vicinity of Colonial Williamsburg. Dennis O'Toole, Cary Carson, and Rex Ellis are three of the professional staff who were critically involved in identifying and wrestling with a far greater range of interpretive questions than those noted here.

6. Several years ago I was invited to the opening of an extraordinary exhibition of African textiles at the Textile Museum in Washington, D.C. I anticipated meeting there a number of Africanist scholars based in the Washington area, but I found myself a fairly solitary member of that community amidst a great number of interior decorators. Drue Fergison has produced a valuable study of one "ground" lying between interior decoration and African cultural practice. See "Chiyavayo: Interior Decorating with the African Mbira," Passages 2 (1991): 2–3.

7. For a valuable inquiry into such issues in a different setting, see Timothy H. Breen, Imagining the Past: East Hampton Histories (Reading, Mass.: Addison-Wesley, 1989). Elsewhere, Carolyn Hamilton has whimsically reflected on the role of academics as arbiters of public interrogation of claims to authenticity, specifically, the claims relating to "Zulu cultural weapons." "[Journalists besieged university anthropology departments, the imagined 'experts' on the matter with urgent questions: 'What is a "cultural weapon"?' 'Is it real, this Zulu tradition "thing"?' Finally, when asked to judge whether 'fold-up spears . . . roughly 50cm long . . . [with] detachable blades that screw into rectangular metal bases, and . . . fit snugly into an easily concealable sheath made of industrial tape' were bona fide 'Zulu cultural weapons,' some of us contemplated unplugging the telephones." See "The Real Goat: Ethnicity and Authenticity in Shakaland," paper presented to the Institute for Advanced Study and Research in the African Humanities, Northwestern University, Evanston, Illinois, March 18, 1992, 36.

papers and paint should be reconstructed, of the specific types of domesticated animals of that period, and the differentiation of status reflected in clothing, footwear, hair-dressing, daily routine, and housing.

The experts of Colonial Williamsburg have, in recent years, faced certain problems that reflect not only upon the entire project of replication but also upon the distinctions in consciousness between eighteenth-century inhabitants of Williamsburg and twentieth-century tourists. One of these problems is the question of dirt and soil. Expert historians recognize that Williamsburg in the eighteenth century was replete with odors, dirt, soiled paint and wallpaper, but would twentieth-century visitors interpret such smells and soiling as authentic replications of the eighteenth century or as negative reflections of the present management of Colonial Williamsburg? Another is the grass; should it be left to grow in a rather wild way in the eighteenth-century manner since, in Williamsburg, there was less of a distinction between meadow or yard and lawn, or should it be trimmed to the twentieth-century specification of what a good home's lawn, or a community's common gardens, should look like? For many twentieth-century Americans, and presumably many visitors to Colonial Williamsburg, the quality of lawn, closely mown, without weeds, is a symbol of social character. Would an unkempt lawn unintentionally reflect negatively upon the folk of eighteenth-century Williamsburg or upon the management of Colonial Williamsburg itself?

A larger problem is what to do about the replication of the slave economy on which the wealth and order of eighteenth-century Williamsburg was based. Historians recognize that Africans were in and around Williamsburg in the eighteenth century in considerable numbers, sometimes doing onerous field labor, sometimes performing services for their masters, sometimes in transport and marketing, sometimes recreating on their "free time," sometimes being bought and sold, and present in various conditions of health and unhealth and in varied dress and undress. How shall Colonial Williamsburg replicate the precise conditions and appearances of oppression and degradation in eighteenth-century Williamsburg with the same replicative control with which it represents wallpaper, crafts, architecture, and cooperage? If one can successfully replicate and portray the blacksmith in apron, how does one deal with the field slave in loincloth in twentieth-century America? Who shall play the field slave and how? And what will the visitor read from the exact portraiture of men, women, and children of African descent, often unclothed, digging in fields adjoining Colonial Williamsburg? Moreover, how will the play, in this instance, affect the players?

The small questions raised here are not intended to undermine the mission of Colonial Williamsburg; indeed, these are issues that have been raised within planning discussions by the staff of Colonial Williamsburg themselves.[8] These questions expose some distinctions between past on the one hand and present consciousness on the other. Portraiture and replications allow a view of some things but not others. We may confer authenticity and accept the legitimacies of certain portrayals through some noticed effects—or clues or signals—which are confirming of the world as we think it ought to be. Things that jar our readiness to believe, as opposed to confirming our senses of what should be there, may be viewed as consequences of shortages of funds or staff or simply poor management (unmown lawns or chipped paint).

Several years ago, I was given permission to observe historical conservators at a National Park Service laboratory in Harper's Ferry, where meticulous work was underway to replicate Booker T. Washington's study at the Tuskegee Institute as it appeared in photographs taken on one day just after Washington's death. Upon completion of the research and gathering of materials, the rehabilitation of the study on the Tuskegee campus was to be done. The conservators were working to the rule of the detail in the photographs; for example, they sought out antiquarian booksellers to acquire the precise editions of books pictured with the intention of putting them on tables and shelves exactly as they appeared in the photographs. The reconstruction would capture a private space in the life of a learned man and produce an image of both quiet and clutter; it would leave an immense silence concerning the haunting controversies in which Washington was involved throughout his days at Tuskegee, with college trustees, townspeople, and contentious intellectuals and nationalists on both sides of the Atlantic.

In these and other situations, one may observe groups of experts or authorities discussing and planning how replications should appear,

8. An article, "Filling in Historical Omissions: Life of Slaves Shown in Tour of Williamsburg," which appeared in the *Evanston Review* (Illinois), February 6, 1992, pages T3–4, reports the growing attention to slavery in Colonial Williamsburg. The author, Irene McMahon, notes, "For decades visitors to the Colony have taken the regular walking tour through the buildings of Williamsburg, an informative tour of the architecture, the historic aspects of the sites, the leaders, the fashions and events of colonial social life ... But, some of the one million visitors who came every year had begun to ask, 'Where did the poorer people live? What kind of work did they do?' Even more telling was the absence of black Americans in the throngs of tourists who visited annually ... Since 1980, a transformation has been happening, moving the ambience of Williamsburg away from an idealized Colonial life to an emphasis on a portrayal of the more realistic Colonial world of that time, riven with class and racial divisions, civility mixed with savagery" (T3).

how the authentic will be presented, how history will be done.[9] These situations recall the far less researched turn-of-the-century replications of African villages in ethnological exhibitions in Hamburg and St. Louis, Wild West touring companies in the cities of the "American East" and Europe, and a 1980s Liberian village in the Baltimore Zoological Park.[10] In the film *Out of Africa*,[11] Denys Finch-Hatton's biplane was reproduced in much the way it appears in a scrapbook photo preserved by Kamante, a servant of Karen Blixen in Kenya.[12] And while the film company worked diligently to match the plane precisely, the producers and director showed no similar concern to match the character of Finch-Hatton in the film to the character known to Karen and others in the early Kenya Colony. Moreover, to the viewer of the film, it is not clear whether the African servants and Kikuyu neighbors of Karen are

(i) portrayed as the film writers and director understood Karen saw them, through close study of her writings; or,

9. Sometimes, the limitations of replication are recognized by those who play the roles, for whom all the skill and ingenuity of playing a part may leave important issues unattended. In "Filling in Historical Omissions," Irene McMahon notes that when Rex Ellis, an actor, "was hired to play a slave who preached in the streets of Williamsburg, he wanted a chance to stop and talk about the character's life, his times and how he related to the people he lived with. After he asked the research department for a chance to talk more about the character he played, the rules were changed to allow actors to abandon their characters periodically and give a brief history lesson."

10. Carolyn Hamilton has been studying "Shakaland" in South Africa. During a presentation of a work-in-progress—"The Real Goat: Ethnicity and Authenticity in Shakaland"—at Northwestern University, March 18, 1992, the members of the seminar were given access to a text of a large sign-board at the entrance to the park. "The romance which surrounds the name of the Zulu nation has lingered on for a century or more since the days in the mid 18 hundreds when their exploits were blazoned in dramatic headlines across the world. The tales of their deeds during those warring years read like the legends of forgotten time. But the Zulu epic is no fantasy! Today below the hills where once stood KwaBulawayo, the great military kraal of King Shaka, lies SHAKALAND." "The Real Goat" refers to a goat on the premises of Shakaland which is reputed to have been in the made-for-television series *Shaka Zulu*.

11. On the second day after the 1986 Academy Awards, in which the film *The Color Purple* got no Oscars after receiving eleven nominations, the Baltimore *Sun* reported that one "Black organization" was continuing to assault the racist stereotypes of "Blacks" in the film while a civil rights organization in Los Angeles was suing the academy for racial discrimination in passing over the film in the awards process. Curiously, as various and sundry individuals picked up the seven Oscars for *Out of Africa* on that Monday night, no mention was made of Kenya, Kenyan actors and staff, and Kenyan cooperation (and distress) in the production of the film.

12. Peter Beard, collector and editor, *Kamante, Longing for Darkness: Kamante's Tales from Out of Africa* (New York: Harcourt Brace Jovanovich, 1975), chap. 16.

(ii)   as they might have been known and understood by those of her time, including the Africans of that time themselves, who have indeed left records such as Kimante's scrapbook and diary; or,

(iii) as a film-going audience in the 1980s would expect to see them; or,

(iv)   according to stock caricature among Hollywood writers and directors; or,

(v)   as some compromise between one of the above conventions and what the Kenyan actors—and the Kenya government—would allow.[13]

While one can recognize different levels of skill in these large and expensive public endeavors in historical production—compare Colonial Williamsburg to the Old Europe component of the nearby Busch Gardens—one perhaps cannot underestimate the enormous power of these productions upon the consciousness of the present. Tremendous public debates developed over the authenticity of images of southern U.S. society in *The Color Purple*, over the depiction of people of Italian descent in *The Godfather* films, and over the presentation of Africans in *The Gods Must Be Crazy*. The debates are not merely about characterization but about whether, because of the characterization, the productions are so charged and venal that the films should be suppressed. In respect to *The Color Purple*, the novelist's and the filmmaker's presentations of African-American family life in the American South in the 1920s invaded the intimate lives of African-American men and women through debates over the accuracy of these images,[14] as have the films of Spike Lee more recently.

Jacqueline Bobo has written on the conflicted reception of Stephen Spielberg's film *The Color Purple* among African-American men and women and also among critics of different orientation. In developing

13. One reviewer, Pat Aufderheide (*In These Times*, January 20–February 4, 1986, 20) wrote that "the movie maunders through its nearly three hours in a style that [director Sydney] Pollack describes as 'pastorale,' in which are revealed 'large truths in very small, specific details.' The details are specific enough, although not necessarily small. But any truths, large or small, remain locked in the same closet where *Out of Africa* is keeping the relationships between colonists, their compatriots in the imperial center, and most crucially the colonized. The culture of colonialism is structured around avoidance of reality, of course. But uncut nostalgia is not a motor for a movie.

14. See, for example, E. R. Shipp, "Blacks in Heated Debate over *The Color Purple*," *The New York Times*, January 27, 1986; Barbara Smith, "*Color Purple* Distorts Class, Lesbian Issues," *Guardian*, February 19, 1986; C. Milloy, "A 'Purple' Rage over a Rip-Off," *The Washington Post*, December 24, 1985; and Michele Wallace, "Blues for Mr. Spielberg," *Village Voice*, March 18, 1986.

her work on the reception of the film, Bobo undertook a number of interviews that helped her construct a view of her audience. One of the black women she interviewed told her,

> When I went to the movie, I thought, here I am. I grew up looking at Elvis Presley kissing on all these white girls. I grew up listening to "Tammy, Tammy, Tammy" . . . And it wasn't that I had anything projected before me on the screen to really give me something that I could grow up to be like. Or even wanted to be. Because I knew I wasn't Goldilocks, you know, and I had heard those stories all my life. So when I got to the movie [Purple], the first thing I said was "God, this is good acting." And I liked that, I felt a lot of pride in my Black brothers and sisters . . . By the end of the movie I was totally emotionally drained . . . The emotional things were all in the book, but the movie just took every one of my emotions . . . Towards the end, when she looks up and sees her sister Nettie . . . I had gotten so emotionally high at that point . . . when she saw her sister, when she started to call her name and to recognize who she was, the hairs on my neck started to stick up. I had never had a movie do that to me before.[15]

Bobo has also closely read texts from popular media discussing the film. She notes that on *The Phil Donahue Show*, of Donahue's panel, Tony Brown, the black television host and columnist, called *The Color Purple* "the most racist depiction of Black men since *The Birth of a Nation* and the most anti-Black family film of the modern film era."[16]

While the representations of African-American women and men in the film, and the distinctive and conflicting reception of these representations among "different audiences," set off extraordinarily powerful and painful debates, relatively few critics have chosen to remark on the representations of Africa in the dream-scenes in the film, which draw on prevalent commercialized American stereotypes of Africa *and* shock some Africans who have seen and commented on the film.[17] Films,

15. Jacqueline Bobo, "*The Color Purple*: Black Women as Cultural Readers," in E. Deidre Pribram, ed., *Female Spectators: Looking at Film and Television* (London: Verso, 1988), 102.

16. "Black Women as Cultural Readers," 90. The *Donahue Show* was aired April 25, 1986.

17. Tejumola Olaniyan, who may write an article on the silences of the critics on the representations of Africa in the dream sequences, has shared some of his observations with me, as has Abena Busia, who was herself on the *Color Purple* film set from time to time because her sister was playing one of the lead roles. One source has noted that within the dream sequence the two Africans are speaking Lingala and Swahili. The words of the Lingala speaker translate, roughly and rather inappropriately—given the dramatic moment—as "what's up, momma?!" I am grateful to Catherine Cole for passing this reading on to me.

as historical confections, are constantly filled with such "history produced"—intentionally, unintentionally, expertly, mythically, and so forth. Stephen Bach, in his recounting of the making of the film *Heaven's Gate*,[18] remarked on how the director Michael Cimino was attracted to the subject—the cattle war in late nineteenth-century Wyoming—by what he saw as the extraordinary issues of class and capital at stake in the struggles between investors and cattle barons on the one hand and landless immigrants on the other. In the making of the film, Cimino swapped the known figures around from role to role with considerable freedom, transforming the life histories and personal chronologies of most of the main figures from the available histories. Indeed, his method was such that the finished film (supposedly the largest commercial failure to that date in the film industry) came to resemble the historical narratives of twelfth-century England, as described by Nancy Partner:

> rambling discursiveness and irrelevance was once appreciated for its variety and elegance, for the general conventions of narrative literature in the twelfth century were easily applicable to history as it was then understood. The looseness of narrative structure, the universal taste for digression, the technique of interlacing, the basic impulse to juxtapose elements in accord with allusion or relations other than strictly logical or subordinating ones—all lent themselves to the materials and point of view historians commonly brought to their work. The expansiveness of narrative forms, their ability to include much diversity, along with an audience accustomed to understand connections or relations we find obscure, to read at length, and to appreciate ornament and digression—all conduced to fit history comfortably with existing narrative forms.[19]

Where Nancy Partner saw these elements composing a genre of historical prose in the twelfth century, the American film critic Pauline Kael saw these elements producing a mess in the Cimino film.

18. Stephen Bach, *Final Cut: Dreams and Disasters in the Making of "Heaven's Gate"* (New York: William Morrow, 1984). Valuable discussion of film and history and National Trust preservation and promotion of important residences in the United Kingdom is to be found in Michael Bommese and Patrick Wright, "'Charms of Residence': The Public and the Past," in Richard Johnson, et al., eds., *Making Histories: Studies in History-Writing and Politics* (Minneapolis: University of Minnesota Press, 1982), 253–301.

19. Nancy F. Partner, *Serious Entertainments: The Writing of History in Twelfth-Century England* (Chicago: University of Chicago Press, 1970), 210–11.

> Tisdale Divide
> Wyoming in the 1880s was an open range controlled by cattle
> kings. Some of the powerful stockgrowers thought rustling was a
> problem, but others were just as concerned about the influx of
> small operators who used government land grants which threat-
> ened the open range. John A. Tisdale, one of the small operators,
> was dry-gulched in a gully just north and east of this spot as he
> returned home from a shopping trip to Buffalo in late November,
> 1891. Locals were outraged by the killing of this respected family
> man.
>   Frank Canton, a former Johnson County sheriff, was accused
> of the murder, but he was never brought to trial. Stock detectives,
> such as Canton, were hired by the Wyoming Stock Growers Associ-
> ation to protect their large herds and to intimidate would-be
> ranchers.
>   The incident, coupled with the murder of Orley E. Jones a few
> days earlier, set the stage for the infamous invasion of Johnson
> County in April, 1992.[20]

About eight miles south of Buffalo, Wyoming, there is a trough in the prairie known in the late nineteenth century as Haywood's Gulch. The site has come to be identified as the Tisdale Divide. It was here on Monday, November 30, 1891, that an assassin stepped from behind cover as John A. Tisdale returned home, driving a wagon laden with Christmas gifts and winter supplies acquired over the previous days in the town of Buffalo. The assassin's first bullet passed through Tisdale's coat from the back, but ricocheted off the handle of the gun Tisdale was carrying under his coat and continued on and struck one of the two horses in the jugular vein. The assassin's second shot killed Tisdale. His body was found two hours later lying atop the load of toys by Howard Roles, Jack Donahue, and Tom Gardner, the three men having been alerted by Charles Basch and Elmer Freeman. From observations made earlier that morning along Tisdale's route home, Basch and Freeman were fearful that Tisdale had run into trouble and they raced to the sheriff's office in Buffalo, whence a search party was sent to investigate.

On Saturday, June 20, 1992, Tom Tisdale, a grandson of John A. Tisdale, stood at the Tisdale Divide before a large gathering, looking down onto the remnants of the track that Tom's grandfather had followed along Haywood's Gulch. The gathering of people from across the United States and Canada heard Tom describe at length and in great detail how his grandfather had died that day, November 30, 1891. The crowd at the

20. Historical marker along a road south of Buffalo, Wyoming.

gulch had been gathered up into buses early in the morning to tour a number of "Cattle War sites" as part of a weekend centennial commemoration of the Johnson County Cattle War of 1892.

The several hundred people looking down into Haywood's Gulch were caught up in the immense power and drama of Tom Tisdale's words. The killing of John A. Tisdale in Haywood's Gulch—"Grandfather was," Tom said, "dry-gulched"—constituted a signal event of the Johnson County Cattle War of 1891–92, which in turn was the subject of Michael Cimino's 1980 film, *Heaven's Gate*.[21] But whatever its moment in late 1891 or mid-1992, the assassination of John A. Tisdale was absent from Cimino's epic treatment.

*

In his 1985 book *Final Cut*, the film producer and Hollywood executive Steven Bach described his own first engagement with Michael Cimino's script.

> as the dining room [of the Polo Lounge of the Beverly Hills Hotel] drained of sun and patrons and we were preparing to leave, Joann [Carelli, a producer working with Cimino at the time—she was credited as "producer" of the finished film] handed me an envelope from her shoulder bag. It was another project, Michael [Cimino] explained, an official submission. He hoped I would like it. No . . . he hoped I would love it, as he did, as he had for several years now. It was a passion of his, he said fervently. It was called *The Johnson County War*, but he thought he could come up with a better title.[22]

In reviewing the discussions concerning the proposed film project, Bach provided a brief view of the historical episode that Cimino's script proposed to treat.

> The script was set in Wyoming in the early 1890s and told the story of a little-known incident in American history called the

---

21. According to most critics, a disaster; and of course the film was withdrawn almost completely from circulation upon its initial release.

22. *Final Cut*, 120. The jacket of the 1985 hardcover edition notes that "At the time of filming of *Heaven's Gate* Steven Bach was the senior vice-president and head of worldwide production for United Artists . . . Apart from the director and the producer, Bach was the only person to witness the evolution of *Heaven's Gate* from beginning to end." Bach relates that this first meeting at the Beverly Hills Hotel was on September 17, 1978 (p. 117). When he began the project of writing an account of the making of *Heaven's Gate*, Bach went back to his logs of meetings, travel, and telephone conversations to reconstruct the sequence and timing of much of the "action" of the narrative.

Johnson County War by those who note it at all. The closing
decades of the nineteenth century saw waves of emigration to
America from Europe, into both urban centers and rural areas.
Homesteading was populating the interior, and animosities
erupted often between homesteaders and prior landed interests—
cattle ranchers occupying vast tracts of western land, much of it in
the public domain. In Johnson County, Wyoming, this familiar cowboy versus settler conflict took a memorable turn when the cattlemen, organized as the Wyoming Stock Growers' Association (most
western states and territories had such groups), coolly hired mercenaries to kill Johnson County settlers suspected of cattle rustling,
a lively activity which had been impossible to stem with spotty
court convictions and fleet-footed defendants.

Though range wars were common enough movie material, what
distinguished this script was its claim that the episode was legally
sanctioned by the governor of Wyoming, the U.S. Congress, and
President Benjamin Harrison. In this context the mercenaries
were special deputies hired to enforce law and order, to suppress
"anarchy" by whatever means. They were to be paid per kill, like
bounty hunters. They were not vigilantes but executioners, and it
all amounted to a modest episode of legalized genocide with
strong class and racial overtones.[23]

Bach then introduced one core element of the Cimino script.

> Cimino's screenplay told this story [of the Johnson County war],
> centering on three fictionalized characters whose lives he lifted
> from contemporary accounts of Johnson County. Through them
> he imposed a love triangle on the vivid and violent massacre and
> battle which ended the script. It later became clear that Cimino
> had hewed very loosely to pure history in developing the script;
> but no one knew that at the time, and it would, in truth, have been
> irrelevant to evaluation of the potential of the drama as Cimino
> told it.[24]

*

Toward the conclusion of Cimino's *Heaven's Gate*, a scene opens with the
character Ella Watson (played by Isabelle Huppert) crouched over the
bullet-ridden body of Nate Champion (Christopher Walken). The character Jim Averill (Kris Kristofferson) rides into the scene on horseback,
dismounts, and approaches Ella. She holds a piece of paper in her hand,

23. *Final Cut*, 122–23.
24. *Final Cut*, 123.

a scrunched note, the text of which the viewer glimpses for just a second:

> Nick died about . . . [indistinct] . . . It don't look as if there is much chance in my getting away. I hope they did not hurt Ella. The house is all fired. Goodbye Ella and Jim if I never see you again. Nathan D. Champion.

While the film does not show Ella pulling the note from Nate Champion's breast pocket, the viewer knows that this is a note that Champion himself hurriedly penned in a small book or diary as flames engulfed his cabin. Champion's friend Nick Ray [or Rae], played by Mickey Rourke, was earlier shot and killed in what is represented in the film as an overpoweringly lethal assault of a force of mercenaries hired by the Wyoming Stock Growers Association. The mercenaries have torched a wagon of hay and pushed it up against Champion's cabin. Champion takes a break from shooting at the attackers to pen an entry in his book, then tears the page from the book and puts the page in his breast pocket. The next glimpse we have of the paper—several scenes later—is as it appears in Ella's hands.

Ella looks up at her lover and comrade Jim Averill and hands him the torn piece of paper, which he reads aloud:

> It don't look as if there is much chance in my getting away. I hope they did not hurt Ella. The house is all fired. Goodbye Ella and Jim if I never see you again. Nathan D. Champion

On April 16, 1892, the *Chicago Herald,* under the by-line of its correspondent Sam T. Clover, published an account of the assault on Nathan Champion's cabin on the KC ranch.[25] The story purported to be an eyewitness report, Clover having accompanied the mercenaries from Cheyenne into Johnson County, Wyoming. The *Herald* reported,

> The roof of the cabin was the first to catch on fire, spreading rapidly downward until the north wall was a sheet of flames. Volumes of smoke poured in at the open window from the burning wagon, and in a short time through the plastered cracks of the log house puffs of smoke worked outward. Still the doomed man [Nathan D. Champion] remained doggedly concealed, refusing to reward them by his appearance. The cordon of sharpshooters stood ready to fire upon him the instant he started to run. Fiercer and hotter grew the flames, leaping with mad impetuosity from

25. Champion's cabin was located a few hundred yards south of what is today the center of Kaycee, Wyoming.

room to room until every part of the house was ablaze and only
the dugout at the west end remained intact.

"Reckon the cuss has shot himself," remarked one of the waiting marksmen. "No fellow could stay in that hole a minute and be
alive."

These words were barely spoken when there was a shout,
"There he goes!" and a man clad in his stocking feet, bearing a
Winchester in his hands and a revolver in his belt, emerged from a
volume of black smoke that issued from the rear door of the house
and started off across the open space surrounding the cabin into a
ravine, fifty yards south of the house, but the poor devil jumped
square into the arms of two of the best shots in the outfit, who
stood with leveled Winchesters around the bend waiting for his appearance. Champion saw them too late, for he overshot his mark
just as a bullet struck his rifle arm, causing the gun to fall from his
nerveless grasp. Before he could draw his revolver a second shot
struck him in the breast and a third and fourth found their way to
his heart.

Nate Champion, the king of cattle thieves, and the bravest man
in Johnson county, was dead. Prone upon his back, with his teeth
clenched and a look of mingled defiance and determination on his
face to the last, the intrepid rustler met his fate without a groan
and paid the penalty of his crimes with his life. A card bearing the
significant legend, "Cattle thieves, beware" was pinned to his
blood-soaked vest, and there in the dawn, with his red sash tied
around him and his half-closed eyes raised toward the blue sky,
this brave but misguided man was left to die by the band of regu-
lars [regulators?] who, having succeeded in their object, rapidly
withdrew from the scene of the double tragedy.

Clover noted that the mercenaries took away some of his possessions
(the firearms, in particular) and found, while searching the corpse, a
pocket memorandum or notebook, blood-stained and with a bullet hole.
Clover reported that under "the printed date of April 9th," one read, in
Champion's own words,

> Me and Nick was getting breakfast when the attack took place . . .
> Nick is shot, but not dead yet. He is awful sick. I must go and wait
> on him. It is now about two hours since the first shot. Nick is still
> alive; they are still shooting and are all around the house. Boys,
> there is bullets coming in like hail. Them fellows is in such shape I
> can't get at them. They are shooting from the stable and river and
> back of the house. Nick is dead, he died about 9 o'clock. I see a
> smoke down at the stable. I think they have fired it. I don't think
> they intend to let me get away this time.

It is now about noon . . . I feel pretty lonesome just now. I wish there was someone here with me so we could watch all sides at once . . . It's about 3 o'clock now . . . I shot at the men in the stable just now; don't know if I got any or not. I must go and look out again. It don't look as if there is much show of my getting away. I see twelve or fifteen men. One looks like (name scratched out). I don't know whether it is or not. I hope they did not catch them fellows that run over the bridge towards Smith's. They are shooting at the house now. If I had a pair of glasses I believe I would know some of those men. They are coming back. I've got to look out.

Well, they have just got through shelling the house like hail. I heard them splitting wood. I guess they are going to fire the house to-night. I think I will make a break when night comes, if alive. Shooting again. I think they will fire the house this time. It's not night yet. The house is all fired. Goodbye, boys, if I never see you again. Nathan D. Champion.

One might directly compare the Champion text momentarily visualized in Cimino's 1980 film with the similar lines reported by Clover as Champion's own words in the 1892 *Chicago Herald:*

Cimino Text	Clover Text
Nick died about . . . It don't look as if there is much chance in my getting away. I hope they did not hurt Ella. The house is all fired. Goodbye Ella & Jim if I never see you again. Nathan D. Champion.	Nick is dead, he died about 9 o'clock . . . It don't look as if there is much show of my getting away . . . I hope they did not catch them fellows that run over the bridge toward Smiths . . . The house is all fired. Goodbye, boys, if I never see you again. Nathan D. Champion.

In his representation of the death of Champion in what has come to be known as "the Johnson County War,"[26] Michael Cimino captured much of the detail of Clover's account: the full day assault, the death of Champion's companion Nick Ray, the firing of Champion's cabin, the penning of the diary entry, the killing of Champion in a hail of gunfire, the finding of the note, and some of the detail and language of the note.

While through a number of scenes of the film, Cimino sought to achieve detailed historical replication and a sense of authenticity, Cham-

26. But is also referred to as the "Johnson County Cattle War," the "Johnson County Invasion," "the Cattlemen's Invasion of Wyoming," "the Powder River Invasion," "the Powder River War," "the war on Powder River," "the Johnson County Insurrection," "the Cattle War of Johnson County," "the Cattle Baron's Rebellion," "the war on the rustlers," "the Wyoming Cattle War," and "the Wyoming Rustlers War."

pion's diary entry most fully unveils the problematical features of his filmic rendering of the past. Where in Clover's account the mercenaries, or invaders, find the diary or notebook as they searched Champion's body, Cimino shows Ella alone, and then with Jim Averill, with the page that Champion was seen to pen amidst the flames engulfing his cabin. And where the Clover text has Champion bidding farewell to the "boys," the Cimino text has Champion saying "goodbye" to "Ella & Jim."

*

On July 27, 1889, some twenty-seven months *before* Sam Clover filed his report from the KC Ranch to the *Chicago Herald*, the *Carbon County Journal*, published in Rawlins, Wyoming, reported that a telegram dated July 24, 1889, had been received by the *Cheyenne Sun*. The telegram, from Douglas, Wyoming, recorded that

> Hanging from the limb of a stunted pine growing on the summit of a cliff fronting the Sweetwater River, were the bodies of James Averell and Ella Watson. Side by side they swung, their arms touching each other, their tongues protruding and their faces swollen and discolored almost beyond recognition. Common cowboy lariats had been used, and both had died by strangulation, neither having fallen over two feet. Judging from signs too plain to be mistaken a desperate struggle had taken place on the cliff, and both man and woman had fought for their lives until the last.[27]

In his book, Bach also drew attention to the hanging of Ella Watson and Jim Averill in 1889, "three years before the Johnson County War." Bach notes from his reading of contemporary sources, including O. H. "Jack" Flagg's 1892 articles in the *Buffalo Bulletin*,[28] that

> Averill . . . was not a federal marshal; he was the local postmaster and surveyor, who owned a general store and "sold a little whis-

27. Helena Huntington Smith, *The War on Powder River: The History of an Insurrection* (Lincoln: University of Nebraska Press, 1967), 125. In some accounts by contemporaries and some by historians, Averill's name is spelled with an *i*; in others, with an *e*. In the end credits to *Heaven's Gate*, Cimino chooses the former spelling: "Averill."

28. Published in Buffalo, Wyoming. Bach himself sees Flagg's writings on the war as the source or inspiration for Cimino's script. Bach writes, Flagg "was a cowboy turned cattleman, was blackballed by the [stockgrowers] association, and eventually earned his place on its death list. He participated in the Johnson County War and was its first historian, breaking into print in the *Buffalo Bulletin* with the first of eleven installments only two weeks after the war had ended. His account . . . is, one suspects, deeply self-serving, but no more so than every other contemporary account. These conflicting and historically ambiguous accounts inspired Michael Cimino's free use of dramatic license in his retelling, the September, 1978, version of which UA bought"; *Final Cut*, 146.

key on the side." He didn't go to Harvard, though one source indicates he may have attended Cornell . . . Ella Watson . . . was Averill's common-law wife, as well as mistress of the local bordello . . .
It is possible she was legally married to Averill but claimed not to
be in order to file her own separate homestead claim. In any event,
the charge that she accepted cattle in payment for her favors is
very likely true, for her nickname in history was Cattle Kate . . .
They hanged her . . . from a cottonwood tree, with Averill, one of
the few recorded instances in American history of the lynching
of a woman. The hanging occurred in the summer of 1889, three
years before the Johnson County War, but Averill and Watson became martyrs, symbols of the ruthlessness of the [stockgrowers]
association toward the homesteaders, and their relationship to
the war is very direct, if quite different from Cimino's reworking
of it.[29]

*

According to Bach's accounts, and from many press and journal reports
that came out during the making of the film, the history of the production of the film was rife with conflict, including the struggles for financial and artistic freedom fought for by United Artists producers and
directors working under new Transamerica Corporation conglomerate
control, the soaring budget (from $7.5 million to $36 million) and poor
monitoring of expenses of *Heaven's Gate*, the expanding and uncontrol-
lable length of the final versions of the film, the collapse of United Artists studio under the weight of the film's expenses, accusations of cruelty
to animals during the filming, the exposure of actors and extras to injury,
the ineptitude of various players, but most particularly those in the principal roles, the failure of the film in the eyes of most prominent film

29. *Final Cut*, 150. In Bach's narrative rendering of the Cimino script and in the final
version of the film, the topography of the events is also shuffled. The film places the
events of 1892 in and around Sweetwater, Wyoming, which was close to the location where
Watson and Averill were hanged in 1889, but Sweetwater is not actually in Johnson
County. The events of 1892 occurred in and around Buffalo. Moreover, the film places the
Stock Growers Association headquarters in Casper, whereas it was in Cheyenne that the
campaign against the residents of Johnson County was organized. The film was actually
shot in Montana and Idaho, and Bach recounts a conflict between the studio and Cimino
over his allegedly unauthorized purchase of 156 acres of land in Montana, for purported
use in making the film. In one biography and filmography of Cimino, it is noted that
Cimino had, in about 1984, a property in Montana where he would spend a great deal of
his time. See John Wakeman, ed., *World Film Directors*, vol. 2, *1945–85* (New York: H. W.
Wilson Co., 1988), 215–20.

critics, and the decision to withdraw the film from the market immediately after its first viewings.[30]

Some observers of the making of the film reflected on the rising costs of the production and the growing conflict between the director on location in Montana and head office, noting that the war between the cattle barons and the settlers was transfigured into one between the studio accountants and the film director and his location assistants.[31] Indeed, in reading Bach's account, which hardly provides expiation for his own participation in the "film disaster" and the collapse of United Artists, one senses the way in which the studio executives (and their financial overseers) may have come to constitute the 1979–80 representatives of the remote capitalist class who were the targets of Cimino's historical dramatization of heroic struggles of settlers on the frontier against the control and discipline of the cattle barons in Cheyenne and the eastern and European investors whose investments framed the struggle but who never set foot in Johnson County or, indeed, Wyoming. The communications between "actors" on the frontier and those "responsible" for finance in remote capitals were occluded by poor communication, intentional distortion and misreporting, and gross misunderstanding of the conditions of production at the site: cattle in 1885–92, film in 1979–80.

In seeking to extend the brief discussion of film as historical confection—a subject that was opened in the 1985 and 1986 drafts of "The Production of History" position paper—I found myself enravelled in a complex array of different interventions in the representation of "The Johnson County War" and of the multiplicity of sites and moments in which such interventions—including my own—were constructed. The lynchings of Jim Averill and Ella Watson were constituted as history through the reports of a young boy in Sweetwater, Wyoming, 1889, and a most interested writer, editor, and historian in Buffalo, Wyoming in 1892. The re-presentation of Ella Watson and Jim Averill in *Heaven's Gate*—with their survival into 1892—constituted an additional production of history, as Michael Cimino sought to reproduce and extend the arguments of O. H. ("Jack") Flagg and Asa Shinn Mercer. And unex-

30. The film continued to be screened in its full length version in a few cinemas abroad, and a videotape version of the full length version eventually was released into the video store and video library markets. It is also occasionally viewed on cable television in the United States. I first saw it in Leicester Square, London, a year after its release.

31. For example, *The Los Angeles Times Sunday Magazine*, August 26, 1979, carried a story entitled, "Shootout at the UA Corral: Artists vs. Accountants."

pected and unsought "interventions"[32] fell "onto my desk" as I was attempting to read the film as itself an intervention. As one entered the field of contest over explanation and representation of "The Johnson County War," from its "prehistory" in the 1880s to the commercialization of some of its perduring images, I came to recognize the multilayered, multisited, and multistranded *experience* of constituting a record and a comprehension of the war. Could one constitute a field of discussion that encompassed a boy in Sweetwater in 1889, an impassioned journalist in Buffalo, Wyoming, in 1892, a filmmaker in Los Angeles in the late 1970s, a marketer of clothing in Wilson, Wyoming, in 1992, and a *grenzgenger* from Evanston, Illinois, in 1991 and 1992?

*

In *Final Cut*, Bach provided several pages of narrative restatement of the Cimino script which, he reports, was handed to him by Joann Carelli at the Polo Lounge in Beverly Hills.[33] Within this narrative Bach offered a view of the scene in which Champion's note is found and read by the Ella Watson and Jim Averill characters, but his narrative engages the one scene with an array of other dramatic incidents:

> Averill, inflamed by Ella's rape [at her homestead by some of the mercenaries] and his realization of the inevitability of mass murder—legal or not—urges the debating factions at the roller-skating rink [which is used for town meetings] to stop arguing, take up arms, and resist the invasion with force. Ella arrives [at the roller-skating rink] with news of the mercenaries' attack on Champion's cabin, taking place as she speaks. We observe Champion's brave resistance and inevitable death in an avalanche of bullets. At the same moment the townspeople mount carriage, wagon, and workhorse, grab whatever weapon is at hand, and ride out of town to wage their rugged battle on the mercenaries, who lie in calm wait . . . The battle begins in blind turbulence. The townspeople, fervent but poorly equipped and badly organized, suffer heavy losses. The mercenaries, crisply efficient and professionally outfitted, pick them off one by one as an "accountant" keeps score

32. Such as a mail order catalogue for "Cattle Kate" clothing and a dramatically contextualized "message" of General Colin Powell to President Saddam Hussein. See discussions, below, in this chapter, and in chap. 7.

33. Bach's rendering of the original Cimino script reads as if it were composed after the completion of the film; it follows the film closely and seems not to reflect the many changes between first script and final product that Bach suggests occurred through the production process.

for the later bounty payments. Averill is wounded but as night falls, he steals from the battlefield to visit Champion's cabin, where he finds Ella mourning over Champion's bullet-riddled body, reading the farewell note we saw Champion scribbling to them in the last moments before his final gunning.[34]

Bach then turned from a presentation of the essential structure of Cimino's narrative to offer a fairly detailed and critical "historically informed" reading of the Cimino script, marking out at a number of points where the Cimino treatment and the historical accounts proceeded along different paths. But against the director's shuffling of historical detail, Bach reported that in 1978 United Artists was less concerned with the "dramatic license" Cimino took in retelling the history of the Johnson County War than with Cimino's three main characters through which "Cimino hoped to weld not only a romantic triangle but also a sort of three-tier class cake that represented a rough American social system of the period: the Harvard-educated eastern aristocrat; the American-bred laborer; the immigrant entrepreneur."[35]

In her December 1980 review of Cimino's *Heaven's Gate*, Pauline Kael provided some brief remarks on the historical grounding of the film:

> The writer-director Michael Cimino uses a garbled version of the Johnson County war as his subject. In Johnson County, Wyoming, in 1892, the Stock Growers Association tried to drive new settlers out of the state. The cattlemen claimed that settlers were stealing their cattle, and when they couldn't get the alleged rustlers convicted in the courts they hired mercenaries to hang them or shoot them.[36]

In his treatment of the life and work of Michael Cimino, John Wakeman noted that the film *Heaven's Gate*

> is based on an actual incident that took place in Johnson County, Wyoming, in 1892, when a group of cattle barons, with the tacit approval of the state government, raised a small army of mercenaries to wipe out more than a hundred German, Bulgarian, Russian, and Ukrainian settlers.[37]

34. *Final Cut*, 149–50.
35. *Final Cut*, 154.
36. Pauline Kael, "The Current Cinema: Poses," *The New Yorker*, December 22, 1980, 100–102; reprinted as "Poses," in Pauline Kael, *Taking It All In* (New York: Holt, Rinehart & Winston, 1984), 112–14.
37. *World Film Directors*, 2:217.

Wakeman's view of the ethnic or national origins of the "settlers" who became targets of the mercenaries in the "actual incident" on which the Cimino film is based is curious for it is a view that seems drawn more from the film, or from the reviews of it, than from sources on the "actual incident." What Wakeman took as the historical basing of the film, Pauline Kael saw as ridiculous inventions:

> Cimino is big on hubbub. The settlers are bizarrely homogeneous: a whole community from some Bulgarian village seems to have moved to Johnson County and another whole community from the Ukraine. The immigrants' languages and customs are intact, along with their choral groups; the women, in white babushkas, are bent low pulling a plow.

*

In the chaos of the town meeting at the roller-skating rink in Sweetwater, Jim Averill (played by Kris Kristofferson) draws the crowd of immigrant homesteaders and townspeople to order. Averill pulls a paper from his pocket and begins to intone a list of names, the death list of immigrants—variously settlers, homesteaders, townspeople, rustlers, tradesmen, family members, according to one's guesses concerning the social composition of the crowd in the roller-skating rink—prepared by the Wyoming Stock Growers Association and somehow obtained by Averill:[38]

Armani, P.
Armani, I.
Gorbistanski, G.[39]

38. Here, there may be an important ellipsis. According to Bach's narrative of the film script, Averill discovers that the governor has made the U.S. cavalry unavailable to him (Averill, the federal marshal), but has reserved authority over them himself. From the cavalry captain, Averill learns that Ella Watson's name is on the death list, and, presumably, he receives a copy of the list at that time, which he pulls from his pocket at the rink. It is possible, also, that Averill obtained a copy of the list while visiting the association headquarters early on in the film. According to discussions at the headquarters in Casper, as represented in the film, 125 names are on the list. In the film, Averill reads aloud the names of only eighteen. As far as this viewer can reconstruct, Averill's own name was not indicated as being on the list. The sheriff of Buffalo at the time of the invasion, W. G. Angus, was prominently figured in all contemporary renderings of the alleged death list.
39. An attempt is made here to transcribe the names accurately, but Kristofferson at points slurs the pronunciations. Moreover, each name is greeted with a volley of distressed voices and shouts, which in part obscure the hearing of the next name. In the case of "Gorbistanski, G.," could this be the same character listed as "Kopestovsky" (played by James Knobelock) in the film credits at the end. One might muse that somewhere amongst the communications of the "Harvard-educated" Averill, the investigators and

Schultz, D. V.
Kaiser, Alvin
Glover, Jr., B.
Schermerhorn, W. R.
Guthrie, W.
Watson, E.
Hastings, B.
Kurj, B.
Shabalaika, C.
Cleveland, T.
Rolly, T.
Koppelman, H.
Fritz, D.
Swan, S.
Korb, P.

In a letter dated November 2, 1913, one of the organizers of the 1892 invasion, W. C. Irvine,[40] wrote,

> We had the record of every man we intended to kill or drive from the country. We have never tried to deny that, and I for one have never had the slightest regret, or made the slightest apology for my part in it.[41]

Charles Penrose, a medical doctor who joined the invasion but then quit, later constructed a memoir of the events, and noted that nineteen names

---

detectives of the Wyoming Stock Growers Association, the Association's Executive Committee, and their scribes (not to say various script writers, editors, and others on the set) there may have been "errors" in the proper recording and pronunciation of the names on the death list.

40. In the film, Irvine's is a large part. He is represented as an alcoholic and sometimes ambivalent participant in the stockgrowers' adventure, and is played by John Hurt, in his first role in an American film. An early Cimino plan had Jack Lemmon playing this role. W. C. Irvine, referred to as "Billy" throughout the film and in some sources, opens the film as class orator at Harvard; the British to mid-Atlantic accent seems not so out of place in the Harvard setting, though Cimino actually filmed the Harvard commencement and Billy Irvine's oration at Oxford.

41. Irvine's letter is quoted in Helena Huntington Smith's *War on Powder River,* 193–94. Smith notes that two decades after the events, Dr. Charles Bingham Penrose, who had initially joined the invasion force as surgeon, but then dropped out, attempted to reconstruct a record of the events, through corresponding with some of the participants, including Irvine. These letters are gathered in the Charles B. Penrose collection at the Western History Research Center in Laramie, Wyoming.In a scene in *Heaven's Gate,* Michael Cimino has Irvine telling Averill that there are "a hundred or so" names on the list, and he refers to them as "emigrants" or "immigrants" depending on how one hears the slurred pronun-

were on the list. George Dunning, who participated in the invasion wrote a sworn confession while in the Johnson County jail in Buffalo. He noted that "30 rustlers in Johnson county" were to be killed and that the invaders "would terrorize the settlers in such a manner that 300 or 400 settlers that owned stock and were in sympathy with the rustlers, would leave the country the best way they could."[42] Another account suggests that seventy names were on the list.[43] Asa Shinn Mercer reported that

> The plan of the campaign, it is believed, was to go direct to Buffalo, kill Sheriff Angus and his deputies and there be reinforced with a large number of co-workers, when they would capture the town, kill twenty or thirty citizens, and then raid the settlements in the county, killing or driving out several hundred more, thus getting rid of all their enemies. After satiating themselves with the blood of Johnson county's citizens, they undoubtedly expected to make detours into Natrona, Converse and Weston counties, where they had dead lists in the hands of the mob, covering many settlers and some business men in each county. Spotters were already in each county locating the men to be killed.[44]

Various questions have arisen in regard to the composition of the death lists. No list, apparently, is extant. There are reports that lists, or

---

ciation of the word. When Frank Canton (played by Sam Waterston) speaks to prospective invaders in a freightyard, he announces to those he is trying to recruit that "We plan to wipe out publicly 125 thieves, anarchists, and outlaws." When Jim Averill reaches the saloon in "Sweetwater, Johnson County" (as the graphic laid over the scene notes, although Sweetwater is and was in Natrona County), where he finds a cockfight under way in the back of the bar, he reports to the saloon keeper that 125 names are on the list, to which he receives a response that that's just about "everybody in the county." In viewing the film for the "nth" time, I wondered whimsically if the cockfight wasn't included by Cimino to invite a reading of the "deep play" in the making of the film. But then, perhaps, it is an oblique reference to one of the leaders of the invasion, Major Frank Wolcott, whom the historian Helena Huntington Smith called "the bloodthirsty little rooster" (*War on Powder River*, 260).

42. The Dunning confession was first published in the *Northwestern Livestock Journal* in October 1892 and then reprinted by Asa Shinn Mercer, publisher of the *Northwestern Livestock Journal*, in his *Banditti of the Plains; Or, The Cattlemen's Invasion of Wyoming in 1892 (The Crowning Infamy of the Ages)* (first printed in Cheyenne, Wyoming, 1894; paperback edition, Norman: University of Oklahoma Press, 1987). The Dunning confession appears as an appendix, 151–95.

43. Robert B. David, *Malcolm Campbell, Sheriff* (Casper, Wyoming: Wyomingana, 1932), 151–52. Helena Huntington Smith regarded David's account of the planning of the invasion as the most detailed and credible account available.

44. Mercer, *Banditti of the Plains*, 47–48.

partial lists, have been published. One writer in Buffalo in April 1892, Mary S. Watkins, reported that the death list was found in Frank Canton's suitcase when the invaders were taken into custody by the U.S. army after the cavalry intervened to stop the siege of the invaders by the residents of Johnson County.[45]

One report has held that the *Boomerang* (Laramie, Wyoming) published a copy of the death list, but this is somewhat ambiguous. The *Boomerang* did publish in April 1892 a list of those who had been "murdered by the cattle associations of the state"; a few days later the *Buffalo Bulletin* published a revised and more complete version of the *Boomerang* list, noting the names of

Sie Partridge
Ella Watson
Jack Averill
Tom Waggoner
Nick Ray
Nate Champion
Jones [Ranger Jones]
Tisdale [John A. Tisdale].

Various sources do indicate that W. G. Angus, Buffalo's sheriff, his deputies (unnamed), Buffalo merchant Robert Roote, and Buffalo newspaper editor Joe DeBarthe were on the stockgrowers' death list along with Nathan D. Champion, Ranger Jones, and John A. Tisdale. If Jones and Tisdale were on the list that Frank Canton is said to have carried with him in a suitcase right through the April 1892 invasion, then the list existed for quite some months, as Jones and Tisdale were killed in November 1891. But, according to Helena Huntington Smith, there has been no trace of the list that Canton was purported to have had in his suitcase.[46] And no list has ever surfaced in any of the dozens of accounts and re-accounts of the events of 1891–92. One opinion voiced in June 1992 was that federal records, in code used by government and military officers allied with the invasion party who were communicating between Cheyenne and Washington, might contain an array of documenta-

45. Mary S. Watkins, whose brother was Buffalo's coroner, was one of the ten founding members of the Union Congregational Church in Buffalo in October 1884. The minister of the church at the time of the invasion in April 1892 was the Reverend Samuel Weyler, who only arrived in Buffalo a month earlier. Reverend Weyler had been born and raised a Jew in Germany, but converted to Christianity while an undergraduate at Knox College in Galesburg, Illinois. See Buffalo's Centennial Book Committee, *Buffalo's First Century* (Buffalo, Wyoming: Buffalo Centennial Committee, 1984), 185–86.

46. *War on Powder River*, 299.

tion, including the lists, which have been suppressed for the past century.[47]

The list that Kris Kristofferson pulled from his pocket and read in the tense scene within the roller-skating rink[48] is clearly imagined. It may not differ in length from some of the lists speculated or reported by various sources. Indeed, the Cimino death list might not differ greatly in its social composition—smallholders, homesteaders, tradesmen, merchants, townspeople, and so forth—from the social composition of the targets of the 1892 invaders (and those who were killed on behalf of the stockgrowers in 1889–91). But beyond this, Cimino's list confirms for him, and for some viewers and critics, the ethnic and national composition of the crowd whose appearance on the Wyoming landscape—in the film version anyway—so inflamed the large cattle companies, investors, agents, and detectives.

Cimino, at enormous expense, cast the smallholders, dirt farmers, homesteaders, and townsmen as struggling immigrants from somewhere in eastern Europe, confounding viewers and critics with unrecognizable tongues, curious customs. Again, Kael, in her review in the New Yorker, pointed out that "Cimino's hearty peasants have their simple, earthly pleasures—a cockfight, spitting on each other, brawling. When it comes down to it, they're just funny foreigners. They don't even discuss organizing themselves against the mercenaries; it takes a Harvard man (Kristofferson) to show them how to fight." In an important sense, Cimino's death list more closely represents the imagined composition of Clairton, Pennsylvania, his composite 1960s steel town, so richly de-

47. Personal communication from a participant in the Johnson County Cattle War centenary symposium in Buffalo, Wyoming, June 1992.

48. *Buffalo's First Century* reports that Mr. and Mrs. Sam Rosenthal moved to Buffalo in 1940 and established a roller-skating rink which they called the "Town Hall." The Rosenthals also operated the Bison Theatre and opened a drive-in cinema in 1950. Newspaper advertisements and notices in the Buffalo newspaper suggest that roller-skating was popular in Buffalo earlier in the century. If a viewer of *Heaven's Gate's* roller-skating excess locates this as another fanciful telescoping and conjuring of historical fiction on the part of Cimino, one might note that, according to the *Encyclopaedia Britannica*, a "great roller-skating craze swept the U.S. and western Europe after 1863." The improvement of the skate, with the patenting of the ball-bearing wheel in 1884, not only made the sport more accessible, but located its new popular growth at the same time as the town of Buffalo was experiencing a period of rapid growth. In the comedy film *Cat Ballou*, "set" in Wyoming in the early 1890s—with multiple references to water rights, rustling, and large-scale British investment—the worn out and drunken gunfighter Kid Sheleen, played by Lee Marvin, decries the decline of the old frontier, and of his old livelihood, remarking, "Why the last time I come through Tombstone, the big excitement there was about the new roller rink they'd laid out over the OK Corral."

veloped in *The Deer Hunter* (1978), than it does the population of Buffalo, Wyoming, in April 1892. Indeed, one may ask if Cimino's view of European immigration on the Sweetwater in 1892 isn't a continuation (or backdrop) to his presentation of Clairton in the 1978 film. Pauline Kael did not point to this comparison, but her earlier review of *The Deer Hunter* is suggestive of an intent on Cimino's part to construct and sustain, through the use of intense detail, extended description, and sweeping visions, particular filmic images of European immigration in nineteenth and twentieth-century America. Kael wrote,

> When we first see the three men [Michael, Nick and Steven], it's 1968, and they are in a steel mill, on the floor of the blast furnace; at the end of the shift, they go from the blazing heat to the showers. It's their last day on the job before they report for active duty [in the U.S. military] and the other workers say goodbye to them. Then they move through the casual sprawl of their hilly mill town, Clairton, Pennsylvania, to their nearby hangout—Welsh's bar—to guzzle a few beers and loosen up. Each step of their day is perceived in ritual terms. The big ritual is to come that night: Steven's wedding at the Russian Orthodox Church and then the celebration at the Clairton chapter of the American Legion . . . We spend about three-quarters of an hour [film running-time] in the church and the hall; the moving camera seems to be recording what's going on in this microcosmic environment—to be giving us an opportunity to observe people as they live their lives. The long takes and sweeping panning movements are like visual equivalents of Bruckner and Mahler: majestic, yet muffled.
> . . . [In the church] and in the Legion hall, there are uninterrupted panning movements in which we see people singing and dancing, flirting and fighting, moving from one group to another. And it has a detailed clarity; we feel that we're storing up memories. There's something nostalgic about this ceremonial view of ordinary American community life even as it's going on . . . The brilliance of his panoramic ensembles sometimes gives us the idea that in seeing so many things so quickly we have come to know these people. They don't actually reveal much more than the convivial crowds in a beer commercial do, yet we're made to feel that what we see is all they are. (A great director would plant doubts in us.)[49]

49. Pauline Kael, *When the Lights Go Down* (New York: Holt, Rinehart & Winston, 1980), 513. In her review of *Heaven's Gate*, Kael is also drawn to Cimino's focus on crowds, but is not quite so respectful of his methodology or prepared to admit a success: "The vistas and the crowd scenes are huge, as in a David Lean Epic, but not so static or literal-minded.

*

In April 1992 a friend in Evanston received a mail order catalogue from "Cattle Kate, Post Office Box 572, Wilson, Wyoming 83014" (tel. 800-332-KATE). On page two of the catalogue, there is a block of text and three photographs. The text reads,

> Cattle Kate designs contemporary clothing to give you the look and feel of the Old West. It is a style conceived through the dreams of a young woman working as a miner in Atlantic City, Wyoming, pop. 45. She lived, much as our pioneer forefathers might have, in a cabin without power, and chopped her own firewood. She soon acquired the nickname Cattle Kate from the townfolks, in memory of another independent woman, Ella Watson, the original Cattle Kate, a colorful Wyoming homesteader of the 1800s. She began sewing old west style dresses and petticoats for fun, and her clothes attracted so much interest when she wore them dancing that the beginnings of today's company were born. Today, Cattle Kate clothing is sold around the country and around the world. All feature fine natural-fiber fabrics and are made in rural America with great attention to craftsmanship and detail. Cattle Kate designs let you wear a little of the frontier sprit, romance and values in today's modern world. Kate hopes you find, in her designs, a little of the quality, honesty and strength that she has found in our frontier past.

Below the text is a color photograph, with a chuck wagon and several models in the foreground.[50] A woman in a long red "prairie dancer dress"[51] is serving coffee and three mustachio-ed male models with three variants of cowboy hats are in different stages of getting coffee or

---

Cimino's is a different sort of madness—he goes for mood, atmosphere, movement . . . Cimino is big on hubbub."

The "planting of doubt" may have been what the directors of the 1985 Budweiser commercial were about in introducing a "mistake" to the advertisement, though not recognizing what "harvest" of criticism Budweiser would receive from the doubters. Of course, before he began directing major motion pictures, Cimino himself was crafting in New York what were regarded as the day's highest quality commercials.

50. At the Cattle War centenary symposium in Buffalo, Wyoming, in June 1992, one of the speakers, Mark Harvey, challenged the identification of Nate Champion in what was purported to be "the only known photograph of Nate Champion in existence." Arguing that this claim was spurious, Harvey showed another photograph of several men at a chuck wagon and pointed to one of the men in the photograph as Nate Champion, noting that this chuck wagon scene contained "the only certain photographic image of Champion."

51. "Cattle Kate" catalog, 21.

"grub." A woman on horseback appears in the mid-background, and snow-covered mountains form a (painted?) backdrop of the prairie landscape.

To the left of the Cattle Kate text is a small inset color photograph of a woman wearing a blue and white print dress, and astride a horse, with the caption, "Cattle Kate, a.k.a. Kathy Bressler, 1990. With her wonder horse Clyde." To the right of the text is a small inset sepia photograph of a woman astride a horse, and she is wearing what appears to be represented on pages 18 and 19 of the catalogue as a

> finely tailored Walking Skirt & Jacket . . . Skirt has two side pockets and is fully gathered in back for a bustle effect. The jacket is very fitted, with piping detail. Fabrics and colors change from time to time; ask what's new when ordering.

There is a caption below the sepia photograph, which reads "Cattle Kate, a.k.a. Ella Watson, circa 1890."[52]

In *Final Cut,* Steven Bach remarked that Ella Watson was called "Cattle Kate" because she was known to have accepted cattle in return for favors at her bordello. Contemporary writers and historians similarly noted the nickname, but Bach also offers that Ella, when "she was dragged from her cabin to be strung up reportedly protested they couldn't hang her because she wasn't wearing her 'new print dress!' They hanged her anyway."[53] In *The War on Powder River,* while not noting Watson's last plea for her "new print dress," Helena Huntington Smith devoted considerable attention to the hanging of Ella Watson and Jim Averill. Smith opened an interrogation of the reputations Watson and Averill "enjoyed" before the lynchings and of the enlarged and diverse reputations that developed after their deaths. Following reports of the

52. In early May 1992, I was in Houston at a conference, Writing the Luo, at the Center for Cultural Studies, Rice University. One evening we went to dinner at the Calypso Caribbean Cuisine restaurant in University Village. The menu is rich in maps and "cultural detail," and each item on the menu is accompanied by the name of an island or country, for example, "Fish Steak with Papaya Salsa—Haiti—Fresh grilled fish steak with papaya, onion, cilantro, and lime." The menu closes with an essay on the Caribbean, its history from 1492, its geography, economy, its foodstuffs, and its cuisine, as well as a paragraph on the origins and meanings of the term "Creole." "Sometimes in the Caribbean it is defined as 'all mixed up and born in the islands' . . . the same amalgam of races that created the population created the Caribbean cooking." As the marketing of Cattle Kate clothes around the figure Ella Watson manages to avoid mention that Watson was lynched, so the Calypso Caribbean Cuisine menu is able to discuss Caribbean cuisine in all its variety, and the Caribbean in the past, with no mention or hint of the history of slavery and the slave trade.

53. *Final Cut,* 151.

lynchings, different groups and individuals attempted to situate the Watson and Averill reputations, or biographies, within arguments for remediation of specific murders, of alleged rustling, of unlawful seizure of land, and of unauthorized butchering of cattle.[54] Writing about Ella Watson, Smith remarked

> Out in the sagebrush near the Sweetwater River Ella kept what the West prettily called a hog ranch. That is, she catered to her customers in their own wild and woolly surroundings instead of amid the lights of town. Twenty-eight years old at the time of her death, she was a farmer's daughter from Lebanon, Kansas, who had gone west and gone wrong as many another young woman had done without getting hung for it. There exists a picture of her,[55] a full-bosomed wench astride a horse with her full calico skirts flowing over the saddle and a sunbonnet on her head. Not bad-looking in a common way, and bright too, according to one who had made her acquaintance, she looked plenty good to woman-starved cowboys who would cover many a mile over dry sagebrush for such an inducement. She died at the end of a rope on July 20, 1889.[56]

The photograph of Ella Watson referred to by Smith is the same photograph as that of "Cattle Kate" in the mail-order catalogue.

*

There were other women on the Wyoming frontier who were known as "Cattle Kate." These women found their activities the preoccupation of lonely men and also of the agents and enforcers of the stockgrowers. At the time that O. H. Flagg was writing his eleven-part account of the Johnson County War, which ran in the *Buffalo Bulletin* in the weeks immediately following the battle at the TA Ranch, Eva Langhoff was defending her husband against charges that he had stolen seventeen

54. See Smith, *War on Powder River*, 121–34.

55. In the Cattle War commemorative symposium in Buffalo, Wyoming in June, 1992, one of the speakers, Mark Harvey, challenged the identification of Ella Watson as the woman in this photograph. Smith, who included the photograph in *War on Powder River*, reported that the photograph is archived at the Western History Research Center in Laramie, Wyoming.

56. *War on Powder River*, 122. According to Smith, page 134, Owen Wister, a Philadelphia attorney whose magazine stories and then his 1902 novel *The Virginian* would establish an essential text for further literary, filmic, and television treatments of justice on the western frontier, noted in his diary for October 12, 1889: "Sat yesterday in smoking car with one of the gentlemen indicted [sic] for lynching the man and the woman. He seemed a good solid citizen, and I hope he'll get off. Sheriff Donell said, 'All the good folks say it was a good job; it's only the wayward classes that complain.'"

horses from a cattle company.[57] The Langhoffs, Eva and Fred, and those they worked with, became targets of the enforcers in the employ of the Swan Land and Cattle Company, which ranched a region of the west stretching from Sidney, Nebraska, to Rock River, Wyoming, something like a half million acres.

In 1892, Fred Langhoff jumped bail and fled and was never found again by—evidently—wife, the law, the enforcers, or historians. In his study of *Tom Horn*, the Cheyenne historian Chip Carlson provided a brief history of the Langhoffs activities on the Wyoming rangeland. For his remarks on the Langhoffs, Carlson drew on an unpublished 1941 manuscript by Leslie Sommer, which he found in the collections of the Wyoming State Museum.[58] Quoting Sommer, Carlson noted that

> There were whispers that the Langhoffs' prosperity far exceeded their visible livelihood . . . There were rumors of the lure Mrs. Langhoff had for the strangers that came within their gates with horses or cattle to sell. Some of these strangers, falling under her spell, fell so deeply in love with her they figured they had received value personally, regardless of the profitless deal they may have made on their business arrangements.[59]

According to Sommer's account, Eva Langhoff was doing quite well, accumulating horses and cattle, even after the disappearance of her husband. Sommer noted that she took on as her foreman a "boy of nineteen" named Lu (or Lou) Bath. Lu "made no secret of his infatuation for his beautiful employer, but [?] it was noticeable that no steadily employed men were hired to work on the ranch after Lu was made foreman."[60]

The next year, 1893, the Swan Company's stock detective Tom Horn[61] arrested Eva Langhoff, Lu Bath, and others, and brought them in for

57. A photograph of Eva Langhoff (appearing to be posed in a studio) is held by the Wyoming State Museum in Cheyenne. The figure in the photograph resembles the woman astride the horse identified by Helena Huntington Smith and the "Cattle Kate" catalogue as Ella Watson. For a reproduction of the Langhoff photograph, see Chip Carlson, *Tom Horn: The Definitive History of the Notorious Wyoming Stock Detective* (Cheyenne, Wyoming: Beartooth Corral, 1991), 23.

58. "The History of the Sybille Country," June 22, 1941.

59. Carlson, quoting Sommer, in *Tom Horn*, 23–24.

60. Ibid., 24.

61. At the time of the stockgrowers' invasion, Tom Horn was said by some of those in and around Buffalo to have aided the invading army through preparatory investigations. Others identified him as one of the invaders; and some identified him as a look-out in the murders of Ranger Jones and John A. Tisdale in November, 1891.

justice on charges of cattle theft and butchering stolen cattle. Sommer recorded that

> Quiet investigation disclosed the fact that Mrs. Langhoff had large contracts for dressed beef in Laramie and Cheyenne. On learning of this Al Bowie [a detective] and Tom Horn decided to visit . . . unexpectedly, with witnesses, and have a look at the cattle being dressed for market . . . There were only three people working by lantern light, Lu, Mrs. Langhoff, and a man by the name of Bill Taylor, a drifter. The lawmen waited until the beef dressing was well under way before they approached the group. There was no chance of a getaway or to hide any evidence, as they were caught indisputably in the act of butchering stolen cattle[62] . . . Young Lu lost his head and started chattering, using the knife he was holding as a defense weapon. Horn ordered him to drop the knife, and on Lu's refusal, Horn gave him the ultimatum of dropping the knife by the count of three, or of being shot without parlaying.[63]

According to Leslie Sommer's account, Eva Langhoff lost her ranch, her cattle, her horses, and all her possessions, though she was not indicted. "Lu swore that he alone was guilty of the cattle stealing—that Mrs. Langhoff could not be held even as an accessory to the crime, as she did not know the cattle were stolen."[64]

On January 30, 1894, Louis Bath was sentenced to 18 months in the state penetentiary in Laramie. He was pardoned on January 8, 1895. According to Carlson, he then entered the University of Wyoming and played "football for the University of Wyoming's 'Never Defeated

---

62. In an early scene in *Heaven's Gate*, one sees a stock detective confronting an immigrant woman and a man cutting and preparing large pieces of meat, and then killing the man. "Behind a shelter of hanging laundry, an immigrant speed-butchers a rustled steer with a hatchet. His wife drags the steaming chunks of meat into their cabin as a child plays nearby. Suddenly the immigrant notices boots approach at the edge of the sheets hung to shield him from view. A rifle blast rips through the sheets, turning the immigrant's face as crimson as the hanging steer's hacked carcass. Nate Champion . . . enforcer for the Stock Growers' Association, puts down his rifle and walks off without a word as the immigrant's wife and child wail over his dead body, bleeding into the frozen earth" (Bach, *Final Cut*, 147).

63. Carlson, 25, citing Sommer. In a memoir which Carlson has read and cites, Gus Rosentreter, one of the two witnesses who went with Horn to the Langhoffs' ranch related many years later, "I went [with Horn and the others], and when we got to the place, they had several beef hanging up in a shed. One man had a big butcher knife in his hand and talked big. Tom Horn told him, 'Drop that knife or I'll put a bullet through your head.' The knife dropped and the show was over, except for watching the prisoners."

64. Carlson, 25, quoting Sommer.

Team'"[65] and participated in the Cheyenne Frontier Days rodeos. Carlson also noted that in 1924, Louis Bath moved to Pasadena, California
"where he worked in the movie industry for four years, appearing in
the now classic films 'Ben Hur' and 'The Sign of the Cross.' He had
seven children and died October 25, 1932."[66]

Louis Bath was not the only participant in the struggles between large
ranchers and alleged rustlers to move to Los Angeles.[67] Sam T. Clover,
the *Chicago Herald* journalist, also moved to Los Angeles, where he died
a wealthy man in 1929. Albert Bothwell, a neighbor of Jim Averill and
Ella Watson on the Sweetwater and one of those arrested on July 25,
1889, on charges of kidnapping and murdering Watson and Averill,
moved to Los Angeles in 1915 and died in Santa Barbara in 1928. Released on bail along with five others accused in the Averill-Watson
lynchings, Bothwell faced a grand jury proceeding in Rawlins, Wyoming, on October 14, 1889. Those charged were released from their indictments when it was discovered that all the witnesses had disappeared.[68] After the lynchings, Bothwell, who served on the Executive
Committee of the Wyoming Stock Growers Association from 1889 to
1902, got possession of Jim Averill and Ella Watson's ranches through a
convoluted land transaction.

In June 1892, O. H. ("Jack") Flagg—a rancher, writer, and newspaper
editor—published an account of the August, 1889, lynching of James
Averill and Ella Watson, as part of an eleven part, nearly instant, account
of "the Causes that Led to the Recent Invasion." Flagg remarked that

> The reason for murdering him [Averill] was the direct result of
> trouble he had with Bothwell over some fine meadow land that
> Bothwell was holding illegally. Averill being a surveyor, had de-
> tected the fraud, and had contested Bothwell's right to the land,
> and the contest had been decided in his [Averill's] favor only a
> short while before he was hung.

65. Carlson, 27.
66. Ibid., 27–28.
67. When Michael Cimino traveled from Beverly Hills to Montana to make *Heaven's
Gate*, did he know that decades before some exemplary participants had taken an opposite path?
68. Helena Huntington Smith, *War on Powder River*, 133, inventories the disposition of
the numerous witnesses to the lynchings, including one witness, Ralph Cole, who was
said to have been shot and his body reduced to ashes as he was seeking to reach a railway
station; and a young boy, Gene Crowder, who is thought to have died by "administration of a slow poison" by those who were claiming to be protecting him from the stockgrowers.

Flagg's source for his account was a young boy who had "rushed into Casper" and reported

> that a man and woman had been hung . . . that he saw and recog-
> nized the parties who hung them . . . prominent stock men, their
> names being Tom Suth, John Durbin, A. J. Bothwell, R. Galbraith,
> and James McLean . . . the boy . . . followed at a safe distance and
> saw those men take the man and woman from the wagon, bind
> them, put ropes about their necks and hang them to a tree; the
> poor woman begging for her life, but in vain; for with a coarse
> jest, that deacon in the Methodist church, John Durbin slapped the
> bound and helpless woman in the face as he threw the rope over
> the limp woman; and thus, with their toes touching the ground
> they were left to strangle slowly to death, while their inhuman
> murderers sat calmly by and gloated over the agony of their
> victims.

Flagg immediately offered some more direct comment on the lynchings, anticipating in important ways the challenge that Michael Cimino would face in translating complex historical experience and multiply-layered accounts into a new, and cinematic, account:

> My readers . . . will naturally ask: "Is this truth or is it fiction?"
> They say "It can't be true, men who rank high in the social and fi-
> nancial world, could not be guilty of such crimes." But it is true,
> every word of it, and the adage, "Truth is stranger than fiction," is
> clearly exemplified in this case.

SEVEN

Tisdale Divide

When I saw *Heaven's Gate* in London in 1981, I was struck by the argument concerning class and capital on the American frontier. The essential argument of the film seemed parallel to a great deal of important revisionist historical writing on eastern and southern Africa, perhaps most specifically the work of Gervais Clarence-Smith, Jacques Depelchin, Gavin Kitching, Mahmoud Mamdani, Shula Marks, Colin Murray, E. S. Atieno Odhiambo, Robin Palmer, Neil Parsons, Stanley Trapido, Charles van Onselen, and Roger van Zwanenberg.[1] While scholars in Africa were attempting to understand the forces of class and capital within what had previously been reckoned racial and ethnic conflicts over the control of labor and land,[2] Michael Cimino seemed in *Heaven's Gate* to have conjured, with considerable success and effect, an integration of ethnic subjects in a class-oriented critique of capital on a preindustrial frontier.[3] A partisan feeling about *Heaven's Gate* also grew perhaps from a sense that the film, having been withdrawn from distribution, had been subjected to a form of censorship or suppression. It had not struck me at the time that, first, *Heaven's Gate* could have possibly been viewed by serious film critics as a cinematic disaster; or, second, that historical representations within the film were substantially warped.

In looking at reviews of the film in 1985 and 1986, I was particularly struck by Phil Hardy's brief remarks published in *The Western*[4] that

1. See, for example, Robin Palmer and Neil Parsons, eds., *The Roots of Rural Poverty in Central and Southern Africa* (Berkeley: University of California Press, 1977).

2. A renewed attention to the role of European capital interests in the constitution of the political geography of southern Africa before industrialization, and to the role of such processes of capital in the constitution of an historical record, has come with the controversies surrounding the research and writing of Julian Cobbing and his students and colleagues. See chapter 3 for a brief discussion of this debate.

3. Perhaps forcing this sympathetic first reading (viewing) of Cimino's film was the context of London in September 1981, when I first saw *Heaven's Gate*. I was attending a conference on the family in Africa at the University of London, organized by Shula Marks and Richard Rathbone. Participants included the European historians David Levine and David Sabean and the American historian Herbert Gutman (who presented a compressed view of his book on the African-American family), along with a number of Africanist scholars, as well as several of those mentioned above. Among the subjects of the meetings were the pressures on norms and practices of family experienced within the capitalist transitions observed in Africa in the late nineteenth and early twentieth centuries and the disjunctures in patterns of small accumulation of households on the moving frontier as they experienced new pressures from capital as well as the exhaustion of resources long important to the regional economies of the African continent. On the day that David Le-

Much of the criticism of the film in America was devoted, not to
the complex and far too elusive structure Cimino hangs his story
on, but to the story's thrust—that a My Lai–type massacre was
only just averted in America—which was roundly (and utterly in-
correctly: the film's factual basis is clear) condemned as historically inaccurate. The script has the characters frequently and awk-
wardly talking about their class position—itself an unusual thing
in a Hollywood film—but Cimino . . . is able to present their grop-
ings and debates with a visual precision that is at times quite stunning. That said, the film's elliptical structure contrasts strongly
with the intense (almost fetishistic) realism of its look and its recreation of frontier life.

There was a sense that the density and complexity of Cimino's vision
simultaneously effected and occluded his argument that, far from finding America an open and welcoming land, immigrants faced, and defeated, the forces of raw oppression and effective genocide.

*

In December 1991, I was in the Great Expectations bookstore involved
in a discussion with Truman Metzel and Jeff Rice, the extraordinary
booksellers who run the operation on Foster Street in Evanston. Upon
my mention of Bach's *Final Cut,* Truman Metzel offered a quick and
vigorous denunciation of Cimino's *Heaven's Gate.* Truman's assault focused on what he saw as the gross inaccuracy of Cimino's representation
of the events in Wyoming. Truman based his critical authority on his
having lived and worked in Wyoming in the 1950s, on his having
learned generally about what happened, and on his having studied a
little book written at the time of the Johnson County war by Asa Shinn
Mercer, who was a witness to the events. Truman related that, in 1954,
when he was teaching school in Glen Rock, Wyoming, 120 miles south
of Buffalo, he had come across a just recently issued edition of Mercer's
account of the war, *The Banditti of the Plains.*[5] Truman wanted to talk with
people around Glen Rock about the war, and also to discuss it with his
students. He was warned off by various people in Glen Rock, who de-

---

vine and I attended *Heaven's Gate* in Leicester Square, I was eyewitness for the first time
to football violence in London, accompanied by racial combat in the streets of North
London, police battering of people of color, and, later in the evening, the savage beating
by cafe patrons of a purse-snatcher in Covent Garden.

4. In *The Film Encyclopaedia* (New York: William Morrow, 1983), 359.

5. First published, in Cheyenne, Wyoming, in 1894; new edition, Norman: University
of Oklahoma Press, 1987.

clared that this was dangerous stuff for those who were descendants of the participants. He was warned to be careful not to start the war all over again. In late 1991 and early 1992, Truman remembered that Mercer himself had been censured and ostracized for producing his book at the time of its first printing. He also recalled that the train which brought the Johnson County "invaders" to the end of the rail line just outside Casper (where they unloaded their horses and supplies) had stopped at Glen Rock, where the telegraph wires were cut and a stationmaster shot to prevent word reaching the Johnson County defenders about the invasion.[6]

I asked Truman to place an order for the Mercer book. In February 1992, the book arrived and I collected it from Great Expectations and began to study its account, setting it against the film, Bach's text on the film script, Bach's treatment of the making of the film, and various reviews, copies of which I had in hand. I was considering the opportunity which the "discovery" of the book held for extending the discussion of the film's representation of the past,[7] cursorily mentioned in the original, 1986, draft of "The Production of History" position paper for the Fifth Roundtable.

In presenting a history of the Johnson County War, Mercer, like Flagg and later Cimino, pilloried the Wyoming Stock Growers Assocation. Mercer, who published Banditti in 1894, developed his account through a critique of the role of capital in the organization of cattle production in eastern Wyoming in the 1870s and 1880s. Mercer, like Flagg, but unlike Cimino, located the changing face of foreign and eastern capital in the context of changing environmental conditions on the prairie, in which agents of the absentee investors as well as the large resident stock growers sought to explain the declining stocks and quality of the herds on the prairie by reference to rustling (theft of branded stock, illegal appropriation of unbranded or maverick stock belonging to the big operations, forged and counterfeit brands) and by blaming small ranchers,

6. Later, Truman Metzel and I found difficulty in confirming these Glen Rock "memories" of the invasion. However, the invasion train certainly passed through Glen Rock (previously known as Deer Creek) on its way to the unloading site at the Casper yards. As a kind of confirmation of Truman Metzel's recollection of the shooting of the stationmaster, Part 2 of *Heaven's Gate* does open with the brutal murder of Cully, the trainmaster (played by Richard Masur), who—while trying to reach Averill to warn him of the invasion—is intercepted by the invading party.

7. I saw an opportunity to model this "reading" of *Heaven's Gate* on Carolyn Hamilton's brilliant critical study of the making of the *Shaka Zulu* television series, "A Positional Gambit: Shaka Zulu and the Conflict in South Africa," *Radical History Review* 41 (Spring 1989), 5–31.

settlers, and even townspeople for declining herds and declining ranching profits flowing to investors in London and in eastern seaboard cities. Mercer's special authority lay in his years of having published a livestock journal and in his participation in securing and publishing a long and detailed confession of one of the invaders, George Dunning. There is no indication that those of Wyoming of the day who observed, and also resented, Mercer's published account of the war (amidst persisting tensions, continuing conflicts, and still threatened prosecutions) knew that Mercer had earlier founded the University of Washington, had been for many years an active proponent and promoter for development of the Northwest (Oregon and Washington), and had for a number of years exercised a most powerful interest in recruiting women to settle in the Northwest.[8]

While studying the Mercer text, I realized that many of the events of the 1892 war had taken place almost exactly a hundred years before. I was also intrigued by the circumstances of the history of the Mercer text itself, which—according to the front-matter added to the book in its later editions—had been suppressed at the time of its first publication, and its author vehemently attacked.[9] The aura of suppression which surrounded the film, the book, and Truman Metzel's experience with the book in Glen Rock, Wyoming, in 1954, suggested an opportunity for setting an inquiry into the programs of suppression of the memory of the Johnson County Cattle War alongside the account of the closing and opening of discussion in Lawrence of the strike of 1912.

*

On March 11, 1992, I telephoned the Johnson County Historical Society, based in the county seat, Buffalo, Wyoming, to see if there were any plans to mark the hundredth anniversary of the Johnson County War. I found two officers of the historical society at the Johnson County Library in Buffalo. Patty Myers, president of the Johnson County Histori-

8. A concise account of the life of Asa Shinn Mercer is to be found in Delphine Henderson, "Asa Shinn Mercer, Northwest Publicity Agent," The Frances Greenburg Armitage Prize Winning Essay, Reed College, 1942–43, *Reed College Bulletin* 23 (January 1945): 21–32. Henderson revives, reproduces, the story of the suppression of *Banditti*, "In 1894 Mercer published *The Banditti of the Plains*, a book which brought down the wrath of the cattle barons upon him because it exposed their plan to monopolize the cattle country and rob the settlers of their share. Copies of the book were seized and burned. Mercer barely escaped with his life, and his business was ruined." I am grateful to the Librarian, Reed College, Portland, Oregon, for providing a copy of the Henderson essay.

9. Mercer himself noted legal problems he had in publishing the written and sworn confession of one of the invaders, George Dunning, in 1892.

cal Society,[10] told me by phone that yes, indeed, they had planned an anniversary ("not a celebration") of "The Cattle War" ("not the Johnson County War") for June 19–21. There was a $48 package fee that would include a bus trip to two sites and registration for the conference. The participants on the panel were to be Jack McDermott, a freelance historian previously based in Washington, D.C., who has been looking at the various texts, historical and fiction, that attempt to recount the war; Colin Keeney, a professor of English at the University of Wyoming; and Mark Harvey, a graduate student at the University of Wyoming who has prepared a multimedia slide show. The organizers were, Patty Myers indicated, trying to produce a dignified program.

> [They are working in] a fairly dignified manner. There are lots of reenactments in the West which are not very dignified. We have many descendants of the participants in the war in Johnson County and we don't want to refight the battle.

I asked Ms. Myers whether there had been an earlier commemoration of the war. She said,

> This is the first and this will probably be the last. There are a lot of people with memories of the war, but they haven't been able to talk about it . . . and we don't expect there will be many people with a strong interest in it fifty or hundred years from now.

Patty Myers agreed to send the information packet on the events. She urged me to respond quickly if I wanted to attend. There were not going to be many tour tickets; there was a problem of moving lots of people and buses across private land to the cattle war sites.

Receiving the material from Buffalo soon thereafter, I discussed a proposed trip with Truman Metzel at Great Expectations. We agreed to go together and to make it a five- or six-day trip.

*

Buffalo, Wyoming, was, in 1992, a town of about 3,300 population. Buffalo is located below the lower slopes of the Big Horn Mountains, at an altitude of 4,600 feet. In June 1992, the protected depression in which Buffalo and its immediately neighboring areas are located appeared a moister and more fertile area than the treeless and poorly watered range lands we observed along U.S. 25 for the 125 miles from Casper to Buffalo. As we drove along U.S. 25, we noted the expansive ranches, defined by fencing and posted by small signs; the lands enclosed by these great

10. P.O. Box 103, Buffalo, Wyoming 82834.

ranch operations were dry in June 1992 (though there had been heavy rains and flooding in Buffalo just a week before the commemoration events), and we spotted but few cattle from the interstate highway. As we approached Buffalo, we did notice large numbers of sheep grazing near the highway. In this part of Wyoming, the human population is not much more than a few persons per square mile; and the greater part of the population seems to be compacted into small communities like Chugwater and Kaycee, and in the county seats like Buffalo.

One of the Cattle War sites, Kaycee, 53 miles south of Buffalo, has a small museum called "Hoofprints of the Past" as well as a couple of bars (The Invasion Bar) and motels (Cassidy Inn) that play off of the era of the Cattle War; a stop at the museum allowed us to view a photographic record of some of the events of the Cattle War, particularly the seige of Nathan Champion's cabin just a few hundred yards south of the museum. While visiting the museum at Kaycee, we noticed two other men working closely through the museum exhibits. We learned later, in Buffalo, that they were very interested in the life of Frank Canton, one of the dark characters of the Cattle War story. They had been for years following his trail from Texas up through the plains. This was their first visit to the Johnson County area.

Buffalo, which is at the intersection of Interstates 90 and 25 and is the nearest town to the recreational areas of the Bighorn National Forest just to the west, has a number of hotels and appears to enjoy a traffic in visitors even when there are no commemoration events planned. Buffalo has a substantial museum located in the old county library building (a Carnegie library built in 1909) and in an adjacent building. Of course, Buffalo developed astride the Bozeman Trail, which brought tens of thousands of settlers into and through the region.

In the center of Buffalo, the Jim Gatchell Museum of the West contains an impressive collection of material and exhibits relating to Buffalo in the late nineteenth century and to the cattle war in particular. There are three dioramas designed and constructed by Juan Menchaca and Paul Rossi, one of which presents a view of the last battle of the Cattle War, the seige of the invaders at the TA Ranch in April 1892. There is also a large three-dimensional topographical rendering of the events of the entire Cattle War from 1891 to 1892. A tape narrative accompanying the topographical display was installed and began running on the morning before the commemoration symposium itself.[11] The photographic record

---

11. Robert C. Wilson, a state employee at Fort Phil Kearny, constructed the topographical exhibit. Patty Myers, president of the Historical Society, did the script. Dave Myers, a local radio disk jockey, did the first recording of the script. In the middle of the day the

of the events and persons of the Cattle War is extensive. In the corner of the old library building, there is a room meant to replicate the early office of the Buffalo sheriffs, and above the doorway are the names and photographs of all of Buffalo's sheriffs including Frank Canton who, after he lost his sheriff's badge in an election defeat, became an important agent and detective of the stockgrowers and a leader of the invasion;[12] and there is a picture of W. G. Angus, the sheriff of Buffalo at the time of the invasion. He was, apparently, one of the individuals on the stockgrowers' death list. The two followers of Frank Canton were also at the Gatchell Museum, and they were asking a staff member for a photograph of Frank Canton, his wife, and his daughter.

The museum buildings, like the bookshop (*The Office*) on the main street, offer a very considerable number of books and other items for sale, and many of the books on display in June 1992 had reference to the Cattle War. At the time of our visit, the Asa Shinn Mercer book and the Helena Huntington Smith book were available at the book shop as well as in the museums. While looking at the books in the museum, I heard a woman tell one of the museum staff, who was handling the till, that she was "in town for the Cattle War." She related, while I browsed nearby, "My grandfather was given important papers about the war by Sheriff Angus who gave them to him for safekeeping because he was afraid of their being taken and destroyed."[13]

Close by the Jim Gatchell Museum is the new building housing the Johnson County Library. Historical society staff are also employees of the library. On one side of the library, there was a large display of books about the Cattle War. The library houses a microfilm collection of regional and local newspapers, and I made arrangements to spend a couple of hours in the morning before the symposium reading microfilms of the *Buffalo Bulletin* of 1891 and 1892. When I went to work on the microfilms, one of the symposium presenters, Jack McDermott, was

tape was changed, and Tom Tisdale, grandson of John A. Tisdale, one of those murdered in November 1891 was the voice reading the script.

12. Canton was accused and formally charged with killings in Johnson County, including the killing of John A. Tisdale, but he was never convicted. The Frank Canton role in *Heaven's Gate* was played by Sam Waterston.

13. On Sunday, June 21, 1992, as I was getting ready to leave Buffalo with Truman Metzel for the trip back to Chicago, a Scots engineer living in Hamilton, Ontario, introduced himself while we were having breakfast and joined us at our table. Colin Campbell is "married to a Buffalo girl." And Campbell said that her father knew Sheriff Angus and that Angus gave the document containing George Dunning's confession to him for safekeeping and that he (Campbell's wife's father) eventually deposited it in the Wyoming State Archives or the university library.

at the next table going over the text of his talk. As he began to put away his things, we introduced ourselves to one another and did some "historians' trade talk" in the course of which I learned that McDermott was previously employed as a historian with the federal government, working on historical conservation and history education programs, that he had left the Reagan administration and moved to Wyoming to work as a freelance historian, and that he had been asked to arrange the afternoon symposium. He also noted that what he had seen in Wyoming is an "absence of a sense of history and a sense of the importance of historical conservation." He was hoping that the afternoon symposium would play at least a small part in helping people understand how important their history is and how much a role they have in keeping the past alive.

*

Jack McDermott opened the symposium, which had been moved to the Buffalo High School gymnasium with the anticipation of a large audience. Chairs had been set up in a radial fashion across the floor, and all but a handful of seats were occupied. Perhaps two hundred and fifty to three hundred persons were there. Most of the audience was older than McDermott, in their sixties and seventies, some older still.

After welcoming the participants to the commemoration and setting out the program for the day, McDermott provided an overview. His opening talk would set the Johnson County Cattle War in a larger American context. He did this by moving through a series of arguments mounted by historians concerning nineteenth-century American capitalism. McDermott brought attention to the centrality of property rights and to the complexities and contradictions of the Homestead Act's concept of entitlement. "Thirty acres and a mule" was a worthless entitlement in the range land of the West, and he noted that from the 1870s on there were various calls to increase the basic grant in the West from what was then 160 acres to 2650.

McDermott defined "the essential conflict in late nineteenth-century America": between concentrations of power such as the capitalists represented—glorified in writings about the Gilded Age—and the processes of mass empowerment that developed from the Jacksonian period and were doubled with the new immigration and the "opening of the West" in the last decades of the nineteenth century. This conflict unleashed a mortal struggle between romantic ideas of the individual on the frontier and ideas of community and society. McDermott described the Cattle War as a deep conflict between the romantic notions of indi-

vidual effort and struggle, which the cattlemen advanced, and the notions of civic democracy, which the granger and merchant groups sought
to foster in new communities in the West such as Buffalo.

McDermott also broadened the field of consideration, introducing
into his discussion the patterns of primogeniture in Great Britain of the
day. Inheritance laws in Britain sent male children far and wide, as both
investors and adventurers in America. The capital that developed the
great ranch operations of Wyoming came substantially from Britain, but
the British aristocracy had no way of knowing about, or dealing effectively with, the changing realities of their investments in a remote area
of the American West.

McDermott also looked at the common law underpinnings of the
range wars, such as the Johnson County struggle, to the notion that was
developing in the West that one had "no duty to retreat" in the face of
a threat of force, that one had a responsibility "to stand one's ground."
He brought attention, as well, to the contradictions of property rights in
the region. Claims to land for smallholding and large-scale ranching
hardly had, in the 1880s, little historical basis, since the rights that settlers and ranchers enjoyed came at the expense of Native Americans.
The ranges in conflict had, generally, been occupied and acquired in
gross violation of treaties between the United States government and
Native Americans. Second, the regulation of rights in cattle through the
assignment and use of brands, through the formalization of programs
and schedules of round-ups, and through the elaboration and revision
of "maverick laws" were all practices operating in a web of imperma-
nence and unenforceability. Rights in law affirmed in courthouses and
association offices in Cheyenne were hardly the same as rights in practice in a wide open range land two hundred and fifty miles away.

McDermott also saw the Cattle War as a Western frontier "civil war
of incorporation." Those in Wyoming who fought for the capitalist interests were typically Republican and Union veterans while those they
sought to discipline, including cowboys who had broken free of the discipline of the large ranch owners and managers, were most often still
identifying themselves with the Southern and Confederate cause.

Finally, McDermott reminded the audience that Wyoming itself was
just going through a process of transition from territory to state, that
there were real issues about the possibility and practicality of regular
legal administration. But, he argued, one should not be fooled that the
Cattle War's cause was "lawlessness" on the frontier. There were real
disputes of interest at work here. The real struggle was not over the
efficiency of the law but rather over the control and ownership of land.

*

Following a short break, Jack McDermott made a second presentation, this one focusing on "the interpreters" of the Johnson County Cattle War from 1892 to the present. The basic theme was that the "Johnson County War is a dream and a nightmare for the historian. There is perfect material. It is full of intrigue and scandal, opposing presuppositions, conflicting frames of reference, and considerable bodies of evidence that can be evaluated and reexamined." But, on the other hand, "There is an untrustworthy and indistinct paper trail, a polarization of memory, a problem of finding truly objective observers . . . The historical record is deeply etched by the effect of time and the lingering search for self-glorification if not expiation."

McDermott focused attention on the journalists of the day, particularly Sam T. Clover of the *Chicago Herald* and Asa Shinn Mercer.[14] Clover's reportage, McDermott asserted, assured that the invasion became a national media event at the time. A. S. Mercer's book, with its very strong point of view—the heady critique of the capitalist barons and their agents—assured that there would be a serious interest in the event long into the future.

Clover traveled with the invasion party, which together numbered about fifty men, comprising paid Texas gunmen (including some law officers), members of the Stock Growers Association, range detectives, teamsters, a surgeon, some hangers-on, and two reporters. Clover had met some of the organizers of the invasion while working on some stories about the Ghost Dance. McDermott related to the audience at Buffalo that Helena Huntington Smith ("the premier historian of the war") considered Clover unscrupulous and a liar, calling him "a cinder in your eye," the worst example of yellow journalism. Clover filed five stories on the war, the best known being that which included the alleged extract from Nathan Champion's diary.

As the fifty or so invaders were surrounded at the TA Ranch by the Johnson County defenders, Sam Clover "went over to the other side." Upon reaching Buffalo, Clover discovered almost immediately that an

14. McDermott here was following Helena Huntington Smith's "method" fairly closely, centering the roles of two key reporters: Sam Clover and Asa Shinn Mercer. Smith, *War on Powder River*, opens her book with a foreword situating these two observers: "The Johnson County war might have been only a footnote on history's page were it not for two writers who, in reporting history, became part of it themselves" (p. vii). In a closing chapter to *Powder River*, 272–80, Smith pursues the role of Asa Shinn Mercer as observer of the war and critic of the Stock Growers Association and examines the controversies and mythologies that grew up around Mercer's report of the invasion.

old friend was at nearby Fort McKinney. From that moment, Clover was somehow involved with getting the cavalry to the site of the TA fight. Having run one day from the TA Ranch, he arrived with the cavalry the next day as they intervened and took the invaders into what became, essentially, protective custody.

While in Buffalo, Clover kept secret his knowledge of the Champion killing and the discovery of the Champion diary (of course, those of the invasion party caught at the TA Ranch knew of the killing of Champion—but of the diary?). However, the invaders did not have access to Clover's telegraphic connections from Buffalo. In Buffalo, Clover evidently induced the army to send a courier to South Dakota with the story of the Champion killing, to be telegraphed to Chicago. Later Clover was received back in Chicago with great praise by colleagues at the *Herald* who had already prepared a story recording his death in the invasion war. In the story he filed on April 13, 1892, Clover seems to have taken sides against the cattlemen for the first time, but as legal proceedings developed he refused to be a witness against them.

McDermott also offered extended remarks on A. S. Mercer, who all through his life had a flair for the dramatic, for the unpredictable. Mercer was, to borrow a Twain phrase, a "charming rascal." McDermott focused attention on Mercer's apparent shift from his being a colleague and ally of the cattlemen (his early publishing work in Wyoming was in service of the stockgrowers) to becoming both a sworn and wholly acknowledged enemy of the stockgrowers. Mercer himself related that in wartime there is no place for fence-sitters, but the turn in Mercer's approach to the war may have developed around personal animosities between himself and key individuals in the Stock Growers Association.

McDermott offered detail on the myth of suppression that had grown up around Mercer's 1894 book, that Mercer traveled around Wyoming for several years openly selling his book personally, that there have been no known court proceedings leading to seizures, that the reports of copies being removed from libraries may have followed the myth of the book's disappearance. Noting that the latest appraised value of a copy of the 1894 edition of Mercer was $2000, McDermott elicited from the audience acknowledgments that three of those in attendance owned copies of the original edition.

McDermott also brought attention to another contemporary observer, Frank Crossthwaite, a federal investigator who was sent to Wyoming to investigate the alleged cowardice of a federal agent in dealing with the invasion. Crossthwaite documented what he called "a pernicious situation in Johnson County," in which there was little likelihood that local courts and juries would successfully prosecute rustlers, but that there was also "unlawful conduct on the side of the cattlemen." Crossthwaite saw as grand irony that "those who were thieves had won the day." The only justification of federal involvement in the conflict was in bringing troops to protect the invaders. Efforts made in advance to join federal troops and cavalry to the campaign against Johnson County were improper; likewise, various intrigues to insinuate federal forces afterwards. McDermott's presentation of Crossthwaite's findings was an opportunity to suggest the still incomplete and ambiguous record of cooperation in the invasion between the power-brokers in Cheyenne and the White House in Washington. One of the principal actors on the side of the stockgrowers was later appointed to the United States Supreme Court "by President Harrison."[15]

After another break, McDermott briefly reviewed the literature coming out since the 1890s which seemed to take one side or another, and brought attention to the still not fully mined sources from family papers. Some of these works reflected the extraordinary tensions and anxieties which marked the war and its aftermath. Some of the writers, like O. H. Flagg, were said to have carried their bitterness against the cattlemen to their graves. Others reconciled themselves to a new postwar order. Fred Hesse, an active invader born in England, resumed his life as a Johnson County rancher, and he and his descendants built positive relationships with the larger community. W. C. Irvine, one of the leaders of the invasion, claimed to have been misled: "We've been played for suckers." In her 1967 study of the war, Helena Huntington Smith felt that time would heal the wounds, but she tended to side with the small, independent rancher.

Then, McDermott looked toward future research on the Johnson County War. He saw valuable new material coming from court records, including better estimates of those involved in the defense of Johnson County. He could see future writing becoming clearer about those "four hundred souls" who surrounded the fifty some invaders at the TA Ranch, producing a better view of this cross-section of Buffalo and Johnson County populations at the time of the invasion. One could look forward to a more sensitive treatment of the history of homesteading: a better understanding of how homesteaders made use of their entitlements, or found that it was necessary to undertake supplemental activities, including rustling and butchering, in order to maintain these home-

---

15. Though McDermott said "Harrison," it was President Taft who made the appointment.

steads. Perhaps most important, one needed to look far more closely at the maps of interpersonal and local conflicts that were developing in the ten years before the invasion: how did these conflicts between individuals and families develop, at times being resolved and sometimes not? What was the material basis of feuding? How did such feuds carry into the alignments and fighting of 1891 and 1892? How do we understand and represent an uprising against concentrated wealth? How did those of the day deal with newcomers?

Finally, McDermott raised the question of "how do we study and write about the war without becoming judgmental?"One has to remember, he noted, that as one looks back to these events . . . "whatever view is taken, the facts are not pretty . . . and they cannot be made so for any of the participants." The larger issue for us is how can we reach an accommodation with the past and learn to resolve our differences.

*

Following another break for refreshments, McDermott introduced Mark Harvey, a graduate student in history at the University of Wyoming, who had been studying the Johnson County War for some years and who had organized a slide lecture reviewing the history of the events and the controversies over the details and their interpretations. Harvey tried to help his audience understand the task at hand: "There are always two sides to a story . . . ask anyone who is married." The task for the historian, and for himself in this lecture, was to tell the story "without getting shot at or without starting another war. There is, in this story, no middle ground." He agreed with Patty Myers, president of the historical society, who held that "this was a class war between two cultures."

Harvey outlined his method: he would deal with the issues by quoting from each side, and to make clear which side he was quoting he would change hats, wearing a white hat when he was speaking from the side of the smallholders of Johnson County, the "rustlers," and a black hat when he was dealing with the stockgrowers, the "capitalists."[16] As Mark Harvey outlined his method, I, as a listener, contemplated the

16. It is curious how fashion and virtue sometimes take divergent and then parallel routes. I later learned from various published sources that the smallholders and cowboys in eastern Wyoming of the day wore *black* hats. Had Harvey used the black hat to represent the voice of the "rustlers," the sensibility of the June 1992 audience in Buffalo might have conferred white hat virtue on the "capitalists." This was clearly not Harvey's intent. It is instructive that a hundred-year interval produces such a symbolic reversal in the "performance" of history.

polarizing process—how such a historian's method in representation and narration would continue and reinforce the polarizing process of the nineteenth-century conflict itself.[17]

Before setting out to depict the views of "the two sides," Harvey, like McDermott, pointed out the paradox of the conflict, noting that the war actually began in 1868 with the simultaneous construction of the railway and the signing of the Fort Laramie treaty which recognized Native American rights over the land of the region.

The early 1880s were a productive period and in 1884 the "rustlers" were noting that this was a plentiful country. Jack Flagg's cattle and horses were fat. And in 1884 a photograph was taken of a group of cowboys, including Nate Champion, at a chuck wagon on the prairie. This is the only undisputed image of Champion. This was a time when virtually all the cattle and all the ranches were owned by less than a dozen British companies. The "rustlers" called the British "B-S," "British subjects." One of the British capitalists talked about the local cowboys who served the ranch companies: "They don't like us and on the whole I don't like them."

But the good times ended. The winter of 1886/87 was a brutal winter, and the herds were heavily depleted by the time the snows melted. This was the time of the painting by Charles M. Russell of the starving cow on the prairie, *Waiting for a Chinook: The Last of the Five Thousand*. Jack Flagg called this the winter that was the watershed of the cattle barons.

With the spring of 1887, settlers started pouring into Buffalo.[18] Cowboys who had no work started to close off sections of land, starting their own herds. Any unbranded cattle were seized by these new ranchers, irrespective of the interpretation and application of the 1884 Wyoming Maverick Law. While "rustlers" complained about dictatorial management from the cattle companies, the "capitalists" complained that rus-

17. While Harvey substantially assuaged this "pre-critique" through the effectiveness of his presentation, other commentators later in the weekend remarked on the complexities of the shifting boundaries between "rustlers" and "capitalists," bringing into view the experiences of Johnson County residents and outside observers whose interests were not clearly or steadily with one side or the other, and also suggesting the underlying interpersonal and internecine struggles and feuds that animated some of the larger conflict. That there were two sides is hard to contest, given the images of the stockgrowers organizing a death list in their club chambers in Cheyenne, and given the configuration of invaders and defenders in combat at the TA Ranch.

18. There was no further elucidation here. Was Buffalo better watered? Were sustenance, work, and protection available in the town to those whose earnings off the prairie had suddenly, and literally, "dried up"? Was the town of Buffalo going through a growth period irrespective of the quality of the surrounding herds?

tlers were so numerous that the cattlemen were "powerless before these thieves and rascals." The "rustlers" said that despite the Maverick Law, and despite new efforts to win its enforcement, there was the old tradition that "the longest rope gets the maverick." While "capitalists" saw themselves being abandoned by labor on their range, the "rustlers," for example Jim Averill, saw the cattlemen as "land-grabbers and land-sharks."

Harvey turned to the photographic record. The captions in Helena Huntington Smith's book needed to be corrected: the so-called Ella Watson photo was incorrect; it was not Watson in the photograph. The once standard photo of Nate Champion was also incorrect. This was not Nate Champion but John Gardner in the photo, Harvey having compared blow-ups of various images. One might also note, in connection with Ella Watson, that "she met a man [Averill] who felt that when a woman acted like a man, she should be treated as such."[19]

Moving into greater detail, Harvey defined a series of conflicts that had developed within Johnson County from 1888 to 1892, bringing out information on the roles of W. C. Irvine, John A. Tisdale, Robert Tisdale (not related to John A.), Tom Waggoner, Col. H. B. Ijams, Nathan Champion, Mike Shonsey, Frank Canton, Charles Basch, Asa Shinn Mercer, Sam T. Clover, and Fred Hesse. In presenting the words of the participants, Harvey succeeded in providing a more complicated picture of the events leading to the invasion, and of the complex social, financial, and labor relations in which many of the participants were mutually involved.

Harvey used the method of the two hats in discussing opinions and reactions to the November 30, 1891, killing of John A. Tisdale, as he returned from Buffalo to his ranch with winter supplies, Christmas presents for his children, and a new dog and puppy. Through Harvey's speakers on the "two sides," one began to see discrete discourses, and also silences, developing around specific episodes. One saw, in particu-

19. Throughout the afternoon symposium, two topics were constantly referenced in a playful way, drawing extemporaneous remarks from audience and speakers: first, the circumstances of women in—and in relation to—the Cattle War, both as authors (like Helena Huntington Smith) and as participants and victims (like the widow of the assassinated John A. Tisdale), and as the unspeaking witnesses of Buffalo; and, second, whether one had died "in his (or her) own bed" or otherwise. One might wonder, as the centennial events unfolded, whether these joking references were not but searches for other ways to divide the population that had experienced the Cattle War in its time and in the 100 years since: shifting the geometry from the uncomfortable distinctions between "rustlers" and "capitalists" to more comfortable and harmonic distinctions between women and men and between those who had died peacefully and those who had died violently.

lar, the problems of sustaining credible witness to the criminal events occurring in Johnson County at the time. People were said to be afraid to speak; witnesses who spoke disappeared or were ushered out of the state; or witnesses changed their stories. Various citations suggest that some of the killings of "rustlers" were really killings of witnesses to previous events.

In respect to the killing of Champion, Harvey succeeded in harnassing a wider range of voices on the attack than Clover, Dunning, and Champion himself, and one could see how quickly individual fates and collective interests might shift. Nick Ray, a "rustler," was, from 1886 to 1891, it seems, a loyal employee of W. C. Irvine, a leader among the "capitalists."

Harvey alerted the audience to continuing mysteries: the never-seen-again Champion diary; the Clover letter which indicates that Clover sent the Champion diary to a man named Blair; the never found death list, though the Buffalo coroner's sister, Mary C. Watkins, claimed to have seen it in Frank Canton's valise; the contents of the coded messages sent between Cheyenne and Washington; the evident relocation of black troops and what looks today like a cooked-up incident to create a disturbance at Suggs, Wyoming, involving black federal troops to try to force martial law on the county.

*

During the commemorative weekend tour of Cattle War sites in Johnson County, a set of maps, diagrams, narratives, and reprints was distributed to participants. One of the narratives, evidently prepared by the staff of the Johnson County Historical Society, reports that Phil DuFran, one of the invaders taken into custody at the TA Ranch on April 13, 1892, arrived at Suggs, Wyoming, near Buffalo, on June 12, 1892, in the company of the Ninth Cavalry, who set up camp just south of Suggs. The text notes that

> On June 1, 1892, six [sic] prominent citizens, Frank Wolcott, Henry May [sic], George Baxter, John Clay and Willis VanDeVanter [sic],[20] wired Wyoming Senator Joseph Carey in Washington, D.C., de-

20. Frank Wolcott was one of the invaders. Henry G. Hay was president of the Manhattan Cattle Company and an active proponent of efforts to get President Harrison to declare martial law in Wyoming. George Baxter was a former territorial governor of Wyoming and an active member of the Wyoming Stock Growers Association; he played a leading role in recruiting the men who made up the invading force. At the time of the invasion, Baxter was in Denver announcing the invasion, providing information on its organization, and a defense of its objectives and methods. John Clay, Jr., a Scotsman, was an active

manding military protection for those with large cattle interests. The telegram read in part, "We want coolheaded men whose sympathy is with us . . . Send six companies of the Ninth Cavalry from [Fort] Robinson . . . to [Fort] McKinney [adjacent to Buffalo]. The colored troops will have no sympathy for Texas thieves, and these are the troops we want."

According to the text, DuFran—whom various residents mistakenly took to be a U.S. marshal armed with arrest warrants—worked quickly to stir up friction between the troops and the people of the town of Suggs, and by June 16 and June 17 tensions had so far developed that "the troops were ready to go into Suggs 'to clean up the place.'" By the next day one of the black soldiers had been killed and another wounded in a gunfight in the town. The text records that many of the townspeople were so frightened of the tensions and gunfire that they fled the town until assured by the commander of the Ninth that they could return home. An inquiry was held and various soldiers provided testimony against DuFran, who was escorted out of the camp. One view of the Suggs episode is that this was a "second invasion" after the first had failed; testimony that DuFran claimed to be a U.S. marshal "with warrants for the arrest of 42 citizens of Wyoming" reinvoked the earlier talk of death list.

The *Buffalo Bulletin*, June 23, 1892, reported the incident at Suggs under the headline: "War at Suggs. A Party of Colored Troops attack the Town in the Night AND ARE ROUTED BY CITIZENS. One Soldier Killed and Several Others Wounded." The report noted one witness from the town saying that he "recognized Phil DuFran among the attacking force and shot at him several times."

In late July 1992, as I was working on this text, National Public Radio's

---

promoter of British investment in the Wyoming cattle operations, and became, according to Helena Huntington Smith, *War on Powder River*, vii, "the historian *par excellence* of that superb folly, the great beef bonanza of the western plains." His memoir, *My Life on the Range*, was privately printed in 1924, and then brought out by the University of Oklahoma Press in 1962. Judge Willis Van Devanter, who had served as Chief Justice of the Supreme Court of Wyoming in its 1889/90 session, and was counsel to the Wyoming Stock Growers Association, defended the invaders when the case against them came to trial in 1893, achieving an acquittal amidst the improbabilities and impossibilites of empaneling a jury. Van Devanter was, in 1910, appointed to the United States Supreme Court by President William Howard Taft (not President Benjamin Harrison, as some in the commemoration symposium audience believed). One of the many odd and, typically, irrelevant "coincidences" met in completing this book is that around the time that President Taft was appointing one of the leading figures in the organization of the invasion to the United States Supreme Court, Mrs. William Howard Taft was organizing support for Camella Teoli and her fellow Lawrence mill workers.

Weekend Edition reported that General Colin L. Powell, chairman of the Joint Chiefs of Staff of the United States Armed Forces, had offered tough remarks warning Saddam Hussein of the consequences of Iraq's alleged failure to honor the United Nations Resolutions. The report noted that Powell was speaking at Fort Leavenworth, Kansas, where he was dedicating a monument honoring the "buffalo soldiers," the black soldiers of the Ninth and Tenth cavalries who pacified the West. On July 26, 1992, the *New York Times* provided a more detailed report of the dedication, also noting that Powell was to give an address later in the evening (July 25) "to several thousand people at the dedication of the monument." The *Times* report described the monument, which was designed by the sculptor Eddie Dixon of Lubbock, Texas, as "a 12-foot bronze statue of a black cavalryman pulling back the reins of a horse." The *Times* also noted that it was General Powell himself, in 1983 when he was deputy commanding general at Fort Leavenworth, who discovered two gravel alleys named for the Ninth and Tenth cavalries. The report notes that

> Though they are hardly to be found in the history textbooks and Wild West movies that shape Americans' image[s] of the frontier, it was soldiers like those of the Ninth and Tenth cavalries who guarded the wagon trains, protected the payrolls and helped build the towns of the West.

A Navy historian teaching at Fort Leavenworth Command and General Staff College, who led the funding campaign for the monument, noted that "One out of every five soldiers in the West was black . . . Above all else the buffalo soldiers [as the black soldiers were called] were patriots."[21] General Powell perhaps could not have known that as he was commenting on one conflict between authority vested in the United Nations and force deployed by the United States, that he was involving himself in another: between authority vested in the United States government and force deployed by the cattlemen.

*

Harvey concluded his lecture by asking his audience, whatever side they are on, to keep speaking about it. "A lot of you [in the audience] have stories and legends. That's what this is all about. Keeping the stories and legends alive."

21. For another view, Bob Marley's "Buffalo Soldiers," from the 1983 posthumous collection *Confrontations*.

Mark Harvey's presentation captured not only the bipolarity of the conflict, but also the bipolarity of accounts of it which developed from 1892 onwards. This construction of the past—one event in the past, but two interpretations, two histories—is expressed dramatically in the unique form of one account/two accounts of the Johnson County War, which I found in the Johnson County Library at Buffalo and was allowed to borrow overnight. When one opens this volume, a cataloguer's nightmare, one notes the title page: Jack R. Gage, *The Johnson County War ain't a pack of lies: The Rustler's Side* (Cheyenne, Wyoming: Flintlock Publishing Co., 1967). If one flips the book over and opens it again (from the "back" or is *this* the "front"?), one reads, Jack R. Gage, *The Johnson County War is a pack of lies: The Baron's Side* (Cheyenne, Wyoming: Flintlock Publishing Co., 1967). On the "rustler's side" of the volume, the book is "dedicated to the memory of Jack Flagg and John H. Smith." On the "baron's side" of the volume the book is "dedicated to F. G. S. Hesse and Billy Irvine . . . two men who made history. You get the idea that they were the kind of men who would have made history wherever they were and their memory will last as long as the history they made."

*

During a break, I went over to Mark Harvey to thank him for his talk and to ask him several questions, but a considerable line gathered ahead of me along the gymnasium wall. A number of people spoke to Harvey about their knowledge of the events:

> A woman says that "Judge Kerr always said that the aftermath of the war was the reason a Wyoming man was put on the Supreme Court."
>
> The grandson of one of those murdered, Tom Waggoner, introduces himself and thanks Harvey for his talk and for his research.[22]
>
> A woman introduces herself as the aunt of Mark Harvey's dissertation adviser, Bill Roberts.
>
> A man tells Harvey that it was at his mother's step-brother's home that William Walker died.[23]
>
> A woman tells Harvey, "Everything you said, I can agree with."

22. On June 4, 1891, Tom Waggoner was taken from his home in Newcastle, Wyoming (not in Johnson County), by three men and was found two weeks later hanging from a tree near his home.

23. "Bill Walker" was one of two men who stayed with Champion and Ray on the night before the invaders struck the KC Ranch and killed Champion and Ray. As Walker and

A man opens and reads aloud to Harvey a section of a book by James Shaw on pioneering in Texas and Wyoming.[24]

While Harvey pushed his way to the door to grab a smoke (and I missed the opportunity to thank him for the beautifully crafted presentation), a woman introduced herself to me. She identified herself as Marge Liberty, the daughter of Helena Huntington Smith, the author of *War on Powder River*. Liberty is an anthropologist by training and practice and has herself written on relations between Native Americans and whites in the region. She lives in the city of Sheridan, Wyoming. She spoke of "the people's rage today that no one paid for the terrible things that were done." She also talked about her mother's research in and around Buffalo as she was working on her book. Her mother would

> "work in the archives all day reading newspapers and she would go out at night with the old boys and when they were loose and drunk she would hit them with their questions and they would open up and say things they wouldn't say otherwise."

Jack McDermott joined the conversation and, in response to a question from me, both McDermott and Liberty said that they had never heard anyone expressing any doubts about the authenticity of the Champion diary.[25]

---

his partner Ben Jones were leaving the ranch, they were seized and held by the invaders. Walker was referred to in the Champion diary as "another man": "Me and Nick was getting breakfast when the attack took place. Two men was with us—Bill [sic] Jones and another man. The old man [Ben] went after water and did not come back. His friend [Walker] went to see what was the matter and did not come back" (*War on Powder River*, 204–5).

Asa Shinn Mercer reports, "Presently a man came out with a bucket and walked down to the creek. He was captured and concealed behind the creek bank. Another man came from the house after a time and walked to the stable. He was captured and held. These men proved to be Jones and Walker, two trappers [other sources say they were out of work cowhands] who had stopped over night at the ranch" (*Banditti of the Plains*, 54).

Curiously, George Dunning's confession, which Mercer included in *The Banditti of the Plains*, offers a different account of the capture of Jones and Walker, and refers to them as "teamsters" (182–87). D. F. Baber, *The Longest Rope* (Caldwell, Idaho: Caxton Printers, 1947), provides another account of the invasion, with a digestion of interviews she did of a very elderly William Walker.

24. In *War on Powder River*, 154–55, Helena Huntington Smith reports that James C. Shaw "had known Champion all his life." She deployed Shaw as a Champion character witness, arguing that Champion had been falsely accused of being involved in a decade of lawlessness before his killing in April 1892.

25. The constitution—throughout the day—of Champion as quintessential victim and pure voice, coupled by the simultaneous "presence" and "absence" of the Champion diary, seemed to suggest the value of questioning the history of the production of the diary.

*

Following the intermission, McDermott introduced Colin Keeney, professor of English at the University of Wyoming, who was to speak about the turn-of-the-century author Owen Wister and *The Virginian,* Wister's 1902 novel, in the context of the Johnson County War.

Keeney opened his remarks by expressing the view that the "Johnson County War was an important event in American culture, as much or more than in American history." The terms and what they stand for are embedded in our culture—concepts like ranch, rustling, cattle barons, these come directly from the Cattle War.

Keeney reviewed the details of Wister's life, saying that it was, first, far more interesting than his fiction and, second, that there could have been no person less likely to write a book such as *The Virginian.* By the time of John A. Tisdale's murder in Johnson County in November 1891, Wister was a confirmed and published author, and much less the Eastern lawyer and banker than he had set out to be. In his first stories it was clear that he had a rough-hewn view of justice on the frontier. "Better a bad lynching than no lynching at all," became a kind of hallmark of his writing. Seven of his early stories were reworked into *The Virginian,* first published in 1902, and the essential elements of *The Virginian,* the eternal struggle between good and evil and the conflict between east and west, are thickly involved with such events as were known to Wister to have been happening in Johnson County in the late 1880s and early 1890s.

One of Wister's chapters, "What is a rustler?" was a discourse repeated again and again in the historic conflicts over law, order, and property in Wyoming during the period. According to Keeney, the Virginian himself was represented as having mixed feelings about riding with the cowboys who were sent to hang the rustlers, and in the Virginian's anxieties were all the threads of complication that run through the lives of various participants in the Cattle War. Wister himself was involved, and also friendly, with several of the invaders, including Frank Canton; Dr. Charles Penrose and other organizers of the invasion offered Wister an opportunity to examine the documentation of the day. Wister was seen as possibly useful to the stockgrowers in telling their side of the story to audiences in the East. Owen Wister had no influence on the Johnson County Cattle War, but the war had an extraordinary influence on him. "Even though Wister did his best to scramble the facts, amidst

---

Does the Champion diary belong to the genre of "writings under seige" which are not quite what they purport to be?

fiction . . . he defended the invaders of the Johnson County War in the way he wrote the events into *The Virginian* . . . this was a lesson he passed down [to us]."

At the conclusion of Keeney's talk, McDermott opened a general question period. A first question concerned Nate Champion's diary. Did it exist?[26]

Harvey said that "there is no way a Chicago journalist could have written that prose." He believes in the facticity of Clover's letter to Henry Blair indicating that he (Clover) had sent the diary to him.

Keeney related that Wister himself attributed rumors he had heard to specific journals; for example, whereas he had heard that baby-switching was a common practice in Texas, Wister told his readers that he had read this in someone's journal.

A second question concerned the role of Mike Shonsey, who "seemed to have wavered from side to side." McDermott and Harvey both remarked that Shonsey's papers have not been published. He was the longest living veteran of the conflict. The questioner had met Shonsey's son.

Another question concerned whether there was any new or recent information on the "pro-rustler" side. One of the panel indicated that some later speakers or witnesses presented problems. For example, in a 1934 interview Charles Basch, who came along to the edge of the gulch where John A. Tisdale was murdered, said that he saw nothing. But in a 1936 interview, he said he saw Frank Canton at the site; in 1938, he said he saw Canton shoot Tisdale.[27] Mark Harvey noted that he had received a call from a Lida Childers just a few days before. She had found a manuscript from May Gardner, Tom Gardner's wife.[28] She was

26. While this was, essentially, the same question I asked Jack McDermott and Marge Liberty during an intermission, another member of the audience posed this question to the panel.

27. A number of those present at the commemoration spoke of these interviews of Charles Basch, but from person to person the dates varied. See below for a brief discussion of a May 1935 interview and subsequent leaks from the sealed interviews.

28. Tom Gardner was an original partner in the HAT Ranch, founded in 1888 with O. H. Flagg and several others, and targeted by the Wyoming Stock Growers Association as one of the worst of the rustling operations. In *War on Powder River*, 171, Smith refers to Tom Gardner as "one of the highly respected middle-of-the-roaders, and a Canton ally." Gardner was one of those who left Buffalo to examine Haywood Gulch, finding John A. Tisdale shot to death. Gardner was the one who notified nearby ranchers of Tisdale's killing, and also was the first to give the news to Tisdale's wife. Gardner was, as well, a principal in removing the former invader George Dunning from the Buffalo jail to a safe-house, Dunning having been recognized by the Stock Growers' agents as a now dangerous informant. In 1902, Tom Gardner was listed as one of the founding stockholders of the new Stockgrowers Bank of Buffalo, a bank which "makes a speciality of looking after the

sending a copy to Mark. He expected that "There is a lot more evidence out there."

Another questioner asked, "Was there a model for the Virginian?" "Well," Keeney responded, "The Virginian was a Virginian who had come out West. Maybe the model was Frank Canton. Frank Canton went from being a sheriff to one of the invaders." At Keeney's mention of "Frank Canton" a large groan came from the audience. A woman a few rows in front of me remarked out loud, "I don't see how he can get from the Virginian to Frank Canton."

Following the symposium, the crowd in the gymnasium, along with speakers, moved to a reception and barbecue at the Gatchell Museum. At the museum, B. J. Earle, an employee of the Bureau of Land Management, a federal agency, introduced herself and said,

> The war is still fully alive in Johnson County. It comes up in all kinds of land issues between public and private uses and rights . . . It has come up in all sorts of conflicts surrounding marriages where people are checking their genealogies . . . It came up in about 1972 when an eighty-year-old woman was convicted of paying for the murder of her nephew. Despite her age she served a year in prison. The Johnson County War was at the center of the case.

*

The following morning, participants in the Cattle War commemoration boarded buses and went on a day-long tour of war sites. A first stop was at the gulch at Tisdale Divide south of Buffalo where John A. Tisdale was shot and killed as he drove his wagon up an incline. This was where Tom Tisdale, John A. Tisdale's grandson, provided a graphic description of the shooting. A witness to Tom Tisdale's remarks that afternoon might be forgiven for momentarily having a sense of witnessing a horrible shooting. Tom Tisdale identified "the exact spot" where Frank Canton stood when he fired at John A.'s back,[29] where the bullets struck, where

---

needs and requirements of Eastern investors and others seeking new locations and business openings" (*Buffalo's First Century*, 162).

29. While this narrative of the commemoration tour was being written, an interview by Clifford Terry of actor and filmmaker Clint Eastwood appeared on pages 5 and 7 of the Arts Section of the *Chicago Tribune*, August 2, 1992. Eastwood, who was in New York promoting his new Western film *Unforgiven*, compared the characters he has played in Western films to those played by the late John Wayne. "My characters, of course, are very different from his. His would never draw first or shoot someone in the back. When Don Siegel was directing *The Shootist* . . . Don says [to Wayne] 'Come up right behind him [a "guy" who comes into a saloon] and nail him.' There's a big silence, and then Wayne says,

Tom Tisdale, June, 1992, at Haywood's Gulch, speaking on the murder of his
grandfather Tom A. Tisdale, November 30, 1891.

'I never shoot'em in the back.' Then Don makes a terrible error. He says, '*Clint* would
shoot him in the back.'" In editing the account of Tom Tisdale's account of his grandfather's murder, I considered the tastefulness of juxtaposing this playful remembrance of
Clint Eastwood against the dead seriousness of Tom Tisdale and the spellbound audience
attending his remarks; but I also considered the effect, and "force," of excluding Eastwood's remarks as if I held some kind of authority to maintain a boundary between the
one recollection, Tisdale's, and the other, Eastwood's.

the blood flowed, how the body fell back on the load. He described how the wagon was loaded. His narration included a description of what Canton did after his grandfather was shot, leading the wagon and horses a bit farther into the gulch and shooting the horses, then killing John A.'s dog that Tom's grandfather had acquired in Buffalo. A puppy, also acquired, was later found in the wagon alive, huddled under a cover on the wagon; it survived and was raised as his father's pet. Tom Tisdale remarked ironically that it was another grandfather who got Canton out of jail on $30,000 bond.[30]

Jim Dillinger, a local historian and descendant of Johnson County homesteaders and storekeepers, offered some comments as well, as the crowd surveyed the site of John A.'s killing. Jim's "grandmother's friend, Mrs. Hogerson,[31] saw Canton's horse in Buffalo later in the morning in a lather in the stable. It had been running hard . . . but the women were afraid to talk about it . . . Fred Hesse may have been a look-out for Canton."[32] Jim Dillinger's wife spoke up too, he related. She said, "I want to ride another bus today, where the truth about these events will be told."

*

The bus party then moved on to Kaycee, to the site of the killing of Nathan Champion in April 1892. At Kaycee, the group was accorded a breakfast at the community center, and after a series of welcomes, Patty

30. Tom Tisdale was evidently referring to the Second District Court proceeding in Laramie, April 3, 1892, just a few days before the invasion, when Frank Canton was charged with first-degree murder and released on $30,000 bail.

31. This was Sarah—Mrs. Charles—Hogerson, who was born in Norway. She had moved to Buffalo with Charles, who opened a blacksmith's shop in the early 1880s after some years moving through the West as a wheelwright employed by the U.S. army. At the time of the invasion the Hogersons were living immediately next door to Henry and Sophia Mikkelson Rothwell in Buffalo. Jim Dillinger's mother Katherine was the eldest Rothwell child. At the time of the invasion, Charles Hogerson was acting mayor of Buffalo.

32. Through various narratives in the commemoration, and in a number of texts, Fred G. S. Hesse, a Johnson County rancher, and perhaps the most active Johnson County participant in the Stock Growers Associations of the day, and also one of the invaders, has been continuously and closely linked to Frank Canton. After an arrest warrant was issued for Canton on fresh charges that he had murdered John A. Tisdale, Canton and Fred Hesse, according to Smith, *War on Powder River*, 175, fled Buffalo on December 17, 1891—though a controversy developed as to whether they were chased out of Johnson County by "rustlers" or were pursued by Buffalo lawmen or were simply traveling together out of town as Canton wanted to catch a train to join his wife in Illinois. On April 3, 1892, Canton appeared in the Second District Court in Laramie, Wyoming, where he was charged with first-degree murder and released on $30,000 bail. The nearby invasion train

Myers introduced relatives of various participants in the Cattle War, including

   (i)   Mike Shonsey, who was implicated by various sources in an earlier and failed attempt to kill Nate Champion, had been known to have been feuding with Champion for months, rode with the invaders, brought word that Champion was in his cabin at the KC Ranch, and was positioned in the ravine among those whose shots would kill Champion as he fled his burning cabin;[33]

  (ii)   Tom Smith, an invader, and the recruiter and leader of the Texans who comprised most of the mercenary party among the invaders, and who directed that a card with the inscription "Cattle thieves, beware" be pinned to Champion's body;

 (iii)   Tom Waggoner, a homesteader in Newcastle, Wyoming, who had been taken from his home and family and hanged from a nearby tree in June 1891;

 (iv)   James C. Shaw, long-time friend of Champion, whose family member present stood and announced that Shaw had boarded the train and tried to argue the invasion leaders out of continuing with their plan . . . an assertion that drew from the president of the historical society the reaction, "Sure . . . sure . . . sure!";

  (v)   William Long(?);

 (vi)   Fred G. S. Hesse, who was a very active Johnson County member of the Wyoming Stock Growers Association and a founder and active member in a parallel organization, and who has been fingered by some as a henchman of accused assassin Frank Canton;

 (vii)   Smith and Taylor [not clear which Smith and which Taylor were being referred to];

(viii)   [Fred] Dillinger, a homesteader in Johnson County and later a clerk at the New York Store in Buffalo.

Patty Myers then introduced Margaret Brock Hanson, a local historian and a daughter of J. Elmer Brock,[34] who wrote on the Cattle War. She addressed the group in the Kaycee community center:

---

left Cheyenne for Casper on the afternoon of April 5, 1892, with Frank Canton and Fred G. S. Hesse aboard. The morning of the ninth, the invading party reached the KC Ranch and Nate Champion's cabin. Hesse was born in England and came to the United States in 1873.

33. I have added these identifications; Patty Myers simply introduced the family members and named their antecedent.

34. It was Brock who in May 1935 interviewed Charles Basch on what he had seen that day on November 30, 1891, at Haywood's Gulch. The Basch interview and other papers

I was much opposed to celebrate the invasion . . . It is those who
stuck it out who should be honored. We don't want people from
outside turning this into a Hatfields and McCoys . . . We are decid-
edly not people gunning for each other . . . Everyone around here
is intermarried. The cause of the war was nothing other than the
high-handedness of foreign owners . . . Grandfather Brock[35] came
out to Wyoming from the east to beat tuberculosis . . . he simply
found himself caught between the outlaws and the barons . . . this
was a tough life out here . . . Americans did not want to be peasants and serfs of foreign owners . . . The British saw Wyoming as a
play-ground for themselves and their investments . . . The mountains west of here were filled with English trophy hunters who
were also, at the same time, collecting trophies from Africa and
Asia. My grandfather said that "basically the problem was economic with changing the law from the six-shooter to the civil
courts."

Hanson then offered a good deal of evidence in support of her grandfather's argument that there was indeed thievery in Johnson County and
that the courts were unable to convict the rustlers. Hanson also noted
that "the invasion was not unplanned in Buffalo." Some of its good citizens wanted the invaders to come in and clean out the bad elements.
But at the last hour these good citizens broke with the invaders and left
them helpless at the TA Ranch.

*

In commencing her remarks by positioning herself against the commemoration, Margaret Brock Hanson broke open a "silence" in noting
that the idea of marking the anniversary of the Cattle War was itself
contested. Hanson's introduction brought back into view Patty Myers's
comments over the phone in March 1992 that in planning the commemoration they had sought to avoid refighting the battle. At the symposium, various members of the audience, and both McDermott and Harvey, spoke in general terms of the tensions and anger that lingered long
after the invasion itself. But I had no sense of palpable conflict—even at
Haywood's Gulch—until Hanson introduced in an angry tone her own

relating to the Cattle War have been in the custody of the Western History Research Center
archives at Laramie, with a provision that they not be opened until 1973. In *War on Powder
River*, 176, Smith cites sections of the Basch interview which she has indicated were leaked
from the archives before that date.

35. This is, presumably, Albert Brock, an early Johnson County settler, who told stories
in support of Champion's integrity.

distaste for the commemoration of *this* past. Later that day, at the banquet, I learned that the historical society had organized a number of small discussion groups through the winter and spring in which members sought to introduce the plans for commemoration to the people of Buffalo.

But I was left wondering what explained the absence within the commemoration of open conflict concerning the interpretation of the events of the 1880s and 1890s, even as people continued to speak of the long aftermath of continuing tension. Was the commemoration planned in a way that such an absence of conflict was a mark of success on the part of the planners? Or was this a commemoration for those who for a long time had viewed themselves as associated with the "inside," under attack in 1891–92 from the "outside"—shifting the terms of the conflict from the framework presented in 1892 and 1894 by Flagg and Mercer (and essentially revitalized in McDermott's talks), with its focus on the role of capital, to a different framework of "us" (those of Buffalo and Johnson County) and "them" (Cheyenne, Englishmen, Washington, the United States army)? Or was it the absence, or the impossibility of presence, of those who would be, or were, associated with the act of invasion and the convocation of a program of genocide?

*

Margaret Brock Hanson's critique of distant and foreign capitalists was partially echoed in the closing remarks of a speaker at Fort McKinney, the site where the invaders were taken for safekeeping, after the United States army intervened and ended the seige of the invaders at the TA Ranch.[36] The speaker related the 1892 war to the 1894–95 closing of Fort McKinney, which came—he said—suddenly, doing great damage to the local economy that had developed around the fort. At a time (1992) when Washington was closing down military bases in Wyoming, including the intercontinental ballistic missile silos (which dot the landscape of Johnson County and neighboring counties), "The lesson of the Johnson County War and its aftermath is that we have to be ever vigilant of those Washington people."

At the closing banquet of the commemoration weekend, Jane Brainerd, from Britain, a historian and archivist at the Wyoming State Archives in Cheyenne, complained that "It is unfair the beating that the British get over this war." In response to Jean Brainerd's remark on the attacks on British capitalists, Patty Myers remarked that during the en-

---

36. Fort McKinney is now a Veterans Home.

tire weekend no one spoke up for Frank Canton, though there were several Canton "followers" at the meeting.

*

Nowhere in my presence did the film *Heaven's Gate* come up for discussion during the weekend's activities until, over dinner at the closing banquet, I finally opened my mouth and asked those at my table if the film had been screened in Buffalo. Patty Myers related that

> *Heaven's Gate* is such a piece of fiction . . . it's really laughable. No one here has seen much of it. The blood and guts[37] had nothing to do with the history of the war. The film makes a big thing about racism, but there was nothing like that here . . . sometimes when *Heaven's Gate* is on cable, the library knows about it, because a few calls come in . . . They [the makers of the film, like the invaders] never came through Buffalo . . . There may be another film on the Johnson County War . . . it's an old black and white film, I think.

Also over dinner, Jean Brainerd of the Wyoming State Archives in Cheyenne said,

> There is a tremendous feeling in Johnson County about the war . . . *Heaven's Gate*, when it is on television, we know about it because people call to find out what ethnic group got wiped out in

---

37. At various points in the weekend one heard speakers noting that only two or so people were killed in the Cattle War and Patty Myers here seemed to be contrasting the slaughter depicted in the Cimino film to the limited loss of life noted in the historical record. But as one sifted the record—and perhaps Cimino went deeper than I did—one begins to stumble upon more and more deaths and disappearances: one of the invaders died of gangrene; John A. Tisdale and Ranger Jones; Tom Waggoner; Ella Watson and Jim Averill; Sie Partridge; various named and unnamed witnesses; at least one soldier at Suggs, and others murdered in the tense aftermath; as well as individuals earlier given frontier justice as "rustlers." This is not to suggest that Cimino got the picture, or the census of death, right; but Cimino's essential argument concerns the deployment of a killing plan by the cattlemen. Had the invaders not been stopped at the TA Ranch, all the evidence suggests that such a slaughter would have taken place. But in contrast to Cimino's evident need to make a point through the depiction of mass slaughter—as in a Sergei Eisenstein film—the participants at the commemoration were deeply affected by the accounting of just three deaths, the murders of John A. Tisdale, Nathan Champion, and Nick Ray, as were many of the contemporaries of the three men. Would the immense production of historical accounts of the war have happened had no one been killed? It seems, from this present angle and this present moment, extraordinary that such an outpouring of interest in the Johnson County conflict, from 1892 to the present, would have developed around the deaths of but three or six or seven or ten principal victims.

the fighting . . . Cimino never came to the archives to try to find
out what really happened.[38]

Jack McDermott walked by the table. Overhearing the conversation he
said, "*Shane* is the best film about the Johnson County War."

*

In June 1992, there was no cinema in Buffalo. Video stores in the town
used marquees and graphics that resembled theater fronts. On June 20,
1992, one of these large boards noted that *City Slickers*, starring Billy
Crystal, was "now showing," meaning "available for rental." *City Slickers*
is a comedy about a group of urban and suburban folk who take a
"dude ranch" vacation in the West that involves a simulated cattle drive.
A "guide" for the "green-horns" is an ancient cowboy, nearing the end
of his time but still speaking and acting the part, played by Jack Palance.[39]

   George Stevens's 1952 film *Shane* offered audiences their first extended view of Jack Palance as a dark Western figure, and it is Palance's
role in *Shane* that is continued, as caricature, in *City Slickers*. *Shane*, based
on a novel by Jack Schaefer, found its material in the struggles in the
West between the "homesteader" or "squatter," represented by Joe Starrett (played by Van Heflin), and the large cattlemen, represented by the
Riker brothers. The film opens with Shane riding toward the Starrett
homestead, which appears well watered, verdant, productive. Shane
(played by Alan Ladd) remarks to Starrett, "Headed north . . . didn't
expect to find many fences around here." One learns from Starrett of the
struggle to maintain a home in the face of the Rikers, the cattlemen.
They "need all the range." "Riker thinks the whole world belongs to
him." But, for Starrett, "Running cattle on an open range can't go on
forever." Starrett tells Shane to "Pick your spot . . . get your land, your
own land . . . we make out, Marian," referring to his wife (played by
Jean Arthur). Starrett declares, "The only way they're going to get me
out of here is in a pine box."

   38. In the credits to *Heaven's Gate*, Michael Cimino gives "Special thanks to the Wyoming State Museum and Archives and A. S. Mercer, George Dunning, Nathan D. Champion, John Clay, and Jack Flagg and all the early reporters who contributed to . . . *Cheyenne
Daily Leader, Casper Weekly Mail, Buffalo Bulletin, The Great Falls Tribune, The Omaha World
Herald, Northwestern Livestock Journal*, the *Western Brand Book*, and the *Annals of Wyoming*."
   39. At the 1992 Academy Awards ceremonies in Los Angeles, Palance received an Oscar
for best supporting actor for his part in this comedy, and in part stole the show by demonstrating—without apparent warning to the hosts and directors of the Academy Awards
program—that at his great age he could do a succession of one-armed push-ups.

Much of the film develops along two axes: first, the male bonding between Starrett and Shane, once a gun-fighter now trying to find another way of life, as he volunteers to help Starrett with the development and protection of the homestead; second, the bonding among a dispersed group of homesteaders, some ready to stick it out at great risk and cost, others close to leaving for fear of the Rikers' potential for violence against their homes, their crops, and their families. If there is a narration in the film, it is provided by the Starrett's only child, Joey (played by Brandon de Wilde), who establishes himself early on in the film as a Greek chorus.

As the homesteaders organize the defense of their farms, the Rikers send a man to Cheyenne to bring a gunfighter to help them break the homesteaders and their new-found defender, Shane. The gunfighter, Wilson (played by Palance), comes into the town and settles himself in the town's saloon, which is, throughout the film the Rikers' headquarters. Wilson baits one homesteader, Stonewall, who challenges the Rikers' gunfighter in the name of the "independence of the sovereign state of Alabama." Stonewall dies in the mud of the town street, first victim of the gunfighter. Shane is baited as well, and at Starrett's homestead there is a struggle among Starrett, his wife Marian, and Shane over what should be done. Starrett announces that he is going to go to town to kill Riker. Shane tries to stop him, as does Marian. Starrett claims that this is his fight, not Shane's, and revisits some of the discussion early on concerning the moral struggle between home and range, proclaiming that there is a contrast between growing beef and growing families. Shane tries to beat Starrett into submission, but Starrett goes off to town anyway. One of Riker's men arrives and announces that he has quit Riker's bunch and has come to warn Shane that if Starrett goes into town he "will be up against a stacked deck." Shane collects his gun and the rest of his possessions, mounts his horse and leaves for town, followed by young Joey Starrett and his dog. The film closes with the by then and still formulaic gunfight in the town saloon, and then Shane rides off into the distance.

As Jack McDermott signaled in Buffalo, *Shane* is in many respects a brilliant reproduction of the Johnson County War. Where Michael Cimino, with *Heaven's Gate*, reached for dense detail and close description to produce the feel of the past, George Stevens produced something of an allegory and may have, through an economy of portraiture and a resolution of some of the essential structures of the Wyoming range war, achieved a mythic text. Cimino moved around dozens of principal characters and thousands of extras; Stevens used but a handful of characters, and scant extras. In *Shane,* each figure is made to stand for a moral universe and a historical process: Stonewall, for example, standing pathetically in the mud, about to die in unfair combat with the gunslinger, is made to represent the old Confederate rabble transplanted to the West and Northwest who, in numerous accounts, were the undisciplined "labor" of the ranches who became targets of the stockgrowers. But the Rikers,[40] the cattlemen, also must lose in this morality tale, because there is no room in the West, finally, for those who will not respect the property rights of common men and women, represented by Joe and Marian Starrett. Shane in all his overt complexity presents an opportunity to explore the several moral dimensions of violence and civility.

Where *Heaven's Gate* portrays a struggle between the interests of capital and the interests of new immigrants to the country, *Shane* reveals in some of its motifs a different contest: and this is one between the dark and destructive arena of the town, with its evil forces and dangers, and the light and hopeful world of family endeavor removed from the spoil of civilization. In *Shane,* George Stevens's portrait of the town is one of a ruinous, mud-filled, decadent, and corrupt world. He uses darkened imagery in each town scene, and in the gunfight between the Palance character and Stonewall, the effects of contrast of dark and light are at their most stunning and most fearsome. On the other hand, the homestead scenes are light and always verdant; there is water and there is moisture, but hardly any mud; the homes are well constructed and well kept. Indeed, Stevens works, or overworks, the contrast between families making good on the prairie and a town world in which there are no families. Good people come to town for necessities, but they stay away from the saloon, and they leave before nightfall. The good homesteaders travel to town in groups for mutual support and protection, and so forth. Starrett and Shane engage in their own fistfight to prevent the other from risking his life by going to town to face the Rikers and their man Wilson. You do not go to town on your own, or casually, unless you are looking to die.[41]

In *Heaven's Gate,* on the other hand, it is the town that carries opportu-

---

40. The "Rikers" as a group are an intriguing and ambiguous quantity. Are they indeed brothers, or is there an elder patriarch and a group of younger men, or are they a sort of clientele organized around and taking the name of a patron? Is George Stevens's intent here to contrast an idealized image of an American domestic family unit with an antiquated and corrupted form of social organization?

41. In his *Sixguns and Society: A Structural Study of the Western* (Berkeley: University of California Press, 1975), Will Wright also identifies the Rikers especially "with society" (50–51), but then argues a distinction between Shane as signifying the untamed, the wil-

nity and new civic culture. It is the town where the defense of community values and interests against the cattlemen is organized. The roller-skating rink is always presented in nearly white light, the sunlight bleached and drawn through the light, translucent roofing. There are artisans, musicians, dancers, business people, and others who have made the town the hopeful receiver and nurturer of new waves of immigrants. One may ask whether, in his zest for "hubbub," Michael Cimino invented a very different world from that which George Stevens imagined in *Shane*. One notation is a report in the *Buffalo Bulletin*, December 18, 1890, that the women of Buffalo's new Methodist Church were sponsoring the first "Merchant's Carnival":

> Forty-one Buffalo firms were represented by the young ladies of the community, who were cleverly robed to portray each business or profession. The Post Office made forty-two. This number did not include any of the 23 saloons, catering to the thirst of soldiers and civilians. A net profit of $140 was realized from the carnival.

And, in the second week of April 1892 it was within the town that four hundred Johnson County defenders organized themselves and then raced to the TA Ranch to surround the invaders and end this particular assault. For John A. Tisdale on November 30, 1891, and for Ranger Jones a few days earlier, it was the prairie and not the town that contained all the world's dangers.[42]

While George Stevens and Michael Cimino both chose to paint the

---

derness, and all the rest of the players as signifying such artifacts of civilization as farms, buckboards, saloons, and stores (58). Where, at the commemoration banquet, Jack McDermott saw *Shane* as grounded in the historical framework of a specific Johnson County Cattle War centering on capital and the control of labor, Wright—deploying a structural analysis—sees *Shane* developing its form through the evolving shape and play of American mythology, a mythology that, by implication of Wright's thesis, makes a greater distinction between wilderness and civilization than between work and capital. One might also consider Colin Keeney's opening argument that the Johnson County Cattle War was a most important *formative* agent in the development of thought and literature about the American West and past, while Will Wright sees the film *Shane* brilliantly *tapping into* that mythology.

42. During the commemoration weekend visit to the site of the assassination of John A. Tisdale, a discussion developed in the audience about whether Tisdale had three or four bullets in his gun at the time of his death, and what additional arms and ammunition he had that day. This discussion was not about whether he could have successfully countered Frank Canton's attack (after all, Canton—if it were Canton—came from behind cover as Tisdale and his wagon passed and then shot him in the back); the question raised was how prepared John A. was for trouble when he left town. For some who took up this discussion, three bullets in his gun suggested that John A. was not expecting trouble, while for others the four bullet hypothesis suggested that he was.

cattlemen as the enemies of a new moral order, they seized distinct and opposed positions in visualizing the program of producing that new order. Stevens saw virtue made powerful through the sustenance and protection of the values of family and home, standing against a cruel and violent urban order. Stevens contemplated the architecture of a new community and society (displacing that of the Rikers) constructed of the solitary efforts of yeoman householders like the Starretts, tilling the land, protecting their fences, building their homes, raising their children. Cimino, on the other hand, located community and social virtue in the collective project of civil order constructed within an urbanizing landscape through the courage of new immigrants oppressed by the violence and racism of the old system.

Where, in this threefold field of dramatically conflicting representation, synthesis, and argument, are the polarized voices of Mark Harvey's two hats?[43] Cimino's argument, in this sense, seems directed not only against the celebration of domestic virtue and individual effort in American culture but also against the programs through which the violence of capital was combed out of American consciousness through such vehicles as the "Western."

43. Or the grounds for pronouncing *Shane* as the "best film about the Johnson County War."

EIGHT

The Constitution of Expertise

An exploration of the space distinguishing, yet also joining, the production of history within and outside the guild, situates in more complex ways notions of expertise. The tensions among intellectuals seeking to manage images, paradigms, and arguments are centered in the issue of acquisition of the map[1] as they also are in the careful work of replication at Colonial Williamsburg and the Harper's Ferry laboratory, and in the reportage of Paul Cowan, Herb Gutman, Lloyd Fallers, Sam Clover, O. H. Flagg, Asa Shinn Mercer, Michael Cimino, George Stevens, and Rea Tajiri.

In the Camella Teoli story that Herb Gutman tabled in Paris, it is possible to see expert knowledge, and also the practitioners of such expertise, moving to and from, into and out of, frames of public and popular discourse over the past. One can ask about the shifting composition of "audiences," about who is listening to whom, and about the struggles for control of vocabularies, grammars, and symbolic materials in the telling and writing of history. In the Lawrence instance, the story of the story is not simply about the reawakening of popular consciousness in Lawrence. It is also about committees, negotiations, mayors and constitutents, public institutions such as the library, the schools and curriculum, dinner dances, forms of radio broadcasting, labor unions and their organizers, television and newspapers. The production of history in Lawrence has an intimate realm but also a heavily socially negotiated and organized one. It is about "insiders" and "outsiders" and about one *Grenzgenger* Paul Cowan who knitted a broader net of relationships between New York and Lawrence, Massachusetts. One can ask how far the social recomposition of collective history requires the intervention of the stranger, indeed how the academy of historical practice produces the historian as stranger. And one can reflect upon historians and anthropologists, trained in the guilds, peering through a story of the telling of stories. One may also see how closely the guild production of history is engaged in the ways the "subjects" of research tell their stories.

The Lawrence story provides a view of the unpredictability, the unintentional amidst so much congested matter and it was surely as unexpected that Paul Cowan would find and link the distinct but deeply intertwined stories of Camella's childhood and her daughter's experi-

---

1. See chap. 5.

ence combing Camella's hair as it was surprising that a simple request to a public museum for a photograph of an item on display would open an array of questions about power, authority, expertise, image, representation, censorship, and the idea of "public." At another level, Herb Gutman could not anticipate what effect his brief telling of the Lawrence story would have on a collection of friends and colleagues.

Nor could one anticipate the effect of a reading of the writings of the Cambridge-trained anthropologist Jean La Fontaine and the writings and political activism of George W. Wamimbi, a schoolteacher and historian living and working in eastern Uganda.[2]

*

In April 1970 a schoolteacher in eastern Uganda, George W. Wamimbi, produced a long and detailed English language manuscript entitled "Modern Mood in Masaaba."[3] G. W. Wamimbi was one of the founders of the Masaaba Historical Research Association and "Modern Mood in Masaaba" was produced as a long and eloquent oration on the culture and past of the people known variously—in anthropological literature, regional historiography, and Uganda administrative practice—as the Gisu or Bagisu or Bamasaaba.

In an interview done by Stephen Bunker on March 7–8, 1970, George Wamimbi related that

> he had started MHRA [the Masaaba Historical Research Association] in 1954 with a group of other students who were in J3 with him at Nyondo TTC [Teacher Training College]. He was then 17. In 1956, the MHRA was extended from a student organization to include adults, but Wamimbi remained president, and has been since.[4]

In early 1971, in a memorandum prepared for Bunker, Wamimbi wrote that the Masaaba Historical Research Association "was founded on 6th

2. This paper develops out of David William Cohen, "La Fontaine and Wamimbi: The Anthropology of 'Time-Present' as the Substructure of Historical Oration," in *Chronotypes: The Construction of Time*, ed. John Bender and David E. Wellbery (Stanford: Stanford University Press, 1991), 205–25. I am grateful to the editors for their counsel and support, and also to Stephen Bunker, Gillian Feeley-Harnik, Suzette Heald, Jonathan Lewis, George Martin, Gabrielle Spiegel, and Michael Twaddle for their early and helpful assistance and comment. Katherine Verdery offered the ultimate guiding question of this paper in response to an early draft of the work on Wamimbi: "Is there a 'native' in this text?"

3. Apparently circulated only in a mimeograph edition.

4. Quoting Bunker's interview notes. The discussion which follows is based on Stephen Bunker's field notes and copies of Wamimbi's memoranda and correspondence. These

February 1954 in St. Peter's College, Tororo in Eastern Uganda by Mr. George Masaaba Wamimbi, who has been its President-General ever since."[5] According to Bunker's notes and memoranda, on January 10, 1962, the association drafted and approved a constitution, with the stated "objectives":

> to collect the past and present history of Bugisu and to establish Masaba Museum; to write books in Lumasaba; to collect and correct common mistakes and develop Lumasaba grammatically; to translate various books from other languages into Lumasaba; to find meanings of names of places and people of Bugisu; and to write down the Geography of Bugisu.[6]

Bunker's notes indicate that the association was—within ten months—petitioning the minister of Regional Administration in Entebbe in a memorandum entitled "Bugisu Land Belongs to the Bagisu." Following a preface on the geography and the early colonial history of the region, the association wrote:

> The Bugisu-Bukedi Boundary Dispute Commission was set up early this year. We willingly co-operated with the Commission but what has happened to its report? The Bagisu are thirsting and longing for the Report. There is a rumour that Bukedi, Bugisu and Sebei Districts might be re-amalgamated. Indeed that is very very unacceptable and can never be entertained by any Mugisu. We shall bitterly and energitically [sic] oppose that move.

---

were passed along to me by Stephen Bunker to whom I am very grateful. The historical writings of George Wamimbi were part of a bundle of materials collected by Franz Rottland which were tabled at the 1985 Johns Hopkins University seminar on Gisu circumcision.

5. One should note here the work of Michael Twaddle, who came across George Wamimbi during his research in Mbale, Uganda, in the 1960s. He found that "during the 1950s a number of young Gisu came together to form the Masaba Research Society in order to collect and collate local traditions of origin relating to Mbale and its ethnic environs. But increasingly this society has become a collection of straightforward antiquaries as its political intentions have been frustrated by official delays. Today its members are attempting to standardize the Lumasaba language, record old circumcision songs, and collect materials for an ambitious History of Bugisu to be edited by the Society's President, George Wamimbi." See Michael Twaddle, "Tribalism in Eastern Uganda," in P. H. Gulliver, *Tradition and Transition in East Africa* (London: Routledge & Kegan Paul, 1969), 202.

6. One notes an effort among some individuals in the area, including Wamimbi, to replace such terms as "Bagisu" and "Lugisu" with "Bamasaba" and "Lumasaba," perhaps an effort at what was viewed as an appropriate modernization and also as a tactical separation of the new literature from older studies, most particularly the works of John Roscoe in the early part of the century (see note below for references to Roscoe's works). Here, Wamimbi interspersed the different nomenclatures.

In December 1965 at Makerere University College in Kampala, George Wamimbi participated in a seminar on "the techniques of collecting and recording local history." In his presentation to the meeting he reviewed the objectives and work of the association, which included the

> Past and Present history of the Basmasaaba and to establish a Museum for all or some of the Kimasaaba materials used by the Bamasaaba . . . In this first aim we devide [sic] our history into (i) that before the Europeans set foot in Bugisu and (ii) that from the coming of Kakungulu and the Europeans in Bugisu and so on.

Wamimbi went on at length to review the achievements of the association, its methods of research, and its future plans. He brought greater specificity to the linguistic agenda, defining the importance of establishing a standard Lumasaaba orthography as a preface to writing and publishing books in Lumasaaba. He also detailed a program of cooperation with parallel organizations elsewhere in East Africa.

Three years later, December 30, 1968, Wamimbi wrote a long memorandum to the Bugisu District Administration in response to a letter from the administration demanding more information before providing fresh funds in subsidy of the Masaaba Historical Research Association. Again, Wamimbi reviewed the objectives and achievements of the association, this time referring to regional conferences held in previous years in the district. More interesting for the present work was the inclusion of a brief report on the progress of a book being produced by the association on the history of Bugisu, to be titled "Bugisu in Modern Uganda," according to Wamimbi. Appropriately, Wamimbi offered the District Administration no account of the political work and political agenda of the association. But there was, indeed, a considerable political agenda: recognition of the Lumasaaba language and standard orthography; the reformation of the school curriculum in the Masaaba area; the reparation of boundaries in eastern Uganda; the organization of district administration; the adjudication of disputes with the government over the timing, regulation, and legality of elements of circumcision campaigns, which had become a critical element in the assertions of Gisu or Masaaba identity within an independent Uganda nation.

For Wamimbi and his colleagues in the Masaaba Historical Research Association, all these problems were seen to be addressable through arguments from history. In the years following, the association produced a seventy-two-page "History," a series of special papers entitled "Malembe," or "Masaba Historical Research Association Presents Its Work," and Wamimbi's "Modern Mood in Masaaba."

*

At the Makerere meeting in 1965, Wamimbi brought his audience's attention specifically to the subject of circumcision:

> Although we have known some facts on circumcision, a lot has to
> be done, for its ceremonies differs [sic] almost from sub-county to
> sub-county. Circumcision is by far the most favourable custom in
> the District. It can be compared to the Olimpic [sic] Games of Old
> Greece. Every Mugisu young or old, female or male must like it
> and every person is forced to join in the dancing and running. (It
> is a wonderful Scene when the time for circumcision has come or
> is approaching.) There is peace and joy all over the District during
> this time of the year. People are happy, impatiently awaiting the oc-
> casion.

In chapter 8 of "Modern Mood in Masaaba," Wamimbi presents an extended, detailed discussion of male circumcision, *Imbalu*, among the people of Masaaba. For Wamimbi, *Imbalu* is the central rite of the people of Masaaba.

Wamimbi's writings on *Imbalu* and his notations on the development of the Masaaba Historical Research Association—the production of a "native voice" and a "native text"—provide an unusual view of the processes of construction of historical and cultural knowledge.

*

In November 1985 serendipity suggested the opportunity of quickly convening a small workshop on the topic of *Imbalu* at Johns Hopkins University, Baltimore, in December 1985. A season of travel to and from academic conferences had positioned several scholars of *Imbalu* within hailing distance of Baltimore. Professor Jean La Fontaine had done anthropological fieldwork between 1953 and 1955 among the people of eastern Uganda known as the Gisu. Her research there had resulted in a Ph.D. dissertation in 1957 and, in 1959, *The Gisu of Uganda*, a volume in the Ethnographic Survey of Africa series.[7] Professor Franz Rottland

---

7. La Fontaine's dissertation was never published. *The Gisu of Uganda* (London: International African Institute, 1959) and subsequent articles on the Gisu were, as a collection, an important contribution to British social anthropology, particularly in the study of initiation ritual. These studies reflected, at the same time, the formative influences upon La Fontaine of the field as it was constituted in the early 1950s, and particularly the interests of her mentor Meyer Fortes in comprehending the ways in which roles become, through ritual, transitional structures. Paradoxically, while La Fontaine's main interest in respect to her Gisu research was with initiation, her mentor Fortes found no initiation rituals among the people he studied, the Tallensi.

of the University of Bayreuth had in 1970 been part of a Makerere University faculty team which had traveled to eastern Uganda to document—from the perspectives and through the practices of different disciplines—a Gisu circumcision campaign. Rottland had maintained a set of some fifteen papers produced by the team, along with copies of typescripts on *Imbalu* produced by eastern Ugandan writers, including Wamimbi. Professor Stephen Bunker, a sociologist and a new Hopkins faculty member, had spent long periods in eastern Uganda working on the peasant economy in the area of Bugisu and had himself interviewed several of the local authorities on *Imbalu* and Gisu history, including Wamimbi. Professor Aidan Southall, a University of Wisconsin anthropologist, had also been a member of the Makerere team. Dr. Suzette Heald, a visitor to the Smithsonian Institution in nearby Washington, had recently done extensive research on *Imbalu* and had produced an ethnographic film which was made available for showing. Professors Gillian Feeley-Harnik of the Hopkins anthropology department, along with her students, and E. S. Atieno Odhiambo, then of the University of Nairobi but at the same time a visiting professor of history at Hopkins, brought special experience and insight to the discussion of *Imbalu*. I had witnessed the Gisu circumcision campaigns in their extensions into Busoga to the west and had examined the Makerere papers during a research visit to the University of Cologne in 1983.

The scholars at the Hopkins seminar drew attention to the differences in accounts and descriptions of *Imbalu*, as noted in the bundle of papers circulated in advance of the meeting. In the discussions, seminar participants commented on the significance of perspectives which different disciplines introduced into the exercise of describing *Imbalu*. Attention was also given to the differences in circumcision practice from one area of Bugisu to another and to the effect of the *locus* of fieldwork observation on the description of *Imbalu*.[8] And there was a very considerable interest in finding methods and sources to unpack the deeper history of circumcision practices in eastern Uganda.

But at the seminar at Johns Hopkins, Professor La Fontaine several times challenged the value of oral evidence for historical reconstruction,

8. In and around the Hopkins meeting, the critique of the ethnographic literature on Gisu *Imbalu* carried some of the flavor of the then recent and remarkable debates surrounding the status of Margaret Mead's Samoan research. Where some voices seemed to develop from a will to dethrone the early authorities such as La Fontaine, other voices appeared to be struggling to produce "objective" explanations of difference—such as the locus or timing of the observation—to preserve, somehow, the scientific standing of anthropological authority as represented in the papers tabled in Baltimore.

with specific reflection on the study of the Gisu past, declaring oral traditions and testimonies "suspect" and "ingenious" and "ungrounded in reality." When asked about the past of the Bagisu before 1954, Professor La Fontaine referred the questioners either to written sources produced by colonial officials and missionaries or remarked on the paucity of written sources which "regrettably limited the opportunities for doing proper history."[9]

*

At the conclusion of the *Imbalu* meeting at Hopkins, I, with the assistance of Jonathan Lewis, reviewed the papers and discussions to see if

9. It is perhaps appropriate to offer some descriptive words about the Gisu, or Bagisu, or Bamasaaba of eastern Uganda. Over several years of writing from her 1953–55 field research, Jean La Fontaine developed a brief, routine, and what she evidently conceived of as a sufficient introductory statement on the people and area she studied: "The Gisu are a Bantu-speaking people who live on the western slopes of Mount Elgon, an extinct volcano which lies across the Kenya-Uganda border, some fifty miles north of Lake Victoria. They number about a quarter of a million and form roughly two-thirds of the population of Bugisu District in the Eastern Province of Uganda" (*Gisu*, 9).

Or, "Since the Gisu have been described in detail elsewhere [*The Gisu of Uganda*], it is only necessary to give a brief recapitulation of the ethnographic background to the discussion. This Bantu tribe, numbering about a quarter of a million, practices settled agriculture on the fertile soil of Mount Elgon, an extinct volcano on the eastern border of Uganda. They are densely settled and land shortage is an old problem that is now becoming acute. The framework of Gisu social organization is a segmentary localized lineage system of which the basic political unit is the village, settled by members of a minor lineage. The minor lineage is segmented into minimal lineages which are the exogamous, property-controlling groups. Villages are not compact settlements but a defined tract of territory over which the homesteads of the inhabitants are scattered. Each village is roughly divided into neighbourhoods" (La Fontaine, "Witchcraft in Bugisu," in John Middleton and E. H. Winter, eds., *Witchcraft and Sorcery in East Africa* [London: Routledge & Kegan Paul, 1963], 187–88).

Compare this with: "The Bagesu are one of the most primitive of Bantu tribes. The Bagesu are a Bantu tribe living upon the eastern and southern slopes of Mount Elgon. They are a numerous people when judged by the numerical standard of other African tribes, being estimated at not less than a million souls. They are a very primitive race and stand low in the human scale, though it is somewhat difficult to understand why they should be so intellectually inferior, surrounded as they are by other Bantu tribes much more cultivated and civilised than themselves" (John Roscoe, *The Northern Bantu* [Cambridge: Cambridge University Press, 1915], 161).

Or "The Bagesu tribe on Mount Elgon is one of the most primitive of the negro tribes of Africa, and was driven from the plains to the east of Mount Elgon by the attacks of the Masai and Nandi. To escape the ravages of these warlike tribes, the Bagesu fled to the mountain, only to find that on the lower slopes they were subject to periodical raids by it were possible to propose a path toward further discussion and publication on *Imbalu*.[10] Early in 1986, as we were closely reading the entire corpus of published and unpublished work tabled at the Hopkins meeting, we were able to discern what appeared to be a relationship between La Fontaine's presentation of *Imbalu* in her 1959 *Gisu* and Wamimbi's account of *Imbalu* in his 1970 typescript "Modern Mood in Masaaba."

What one notes, in setting the La Fontaine text and the Wamimbi script side by side, is that the La Fontaine text of 1959 and the Wamimbi text of 1970 resemble one another in important ways. We continued to examine the texts more closely, and compared the two authors' accounts of Gisu initiation with all other accounts which we could find, both published and unpublished. Recognizing that the two texts were clearly *not* independently derived, we were interested in establishing the parentage of the two texts.

La Fontaine	*Wamimbi*
The rite of circumcision was performed at different times in different lineages, which had their traditional order for the performance of the ceremonies in the preceding lineage. The order was not rigidly fixed but, in general, was as follows: Bu-Ngokko, -Soba, -Siu, - —Sano, -Shiende,	The rite of circumcision is done at different times in various clans according to the wishes of the clan elders or *basukhulu*. In the days gone by circumcision was performed almost from clan to clan and in that way a lot of useful time was wasted. Really people in Bugisu cannot dare

the Abyssinians and those tribes who inhabited the borders of Abyssinia. They therefore made their way to the less easily accessible heights" (Roscoe, *The Bagesu* [Cambridge: Cambridge University Press, 1924], 1).

Or "The Gisu, numbering some 500,000, are Bantu-speaking agriculturalists living on slopes of Mount Elgon on the Ugandan side of the border with Kenya (Suzette Heald, "The Ritual Use of Violence: Circumcision among the Gisu of Uganda," [in press]).

And "The Bagisu, a Bantu people numbering over 500,000, occupy Bugisu District, which covers 1,170 square miles of eastern Uganda and includes the western and southern slopes of Mount Elgon. The earliest Bagisu settlements were on the mountain, but during the last century many of the Bagisu moved down onto the plains. They first located in the southwest and then moved around the mountain to settle the central and later the northern areas" (Stephen G. Bunker, *Peasants against the State: The Politics of Market Control in Bugisu, Uganda, 1900–1983* [Urbana and Chicago: University of Illinois Press, 1987], 32).

10. The papers tabled at the meeting were not publishable as a group. They were, to begin with, of different quality, some having been quickly penned as notes immediately after or during the Makerere field exercise. The authority to edit and publish the Makerere papers has been circulating among several scholars on the European and African continents. But there were opportunities for students of *Imbalu*—and also anthropologists and historians interested in the construction of ethnographic knowledge—to draw fresh evidence and insight from the papers and the discussions at Hopkins.

-Wagogo, -Tta, -Gobero, -Tiru . . . work if there is joy, dancing, singing
(41) and drumming in the country side.
People feel free and feel happy.
When the Government realised this,
they stepped in and each sub-county
or Gombolola was given a day on
which circumcision must take place.
Sundays were excluded. The Bamu-
toto clan of Bungokho must always
of necessity open up the circumcision period because this important
custom began in their clan, and so
the whole of Central Bugisu comes
first before the rest of the District.
Circumcision is taken in the following order on the days and dates actually specified by the Bugisu District
Administration: Central Bugisu: Bungokho, Busoba, Busiu, Bukhiende,
Bufumbo . . . (7/2–3)

There seemed a possibility that either La Fontaine or Wamimbi might
have been parent to the other text or that there may have been another
text—whether accessible to us or not—which might have been accessible to both authors.[11] We were interested in the identity (and the "moment") of the original inscription and in the process by which an original text was adapted and inscribed within a new version.

Amidst months of investigation of *Imbalu* texts, speculation, and discussion, we concluded that La Fontaine's text had, indeed, preceded
Wamimbi's and that Wamimbi paraphrased La Fontaine rather liberally
in building his own account of *Imbalu*.[12] In important ways, Wamimbi's
text appears to read as if its authority is seated firmly upon the authority of La Fontaine's ethnography.

Where some historians might be driven by the protocols of their discipline to disregard the derivative version and to focus attention on the

11. And we surveyed considerable speculation that a "parent account" was deposited
at some time in the district archives to which both La Fontaine and Wamimbi might have
had access.

12. Where we concluded that Wamimbi's text on *Imbalu* is written out of La Fontaine's
Gisu, there was of course no way to assure ourselves that earlier texts unknown to us may
have influenced either or both authors to some extent. Neither author cites any earlier
author who might have influenced their texts, though, as noted below, La Fontaine does
refer to John Roscoe's writings in her exposition.

original, what is significant in the comparision of La Fontaine and Wamimbi is that Wamimbi has expanded boldly on the La Fontaine text at a number of points; indeed, where La Fontaine's *Gisu* presents four pages on *Imbalu*,[13] Wamimbi's text is perhaps twice the length. Once one recognizes the path of inscription, one recognizes that Wamimbi has, without explaining his rhetorical operation, adapted the La Fontaine text to his own purposes. One may further speculate that the La Fontaine text has empowered Wamimbi's own text, and one may argue that La Fontaine's anthropological writing has actually made possible the Wamimbi text.

*

In "rewriting" the ethnography of Jean La Fontaine, the Cambridge-trained anthropologist, George W. Wamimbi, the Ugandan schoolteacher, has implicitly defined an important field of *difference* yet at the same time unveiled a latticework of *connection*. Wamimbi has imposed a different theory of practice on top of La Fontaine's text. What is evident from the comparison of the pair of texts above is that where La Fontaine has asserted the power of the "traditional" in establishing the order of timing of rites from lineage to lineage, Wamimbi has revised La Fontaine and introduces "agency": "the wishes of the clan elders." The Western sense that Africans governed their lives by "tradition" and "custom" is confounded as we notice that it is the Cambridge-trained anthropologist who has made the case for the determination of the "traditional" while the local writer has revised her work to introduce an entirely different perspective.

One might say that Wamimbi has gone still further, alerting the reader to the opening of a contest over the value of Time in the colonial period with the confrontation between the effects on the use of time rendered by the agency of clan elders and the notion that "useful time was wasted" which brought the "Government" to introduce regulations over the time of the rites. What is perhaps intended yet implicit in Wamimbi is an acknowledgment of an *economy of circumcision* which the new "government" policy affected: circumcision periods were made more uniform; the peripatetic character of the circumcisor's activity was substantially reduced; a shortage of circumcisors became evident; and a certain anxiety was noted in regard to the speed of cutting required for the circumcisors to get the job done.[14]

13. *The Gisu*, 41–45.
14. As noted earlier, I am most grateful to Professor Stephen Bunker for these observations which come from his fieldwork in Bugisu, done at approximately the same time as Wamimbi was drafting his manuscript.

Wamimbi has, in his writings, begun the reconquest of Time,[15] largely relieving the text from the burden of the "anthropological time-present" and the anthropologist's occasional use of the past tense. Wamimbi's reconquest of Time is both explicit and implicit. For one, he has introduced considerable temporal specification into the La Fontaine treatment of *Imbalu*. But also, where he utilizes the present tense, it may mean both more and less than La Fontaine's "time-present." For one, Wamimbi has an unconscious and consequential disregard for the conventions in ethnography concerning the use of the "anthropological time-present"; in an important way he helps us see La Fontaine's "time-present" as artificed synchrony. Moreover, Wamimbi has a longer span of time to establish the currency or continuity of aspects of *Imbalu* as described a decade and a half earlier by La Fontaine. And Wamimbi has established in his text very powerful concerns, indeed a political and cultural agenda, relating to the distinctions between present and past.

La Fontaine	*Wamimbi*
The rituals take place after the main harvest, which lasts from June to September, but formerly if there were a bad harvest the ceremonies would have been postponed a year. Today they are held regularly every other year, but it seems likely that formerly they were held less often. (42)	In all cases circumcision always takes place after the main harvest of millet (bulo) particularly between June and September. But when there is very serious shortage of food ceremonies can be postponed until further notice. For instance, there was very serious famine between 1917 and 1919 and because of the seriousness of that famine (inzala iya Kakutiya) boys and the uncircumcised men were not circumcised in 1919 which was supposed to be the year of circumcision, and so changed the order from odd years as it was formerly done to even years up to the present moment. (7/3)

Set next to valorizing and prescriptive sentences of Wamimbi, La Fontaine's text suggests the chilling quality of certain forms of ethnographic exposition. Where agency may be effaced through use of the "time-present," practices which still carry meaning and value may be interred through the simple rhetorical operation of the past tense.

15. This discussion of the treatment of Time in the two texts is more fully developed in David William Cohen, "La Fontaine and Wamimbi: The Anthropology of 'Time-Present'

La Fontaine	*Wamimbi*

Men circumcised in the same year, and particularly in the same village, were expected to behave towards each other as brothers. They called each other by a special term, magoji, and might not marry each other's daughters. The children of two magoji might not marry, but the grandchildren were allowed to do so. Magoji were expected to make certain gifts to one another, of which the most important was a cow at the circumcision of the son of one of them when he has the obligation to feast his age-mates with meat and beer. The ruling of the African Local Government in 1954 that there were to be no more such gifts caused widespread complaint. (42)

The boys and the men who undergo this intolerable and unforgettable pain in the same year regard themselves as real brothers—Bamakoki or Magoji. We can regard them as people of the same age-group. They are not allowed to marry each other's daughters and even their children may not marry one another. This tradition is very strong and began at the time when circumcision began in Bugisu. There are other rules and beliefs in connection with Bamakoki. They were not allowed to wrestle with one another. It was forbidden for these men to meet in the latrine or any other places of excretion. It was unlawful for them to find one another on the roof of a hut thatching the roof. It was considered illegal for one to find his Magoji bathing at the stream. If one of the above rules was violated, then the offender was asked to pay a fine to his magoji. The fine was to be negotiated between those concerned. Usually amicable agreement was reached. A man was almost compelled to give his Bamagoji things in the form of money, meat, chickens and beer if he had a son who had been circumcised that year. In some parts of the District, this practice is still carried on a very high scale. It is therefore important to remember that circumcision as a custom of the Bamasaaba creats [sic] a sense of fellow-feeling among men who are circumcised and initiated during the same year and these same people sincerely

---

as the Substructure of Historical Oration," in John Bender and David Wellbery, eds., *Chronotypes*, 205–25.

retain a sense of corporate
identity. (7/4)

On the other hand, Wamimbi was in a struggle to revive the past and
hold back the present. His reconstitution of tense forms allows him to
introduce and assert affect, and affect is substantially absent from the
La Fontaine passages. But, Wamimbi seems to have been after more than
simply a romance with the past. Here and elsewhere, Wamimbi has
used tense demarcation as a means of distinguishing the realm of government program and influence from internally sustained—and what
he has projected as valued—elements in the rituals of circumcision.
Where La Fontaine's treatment may be read as an epitaph reporting the
disappearance of a cultural practice, Wamimbi's text here begins and
ends as an oration on its high and continuing importance, though in the
discussion of rules established within, as opposed to those pressed into
service by government, he has shifted to the past tense. By transforming
La Fontaine's general temporality into the specific reporting of government edicts, and by introducing specific dates Wamimbi has altered the
nature of La Fontaine's exposition, making it possible for him to assert
the significance of historical contingencies.

In another segment of her treatment of *Imbalu*, La Fontaine turned
to John Roscoe's work for assistance in developing a description of the
circumcision ritual. "The account here," she writes, "is based on personal observation, with references to Roscoe where significant variations
occur."[16] There is some irony in the fact that as Wamimbi (who himself
went through the circumcision ritual and had occasion to participate in
and observe perhaps a dozen cycles up to 1970) turned to La Fontaine
(who observed but one cycle during her two years of fieldwork) for
description so La Fontaine turned to John Roscoe, who, forty years earlier, though a fine observer, was no expert on the Gisu specifically. It is
upon this revealed sequence of dependence in the series of observations
of *Imbalu* that one commences to ask if it would have been possible for
Wamimbi to write his "native text" without having the "guild text" of
La Fontaine upon which to develop his own text and from which to give
his text the authority which his political agenda required.

La Fontaine	Wamimbi
The first phase is occupied entirely with dancing. The novices dress up in the traditional costume and dance	The intending boys traditionally dress and dance in their local vil- lages at special places. They wear

16. Roscoe, *The Northern Bantu* (Cambridge: Cambridge University Press, 1915), 23.

on the village greens, under the direction of an older, already circumcised man, who leads the songs and
instructs the novices in the dances
and songs they will have to sing. Roscoe states that the initiates are given
formal instruction by the elders before circumcision, but I did not observe this and I do not think it ever
occurred. The dress of a novice con-
sisted of a headdress made of the
skin of a colobus monkey; cross-
bands made of the nuts of a tree or
beads used by women for the girdles
worn by all women round the hips
under the main clothing. (42)

bells—bizenze or zikuuma—which
are always worn on the thighs or kamakimba which are always used in
the hands. The majority of the boys
in Bugisu use the former type of
bells. But kamakimba are used
chiefly in Bumbo and Bubutu, but
they may be used in Butiru or Bu-
wabwala. The first type of dance is
called "isonja." The boys hire an expert man who is already circumcised—usually called by different
names of Khyilali, Namwenya or
simply Umwimbi according to various parts in the District. Besides
bells worn by the initiates, they wear
a head-dress—lilubisi—made of the
skin of a colobus monkey; then
cross-bands from special seeds or
nuts of a particular tree—kamaliisi
or beads formerly known as ma-
dongo. (7/4)

One observation is that while La Fontaine—at the Hopkins seminar—
saw her sources without value as materials for the reconstruction of the
past, and at no point made any claim that her ethnographical writings
could lay the groundwork of an historical exposition, Wamimbi saw her
materials, as digested into an ethnographic genre, as an important
means of valorization of the past. Where La Fontaine appears to have
considered those stories that were presented to her as speaking to present social and cultural concerns rather than as opening toward a reconstruction of the past, Wamimbi saw La Fontaine's materials as making
possible a strong and controlled appreciation and powerful use of history among the Bagisu. Those African, American, and European scholars at the December 1985 *Imbalu* seminar at Johns Hopkins heard La
Fontaine's perspective on her own texts as a distinctly and enduring
ahistorical one, while Wamimbi saw La Fontaine's *Gisu* as a powerful
basis for producing history.

Wamimbi made sense of La Fontaine's analysis not through an appreciation of "structures" and "functions," but through a realization
of the openness of Bugisu ritual. Wamimbi produced in one sense a
"double narrative." He worked within the conventions of presentation
of La Fontaine's ethnography, building upon the authority of her printed

work; yet he sought to construct another and very different work, with a concern for presentation of the constraints and contingencies which produced variation and made vulnerable what he saw as valued elements of circumcision ritual. He was also concerned to reintroduce into the treatment of circumcision the emotional, or affective, aspects of the ritual, the tumultuous qualities and pleasures of experiencing circumcision as audience and as initiate.[17]

*

The potential force of a written and published work such as La Fontaine's ethnography upon the oral expression and early writings (such as Wamimbi's "Modern Mood in Masaaba") of a newly literate culture has been well noted. In *The Chronology of Oral Tradition*, the historian and archivist David Henige examined ways in which "oral traditions arose in response to a broad range of stimuli."[18] Henige took the printed word as one, and a very significant one, of these stimuli, and he termed the process "feedback" by which oral tradition was influenced or remade by the written and published word. Henige asserted that "Feedback may be defined as the co-opting of extraneous printed or written information into previously oral accounts. The process occurred very widely, if not obviously."[19] Henige cited numerous examples from around the world which suggested to him, first, the power of the written and published word for people not yet, or just recently, exposed to literacy, and, second, examples of instances where written, and often newly written and sometimes inexpert sources, are cited by and incorporated into oral traditions.

> Examples of this propensity to incorporate the written word into putatively oral traditions, or to base these "traditional" accounts entirely on printed or written sources can be found wherever liter-

17. One is tempted to consider Mikhail Bakhtin and the expressions of popular culture, resistance, and opposition to authority in the boisterous, carnivalesque oppositions to authority. *Rabelais and His World*, trans. Helene Iswolsky (Cambridge: Harvard University Press, 1968). Later in his text on *Imbalu*, Wamimbi has written, "At this moment the onlookers keep up shouting and yelling and the atmosphere is mixed with great excitement full of joy, worry and great expectations. The noise made by the spectators is extremely deafening." Here and there, in the context of his longer text, Wamimbi resets such images against the surveillance and regulation of the state, and also, in a sense, against the rather cold descriptive form of La Fontaine's ethnographic text. In the section from which Wamimbi has inscribed the sentences above, La Fontaine wrote, "The spectators, both men and women, keep up a deafening noise of shouts and exhortations" (44).

18. Henige, *The Chronology of Oral Tradition* (Oxford: Clarendon Press, 1972), 95.

19. Ibid., 96.

acy has occurred in Africa, not only in areas of European language penetration but of Arabic influence as well.[20]

Henige's point in this discussion was to demonstrate the vulnerabiliity
of what he has taken to be pristine oral tradition to the printed word.
Henige warned that the historian using oral tradition can become victim
of a circular effect in the production of the historical source and that the
facts which the historian seeks to uncover from oral sources may in fact
derive from less expert and possibly interested sources from outside the
society: missionaries, explorers, educators, government authorities, and
so forth. At a deeper level, ideas and structures may be lifted from
books, most particularly the Bible, and may then set the structure and
content of oral tradition or of literary works based on oral tradition.

The connection between Wamimbi's production of a text on *Imbalu*
and Henige's admonitions concerning the influence of a written text
upon an oral one is of course imperfect. Wamimbi's text is itself a written
one. Henige's discussion draws one into the subject of influence, but,
certainly, the relationship between La Fontaine and Wamimbi suggests
that there is much more to this discussion. Historians and others interested in contact between literary and nonliterary traditions can hardly
live with the simplifications and reifications involved in the simplistic
dichotomy of written and oral. Wamimbi's rewriting of La Fontaine
alerts one to the complexity of discourses which develop in innumerable
settings between source and source, between book and memory, between a written record and an oral testimony, between a work of guild
scholarship and a reformulation of that work for a different audience.[21]

A useful argument, and one in sharp conflict with Henige's view of
the influence of the written word on the oral, may be drawn from Carlo
Ginzburg, *The Cheese and the Worms: The Cosmos of a Sixteenth-Century
Miller*. Ginzburg constructed his subject, the miller Menocchio, as an
avid and eclectic reader. Ginzburg explored the relationships among the
ideas about the world that Menocchio articulated (and reproduced for
the Inquisition) and the published sources and knowledge circulating
through a still existing "oral culture."

> In Menocchio's talk we see emerging, as if out of a crevice in the
> earth, a deep-rooted cultural stratum so unusual as to appear al-

20. Ibid., 103.
21. The discussion here is stimulated by Dominick LaCapra, "Rethinking Intellectual
History and Reading Texts," in Dominick LaCapra and Steven L. Kaplan, eds., *Modern
European Intellectual History: Reappraisals and New Perspectives* (Ithaca, N.Y.: Cornell University Press, 1982), 47–85.

most incomprehensible. This case . . . involves not only a reaction filtered through the written page, but also an irreducible residue of oral culture. The Reformation and the diffusion of printing had been necessary to permit this different culture to come out to light. Because of the [Reformation], a simple miller had dared to think of speaking out, of voicing his own opinions about the Church and the world. Thanks to the [diffusion of printing], words were at his disposal to express the obscure, inarticulate vision of the world that fermented within him. In the sentences or snatches of sentences wrung out of books he found the instruments to formulate and defend his ideas over the years.[22]

In rather less stunning ways, there are resonances with Wamimbi's production of a unique and historically sensitive oration out of the words and structure of a carefully fashioned and ahistorical ethnographic text.

In 1982, Roger Chartier brought attention to Ginzburg's close study of Menocchio as a reader of diverse sources and to the significance of reading in the passage of knowledge from one field or system to another.

As Carlo Ginzburg has shown, what readers make of their readings in an intellectual sense is a decisive question that cannot be answered either by thematic analyses of printed production, or by analysis of the social diffusion of different categories or works. Indeed, the ways in which an individual or a group appropriates an intellectual theme or a cultural form are more important than the statistical distribution of that theme or form.[23]

It is clear that the discourse between the Wamimbi text and the La Fontaine text was not a simple one of adaptation of ethnographic data from one source into another.

*

A question arises of to whom Wamimbi's work was addressed. Who constituted the audience for Wamimbi's text? A first point is that the Wamimbi text was drafted and reproduced in English. Here Wamimbi sat amidst a tangle of contradictions inherent in colonial and postcolonial intellectual life. To address questions of power or authority in the

22. Ginzburg, *Cheese and the Worms* (Baltimore: Johns Hopkins University Press, 1980), 58–59.

23. Chartier, "Intellectual History or Sociocultural History? The French Trajectories," in Dominick LaCapra and Steven L. Kaplan, eds., *Modern European Intellectual History: Reappraisals and New Perspectives* (Ithaca, N.Y.: Cornell University Press, 1982), 15–46, esp. 30.

defense of culture, territory, local governance, ethnicity, one had to speak or write in the language of the colonial power or, with independence, the national government. To speak into the face of authority Wamimbi could not at the same time address his own communities in their language. Wamimbi's position was the more complicated because to attempt to write in Lumasaaba or Lugisu before achieving an accord on orthography was to give preeminence to one dialect cluster of Lumasaaba and thus one subregion of Bugisu. Moreover, Wamimbi's prose may seem to be produced for, and directed toward, an audience of one: the magistrate or district commissioner. If Wamimbi "heard" La Fontaine well, who indeed "heard" Wamimbi?

Given the specific contradictions that surrounded and marked the intellectual production of Wamimbi, given the constraints on his writing in Lumasaaba, given the reading of La Fontaine, one may well ask what is the meaning of "native author" in this setting? The dichotomy between "native" and "guild," which seems so natural within the discourse of the academy, is opened to challenge. The "native" character and authority which attaches to Wamimbi's text is not a consequence of his birth, or of a socialization to a cluster of core values. To address with power the officials of the Uganda government, Wamimbi constructed and seized the authority which he saw located in the construction of a "native" voice out of an ethnographic text. The "native" voice is here not given but constituted. In his December, 1968, memorandum addressed to the District Administration, Wamimbi wrote,

> I assume you are quite aware that however able and sympathetic the foreign observer may be, he can never fully interpret the thoughts and aspirations of another tribe or country. Therefore, the Masaaba Historical Research Association is the very capable organisation to write a thorough history of Bugisu as the majority of its members are Bamasaaba themselves.

In this sense, the Masaaba Historical Research Association was a complex and well-organized device to induce an authoritative "native" voice from the murky social and cultural field which was the Uganda of the late 1960s. What we see is that to produce his text Wamimbi, the "native author," commanded his own reading of an ethnographic text, reaching for its authority, but simultaneously commanded the forms and values of "native" discourse within Uganda. To achieve his object, he came to assemble these two textual modes, to make out of them a new and singular text with the doubled authority of the "native account" and the expert ethnography. The question of intertextuality moves to a more challenging plane. These are not simply two texts, one read and written out of the other, but a confrontation of modalities, of the ways knowledge is rendered, marked with authority, and transformed into literature.

*

On Friday, February 13, 1987, Justice S. E. O. Bosire of the High Court presented his judgment[24] in the S. M. Otieno case.[25] The final text of the judgment contains extensive comment on the standing of various witnesses and their testimony, including that of two men: Albert Ong'ang'o, a gravedigger in Alego, Siaya, seventy-nine years old, and Professor Henry Odera Oruka, a member of the Department of Philosophy, University of Nairobi, forty-two years old. While Ong'ang'o and Odera Oruka were both witnesses for Ougo and Siranga—that is they advocated burial in the land of S. M.'s birth in western Kenya—the ways in which they presented themselves and the ways in which they were viewed within the practice of the court offer further openings to the study of the ways in which knowledge, or expertise, are read. In Bosire's "opinion,"

> The Umira Kager Clan comprises a large number of people. Even if I were to accept what Professor Henry Odera Oruka said, that the clan sages take the decision, who is to decide that a particular person should be called upon to give direction with regard to burial as required? To my mind it will be idle to say that the clan takes a decision as to where and how a deceased person is to be buried. A line must be drawn somewhere to show who are involved in making the crucial decisions with regard to burial.[26]

24. Officially the case is known as *Virginia Edith Wambui Otieno v. Joash Ochieng Ougo and Omolo Siranga*. The Bosire judgment was an interim one. The case was appealed by Wambui to the Court of Appeal, Kenya's highest judicial authority, which ruled in the clan's favor rather than Wambui's, that Otieno was to be buried at Nyamila village, Nyalgunga, Alego, in Siaya.

25. For an extended treatment of the conflict over the corpse of S. M. Otieno, see David William Cohen and E. S. Atieno Odhiambo, *Burying SM: The Politics of Knowledge and the Sociology of Power in Africa* (Portsmouth, N.H.: Heinemann, 1992), particularly 75–87; and chaps. 4 and 5, above. At an early stage in the development of the jointly authored book, this section was drafted by me as part of a paper, "The Surveillance of Men," presented to the Conference on the Male Gender in Africa, organized by Luise White at the University of Minnesota. Clearly, much acknowledgment is due my co-author E. S. Atieno Odhiambo for his collaboration in all aspects of my work on the Otieno litigation.

26. Justice Bosire, in Sean Egan, ed., *S. M. Otieno: Kenya's Unique Burial Saga* (Nairobi: National Newspapers, c. 1987), 111. The Egan volume contains transcripts of the Otieno litigation as published in the *Daily Nation*.

And, Bosire also noted,

> Albert Ong'ang'o, a mason in Siaya District and a cousin of the deceased, also testified that the deceased did intimate to him that he wished to be buried next to or near his father's grave. Ong'ang'o was at the time cementing the grave of the deceased's elder brother, Simon, who was then awaiting burial. The witness testified that the deceased expressed his wish in the following words or words to that effect: "Albert, Albert, you have now prepared my brother Simon's grave. In case I die prepare a grave for me next to that of my father."
>
> Those words were spoken to the witness, so he said, when he was inside the grave which was under construction. The court moved to Westlands Cortage Hospital where the witness was admitted, having had a prostate operation, to receive his evidence. He testified as he lay on his back in his hospital bed. In spite of being in that condition he had no difficulty expressing himself. He impressed me a lot. He appeared candid and truthful. I had no reason to doubt his testimony.[27]

The juxtaposition of these two individuals, one the elderly gravedigger Albert Ong'ang'o, the other the youthful Professor Henry Odera Oruka, challenges one to readdress issues of expertise and authority in the production of knowledge. While one may read Bosire's commentaries *within* the practice of a court, the present reading of these testimonies, along with the reading of Bosire's "reading" of the testimony of these two witnesses, draws out an additional cluster of arguments.[28]

First, the testimony of each of these two men does not stand outside its performance. And the performance does not stand independent of the programs of counsel to construct and deconstitute authority within the practice of the courts. For Judge Bosire, the very context of the examination of the gravedigger in Westlands Hospital "speaks for itself." The very body and posture of the elder contributed to his words' appearing candid and truthful.

For the witness Odera Oruka, the erect and formal posture of the sprightly and energetic philosopher was not sufficient to affirm the authority of his testimony. An extensive transcript of his career and his

---

27. Ibid., 110.

28. One might draw a comparison between Justice Bosire's evaluation of different forms of authority and that of the United States Federal Court in the Mashpee case, reported by James Clifford, *The Predicament of Culture* (Cambridge: Harvard University Press, 1988); and consider further Roger Chartier's reading of Carlo Ginzburg as a reader of Menocchio and his sources, discussed above.

scholarly work was adduced in a prefatory questioning by Richard Kwach, the lawyer for the clan. In his introductory questions to his own witness, Kwach drew out that Odera Oruka is "of Nairobi University," a "professor of philosophy," "of the Kenya National Academy of Sciences," "a holder of [the] B.Sc. degree in philosophy and science from Uppsala University, Sweden," that he "co-authored a number of articles," that he has taught "for sixteen years" at the university, that he has been chairman of his department "for six years," and that he has "researched on African customs and traditions in Kenya."[29]

There are other angles of view into Professor Odera's testimony before the High Court. A letter writer to the *Weekly Review* pointed to:

> The rare spectacle of a professor in our national university declaring publicly his belief in ghosts and spirits . . . is a sad reality . . . that we have to face in a society which, though fast changing to the modern, has a history deeply rooted in mysticism and belief in the supernatural.[30]

In cross-examination, Wambui Otieno's counsel, John Khaminwa, drew out that Odera Oruka's research had mainly focused "on rural areas," that he has interviewed "some sages, wise men," that "some of them were interviewed by students," that "his research covered Siaya, South Nyanza, and a bit of Kisumu," that "the local community" determined "who qualified" as sages, that "about ten students" were involved in the research, that "the students . . . would ask the community who the sages were, interview them and ultimately the students would decide the best of the sages," "subject to his [the sage's] approval"!

In discussing the value and credibility of these two witnesses, Bosire appears to have seen the essential quality of Ong'ang'o's testimony as fully embodied in the person as represented before him: elderly, infirm, prostrate. And he appears to have regarded Odera Oruka's testimony as contingent on the status of an array of credentials, histories, and arrangements outside his very body. Through examination and cross-examination, with various interventions by the judge, we are confronted by two distinctive modalities through which the person, represented by these two men, has been constituted before the court and its broad national audience.

Second, the testimony, within performance and within the program of legal practice, was silently but powerfully valenced by other significant factors, most important being the meanings attached to the ways in

29. See Egan, 79–82.
30. *Weekly Review,* May 1, 1987, 2.

which the two lives were "grounded" within western Kenya. Here one may see the category of "man" disaggregated into two distinctive cultural fields: Ong'ang'o's authority drew on his age, but also upon his manual work and ability, and with reference to his connection with the earth of the grave and to the dead. Unspoken, his relationship to the dead was multiply expressed, through the site of the hospital, through his sickly appearance, through his remembrance of being at the grave, through his represented voice from the grave, and through his association with the disposition of the corpse of Simon Odhiambo (S. M. Otieno's brother).

Odera Oruka's authority drew on the privileges conferred by the scientific method and on achievement in and through the academy. While his research work was based in Siaya and other Luo-speaking communities of western Kenya, Odera Oruka was grounded not in the material world of western Kenya but rather in the world of the academy. He was presented, and represented himself, as vigorous and active, as organizing teams, groups, and elaborate research methodologies.[31] In his physical mastery of his profession, he disappropriated the very meaning and force of his body.

Kwach and Ong'ang'o were, on the other hand, situating the gravedigger Ong'ang'o's testimony differently. He was presented as one, as whole, in the world, his life and his discourse uninflected by the contradictions of speaking of one world while trying to live in another. In his cross-examination, Wambui's counsel, John Khaminwa, attempted to unveil contradictions in Ong'ang'o's life and testimony, but the gravedigger in his responses cleverly unveiled the contradictions in Khaminwa's practice and knowledge. In one lovely example, the widow's counsel John Khaminwa tried to lead the gravedigger Albert Ong'ang'o into admitting that Luo funerals rest on superstitions concerning "spirits and ghosts of dead people," but found his witness exceedingly cagey. Abandoning that line of examination, Khaminwa proceeded along other tangents, including attempting to lead the witness to admit that his testimony had been rehearsed with counsel and other witnesses. Eventually, Khaminwa took the cross-examination of Ong'ang'o in a different direction and found the tables turned on himself:

KHAMINWA: Now, this illness you are suffering from, do you think
    it has anything to do with Mr. Otieno's death?

31. One recognizes, with Parker J. Palmer, the problematic inherent in trying to "recover the human"—read "sagacity"—through "science." See "A Critic of Academics Wins Applause on Campus," *New York Times*, September 12, 1990, B7.

ONG'ANG'O: It might be because I was okay at home. But when I
    arrived in Nairobi, I got a strange illness.
KHAMINWA: Then let us pray to the Almighty God.
ONG'ANG'O: Go ahead and pray for me so that when I leave hospital,
    I will be able to accompany the body of Otieno back home to
    bury him there.
KHAMINWA: I put it to you Mzee Ong'ang'o, that Otieno never told
    you he wanted to be buried at home.
ONG'ANG'O: May I ask you a question?
KHAMINWA: Go ahead, Mzee Ong'ang'o, you are at liberty.
ONG'ANG'O: Have you ever stopped at the home of Otieno at Nyal-
    gunga [at Nyamila in western Kenya]?
KHAMINWA: I haven't.
ONG'ANG'O: Then how can you be talking about a thing you don't
    know about? Give back our son so we can go and bury him
    at home! You can join us on the way to Nyalgunga. I will take
    care of your stay there![32]

Third, the program of litigation, by which counsel "managed" this
testimony and its performance, anticipated different and yet simultaneous "readings" by the court. Bosire made clear that it was the infirm
body and its presentation of a voice that gave authority to the story that
Ong'ang'o intended to tell. He did not choose to enter and examine the
text of Ong'ang'o itself, to evaluate its inner meanings and logic. But,
with Odera Oruka, he was drawn into discourse over the meanings,
logic, and practical implications of the professional representations of
"Luo culture" and "Luo philosophy."

> Even if I were to accept what Professor Henry Odera Oruka said,
> that the clan sages take the decision, who is to decide that a partic-
> ular person should be called upon to give direction with regard to
> burial as required? To my mind it will be idle to say that the clan
> takes a decision as to where and how a deceased person is to be
> buried. A line must be drawn somewhere.[33]

In a sense, Odera Oruka himself—through the Kwach examination—
forced the court's examination into the deeper evaluation of his report.
While Odera Oruka related that he drew knowledge of "Luo culture"
and "Luo philosophy" from "wise men who are . . . recognised by the
community,"[34] he applied a different validation method than did Bosire
in respect to Ong'ang'o's testimony before the court.

32. Egan, 86.
33. Egan, 111.
34. Odera Oruka, in Egan, 79.

Fourth, the testimony, and its performance, connected to broader "readings" beyond the court, addressing other parties and other issues which have no direct and immediate place in the formal setting of the court. These materials can be read more deeply by Kenyans and other observers as touching and evoking critical elements in the ways in which person, gender, and society are constituted. One has seen that Bosire convened a different "reading" for Ong'ang'o than the reading he gave to Odera Oruka. From a removed observational position, one may play with the testimony in different ways than Bosire himself had available; for example, one may compare the manner in which Bosire "read" the elderly gravedigger with the way in which another authority, the philosopher Odera Oruka, "read" his sages. One may observe, for example, how Justice Bosire situated Ong'ang'o's words within the material facts of his infirmity, maintaining Richard Kwach's very embodiment of those words as he had organized Ong'ang'o's testimony from his hospital bed. One may note, through closer reading of his extended testimony, how Odera Oruka disembodied the voices, the words, and authority of his elderly sages, abstracting them from the material contexts in which they were voiced. For Odera Oruka, the very practice of philosophy, in his hands, obscured these material facts of his interrogations.

Odera Oruka began his research with the view that his sages would pass on to him knowledge which they have learned from older sages, and there is a further obscuring by virtue of use of student interviewers carrying formulaic methodologies to the field. By advancing one frame of authority, that of the scholar and the scholarly apparatus, Odera Oruka and Richard Kwach obscured the very elements of the work of the sages which would give their texts authority within Bosire's court in the sense which Bosire had chosen to read it.

Through a comparison of two witnesses for the one side of the litigation, we are better positioned to form a close and extended surveillance of the two witnesses, counsel, and the judge. It would be a mistake to see Ong'ang'o and Odera Oruka as occupying symmetrical and opposed positions. There are no substantive differences between the positions of Ong'ang'o and Odera Oruka but, in another sense, everything is different. Odera Oruka has committed himself to an academic revival and valorization of a cultural tradition, the recapture of a "traditional world" through which only the trained and expert reportage of the sages can provide access. To do so he has appropriated the tools and adopted the habitus of what would be taken to be the "modern world." While arguing the case for the standing of "traditional authority" and bringing into parlance the ideas of a "traditional world," Odera Oruka has entered fully the world which Wambui Otieno, her counsel, and witnesses claim to have been the world which S. M. Otieno inhabited as a "modern individual" living far from, and outside the bonds, of "tradition and custom." He has become "civilized"—*Ng'ato molony!*

With the Otieno case, the debates may still be more complex, for the participants themselves—whether within the courtroom or far removed—were recognizing the different positions taken, and at the same time defining and interpreting the substance and meaning of difference. They were "reading" and also "writing" history.

Since the 1960s, anthropologists   CONCLUSION
and historians have found im-
portant stimulation in the recognition of shared interest in such subjects
as family, class, domination, and gender. If one cannot yet notice the
once anticipated merging of method and theory, research in both disciplines has been strengthened through collective approaches and
through the "conversations" that have developed across disciplinary
boundaries.

Among subjects of these conversations, anthropologists and historians have in recent years found common interest in *the authority of the
text*, previously the province of the philosophy of history and literary
criticism. The attention to the *text* and to its *authority* seems to develop
from at least two sources: first, the recognition of the possibilities and
difficulties of close readings of historical sources such as have been undertaken by Natalie Zemon Davis, Carlo Ginzburg, Emmanuel LeRoy
Ladurie, among others, which seem in turn to draw on "interpretive"
approaches in anthropology exemplified by Clifford Geertz's "thick description" of cultural practice; and, second, the self-critical or reflexive
turn in anthropology and other disciplines of the humanities and social sciences.

The questions raised within these discussions concerning *the authority
of the text* are, almost transparently, readdressable to the larger programs
and standing of academic scholarship. While such reflexive work has
embroiled the academic guild in both explicit and implicit contests over
questions of ethics, value, and authority,[1] it has raised more significant
questions concerning the relationships between guild practice and the
notional and actual audiences for scholarship. Moreover, the relationship between popular productions of knowledge and those of the guild
has been prominently implicated as historians and anthropologists observe closely the ways in which their own texts are socially constituted
as authority.

One of the additional sources of scholarly interest in *the authority of
the text* is surely the broadening recognition of the power of popular,
and also official, constructions of the past in memorials, reenactments,
museum exhibitions, film and television accounts, popular biography,

1. For a site of discussion of these issues, see the recent debate (is it an example of a
bipolar or tripolar debate?) in *Past and Present*, 1991 and 1992, among Patrick Joyce, Catri-
ona Kelly, Lawrence Stone, and Gabrielle Spiegel. Catherine Cole at Northwestern University has studied the texture and process of this debate, which began with a response from
Joyce and Kelly to brief remarks in which Stone wrote of a recent paper by Spiegel on the
textualization of the past.

and advertising.[2] The role of academic research on the past, on history, is made problematic and at the same time given extraordinary moment by the capacity of nonacademic producers to generate alternative and competing historical and cultural accounts. One might imagine that scholars will look back on the past sixteen years, that is, from 1976 to 1992, as exceptionally marked by the search for reawakened authority and value in the constitution and deconstruction of a clot of commemorative events—1776, 1783, 1945, 1939, 1789, 1492—in the United States and in Europe which have surely filled a number of academic calendars.[3] The packing of commemorations of both enormous and modest scale has, clearly, engendered important debates over the meanings of these "events" and of the force of commemoration in the constitution of historical knowledge.[4] The dense schedule of commemorative events and the growing attention to commemorative practice by anthropologists and historicians have, certainly, heightened the capacity to read interest and power within the act of commemoration.[5] But, additionally, the meanings that organizers and participating scholars have attached to particular commemorative activities have generated responses, alternative activities, reinterpretations, denunciations, and deep conflicts, as well as forums, seminars, exhibitions, festivals, parades, workshops, symposia, conferences, lecture series, and publication projects.

Scholars have also been awakened to the significance for the anthro-

2. This discussion builds upon, with both extension and revision, "the conference call" for the Sixth Roundtable in Anthropology and History, August 31–September 4, 1989. The call itself drew on earlier discussions on "the production of history" at the Fifth Roundtable held in Paris in July, 1986.

3. Note the tumult stirred by the plan for the Reagan visit to the Bitburg military cemetery on the date of the fortieth anniversary of the end of the Second World War and the additional significance for a broad spectrum of parties which attached symbolic force to the venue.

4. Ciraj Rassool and Leslie Witz have been exploring the important political convulsions surrounding the 1952 Jan van Riebeeck Tercentenary Festival, and they note the decision in April 1992 of the mayor of Cape Town to cancel the three hundred and fortieth anniversary celebrations because "it would be 'divisive' to focus on a one-sided Eurocentric founding of Cape Town." See their forthcoming article "The 1952 Jan van Riebeeck Tercentenary Festival: Constructing and Contesting Public National History," a paper presented at the African Workshop, University of Chicago, November 17, 1992.

5. While papers tabled at the Fifth and Sixth Roundtables were substantially silent on these *big* commemorations (the organizers invited several scholars who were actors and authorities in these commemorations but they were all "fully booked") many of the papers *did* examine lesser commemorations. With considerable acuity, participants brought attention to the very process of commemoration, with an interest in comprehending the sociology of struggles over meaning, value, and truth.

pological and historical guilds more generally of the processes of the constitution of histories in the new nations of the world.[6] Scholars are alerted to the paradoxes and contradictions in the notions of "giving history" to peoples called "without history"—to note a portion of the title of Eric Wolf's 1982 tome.[7] In recognizing how histories have been—and are being—produced in other places and other times, historians are discovering a mirror effect: their own scholarly craft being demystified. Such is patently clear in the important ripple effect developing around Edward Said's 1979 volume *Orientalism*, which unveiled in a unified critique the institutional structure of Western knowledge production about the non-Western world.

But the production of history has continued in all kinds of settings beyond this formal and quite visible institutional structure. In many of these settings, such as situations of decolonization, the practices of liberating knowledge production have themselves contained the impulses and grammars of the established imperial frameworks. One can find no more obvious continuity than in the structuring of academic disciplines in the universities of the former colonies and in the accompanying modes of formal evaluation of scholarship within the "new" academies.

More significantly, the Western power system that Edward Said, with others, has seen as regulating local knowledge practices in, and in reference to, non-Western areas (simply by reference to the evidenced grand distinctions in all kinds of powers between the old metropoles and the new societies) was in no way complete.[8] As one notes throughout the examples offered within this volume, ethnographies were being rewritten into histories; court litigants were operating their own discourses

6. When this sentence was entered into "the conference call" for the Sixth Roundtable in early 1989, the reference was to the new nations emerging with the end of the old empires. There was, admittedly, no prediction here of the extraordinary changes that would sweep across eastern Europe and the former Soviet Union and of the new conditions and possibilities of *history* as old contradictions and mythologies came to be replaced by new ones.

7. *Europe and the People without History* (Berkeley: University of California Press, 1982).

8. Karin Barber has opened an important argument with recent postcolonial literary criticism on its approaches to literary and cultural production "at the margins" or within the paradigms of "the empire writes back," "writing to power," or "writing to the center." She sees these constructions, and notions of "the silenced, muted post-colonial subject," as offering no break at all from the European, Commonwealth, and imperial paradigms and institutions of knowledge and power that Said identified and critiqued in *Orientalism*. The privileging of metropolitan languages—even in the search for oppositional, anti-colonial, and alternative discourses—robs postcolonial literary studies of a regard for the rich cultural, literary, and artistic productions ongoing in non-metropolitan languages in Africa and in other parts of the world. See Barber, "Post-Colonial Criticism and Yoruba

outside, within, and beneath the practices of colonial courts; and anthropological learning and expertise were being debated in courtrooms and in the streets. One may ask how far the widely observed reflexive turn across many disciplines is really, as some have observed, a self-centered and self-indulgent digression, or, examined from a different perspective, a piece of broader and more diverse critical practice around the globe involving powerful productions of historical and cultural texts, including those in eccentric spaces both in the past and the present.

Historians, and anthropologists concerned with the past and with history, will in future years have to confront more directly the ways that popular and official constructions of the past, as well as political suppressions of historical knowledge, shape and deform the processes of knowledge production and the general knowledge of the past in the world. The debates over interpretations of the "Mau Mau revolt" in Kenya and "Horea's revolt" in Romania or the *mfecane* in South Africa or the appropriate history for a postwar Germany appear at one glance to be the activities of academics battling over recondite sources and evidence, but on closer inspection, they are primary, and singular, sites of critique of deeply felt and broadly held ideas, principles, and values. Through such debates, elaborated across several fields or media, the past is managed and the future imagined. Moreover, states and nations and cultures—never easily defined—are constructed beyond the formulae through which scholars have discussed them.

In complex and diverse ways, historians, in their praxis, give attention simultaneously to what some might call their traditional object—the reconstruction of the past—and to the nature and work of their audiences. Actual, and imagined, audiences work upon the productions of history in powerful ways, introducing critiques, rereadings, corrections, value, and meaning. In looking at ways in which language and social practice give form to the relationships between scholar and audience, scholars open a vital path in the reconstitution of history as a field and as a discipline.

The production of history—a frame of reference that is intended here to augment the conventional senses of meaning of history and historiography—refers to the processing of the past in societies and historical settings all over the world and the struggles for control of voices and texts in innumerable settings which animate this processing of the past. This

---

Popular Culture" (Institute for Advanced Study and Research in the African Humanities, February 17, 1993).

field of practice—*the production of history*—encompasses conventions and paradigms in the formation of historical knowledge and historical texts, the organizing sociologies of historicizing projects and events including commemorations, the structuring of frames of record-keeping, the culturally specific glossing of texts, the deployment of powerfully nuanced vocabularies, the confronting of patterns and forces underlying interpretation, the workings of audience in managing and responding to presentations of historical knowledge, and the contentions and struggles which evoke and produce texts and which also produce historical literatures.[9]

Looking back to where this project of writing began in 1985, there was, in the particular conceptualization of this notion of "the production of history," an analogy being drawn to processes of labor, work, and production that were the central concerns of the earlier Roundtables in Anthropology and History. As the work of the Roundtables shifted toward the examination of the production of history," the challenge posed to anthropologists and historians was how as "producers" they could stand both *within* and *outside* the production process, drawing attention to both the *inner* dimensions of production relating, for example, to the definition of topic, the conceptualization of audience, research methods, archival practices, writing, and publication, and the *outer* dimensions of production relating to guild routines and constrictions, official regulation, capitalization of research, the workings of audience, debate and contest, the dissemination of knowledge, and so forth. Here was an opportunity for the coupling of a reflexive concern for the ways in which academic practice disguises its very own organization of production with a similarly critical attention to the ways in which histories of various kinds are produced outside the academy and, from this, an enlarged sense of how historical knowledge is produced or unfolds, and how value, force, power, utility, and opportunity become attached and detached from such knowledge of the past.

At the same time, there is an interest in the "walls and passageways" that close and open fields of guild and nonguild history production to one another. Across the materials in the present book, it is seen how rich and complex and powerful these walls and passageways can be, whether one is inspecting the *Historikerstreit* in Germany in the late 1980s or one is considering the ways in which the expulsion of the "digressive mode" from guild historical practice has altered the shape of

9. This conceptualization of a field termed "the production of history" developed in the planning for the Fifth Roundtable during 1985 and 1986. While the paper was circulated to

the historical text or one is rethinking concepts of "forgetting" and "remembering."

*

Across the work contained in this volume—and in the work of the Fifth and Sixth Roundtables—two fields of discussion—*commemorations* and *silences*—have come to the fore again and again.[10] It can be argued that anthropologists and historians work in an interstice between the usurpation of knowledge and the restoration of knowledge. The "combing" of history is offered as a metaphor, the "comb" representing simultaneously the power to cover and veil knowledge from inspection, but also the power to restore it in practice.

Commemorations bridge this "space" between usurpation and restoration. Commemorations are socially constructed events in which struggles for the control of knowledge may break out into the open, yet may also be regulated and contained. In confrontations with those outside the guilds (for example, over participation in the planning of a monument), scholars may find that historical knowledge (or the commitment to certain knowledge and certain histories) may be difficult to unravel, dismantle, or deconstruct. Invisible communities, inchoate factions, may emerge amidst the contests over the form, content, timing, and manner of commemoration. In these confrontations, history is remade as a paradialect of property; in struggles over the production of history there is often a pathology of ownership. At the same time, deeply rooted commitments to privacy and secrecy are jeopardized. Intimate and dangerous knowledge may be lifted onto the surface, handled, massaged, violated. But the force of suppressed knowledge, of secret knowing, may be exploded and dissipated in public acknowledgment. Commemorations may restore general knowledge but may also produce a hollowing effect on the power and meaning of such knowledge.

As commemorations become the subject of close inspection, they may be seen to enclose differing and conflicting temporalities in common social settings in which, for some, experience seems remote or distant, while, for others, it may seem close and intimate. Differing temporal subjectivities within common settings may force negotiations about the

---

all the participants in the Fifth and Sixth Roundtables, and hundreds of photocopies of the "final" March 31, 1986, text have circulated, it has not been published intact.

10. The comments here develop from, and have been stimulated by the interventions of colleagues in the Fifth and Sixth Roundtables.

order and logic of associative activity, of what "belongs" and with what weight, within a commemorative program. In addressing *commemorations* as productions of history, one is examining the ways in which memorials and celebrations produce history, the ways in which such production is socially negotiated, and the paradox of the imposition of meaning in the workings of commemorations. In recognizing that commemorations are socially produced, one may come to recognize more clearly—and in one's own "time" and "space"—the ways in which historical knowledge, a sense of past, descend in time as inheritance, legacy, pathology, encumbrance, and ideology. As attention is brought to the social processes through which expert knowledge gathers authority, the naturalized and privileged sense of history constituted by guild professionals comes to be demystified.

Silences present other challenges. Silences may be specific and singular, but they nevertheless demand attention to an enormous range of experience and possibilities. Silences have multiple sources. They may develop from particular and transient conditions; they may be an element of structure. Silences may be a claim of some who would want to seize an authority to speak for others; but silences may also actually involve a willed reticence to speak. Silences may be produced by the effect of suppressive forces yet they may also derive from the condition that not everything is explainable or speakable. Some silences may derive from the selectivities and impositions of archives or from systems of preservation. Indeed, systems of preservation may make the most eloquent statements about the selectivities by which some, but not all, "pasts" are transformed into "histories." It is clear that ethnography, even where well practiced, may silence whole areas of culture, while histories may produce vast silences of others' lives out of unrecognized and unmediated silences in the societies in which the historians are raised and trained. The *Historikerstreit* in Germany and the *mfecane* debate in South Africa are about the reconstitution and the interruption of silences.

To take up the question of silence is at the same time to take up in a very specific way the general problem of how people handle and deploy knowledge. This is a complex moral and ethical ground. Within the material of this volume, one can see this in the complex interpersonal silence in family memory of working-class experience in Lawrence; or in the silence that Rea Tajiri's mother constructed around her experience in the Poston, Arizona, internment camp. Silences may be communal, as in the Lawrence example; or in more complex ways may involve, simultaneously, personal, communal, and national experience as in the silences attacked by Sonya Rosenberger in *The Nasty Girl* and by Utz Jeggle in Baisingen. The examples of Rosenberger and Jeggle open to view the ways in which powerful silences may be jointly constructed through personal, communal, official, and also, academic practices.

To grasp the challenge to unlock silences is to intervene dramatically in the forms of knowledge of others. Apart from the unanswerable indictments of individuals, groups, and nations that may come from silences broken, scholarly appropriations and magnifications of subdued voices can become part of a process of domination of which a silence may stand as critical resistance.

One can situate a series of questions concerning such "silences." What is the nature of force in these silences? Are silences thus to be conceived as something quite different from "forgetting"? What are the risks or dangers for audiences and producers in the investigation, interpretation, and unveiling of silences within "the production of history"? How is the dignity, and not merely the security, of silences to be weighed and understood? Why, indeed, should people not be silent, under many circumstances, about their pasts? To what extent does the power in silences involve the sometimes ominous, subversive, and seditious qualities and intentions of speaking?

*

The papers in this volume are diverse. They probe, and also skate across, settings very different in location and temporality. The treatments are in places intentionally eccentric. In places, digression is prized and celebrated. Narratives and expositions are burdened by frequent references to the paraphernalia of production of the text, as if one's new car came from the showroom with leftover parts, discarded but still useful tools, a worker's lunchbox, and the shop steward's notes from a management training session—and with no operator's manual.

There is, within this text, an enchantment with the notion of economy: that the conventions of research, interpretation, analysis, exposition, presentation, and argument are seated in complex, and often unspoken and effectively naturalized processes, themselves constructed out of routines relating to time, value, labor, property, and cost. Such naturalizing processes leave much important matter to the side as authors, directors, performers, and orators seek to achieve economy, precision, accuracy, authenticity, credibility, and authority through the workings of an historical production.

In a recent article the historian Achille Mbembe has cited a newspaper report in the Nairobi *Standard* about a Kenyan schoolteacher who was publicly humiliated by a district commissioner because he was wearing a goatee—and then professionally pilloried by the teachers' service.[11] Mbembe deploys his reading of the teacher's trauma as a means of showing how the state in the "postcolony" affirms its power over its subjects. In Mbembe's analysis the "political community" is reduced to the small assortment of players contesting the fact of a goatee. What is lost in Mbembe's analysis is the presence of the reporter, the reporter's act of observing and describing, the newspaper's act of publishing, the implied or overt critique of the district commissioner and the teachers' service, the sense of the larger and different and more complex political universe that the fact of the found article from the *Standard* manifests, not to speak of the workings of the newspaper's audiences in digesting and remaking the account to their own purposes (which may be different from Mbembe's or the state's).

To quote Richard Avedon one last time,

> These disciplines, these strategies, this silent theater, attempt to achieve an illusion: That everything embodied in the photograph simply happened, that the person in the portrait was always there, was never told to stand there, was never encouraged to hide his hands, and in the end was not even in the presence of a photographer.[12]

This book has sought to relieve Avedon of the burden of his authority over his subject, through suggesting a means of realizing the *production* of history, not meaning simply a restoration of the subject's hands to the photograph, but capturing the processes of production—in all its senses—through which the hands became an absence. In search of a comprehension of such production, this collection of papers has advanced an argument, both explicit and by example, for venturing into eccentric domains, for experimentalism in analysis and exposition, including evaluating in practice the interpretative and expository powers of juxtaposition and digression.

A century before Avedon penned his introduction to *In the American West*, a young woman, Olive Schreiner, wrote, as preface to her *Story of a South African Farm* that

> Human life may be painted according to two methods. There is the stage method. According to that each character is duly mar-

---

11. Achille Mbembe, "The Banality of Power and the Aesthetics of Vulgarity in the Postcolony," *Public Culture: Bulletin of the Center for Transnational Cultural Studies* 4 (Spring 1992): 19–20.

12. Richard Avedon, Foreword, *In the American West* (New York: Abrams, 1985).

shalled at first, and ticketed; we know with an immutable certainty that at the right crises each one will reappear and act his
part, and, when the curtain falls, all will stand before it bowing.
There is a sense of satisfaction in this, and of completeness. But
there is another method—the method of the life we all lead. Here
nothing can be prophesied. There is a strange coming and going
of feet. Men appear, act and re-act upon each other, and pass
away. When the crisis comes the man who would fit it does not return. When the curtain falls no one is ready. When the footlights
are brightest they are blown out; and what the name of the play is
no one knows. If there sits a spectator who knows, he sits so high
that the players in the gaslight cannot hear his breathing. Life may
be painted according to either method; but the methods are different. The canons of criticism that bear upon the one cut cruelly
upon the other.[13]

13. Olive Schreiner, *The Story of an African Farm* (London: Chapman & Hall, 1883), preface. I am grateful to my late aunt Rhoda Finkel for long ago introducing me to Olive
Schreiner's writing and giving me her own well-read copies of the early editions of two
of her books, including *The Story of an African Farm*.

Abuor, C. Ojwando. *White Highlands No* BIBLIOGRAPHY
More: A Modern Political History of
Kenya, vol. 1. Nairobi: Pan African Researchers, 1970.

Appiah, Kwame Anthony, "Is the Post- in Postmodernism the Post- in Postcolonial?" *Critical Inquiry* 17 (Winter 1991): 336–57.

Aufderheide, Pat. "Review." *In These Times*, January 20–February 4, 1986, p. 20.

Avedon, Richard. *In the American West*. New York: Abrams, 1985.

Baber, D. F. *The Longest Rope*. Caldwell, Idaho: Caxton Printers, 1947.

Bach, Stephen. *Final Cut: Dreams and Disasters in the Making of "Heaven's Gate."* New York: William Morrow, 1984.

Bakhtin, Mikhail. *Rabelais and His World*, trans. Helene Iswolsky. Cambridge, Mass.: Harvard University Press, 1968.

Bal, Mieke, "Telling, Showing, Showing Off." *Critical Inquiry* 18 (Spring 1992): 556–94.

Barber, Karin. "Post-Colonial Criticism and Yoruba Culture." Paper presented to the Institute for Advanced Study and Research in the African Humanities, February 17, 1993.

Beard, Peter, collector and editor. *Kamante, Longing for Darkness: Kamante's Tales from Out of Africa*. New York: Harcourt Brace Jovanovich, 1975.

Benjamin, Walter. "Theses on the Philosophy of History." In Hannah Arendt, ed., and Harry Zohn, trans., *Illuminations*. New York: Schocken, 1969.

Berdahl, Robert et al., eds. *Klassen und Kultur. Sozialanthropologische Perspektiven in der Geschichtsschreibung*. Frankfurt: Syndikat, 1982.

Berman, Bruce, and John Lonsdale. *Unhappy Valley. Book One: Violence and Ethnicity; Book Two: State and Class*. London: James Currey, 1992.

Berman, Paul, ed. *Debating P.C.: The Controversy over Political Correctness on College Campuses*. New York: Dell, 1992.

Blount, Ben G. "Agreeing to Agree on Genealogy: A Luo Sociology of Knowledge." In Mary Sanches and Ben G. Blount, eds., *Sociocultural Dimensions of Language Use*. New York: Academic Press, 1975.

Blount, Ben G. "Aspects of Luo Socialization." *Language and Society* 1 (1979): 247–48.

Bobo, Jacqueline. "*The Color Purple:* Black Women as Cultural Readers." In E. Deidre Pribram, ed., *Female Spectators: Looking at Film and Television*. London: Verso, 1988.

Boltanski, Luc. *The Making of a Class: Cadres in French Society*. Translated by Arthur Goldhammer. New York: Cambridge University Press, 1987.

Bommese, Michael, and Patrick Wright. "'Charms of Residence': The Public and the Past." In Richard Johnson et al., eds., *Making Histories: Studies in History-Writing and Politics*, 253–301. Minneapolis: University of Minnesota Press, 1982.

Bourdieu, Pierre. *The Field of Cultural Production: Essays on Art and Literature*. Edited by Randal Johnson. New York: Columbia University Press, 1993.

Breen, Timothy H. *Imagining the Past: East Hampton Histories*. Reading, Mass.: Addison-Wesley, 1989.

Browning, Christopher R. *Ordinary Men: Reserve Police Battalion 101 and the Final Solution in Poland.* New York: HarperCollins, 1992.

Buffalo's Centennial Book Committee, *Buffalo's First Century.* Buffalo, Wyoming: Buffalo Centennial Committee, 1984.

Bunker, Stephen G. *Peasants against the State: The Politics of Market Control in Bugisu, Uganda, 1900–1983.* Urbana and Chicago: University of Illinois Press, 1987.

Cameron, Ardis. "Bread and Roses Revisited: Women's Culture and Working-Class Activism in the Lawrence Strike of 1912." In Ruth Milkman, ed., *Women, Work and Protest: A Century of Women's Labor History*, 42–61. Boston: Routledge & Kegan Paul, 1985.

Carlisle, Olga. "The Perestroika of Memory." *Il Aperture*, Fall, 1989, 40–45.

Carlson, Chip. *Tom Horn: The Definitive History of the Notorious Wyoming Stock Detective.* Cheyenne, Wyoming: Beartooth Corral, 1991.

Chakrabarty, Dipesh. "Postcoloniality and the Artifice of History: Who Speaks for 'Indian' Pasts?" *Representations* 37 (Winter 1992): 1–26.

Chartier, Roger. "Intellectual History or Sociocultural History? The French Trajectories." In Dominick LaCapra and Steven L. Kaplan, eds., *Modern European Intellectual History: Reappraisals and New Perspectives*, 15–46. Ithaca, N.Y.: Cornell University Press, 1982.

Clay, John, Jr. *My Life on the Range.* Private imprint: 1924; Norman: University of Oklahoma Press, 1962.

Clifford, James. *The Predicament of Culture: Twentieth-Century Ethnography, Literature, and Art.* Cambridge, Mass.: Harvard University Press, 1988.

Cobbing, Julian. "The Mfecane as Alibi: Thoughts on Dithakong and Mbolompo." *Journal of African History* 29, 4 (1988): 487–519.

Cobbing, Julian. "Overturning 'The Mfecane': A Reply to Elizabeth Eldredge." Paper presented to the Colloquium on the "Mfecane" Aftermath, University of the Witwatersrand, September 6–9, 1991, 36.

Coetzee, John. *Waiting for the Barbarians.* New York: Penguin, 1982.

Cohen, David William. "'A Case for the Basoga': Lloyd Fallers and the Construction of an African Legal System." In Kristin Mann and Richard Roberts, eds., *Law in Colonial Africa*, 238–54. Portsmouth, N.H.: Heinemann, 1991.

Cohen, David William. "Doing Social History from Pim's Doorway." In Olivier Zunz, ed., *Reliving the Past: The Worlds of Social History*, 191–232. Chapel Hill: University of North Carolina Press, 1985.

Cohen, David William. "La Fontaine and Wamimbi: The Anthropology of 'Time-Present' as the Substructure of Historical Oration." In John Bender and David Wellbery, eds., *Chronotypes: The Construction of Time*, 205–24. Stanford: Stanford University Press, 1991.

Cohen, David William. "*Pim's* Work: Some Thoughts on the Construction of Relations and Groups—the Luo of Western Kenya." Paper presented to the Conference on the History of the Family in Africa, School of Oriental and African Studies, London, September, 1981.

Cohen, David William. "The Production of History." Position paper prepared for the Fifth International Roundtable in Anthropology and History, Paris, July 2–5, 1986.

Cohen, David William. *Toward a Reconstructed Past: Historical Texts from Busoga, Uganda.* London: British Academy and Oxford University Press, 1986.

Cohen, David William. "The Undefining of Oral Tradition." *Ethnohistory* 36 (Winter 1989): 9–17.

Cohen, David William. "Words Spoken Become History: Memory, Oral Tradition, and the Reconstruction of the African Past." National Museum of African Art, Washington, D.C., February 9, 1988.

Cohen, David William, and E. S. Atieno Odhiambo. "Ayany, Malo and Ogot: Historians in Search of a Luo Nation." *Cahiers d'Etudes Africaines* 27, 3–4, 107–8 (1987): 269–86.

Cohen, David William, and E. S. Atieno Odhiambo. *Burying SM: The Politics of Knowledge and the Sociology of Power in Kenya.* Portsmouth, N.H.: Heinemann; London: James Currey, 1992.

Cohen, David William, and E. S. Atieno Odhiambo. *Siaya: A Historical Anthropology of an African Landscape.* London: James Currey, 1989; Nairobi: Heinemann Kenya, 1989; Athens, Ohio: Ohio University Press, 1989.

Comaroff, John. "Dialectical Systems, History and Anthropology: Units of Study and Questions of Theory." *Journal of Southern African Studies* 8, 2 (1982): 143–72.

Comaroff, John, and Jean Comaroff. "The Madman and the Migrant: Work and Labor in the Historical Consciousness of a South African People." *American Ethnologist* 14, 2 (1987): 191–209.

Cook, David, and Michael Okenimkpe. *Ngugi was Thiong'o: An Exploration of His Writings.* London: Longman, 1983.

Cowan, Paul. *An Orphan in History: One Man's Triumphant Search for His Roots.* New York: Doubleday, 1982.

Dakhlia, Jocelyne. "Des prophètes à la nation: la mémoire des temps anté-islamiques au Maghreb." *Cahiers d'Etudes Africaines* 27, 3–4, 107–8 (1987): 241–67.

David, Robert B. *Malcolm Campbell, Sheriff.* Casper, Wyoming: Wyomingana, 1932.

Davidson, Glen W. "Human Remains: Contemporary Issues." *Death Studies* 14 (1990): 491–502.

Davison, Patricia, "Human Subjects as Museum Objects: A project to make life casts of 'Bushmen' and 'Hottentots', 1906–1924." *Annals of the South African Museum,* forthcoming.

De Certeau, Michel. *Heterologies: Discourse on the Other.* Translated by Brian Massumi. Minneapolis: University of Minnesota Press, 1986.

Dening, Greg. "A Poetic for History." Paper presented to the Fifth Roundtable in Anthropology and History, Paris, July 2–5, 1986.

De Bolla, Peter, "Disfiguring History." *Diacritics,* Winter 1986, 49–58.

Egan, Sean, ed. *S. M. Otieno: Kenya's Unique Burial Saga.* Nairobi: Nation Newspapers, c. 1987.

Eldredge, Elizabeth. "Sources of Conflict in Southern Africa, ca. 1800–1830: The 'Mfecane' Reconsidered." *Journal of African History* 33, 1 (1992): 1–35.

Fallers, Lloyd A. *Bantu Bureaucracy: A Century of Political Evolution among the Basoga of Uganda*. Chicago: University of Chicago Press, 1965; orig. publ., Cambridge, U.K., 1956.

Fallers, Lloyd A. *Inequality: Social Stratification Reconsidered*. Chicago: University of Chicago Press, 1973.

Fallers, Lloyd A., ed. *The King's Men: Leadership and Status in Buganda on the Eve of Independence*. London: Oxford University Press for the East African Institute of Social Research, 1964.

Fallers, Lloyd A. *Law Without Precedent: Legal Ideas in Action in the Courts of Colonial Busoga*. Chicago: University of Chicago Press, 1969.

Fergison, Drue. "*Chiyavayo:* Interior Decorating with the African *Mbira*," *Passages* 2 (1991): 2–3.

Fischer, Michael M. G., and Mehdi Abedi. *Debating Muslims: Cultural Dialogues in Postmodernity and Tradition*. Madison: University of Wisconsin Press, 1990.

Fraser, Nancy. "Sex, Lies, and the Public Sphere: Some Reflections on the Confirmation of Clarence Thomas." *Critical Inquiry* 18 (Spring 1992): 594–612.

Freedman, James A. "Orality versus Textuality in the Reformation: The Origin and Influence of Textuality on Theological Perspectives in the Reformation." Ph.D. thesis, Department of Religious Studies, Rice University, 1990.

Geertz, Clifford. "Deep Play: Notes on the Balinese Cockfight." *Daedalus* 101 (1972): 1–37.

Geertz, Clifford. *The Interpretation of Cultures: Selected Essays*. New York: Basic Books, 1973.

Geertz, Clifford. "Ritual and Social Change: A Javanese Example." *American Anthropologist* 61 (1959): 991–1012.

Ginzburg, Carlo. *The Cheese and the Worms: The Cosmos of a Sixteenth-Century Miller*. Baltimore: Johns Hopkins University Press, 1980.

Graff, Gerald. *Beyond the Culture Wars: How Teaching the Conflicts Can Revitalize American Education*. New York: W. W. Norton & Co., 1992.

Graff, Gerald. *Professing Literature: An Institutional History*. Chicago: University of Chicago Press, 1987.

Greene, Jack P. "The New History: From Top to Bottom." *The New York Times*, June 8, 1975, 37.

Gutman, Herbert G. *Power and Culture: Essays on the American Working Class*. Edited by Ira Berlin. New York: Pantheon, 1987.

Habermas, Jürgen. "A Kind of Settlement of Damages (Apologetic Tendencies)," July 11, 1986. Reprinted and translated in *New German Critique* 44 (1988): 25–39.

Habermas, Jürgen. *The New Conservatism: Cultural Criticism and the Historian's Debate*. Edited and translated by Shierry Weber Nicholsen. Cambridge, Mass.: MIT Press, 1989.

Hagopian, Patrick. "The Social Meaning of the Vietnam War" Ph.D. diss., Johns Hopkins University, 1993.

Hall, Martin. "Small Things and the Mobile, Conflictual Fusion of Power, Fear, and Desire." In Anne Elizabeth Yentsch and Mary C. Beaudry, eds., *The Art and Mystery of Historical Archaeology: Essays in Honor of James Deetz*, 373–99. Ann Arbor, Mich.: CRC Press, 1992.

Hamilton, Carolyn. "Authoring Shaka: Models, Metaphors, and Historiography." Ph.D. diss., Johns Hopkins University, 1993.

Hamilton, Carolyn A. "'The Character and Objects of Chaka': A Reconsideration of the Making of Shaka as 'Mfecane' Motor." *Journal of African History* 33, 1 (1992): 37–63.

Hamilton, Carolyn. "Ideology, Oral Traditions and the Struggle for Power in the Early Zulu Kingdom." M.A. thesis, University of the Witwatersrand, 1985.

Hamilton, Carolyn. "A Positional Gambit: Shaka Zulu and the Conflict in South Africa." *Radical History Review* 41 (Spring 1989): 5–31.

Hamilton, Carolyn. "The Real Goat: Ethnicity and Authenticity in Shakaland." Paper presented to the Institute for Advanced Study and Research in the African Humanities, Northwestern University, Evanston, Illinois, March 18, 1992.

Handler, Jerome, and Robert S. Corrucini. "Plantation Slave Life in Barbados: A Physical Anthropological Analysis." *Journal of Interdisciplinary History* 14 (Summer 1983): 65–90.

Harley, J. B. "Deconstructing the Map." *Cartographica* 26 (Spring 1989): 1–20; reprinted in *Passages* 3 (1992): 10–13.

Harrington, Spencer P. M. "Bones and Bureaucrats." *Archaeology* 46, 2 (March–April 1993): 28–38.

Hauser, Eva. "Ethnicity and Class Consciousness in a Polish American Community." Ph.D. diss., Johns Hopkins University, 1981.

Heald, Suzette. *Controlling Anger: The Sociology of Gisu Violence*. Manchester, U.K.: Manchester University Press, 1989.

Henderson, Delphine, "Asa Shinn Mercer, Northwest Publicity Agent." The Frances Greenburg Armitage Prize Winning Essay, Reed College, 1942–43, *Reed College Bulletin* 23, Jan., 1945, 21–32.

Henige, David. *The Chronology of Oral Tradition*. Oxford: Clarendon Press, 1972.

Holquist, Michael. "From Body-Talk to Biography: The Chronobiological Bases of Narrative." *Yale Journal of Criticism* 3, 1 (1989): 1–35.

Hoskins, W. G. *English Landscapes*. London: British Broadcasting Corporation, 1973.

Hoskins, W. G. *Fieldwork in Local History*. London: Faber & Faber, 1967.

Hoskins, W. G. *The Making of the English Landscape*. Baltimore: Penguin Books, 1955.

Isaac, Rhys. *The Transformation of Virginia, 1740–1790*. Chapel Hill: University of North Carolina Press, 1982.

Jeggle, Utz. "Recollecting State Terror: Local Memories of the Persecution of the Jews in the So-called 'Reichskristallnacht,'" paper presented to the Sixth International Roundtable in Anthropology and History, Bellagio, Italy, August 31–September 4, 1989.

Kael, Pauline. "The Current Cinema: Poses." *The New Yorker*, December 22, 1980, 100–102; reprinted as "Poses." In Pauline Kael, *Taking It All In*. New York: Holt, Rinehart & Winston, 1984.

Kael, Pauline. *When the Lights Go Down*. New York: Holt, Rinehart & Winston, 1980.

Karp, Ivan, and Steven A. Lavine, eds. *Exhibiting Cultures: The Poetics and Politics of Museum Display*. Washington, D.C.: Smithsonian Institution Press, 1991.

Karp, Ivan, Christine Muller Kreamer, and Steven D. Lavine, eds. *Museums and Communities: The Politics of Public Culture*. Washington, D.C.: Smithsonian Institution Press, 1992.

Kitching, Gavin. *Class and Economic Change in Kenya: The Making of an African Petite Bourgeoisie, 1905–1970*. New Haven, Conn.: Yale University Press, 1980.

Krohe, James, Jr. "Skeletons in Our Closet." *The Reader: Chicago's Free Weekly* 21, 19 (Friday, February 14, 1992): 1 ff.

LaCapra, Dominick. *"Madame Bovary" on Trial*. Ithaca, New York: Cornell University Press, 1982.

LaCapra, Dominick. "Rethinking Intellectual History and Reading Texts." In Dominick LaCapra and Steven L. Kaplan, eds., *Modern European Intellectual History: Reappraisals and New Perspectives*, 47–85. Ithaca, N.Y.: Cornell University Press, 1982.

La Fontaine, Jean. *The Gisu of Uganda*. London: International African Institute, 1959.

La Fontaine, Jean. "Witchcraft in Bugisu." In John Middleton and E. H. Winter, eds., *Witchcraft and Sorcery in East Africa*. London: Routledge & Kegan Paul, 1963.

Little, Peter D. "Woman as Ol Pa'yian [Elder]: The Status of Widows among the Il Chamus (Njemps) of Kenya." *Ethnos* 52, i–11 (1987): 81–102.

Lowenthal, David. *The Past is a Foreign Country*. Cambridge, U.K.: Cambridge University Press, 1985.

Lüdtke, Alf, ed. *Herrschaft als soziale Praxis*. Göttingen: Vandenhoeck & Ruprecht, 1991.

Lüdtke, Alf. "Industriebilder—Bilder der Industriearbeit? Zur Industrie- und Arbeiterfotografie ca. 1890–1940." *Historische Anthropologie: Kultur-Gesellschaft-Alltag* 3 (1993).

Lüdtke, Alf. "Zu den Chancen einer 'visuellen Geschichte,'" *Journal für Geschichte* 3 (1986): 25–31.

Maalki, Liisa H. "Body Maps of Good and Evil: Violence, Race, and the Narrative Construction of Moral Community among Hutu Refugees in Exile." Paper presented to the African Studies Workshop, University of Chicago, December 4, 1990.

McMahon, Irene. "Filling in historical omissions: Life of slaves shown in tour of Williamsburg." *Evanston* [Illinois] *Review*, February 6, 1992, pp. T3–4.

Mann, Kristin, and Richard Roberts, eds., *Law in Colonial Africa*. Portsmouth, N.H.: Heinemann, 1991.

Mbembe, Achille. "The Banality of Power and the Aesthetics of Vulgarity in the Postcolony." *Public Culture: Bulletin of the Center for Transnational Cultural Studies* 4 (Spring 1992):1–30.

Medick, Hans, and David Sabean, eds. *Interest and Emotion: Essays on the Study of Family and Kinship.* Cambridge: Cambridge University Press, 1984.

Mercer, Asa Shinn. *The Banditti of the Plains Or the Cattlemen's Invasion of Wyoming in 1892 (The Crowning Infamy of the Ages).* Norman: University of Oklahoma Press, 1954, 1987; orig. pub. Cheyenne, Wyoming: 1894.

Miller, Judith. "Erasing the Past: Europe's Amnesia about the Holocaust." *The New York Times Magazine,* November 16, 1986, 30–40, 109–11.

Miller, Marc S., ed. *Working Lives: The "Southern Exposure" History of Labor in the South. . .* New York: Pantheon, 1981.

Mintz, Sidney W. *Worker in the Cane: A Puerto Rican Life History.* First ed., 1960. New York: W. W. Norton, 1974.

Moore, Sally Falk. "Explaining the present: Theoretical dilemmas in processual ethnography." *American Ethnologist* 14, 1 (1987): 727–36.

Moore, Sally Falk. *Social Facts and Fabrications: Customary Law on Kilimanjaro, 1880–1980.* Cambridge, U.K.: Cambridge University Press, 1986.

Morrison, Toni, ed. *Race-ing, Justice, En-gendering Power: Essays on Anita Hill, Clarence Thomas, and the Construction of Social Reality.* New York: Pantheon, 1992.

Mutai, Chelagat. *Viva* magazine, April, 1979, pp. 10–12.

Nader, Laura and Harry F. Todd, Jr. *The Disputing Process: Law in Ten Societies.* New York: Columbia University Press, 1978.

Ngugi wa Thiong'o and Micere Mugo. *The Trial of Dedan Kimathi.* London: Heinemann, 1976.

Niethammer, Lutz. *Posthistoire: Has History Come to an End.* Translated by Patrick Camiller. New York: Verso, 1992.

Nolan, Mary. "The *Historikerstreit* and Social History." *New German Critique* 44 (1988): 51–80.

Novick, Peter. *That Noble Dream: The 'Objectivity Question' and the American Historical Profession.* New York: Cambridge University Press, 1988.

O'Brien, Jay, and William Roseberry. *Golden Ages, Dark Ages: Imagining the Past in Anthropology and History.* Berkeley: University of California Press, 1991.

Ocholla-Ayayo, A. B. C. *Traditional Ideology and Ethics among the Southern Luo.* Uppsala, Sweden: Scandinavian Institute of African Studies, 1976.

Odaga, Asenath B. "Some aspects of the Luo traditional education transmitted through the oral narratives—*sigendini*," UNESCO Seminar on Oral Traditions, Past Growth and Future Development in East Africa, Kisumu, Kenya, April, 1979.

Odhiambo, E. S. Atieno. "Democracy and the Ideology of Order in Kenya, 1888–1987." In Michael G. Schatzberg, ed., *The Political Economy of Kenya.* New York: Praeger, 1987)

Odhiambo, E. S. Atieno. "Kenyatta and Mau Mau." *Transition,* 53, 1991, pp. 147–52.

Odhiambo, E. S. Atieno. "The Production of History: The Mau Mau Debate." Prepared for the Fifth International Roundtable in Anthropology and History, Paris, July 2–5, 1986.

Odinga, Oginga. *Not Yet Uhuru: An Autobiography.* New York: Hill & Wang, 1969.

Ojwang', J. B. *Constitutional Development in Kenya: Institutional Adaptation and Social Change.* Nairobi: ACTS Press, Centre for Technological Studies, 1990.

Ojwang', J. B., and J. N. K. Mugambi, eds. *The S. M. Otieno Case: Death and Burial in Modern Kenya.* Nairobi: Nairobi University Press, 1989.

Oliver, Roland. *The African Experience.* London: Weidenfeld & Nicolson, 1991.

Ozouf, Mona. *Festivals and the French Revolution.* Translated by Alan Sheridan. Cambridge, Mass.: Harvard University Press, 1988.

Palmer, Robin, and Neil Parsons, eds. *The Roots of Rural Poverty in Central and Southern Africa.* Berkeley: University of California Press, 1977.

Parkin, David. *Cultural Definition of Political Response: Lineage Destiny among the Luo.* London: Academic Press, 1978.

Petty, Sheila, *Identity and Consciousness: (Re)Presenting the Self.* Regina, Saskatchewan: Dunlop Art Gallery, 1991.

Partner, Nancy F. *Serious Entertainments: The Writing of History in Twelfth-Century England.* Chicago: University of Chicago Press, 1970.

Price, Richard. *Alabi's World.* Baltimore: Johns Hopkins University Press, 1990.

Price, Richard. *First-Time: The Historical Vision of an Afro-American People.* Baltimore: Johns Hopkins University Press, 1983.

Price, Sally. *Primitive Art in Civilized Places.* Chicago: University of Chicago Press, 1989.

Rabinbach, Anson, ed. "Special Issue on the *Historikerstreit.*" *New German Critique* 44 (1988): 1–192.

Rassool, Ciraj, and Leslie Witz. "The Jan van Riebeeck Tercentenary Festival: Constructing and Contesting Public National History." Paper presented to the Africa Workshop, University of Chicago, November 17, 1992.

Richards, Thomas. "Archive and Utopia." *Representations* 37 (Winter 1992): 104–35.

Rosaldo, Renato. "Doing Oral History." *Social Analysis* 4 (September 1980): 89–99.

Roscoe, John. *The Bagesu.* Cambridge: Cambridge University Press, 1924.

Roscoe, John. *The Northern Bantu.* Cambridge: Cambridge University Press, 1915.

Said, Edward. *Orientalism.* London: Routledge & Kegan Paul, 1978.

Schreiner, Olive. *The Story of an African Farm.* London: Chapman & Hall, 1883.

Scott, Joan W. "The Evidence of Experience." *Critical Inquiry* 17 (Summer 1991): 773–97.

Simmonds-Duke, E. M. "Was the Peasant Uprising a Revolution? The Meanings of a Struggle over the Past." *Eastern European Politics and Societies* 1, 2 (1987): 187–224.

Singh, Jyotsna. "Different Shakespeares: The Bard in Colonial/Postcolonial India, *Theatre Journal* 41, 4 (December 1989): 445–58.

Smith, Helena Huntington. *The War on Powder River: The History of an Insurrection*. Lincoln: University of Nebraska Press, 1967.

Sontag, Susan. *On Photography*. New York: Anchor Doubleday, 1989. From articles in first published in *The New York Review of Books*, 1973–77.

Soyinka, Wole. *Ake: The Years of Childhood*. New York: Aventura Vintage, 1981.

Spiegel, Gabrielle M. "History, Historicism, and the Social Logic of the Text in the Middle Ages." *Speculum* 65 (1990): 59–86.

Spiegel, Gabrielle M. "History and Post-Modernism." *Past and Present* 135 (May 1992): 194–208.

Spiegel, Gabrielle M. *Romancing the Past: The Rise of Vernacular Prose Historiography in Thirteenth-Century France*. Berkeley: University of California Press, 1993.

Stamp, Patricia. "Burying Otieno: The Politics of Gender and Ethnicity in Kenya." *Signs* 16, 4 (1991): 808–45.

Stewart, Susan. *On Longing: Narratives of the Miniature, the Gigantic, the Souvenir, the Collection*. Durham, N.C.: Duke University Press, 1993.

Thomas, Lynn M. "Contestation, Construction, and Reconstitution: Public Debates Over Marriage Law and Women's Status in Kenya, 1964–1979." M.A. thesis, Johns Hopkins University, Baltimore, Md., 1989.

Tilly, Charles. *As Sociology Meets History*. New York: Academic Press, 1981.

Tompkins, Jane. *West of Everything: The Inner Life of Westerns*. New York: Oxford University Press, 1992.

Torpey, John. "Introduction: Habermas and the Historians." *New German Critique* 44 (1988): 5–24.

Twaddle, Michael. "Tribalism in Eastern Uganda." In P. H. Gulliver, *Tradition and Transition in East Africa*. London: Routledge & Kegan Paul, 1969.

Ubelaker, Douglas H., and Lauryn Guttenplan Grant. "Human Skeletal Remains: Preservation or Reburial?" *Yearbook of Physical Anthropology* 32 (1989): 249–87.

Vansina, Jan. *Oral Tradition: A Study in Methodology*. London: Oxford University Press, 1965.

Vansina, Jan. *Oral Tradition as History*. Madison: University of Wisconsin Press, 1985.

Vansina, Jan. "Some Perceptions on the Writing of African History: 1948–1992." *Itinerario* 16, 1 (1992): 77–91.

Verdery, Katherine. *National Ideology under Socialism: Identity and Cultural Politics in Ceauşescu's Romania*. Berkeley: University of California Press, 1991.

Wakeman, John, ed. *World Film Directors*. Volume 2: *1945–85*. New York: H. W. Wilson Co., 1988.

Williamson, Judith. *Decoding Advertisements: Ideology and Meaning in Advertising*. New York: Marion Boyars, 1984.

Wills, Garry. *Lincoln at Gettysburg: The Words that Remade America*. New York: Simon & Schuster, 1992.

Wister, Owen. *The Virginian*. Lincoln: University of Nebraska Press, 1992; orig. pub. Macmillan, 1902.

Wright, Will. *Sixguns and Society: A Structural Study of the Western.* Berkeley: University of California Press, 1975.

Wolf, Eric. *Europe and the People without History.* Berkeley: University of California Press, 1982.

Zonabend, Françoise. "Childhood in a French Village." *International Social Science Journal* 31 (1979): 492–507.

Zunz, Olivier, ed. *Reliving the Past: The Worlds of Social History.* Chapel Hill: University of North Carolina Press, 1985.

African law, 30–34, 48–49
anthropology and history, xvi–xvii n, 1, 4,
  96, 105, 105 n, 241–42; international
  roundtables, xvii, 1, 1 n, 3, 5, 184, 242–
  43 n, 245–46; "interpretive" vogue in,
  126–27, 241
argument, 34, 41–42, 47, 67, 103–4; tradition and agency, 225
audience, 21, 147–49, 155–57, 244
authenticity, xx, 136–41, 147–49, 151–52,
  201; and "native" voices and texts, 220,
  228, 233–34; replications, 151–55
Avedon, Richard, 24–25, 30, 133, 249

Bach, Stephen, 157, 159–60, 159 n, 164–68,
  164 n, 165 n, 167 n, 169 n, 183
Bitburg, 7, 7–8 n, 64–65, 72
Bosire, Justice S. E. O., 234–40
Buffalo soldiers, 197–200, 199 n
burials and reburials, 64–66, 76–77, 78–
  111; Barbados, 79–81; Bitburg military
  cemetery, 64–65; Buganda, 90–91; Dick-
  son Mounds, 81–86; El Negro, 92–93;
  Ethiopian, 93 n; Gettysburg battlefield,
  65–66; Luo practice, 104–6, 105 n;
  Native American remains, 78–86, 92 n;
  Negro Burial Ground, 86–90; S. M.
  Otieno, 94–111

Cameron, Ardis, 12–13
Cattle Kate, 175–81
circumcision, 220–35
Cimino, Michael, xx, 157, 159–81, 159 n,
  165 n, 167 n, 170–71 n, 173–74, 175 n,
  180 n, 210 n, 211 n, 212–15
class, 104, 104 n, 107–8, 166–68, 182–85,
  194; and capital, 189–90, 191–92, 194–
  96, 194 n, 207–8, 213–15
Clifford, James, 25, 27–28
Clover, Sam T., 161–64, 180, 191–92
Cobbing, Julian, 70–75
colonialism, colonial rule, 28, 31–33
commemoration, xxi, 15, 23, 76, 242–43,
  242–43 n, 246–47; Bitburg, 64–65; Cattle
  War symposium, 158–59, 175 n, 185–
  215; Horea, 56–59, 58 n

consent, 30, 32, 34, 48, 134–35 n
courts, and courtrooms, 28–49, 94–111;
  alternative discourses within, 33;
  and S. M. Otieno case, 94–111, 234–
  40; Uganda Protectorate, 28–49,
  53–54
Cowan, Paul, xvii, 8–12, 15–21, 18–19 n,
  132, 216

death lists, 169–73, 210 n
debate, xviii, 52–55, 53 n, 76–77, 155–57,
  244; asymmetry of, 54, 63–64, 67,
  73–74; bipolarity of, 54–55, 54–55 n, 73–
  74, 75–76, 199–200, 215; Budweiser commercial, 147–49; Color Purple, 155–57;
  Dickson Mounds, 82–86; El Negro,
  92–93; Historikerstreit, 64–70, 72, 74 n,
  245–46, 247; Luo custom and culture,
  99, 104–6, 105 n, 106–8, 106–7 n,
  237–40; Mau Mau, 59–64; mfecane, 56,
  56 n, 70–75; modernity and tradition,
  95, 97–98, 103–4, 109–11, 234–40; nationalist, 56, 56 n, 58–59, 76–77, 96; Otieno's
  remains, 94–111, 234–40; rights of
  women in Kenya, 108–11, 111 n
Dickson Mounds (Illinois), xix, 81–86,
  145–46, 146 n
digression, xxi–xxii, 157, 245–46, 248
Ditmar, Art, 147–49, 149 n

economy, 248; of circumcision practice,
  225; of debate, 75; of history production, 52–54, 76–77; of juridical practice,
  30, 46–48, 51
Eldredge, Elizabeth, 73–74, 73 n
events, 20, 20–21 n, 123–24
expertise, xxi, 40, 58, 75–76, 103–4, 247;
  and landscape, 128–30; philosopher
  and grave-digger, 234–40; and pim,
  112, 115–16; in replication, 151–54;
  Wamimbi and, 217–34

Fallers, Lloyd A., 30–35, 39–40, 47–49;
  "discovery" of Weber, 31
film, video, television, xx, xxii, xxiv, 61,
  130–35 n, 177 n; Bad Day at Black Rock,

film, video, television (*continued*) 131–32, 134 n; Budweiser commercial, 147–49, 175 n; *Cat Ballou*, 173 n; *City Slickers*, 211–15; *Color Purple*, xx, 154 n, 155–57, 156 n; *Come See the Paradise*, 132, 134–35; *The Deer Hunter*, 173–74; *Heimat*, 67–68, 70; *Heaven's Gate*, xx, 157, 159–81, 179 n, 183–84, 188 n, 210–15; *History and Memory: For Akiko and Takashige*, 130–35, 145; and narrative, 157; *The Nasty Girl*, xxiv, 247–48; *Out of Africa*, 154–55, 154 n, 155 n; and representation of African-Americans, 155–57; *Shaka Zula*, 107 n, 154 n; *Shane*, 211–15; *The Shootist*, 204–5 n; United Artists/Transamerica Corporation, 165–66; *Unforgiven*, 204–5 n

Flagg, O. H. ("Jack"), 164–65, 177, 180–81, 193

"forgetting," xiii–xiv, xxiv, 22, 245–46

Geertz, Clifford, 20–22, 23 n, 59, 106, 126 n, 127, 241

Ginzburg, Carlo, 101, 150 n, 231–32

Graff, Gerald, 51, 52, 53 n

Gutman, Herbert G., xvii, 2–3, 5–8, 17, 19–20, 24, 132, 182–83 n, 216

Habermas, Jürgen, 64–68

Hamilton, Carolyn, 56 n, 72 n, 107 n, 151 n, 154 n, 184 n

Handler, Jerome, 80–81

Harley, J. B., 141–43

Harvey, Mark, 177 n, 186, 194–97, 194 n, 195 n, 199–201, 203, 215

Haverford College, 103–4 n

Henige, David, 230–32

Hill, Anita, 150, 150 n

historiography, 1, 2, 50–55, 66, 75–77; African past, 139–40; and American west, 189–90; "history" and "past," 129–30 n; and landscape, 128–30; and Johnson County cattle war, 159–60, 184–85; nationalist, 56, 56 n, 60, 76–77; southern African, 70–75

history and anthropology. *See* anthropology and history

Hoskins, W. G., 128–29

Imbalu (circumcision), 220–35

Issac, Rhys, 129–30

Japanese-American internment, 130–35

Jeggle, Utz, 69–70, 247–48

Johnson County (Wyoming), xxi, 185–215; Historical Society, 185–86

Kael, Pauline, 157, 168, 173–74, 174–75 n

Keeney, Colin, 186, 202–4

Kenya, 94–111; ethnic politics, 107–8; national historiography, 59–64; women's rights, 108–11, 111 n

Kundera, Milan, xiii–xiv

La Fontaine, Jean, 217–34, 220 n, 221–22 n

Lawrence (Massachusetts) strike, xvii, 5, 8–12, 13–20, 24, 27, 216–17, 247–48

Leakey, Louis, 119–20

Lincoln, Abraham, 65–66

literacy, 5, 231–32

litigation, xix, xxi; *Namuluta v. Kazibwe*, 28–49; *Virginia Edith Wambui Otieno v. Joash Ochieng Ougo and Omolo Siranga*, 76–77, 94–111, 234–40

Lüdtke, Alf, 3, 24–28, 26–27 n

maps, 135–43

Masaaba Historical Research Association, 218–20, 218 n

Mau Mau, 59–64, 62 n, 63 n, 130

Mbembe, Achille, 248–49

McDermott, Jack, 186, 188–89, 189–94, 201, 202, 203, 211

memory, xvii, xix, 117, 123, 184, 200; of internment, 131–32, 132 n; in Lawrence, 13, 16, 18, 23; public, collective, 12, 19, 100

Mercer, Asa Shinn, 171 n, 183–85, 185 n, 191–92, 191 n

Metzel, Truman, Jr., 183–84, 184 n

mfecane, 56, 56 n, 70–75

Mintz, Sidney W., 21–22

Mofokeng, Santu, 135

Moore, Sally Falk, 20–21

museums, 78–80, 89–90, 150–51; in Banyoles, 92–93; Dickson Mounds, 81–86, 146; and Johnson County cattle war,

187–89; Maryland Historical Society, 143–45; National Museum of African Art, 135–43; and representation, 135–41, 143–45

Nasty Girl, The, xxiv, 247–48
National Museum of African Art, xx, 90, 90 n, 135–43
Native Americans, xviii–xix, 78–81, 92 n, 190, 195
Negro Burial Ground (New York City), 86–90
newspapers, magazines, 132 n, 138, 141, 144; and Budweiser commercial, 147–49; and "call-out," 122–27; coverage of Johnson County cattle war in, 161–64, 164 n, 172, 177, 180–81, 198, 201; and debate, 62–63, 63 n, 64, 67, 69; and Dickson Mounds issue, 82, 83–84 n; and Negro Burial Ground, 86–90; and Otieno litigation, 92–94, 97, 97–98 n, 100, 107
Ngugi wa Thiong'o, 60–61

Odhiambo, E. S. Atieno, 60, 62 n, 63 n, 97 n, 221
Odinga, Oginga, 104 n, 106–8, 106 n, 113
On'gang'o, Albert, 234–40
oral history, tradition, xiv–xvi, 21 n, 90–91, 90 n, 115 n, 221–22, 230–32; in Lawrence, 12, 14 n
Oruka, Henry Odera, 234–40
Otieno, S. M. (Silvanus Melea), xviii, xix, 76, 94–111, 112, 234
Otieno, Wambui, xix, 94–95, 97, 101, 104 n, 108–11, 112–13
Ouko, Robert, 97

Parker, Alan, 132
photography, 24–28, 26 n, 119–22, 122–27, 132–35, 134 n, 153, 175–77, 178 n, 196, 249
pim, xix–xx, 112–19
Powell, General Colin L., 199

radio, 14–15, 78–79, 199
Rathbone, Richard, 12–13 n, 130
reading, 121–22, 126, 216–17, 239–40; of landscape, 128–30; maps, 141–43; the

museum, 143–45; narrative, 7, 7 n, 157, 229–30; Wamimbi, of La Fontaine, 217–35
Reagan, President Ronald, 7, 7–8 n, 64–65, 72
roller-skating, 173, 173 n
Rosaldo, Renato, 21 n

Said, Edward, 243–44, 243–44 n
Schreiner, Olive, 249–50
Sider, Gerald, 5 n
silences, 6, 6 n, 121–22, 125, 153–54, 246–48; in colonial courts, 40, 44–46, 48–49; in Johnson County commemoration, 196–97, 208–9; jointly enacted, 44–45, 104, 150; in Lawrence, 14, 18, 28, 29; maps and, 141–42; in Otieno litigation, 96, 104–8, 104 n, 106–7 n
Smith, Helena Huntington, 164 n, 170–71 n, 172, 176–77, 177 n, 191, 191 n, 196, 198 n, 201 n
Smithsonian, xviii–xix, 78–79, 135–43, 144 n
Sontag, Susan, 133
Spiegel, Gabrielle, xxiii, 91 n
Stevens, George, 211–15
Strand, Paul, 134, 134 n
suppression, 6, 9, 13, 44–46, 105 n, 184–85, 192, 244, 246

Tailhook, 126–27
Tajiri, Rea, 130–35, 145, 247
Teoli, Camella, xvii, 9–12, 18–20, 18–19 n, 132, 198 n, 216–17
testimony, 6 n, 47–49, 97–101, 115–16, 235–37; discordant voices, 47–48
Tilly, Charles, 118–19, 119 n
Tisdale, Tom, 158–59, 204–6, 204–5 n
Tuskegee Institute, 153

Vansina, Jan, xv n, xvi n
Verdery, Katherine, 56–59
Verhoeven, Michael, xxiv
Village Voice, 8, 18, 18–19 n, 19, 20

Wamimbi, George W., 217–35; and affect, 228; and agency, 226; and the "native" text, 228; and time, 225–26

Williamsburg, Colonial, xx, 150–53, 151 n,
    152 n, 153 n; and representation of
    blacks, 152–54, 154 n
Wilson, Fred, 143–45

Wisconsin, University of, 122–27
Wister, Owen, 177 n, 202–4
Wyoming, cattle war, 158–81, 182–215